✻

"In *The One Year Sweet and Simple Moments with God Devotional*, Kim gives us a fresh reminder of well-loved Scriptures, rediscovered with new blessings and with practical application of truth for all of us. Kim's delightful, gentle reminders of things we have forgotten are daily delights. The readings sweetly nudge us toward a deeper understanding and love for Jesus our Lord."

JILL BRISCOE Author and speaker

"Believers want to follow Jesus every day. But how? What does that look like? It's helpful to find someone with a vibrant walk with God who lives what they believe and shows what following Jesus looks like in the contemporary world. Kim Newlen is such a person. She's Barnabas in pink. Kim Newlen is not like a box of chocolates because you know exactly what you're getting: solid, biblical encouragement for everyday life!"

CHRIS FABRY Syndicated radio host and bestselling novelist of six books, including *June Bug*

"I'm a big fan of Kim Newlen and her love of the Lord. Read *The One Year Sweet and Simple Moments with God Devotional* and you'll fall in love with both!"

KEN BLANCHARD Coauthor of *The One Minute Manager*® and *Lead Like Jesus*

"A breath of fresh air for weary souls! Kim's devotional expresses genuine feelings, uses rich metaphors, and always points us to Christ. A great way to start your day!"

SUSAN A. YATES Speaker and bestselling author of many books, including *Raising Kids with Character That Lasts*

"Growing up in the same neighborhood with Kim was inspiring to me because I got to see the brightness of her faith. My mom and hundreds of other women would pile into Kim's house to share the miraculous Word of God. To this day, I read Kim's daily devotionals which allow me to prepare, relax, and focus on Jesus. *The One Year Sweet and Simple Moments with God Devotional* is a must-read, whether you are a starting quarterback in the NFL, a Christian looking to grow, or one who needs inspiration from above."

RUSSELL WILSON NFL quarterback for the Seattle Seahawks

about precious moments in her stirring faith journey—moments to which we all can relate. She helps us see the sacred in the secular."

ANNA B. BILLINGSLEY Writer and university administrator

"*The One Year Sweet and Simple Moments with God Devotional* almost bursts with Kim Newlen's enthusiasm and love for God. We all know there is nothing 'sweet and simple' about many of life's difficulties, but somehow in this book we are led back daily to the truth that nothing in our lives is too large or small to bring to God: Kim writes with the same trust and faith about putting on lipstick as she does about losing her hair to chemotherapy. These devotions are refreshingly simple, yet reflective of a profound and powerful faith."

MARY MCDANIEL CAIL, PH.D. Author of *Alzheimer's Disease: A Crash Course for Friends and Relatives*

"Kim Newlen is one of the most inspirational women I've ever met. She is fearless in talking about her faith and using it to encourage other women. *The One Year Sweet and Simple Moments with God Devotional* will allow to her reach even more women with her infectious enthusiasm for life and God."

STEPHANIE ROCHON CBS 6 news anchor and reporter, Richmond, Virginia

"Kim Newlen's Sweet Monday ministry has been a blessing to thousands. *Sweet and Simple Moments* will prove to be a blessing to many more."

KENNETH G. ELZINGA Author and Robert C. Taylor Professor of Economics, University of Virginia

"Kim Newlen is a humble and authentic ambassador for God. Sometimes there are curves or bumps in her path, but her ultimate destination and purpose never wavers. She understands that obstacles are expected, and trusts that when needed or appropriate, God will supply her with the tools she needs to move forward and closer to Him. Kim's words encourage you to stop, look around, and see the simple pleasures God provides every day. Her attitude toward her life's purpose is infectious. What a blessing!"

DEBBIE THARP FISHER Associate director, MBA Program, Robins School of Business, University of Richmond

"Kim knows Jesus and His love in a profound way, and she demonstrates that through her simple faith in His Word and promise. This book is a great tool to help you ground yourself every day in the goodness and love of God. It will remind you that you are not alone and that your Heavenly Father sees you and hears you."

STEVE SHELBY Pastor, West End Presbyterian Church, Richmond, Virginia

"I am so excited to know that Kim Newlen has been led by the Spirit to release this wonderful devotional book. Now Sweet Monday can take place 365 days a year! You will be blessed and encouraged on a daily basis. Kim's love for Christ leaps from the pages."

DR. HENRY P. DAVIS III Pastor, First Baptist Church of Highland Park, Landover, Maryland

"Kim's passion is twofold—for Jesus Christ and for women. Kim doesn't want women to just survive the challenges that come, but to actually thrive and press in toward a deeper relationship with Christ. In a winsome, 'chat over coffee' style, Kim's devotions encourage women in every life stage to embrace each moment with anticipation for what God has in store for them. Transparent, honest, and rooted in Scripture, Kim is a gifted communicator!"

EMMITT FOWLER Station relations manager, *FamilyLife Today* radio program

"Kim Newlen's sweet spirit and love for God shine through on each page. Her witty and encouraging messages will help readers find rest and contentment in God's Word. This devotional will guide seekers to look for God in simple and significant moments, and to pursue an intimate relationship with Him at every stage of life."

STACY HAWKINS ADAMS Author of *Lead Me Home* and *Who Speaks To Your Heart?: Tuning In to Hear God's Whispers*

"Kim Newlen reads the Bible as many would read a favorite thriller, unable to put it down. Her genuine love for women and heart for evangelism are part of her life and are evident in every page of this book. As you read, you just might be more grateful that you know God, and if you aren't sure you do, you will understand how the God of the universe desires to be in relationship with you."

FAYE RIVERS Teaching director, Community Bible Study

"Kim's deep passion for God is matched by her concern and love for the reader. While the devotions may be sweet and simple, they will nourish and bring life."

NATHAN CLARKE Video director, *Christianity Today*

"I can unequivocally say that this book is not just fluff. Kim takes you straight to the Word of God. She's written each devotion as if she were sitting on the couch, sharing a cup of tea or coffee with you. In her sweet way, she encourages you to grow deeper in your own relationship with the Father and to live out a love for Him and your fellow man."

HANNAH ELLENBURG Coauthor of *Sweet Monday, Collegiate Socials on a Shoestring . . . Tied to a Generous God* (College Edition)

THE ONE YEAR®

Sweet & Simple Moments with God

DEVOTIONAL

KIM NEWLEN

Founder of
Sweet Monday®

TYNDALE™
MOMENTUM

An Imprint of
Tyndale House Publishers, Inc.

Visit Tyndale online at www.tyndale.com.

Visit Tyndale Momentum online at www.tyndalemomentum.com.

TYNDALE, The One Year, and One Year are registered trademarks of Tyndale House Publishers, Inc. Tyndale Momentum, the Tyndale Momentum logo, and The One Year logo are trademarks of Tyndale House Publishers, Inc. Tyndale Momentum is an imprint of Tyndale House Publishers, Inc.

The One Year Sweet and Simple Moments with God Devotional

Designed by Beth Sparkman

Edited by Erin K. Marshall and Bonne Steffen

ISBN 978-1-4143-7332-4 softcover

Printed in the United States of America

19	18	17	16	15	14	13
7	6	5	4	3	2	1

Dedication

In awe and wonder of such a BIG, PATIENT GOD,
the only One who works marriage miracles and can take
two sinner opposites and make them one!

To my husband of twenty-eight years and literal knight in shining armor
Mark
who has always seen things in me I couldn't see and who said to me
almost twenty years ago (after the first year of Sweet Monday in
our home), "Kim, write your ideas down. This outreach has been so
successful in our home, other women can do it. If you write it down,
I will go and make fifty copies." And the rest is sweet history . . .
I love and respect you, Markie.

And to Kali, my sweet Special K, the greatest earthly gift God
has given me. I love you—BSSYP!

Finally, to my sweet office manager JJ—Joyful Jamie
Breeden—the only person who can read my handwriting
and my heart at the same time. I love you too!

Introduction

A Sweet Monday Every Day in Christ

Dear Sweet Reader,

I wish you could see my so-excited face as I share with you this simple, sweet devotional. It's really not the words I am excited about sharing—it is the *Lord*, our Creator, the one true God, who sent Jesus, His only Son, not only to save us from our sin, but also to give us a personal relationship with Himself now and forever.

I came to accept God's free gift of salvation in Christ at an early age, but I did not begin to grow in my love for Him through His Word until I was a young adult. I try to live life with no regrets, but I do regret that I did not plunge into reading His Word every day a lot sooner. Getting to know God has been the greatest adventure of my life! The wildest thing is that the more difficult life is at times, the sweeter He becomes to me!

About ten years ago, I decided that I wanted to read through the Bible. I had never read cover to cover the greatest book ever written. If I could read so many other books, why not the only living and active book breathed by God? I picked up *The One Year Bible* because I loved that it was so simple to follow. Since I cannot remember numbers very well, I loved that the date was there. Not only did I get a New Testament reading along with an Old Testament reading, but there were portions from Psalms and Proverbs every day too.

At first, when I was crawling through 1 and 2 Chronicles, I encouraged myself with the thought that I had readings from the New Testament, Psalms, and Proverbs to look forward to. Over the years, I have grown to love the Lord in Chronicles, too! He is the same unchanging God who is still committed to His people—that's you and me in Christ. He loves us and forgives us. He helps us and changes us. He always has our backs and always has our best interests at heart. This *One Year* plan has now become a staple, a habit, not on my "to-do" list but on my daily "want-to-do" list.

My hope and prayer is that we will all know and grow in Christ together in the sweet days ahead. Please put your Bible and your favorite cup of tea or coffee alongside this devotional and begin spending every day with Him through His Word. We do not want to miss Him. We do not want the world to drown out His voice in our lives. We want our relationship with God to be above all others, instead of being lukewarm or a "have-to-do" Sunday appointment. Let's place Him highest on our "want-to-be-with" list and not look back with regret, saying, "I wish I had."

I already know that the hardest thing about writing this devotional will be not seeing your sweet face in my home and hearing how God through His Word has followed you around too! But I know we will all be under the same roof one day when He chooses to bring us to our heavenly home for all eternity.

His,

Kim ☺

BSSYP (Be Sweet & Say Your Prayers)

SP (Sweet Pea): I know it is not fashionable to talk about yourself, but it is in the spirit of Psalm 66:16—His Spirit—that I share these simple devotions with you. "Come and listen, all you who fear God, and I will tell you what he did for me."

Lifetime Resolution

> *May God give you more and more grace and peace as you*
> *grow in your knowledge of God and Jesus our Lord.*
>
> 2 PETER 1:2

More and more grace and peace! More and more growth in my knowledge of God and Jesus my Lord. Doesn't that sound wonderful? It is a lifelong New Year's resolution for me. Don't we all long for more grace and peace in our personal lives, in our families, in our world?

Sometimes it is difficult to describe the deep meaning of those words, but I sure know when I am *not* experiencing God's peace. "His peace will guard your hearts and minds as you live in Christ Jesus" (Philippians 4:7).

His peace is a gift we can share with others, something that I don't always do consistently. The same is true for God's grace. I sure know when I am not extending God's grace to people, although I usually discover it after the fact. I am stingiest with grace when I am on the phone with a technician on the other side of the globe who is remotely troubleshooting a problem with my computer, television, or phone. I am ashamed to say I have had to call a technician back and humbly apologize for my irritation and curt responses. My forever New Year's resolution is to know Jesus more and more—to open my heart to receive His grace and peace, be renewed, and never miss anything He has for me!

How do we get to know God? After receiving Christ by faith, we become part of His family. As we read the Bible, we experience Him more personally, especially understanding how He deals with His people and what we need to do to live for Him. Why would any of us want to miss out on anything God Almighty has planned?

 Know Jesus and grow! Discover how knowing Jesus and staying close to Him affects every area of your life by reading John 15:1-17.

God's Girl

Everyone who acknowledges me publicly here on earth,
I will also acknowledge before my Father in heaven.

MATTHEW 10:32

For so long in my life, I was afraid of being who I really am: "God's girl." At nine years old, I prayed and invited Jesus Christ into my life, by faith, believing that He died on the cross for my sin and that He was the only way to God. Yet I was quiet about my faith for years. You see, I wanted people to like me. I didn't want to offend anyone. I basically did not want to dissociate myself from Christ, but I didn't want to identify myself with Him either. Sounds a little lukewarm to me!

During my first year of college, when I started reading the Bible regularly and spending time with other girls who were also growing in their faith, I prayed the second most honest prayer I think I have ever prayed: "God, I want to be Your girl every day—not just on Sunday. I want to receive all You have to give, and I want to give myself to You." This simple prayer was a turning point in my life, from desiring to chart my own course to trusting in God's plan for me—moving toward Him, not away from Him. I began taking a lot of baby steps of faith in His direction.

At the core of my being, I rejoice that I know who I really belong to for all of eternity. And I am bolder to acknowledge Him, which is one big way He is changing me!

 Memorize and act on Ephesians 6:19. Let's be bold and embrace who we really are—God's girls!

Sew Sweet

*I am certain that God, who began the good work
within you, will continue his work until it is finally
finished on the day when Christ Jesus returns.*

PHILIPPIANS 1:6

My home economics class in college was wonderful! I wish that subject would make a comeback. If nothing else, you learn sewing basics. Although I wasn't an accomplished seamstress, I did construct a complete pantsuit. (Remember those?) It was the prettiest polyester pantsuit you have ever seen—if you like the color burnt orange! The suit had all the things needed to pass the class: a collar, a zipper, and buttonholes.

Of course, I had plenty of assistance from the skilled professor, but I know my mother, who was an excellent seamstress, was pleased with my finished product too. With budding confidence, I moved on to my next project—a dress that looked adorable on the front of the pattern package. I was going solo this time, without my experts' guidance. I failed miserably. It drooped where it should have draped and stayed where it should have swayed. It was the ugliest outfit I have ever seen to this day, and I threw it right into the trash can. When I recuperated from the initial shock, I realized I had used the wrong kind of fabric!

We sometimes try so hard to mend ourselves without the help of our Creator—our Designer and the Finisher of our faith. We can't fix ourselves any more than we can fix outfits made with the wrong fabric. Jesus made the pattern! He sews, mends, fixes, and completes us here, in preparation for all eternity. Sew sweet!

 The next time you sew on a button (or lose one, if you don't sew), meditate on the fact that the biggest mending job in your life was completed by Jesus on the cross!

The Mixed-Up Chameleon

Oh, don't worry; we wouldn't dare say that we are as wonderful
as these other men who tell you how important they are!
But they are only comparing themselves with each other, using
themselves as the standard of measurement. How ignorant!

2 CORINTHIANS 10:12

In this verse, Paul was defending his authority because he was taking some heat from critics for both his appearance and his oratorical delivery, which others thought was lacking. I have to confess that I used to have a bad habit of comparing myself with other women, which would make me feel woefully inadequate. I wanted to attain Diane's professionalism, Katherine's taste, Brenda's typing skills, Shawn's sense of style, Pam's beauty, Grandma Hazel's cooking skills, Faye's wisdom, Sherry's skin, my mama's legs, and my daughter's memory. I believed that when I did, I would be so much stronger and better.

It reminds me of Eric Carle's picture book *The Mixed-Up Chameleon*. In the story, the chameleon tries on the trunk of an elephant, adds the bushy tail of a fox, then dons the pink legs of a flamingo. As more and more unnatural things are added, the chameleon is so weighed down with his creative new look that he can no longer change colors or catch a fly with his tongue. He was one ugly reptile.

This book hit close to home. As I looked at other women and wished I had what they had, pretty soon I was a Mixed-Up Mama, and I looked ugly too. I became ineffective and unable to accomplish what God had prepared for me to do. Now I've learned we can all celebrate what other women have, what God has given them, and we all look better for it.

The Lord knit together each of us in our mothers' wombs. We are "fearfully and wonderfully made" (Psalm 139:13-14, KJV). We are perfectly put together, whether we feel like it or not. "Thank You, Lord, that in obedience to You, we don't need to compare ourselves to others, but we can live each day in gratefulness for our uniqueness. Thank You that You love us and use us just as we are."

Let's ask a friend to gently remind us if we are comparing ourselves to others.

Christ Confidence

Don't be afraid, for I am with you. Don't be discouraged,
for I am your God. I will strengthen you and help you.
I will hold you up with my victorious right hand.

ISAIAH 41:10

Are you a confident person? Throughout my life there have been so many times when my lack of confidence and my sheer fear held me back from doing things I really wanted to do. I missed out on not only the experiences but also the possibilities of being a blessing and being blessed. To this day I'm shy about picking up a tennis racket, because I never really learned how to play. In college, cute boys would occasionally ask me to play a match with them, and I would decline because I was too afraid I'd fail. Failing alone is hard, but failing in front of someone is *horrible*!

That happened at my first piano recital. I had been taking piano lessons for about a year when my teacher said we would be preparing a piece for that event. I was terrified just thinking about it. I got a new dress and, at my mom's insistence, spent a day at the beauty parlor in preparation for the occasion. At the recital when it was my turn to perform, I walked onstage in a full auditorium, sat down on the bench, put my hands on the keys for a moment, then got up and walked off without even playing a note! (But I thought I deserved their sweet round of applause just for walking across the stage.)

A personal relationship with Jesus Christ replaces our earthly confidence with Christ confidence. He gives us strength to do everything He has planned for us. And when we need a boost, He's always there to provide it. His strength is truly one of the greatest visible changes He has made in my life—from having no earthly confidence to embracing robust Christ confidence!

What areas are we ready for Him to change in our lives today? Make a list right now and confidently share those areas with Christ.

Piles to Go before I Sleep

For everything there is a season, a time for every activity under heaven. . . . A time to keep and a time to throw away.

ECCLESIASTES 3:1, 6

At some point in my education I had to memorize Robert Frost's famous poem "Stopping by Woods on a Snowy Evening." I like the images that the poet created, but to be honest, that's not my life. Forgive me, Mr. Frost. I've changed the last two lines of your poem from "*miles* to go before I sleep" to "*piles* to go before I sleep, and *piles* to go before I sleep." That's a truer description of what I face each day.

Can you relate? Many of us have big and small piles around us, whether they're on the desk, in the sink, or by the bed—piles of papers, piles of dishes, or piles of reading materials. If you are a crafts person, you might have piles of projects, piles of photos, or piles of fabric. If you are into the latest beauty products, you might have accumulated piles of lipstick (that really won't come off when you eat!) or piles of "age defying" makeup.

There is nothing wrong with material things. There is a time to keep things and a time to throw them away (Ecclesiastes 3:6). Anything around us that distracts us from God's specific plan for our lives is clutter and needs to be discarded. I think it is that simple. Your clutter might not look like my clutter, but that's okay. We need to stop comparing piles and allow God to help us clean up our own. This frees us for simple priority living, investing our time in God, His Word, and people.

 Identify one physical and one spiritual pile today that weighs you down. Then take action. Maybe it's time to drop off a donation at the local resale shop. And if you have lost your temper with someone, ask for forgiveness.

What to Wear?

I am overwhelmed with joy in the LORD my God! For he
has dressed me with the clothing of salvation and draped
me in a robe of righteousness. I am like a bridegroom
dressed for his wedding or a bride with her jewels.

ISAIAH 61:10

What to wear? What to wear? What to wear!

As a little girl (and now, as a big girl), I have always wanted to have the genie-like powers I used to see on the television show *I Dream of Jeannie*. With just a nod of her head, Jeannie would be able to change from her harem pants to the perfect attire for any occasion.

Like most women, I enjoy looking nice and feeling put together. My problem is that I do not like to spend time getting ready! But more important than being well dressed and ready to meet the world is being right with God and ready for eternity. It's a matter of life and death because it is inevitable that each one of us will die. In the blink of an eye, our lives on earth will be over, and either we will be in the presence of God forever or we will spend eternity without Him. Oh, it doesn't sound very sweet, but it is true. We should ask ourselves now instead of later, *Am I ready?*

There is only one way to be ready for eternity with God. Today's prophetic song from Isaiah beautifully describes Christ's return to redeem our lost world. When we accept Christ, we are clothed with garments of salvation and robes of righteousness. Instead of fretting over what to wear from our closet, we should delight in the Lord's gift. It is a reason to be joyful!

What are you wearing today? Make sure you have Jesus' garment of salvation and thank Him every day for that gift.

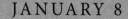

Hairdos and Hairdoozies

The very hairs on your head are all numbered. So don't be afraid;
you are more valuable to God than a whole flock of sparrows.

LUKE 12:7

I'm so grateful this very personal verse was planted in my heart at a young age, especially since I've been self-conscious about my hair for most of my life.

When I go to the hairdresser, I am afraid of what I'll look like when I come out of that swivel chair! Don't get me wrong. It's not that I don't have confidence in the skills of my hairdresser; it's just that I don't "talk" hair very well. For years, I have collected cute-hair pictures from magazines and catalogs so I can show the hairdresser a picture. At the insistence of a tasteful friend, my cluttered collection has turned into a small, one-of-a-kind book I call *Hairdos and Hairdoozies*! The hairdos are magazine pictures I like. The hairdoozies are the actual, awful photographs of me with bad hair. Now ladies, my little handmade book will never make it onto the bestsellers list because I have the only copy, but friends have actually borrowed it when they are thinking of changing up their hairstyles because it is helpful.

As useful as this book is, the most helpful book in my life is the Bible, God's Word. I meditated on this very verse when I lost every hair on my head through chemotherapy. How precious that God knows the number of hairs on my head since He knows the exact number of hairs that were falling out in clumps. That truth brought me great comfort and helped alleviate my fear. God has me covered! It doesn't get any better than that!

The next time you go to the hairdresser, repeat today's verse to yourself or—even better yet—share it with your stylist. Praise God that He created you and knows every detail about you.

Snow Day

Be still, and know that I am God! I will be honored by
every nation. I will be honored throughout the world.
PSALM 46:10

One of my favorite things has always been snow days. I grew up in the South, where snow days are a rare and celebrated event, especially if you're a child. When it happens, schools are closed and everyone is encouraged to stay home while snowplows clear the roads. Since I married a teacher, a snow day means everyone gets to stay home, sleep late, and eat snow cream for breakfast. Whenever the TV weatherman even hints about an upcoming snowstorm, I'm so excited I can't sleep! To this day, if an overnight storm is predicted, I get up throughout the night to peek out the window, watching for the first snowflakes.

I love it when snow blankets our neighborhood, and I'm amazed by the stillness it creates. For me, it's a visible reminder of the command to be still and know that God is God.

But lately I have found how difficult it is in life to capture that snow-day stillness year-round, regardless of the weather. That's when God reminds me that His commands are timeless and are not dependent on the seasons, or our schedules, or how we're feeling at the moment. The many times I find I have overcommitted myself and am *not* forced to be still by inclement weather or ill health, I quickly forget who is in control of each day I am given. It's then that I need to pray, "Help me, God, each and every day to stop, be still, and know You are God!"

Whether it's a snow day or not, stop whatever you are doing. Go sit in the car, the tub, or your favorite chair—and be still. Spend a few minutes thinking only about God.

A Beauty-Full Evening

I will extol the LORD at all times; his praise will always be on my lips.
PSALM 34:1, NIV

Is it, Lord? Is Your praise always on my lips? Every time I put on my lipstick, I can think about You! This is something we all can remind ourselves to do. We need to put on lips of praise. As far back as I can remember, my mama and daddy told me that it was more important to be pretty on the inside than pretty on the outside. I'm thankful that at a very early age, I began to have this biblical principle of ongoing praise instilled in me—I just didn't know it!

Two of my favorite beauty items are my Bible and my lipstick. At first glance, they probably don't appear to have much in common, but they really do. Both are used to enhance the women God created us to be—applying spiritual beauty on the inside and physical beauty on the outside. I have discovered that putting on lipstick is a quick routine that helps me focus on God's truth to praise Him.

As much as I appreciate a good night's sleep, I always look forward to the next day because it gives my lips another opportunity to praise God! And when it's one of those days when my praise list seems to come up short, I look around and begin praising God for everything that I see, the people I know, and most of all, for Him.

The next time we apply our lipstick, let's make it a visual reminder for our lips to praise God. We can't help but smile when we offer praise to our Creator!

Let's start our own "Lips of Praise Lists" right now! (I think I just wrote a lip twister!)

I Live You

Those who obey God's word truly show how completely they love him. That is how we know we are living in him. Those who say they live in God should live their lives as Jesus did.

1 JOHN 2:5-6

It happens repeatedly to me when I'm texting on my phone's teeny keyboard. I hit the *i* key instead of the *o* key and sign off my messages with "I *live* you" instead of "I *love* you." I've thought about my unintentional misspelling in terms of my relationship with God. We *love* Him when we *live* Him. We *live* Him when we *obey* Him. And when we *obey* Him, we *love* and *live* Him. That's all there is to it! The best part is that when we have given our lives to Christ, His Spirit inside us gives us the "want to." We want to do His will. "God is working in you, giving you the desire and the power to do what pleases him" (Philippians 2:13). Isn't this wonderful news? We want to please Him, and even that desire comes from Him! God is always at work in His children's lives.

It makes sense. If you're like me, you want to show your family and close friends how much you love them. We want to please them, so we do things that we know they like. Here's a simple example: I try to remember to clean off my clutter from our small bathroom counter so my husband, Mark, has room for his things. All of us have choices, and when we choose to take God's high road in the big and small things, we live Him over and over again. What a wonderful, freeing way to live!

What small change do you need to make to live God before a family member or friend? Try to implement it quickly and live Him.

Been Bumped Recently?

The LORD will go before you, the God of Israel will be your rear guard.

ISAIAH 52:12, NIV

I am so glad that God is my rear guard. I need one! Have you ever gently backed out of your driveway while trying to put on your lipstick? It shouldn't be that hard, right? Fair warning: you're asking for trouble. I know from experience! That last-minute beauty application has been such a routine for me for so long, I didn't give it a second thought. That is, until I put my car in reverse and bumped into my neighbor's car, forgetting it was back there—somewhere. Ugh! The gentle impact not only took me by surprise, it also taught me not to apply lipstick while in motion. I was relieved that our daughter, Kali, who was a teenager at the time, wasn't in the car to witness my distracted driving.

Thankfully, there were no big dents on either car. After my sweet neighbor assured me that all was well, I breathed a sigh of relief. I thanked God for car bumpers that take the brunt of a fender bender and was grateful mine did its job well. Bumpers act as front and rear guards, protecting us as well as the other car. My husband, Mark, has taken it one step further with an added safety feature on his car—it beeps loudly when there is any object close behind him.

As much as we rely on car manufacturers to design safer vehicles, I take greater comfort in the promise that "the LORD keeps watch over [me] as [I] come and go, both now and forever" (Psalm 121:8). He never takes His eyes off us. He is our rear guard, our bumper, to protect us as we hit the bumps of life.

 Celebrate today if you are in Christ and the Lord is your protection on all sides, now and forever. Thank Him specifically for one protection He provides for you today.

Dry Skin

*All the trees will know that it is I, the LORD, who cuts the
tall tree down and makes the short tree grow tall. It is I who
makes the green tree wither and gives the dead tree new life.
I, the LORD, have spoken, and I will do what I said!*

EZEKIEL 17:24

I have a never-ending battle with dry skin. I know what to blame: my heated and
air-conditioned house. Don't get me wrong. I am thankful for my furnace and my
AC, but they do suck the moisture out of my skin when I'm inside. I remember
the first time I spotted a sign of dryness on my legs. I immediately headed to the
drugstore and asked the pharmacist which lotion to buy. For two weeks, I applied
the recommended lotion. I wasn't dabbing a little here and a little there; I was
using a liberal amount and rubbing it in every day. It did the trick—no more dry
skin! As long as I was consistent, the problem was taken care of.

What about our hearts? Do they ever feel dry? We need to be revitalized by
God's Word. When we spend time in God's Word, committing Scripture to heart,
the nourishing power of the Holy Spirit will shine through us. People will notice
if we do it consistently because the change will be visible to them.

There is no way to live an abundant, consistent Christian life apart from
Christ. And there is no way to know what He says unless we read His Word.
I am afraid there are a lot of scaly Christians running around who need to rub
in God's Word. We must let it soften and penetrate our brittle hearts. Before
long we will notice that our priorities change and our attitudes toward others
do too. It's Jesus, the Living Water, hydrating us and making us flourish.

Let's start moisturizing every day with God's Word! Read more
about God's hydration plan for us in Psalm 1:1-3.

What Is a Sweet Monday?

That is what the Scriptures mean when they say, "No eye has seen, no ear has heard, and no mind has imagined what God has prepared for those who love him."

1 CORINTHIANS 2:9

Nineteen years ago, I was a young mother busy with our daughter, Kali, at home while my husband, Mark, was at his job at school. At times, I felt isolated and lonely for the company of other women. I knew I couldn't be the only woman feeling this way . . . and I knew Jesus! So I decided that with God's help, I would open our home the first Monday night of the month for an hour and a half to any woman who would come—neighbors, church friends, acquaintances, women of all ages and stages of life. Since our household income had been significantly reduced when I stopped teaching, I called the get-together "Sweet Monday, Women's Socials on a Shoestring . . . Tied to a Generous God." I served a simple dessert (full of fat and sugar), decaf coffee, and candy to go along with the theme. Because God promises that His Word never returns void (Isaiah 55:11, KJV), I shared a five-minute gospel message to point us all to Christ as the one and only lasting Sweetener of life!

The night before that first Sweet Monday, I dreamed that I was sitting on the front porch in a rocking chair, waiting and waiting for someone to come. Not one woman showed up! It was a terrible dream, but thankfully it wasn't what actually happened. The next night the room was crowded, and new women continue to come to this day.

What about you? We can all have a Sweet Monday any day of the week by reaching out to another woman for Christ, one sweet invitation at a time! If we who have Christ living inside us aren't connecting other women to Him, who will? Let's invite women into our lives, into our homes, and into our churches by faith!

Extend an invitation to a woman this week for coffee or tea. It may lead to a regular Bible study or Sweet Monday in your home. But start with allowing the Holy Spirit to encourage her through His life in you.

Be a Cheerleader

*Encourage each other and build each other
up, just as you are already doing.*
1 THESSALONIANS 5:11

I loved being a cheerleader in middle school, high school, and college. Early on, my sweet mama told me that I couldn't be a cheerleader all my life. She knew the kind of commitment it took. But this is probably the only time Mama's been proven wrong. You see, I'm married to a wonderful schoolteacher and coach, so I'm always cheering for his basketball and tennis players as well as the team representing his alma mater! As a mother, my cheerleading responsibilities have doubled. Even though I don't always jump up at the right time, I try to let my husband and daughter know in different ways that I'm always on their team.

One way to "cheer" for my family is to care about the things they care about. My sweet mother taught me this gracious principle by example. I remember as a middle-school student telling her about my eyebrows growing together. Instead of telling me to get over my bushy eyebrows, she immediately took action. She cared about what I cared about at a very self-conscious stage in my life. I've been indebted to her ever since!

Our world is full of negative people and bullies—large and small. As daughters of our heavenly Father, we can practice His example and build up our family members first, then others. Each day we face many choices about whether to act as a "go girl" encourager or a "boo girl" discourager.

As believers in Christ, we are all on the same team, and we need to cheer for each other throughout this game of life. God so sweetens our lives through the genuine encouragement of others. We all need to practice our cheerleading skills and care!

Today, let's root for one or two people who could use a boost of encouragement. Show you are interested in what they care about! Pray for them, and let them know that God put them on your heart.

Sweet Assurance

This is what God has testified: He has given us eternal life, and this
life is in his Son. Whoever has the Son has life; whoever does not have
God's Son does not have life. I have written this to you who believe in the
name of the Son of God, so that you may know you have eternal life.

1 JOHN 5:11-13

By the time I was nine years old, I think I had asked Jesus into my heart multiple times! I didn't tell anyone because in our small hometown church, when someone asked Jesus into their heart, they had to walk down the aisle and make a public profession of their faith. I was such a scaredy-cat. I could not bring myself to get up off the pew. One Sunday when my older brother, Ryan, got up to profess his faith publicly, I immediately jumped up to join him. Finally, someone I could walk down the aisle with so I would never have to walk it alone.

That summer, I attended a Girls' Auxiliary camp in Aiken, South Carolina. The camp director told us that there was a minister available to us all week and we could go to him with any problem we had or ask him any questions. I rallied up every bit of courage for my first visit to the preacher. I was worried that my eternal salvation was in jeopardy and my baptism "did not take" because I had gone forward with my brother and not on my own.

The minister asked me if I believed that Jesus died on the cross for my sin and if I had invited Him into my life. When I said yes, he assured me that I was saved for sure!

God wants us to be assured of our eternal life in Christ. That happens when we receive Him by faith, believing He died on the cross for our sin. Buy a small jar of honey and write "Forever" across the glass. When you see it in the cupboard, be reminded that, just as honey doesn't spoil, your salvation in Christ lasts forever.

Where's the Light?

He is a light to reveal God to the nations, and
he is the glory of your people Israel!

LUKE 2:32

A picture of life lived in darkness without the light of Christ was recently illumined for me in the most personal and practical way.

My family was traveling by car on unfamiliar roads in a foreign country, anxiously looking for a rest area. When we finally found one, we made our way to the restrooms. I was thankful that I could figure out which door led into the men's restroom and which door led into the women's. When I opened the door, though, the room was pitch black. That is darker than dark!

I felt around for a light switch on the wall inside of the door, then outside. Nothing! I was scared to go into the facility, but I needed to. So I put my right foot in and took a tentative step forward—it was still dark and scary. Then I put my left foot through the door, and all of a sudden, there was *light*!

The light did not appear until both feet were firmly placed through the door. After I uttered, "Thank You, Lord," it occurred to me what it must feel like to be walking through life in darkness apart from the light of Christ.

To choose to follow Jesus, even when there are unknowns that frighten us, we must take the step of faith with both feet. We must intentionally leave the darkness behind forever. Only then are we able to reflect God's glory. There is no other way to gain salvation and security for the future, as well as peace, joy, and hope now.

Darkness or light? We must make the choice to be included in His great grace.

Let's live in the light of Christ's light in this dark world—for our own security but also so others can learn to step out in His light of faith too!

Little Things Mean a Lot

Well done, my good and faithful servant.

MATTHEW 25:21

I will never forget an early motherhood moment centered on our small kitchen table. I had been home full-time about a year after ending an almost-ten-year teaching career to be home to raise our baby. My husband, Mark, who is also a schoolteacher and coach, agreed with me on this *big* step of faith.

That particular summer day, I was attempting to add some color and cheer to our kitchen table. I couldn't buy anything, so I needed to be creative. I put out a fresh set of placemats, picked some dandelions from the yard, and placed them in a small vase at the center of the table. When the task was done, I got busy with something else. Then three-year-old Kali came into the kitchen, walked by the table, patted it with her sweet little hand, and said, "Pretty, Mommy. Pretty, Mommy." My heart swelled and tears came to my eyes as I breathed a quick "Thank You, Lord" for her precious affirmation that I had done well by adding His touch to our table.

Words of encouragement are so powerful. Anytime we look beyond our own interests and take an interest in others (Philippians 2:4), God is pleased! Our efforts reveal His Spirit at work inside of us.

When my young child said, "Pretty, Mommy," I heard God's voice echo in my mind, *Well done! Well done!* I sensed His pleasure. Even though He was the only One who witnessed that moment, I felt His encouragement.

Soak in His words today, and act on the things that God stirs in your heart to do, no matter how big or small they are. Experience the joy that comes from responding to His prompting.

High Hopes

Let all that I am wait quietly before God, for my hope is in him.
PSALM 62:5

The first ten years of Mark's and my marriage were definitely not a perfect ten. One of our biggest problems was my unfair, high hopes and expectations of my true "knight in shining armor" husband.

Unfortunately for Mark, he had a very tough act to follow—my daddy. My sweet but "all man" daddy not only fixed breakfast with fresh fruit every morning for our family, he also polished our shoes left outside his bedroom door. Can you imagine the reaction from my new husband when I took my shoes to him right after the honeymoon was over? He wasn't in the habit of polishing his own shoes very much, since he's a physical education teacher and coach who wears tennis shoes almost every day. And then his young bride shows up with these expectations.

It wasn't like I had come into marriage unprepared. I had read so many Christian books on marriage. I was marrying a wonderful Christian man, and I was a Christian, too, so what real problems could we have? Surely our Christian marriage would be perfect! It didn't dawn on me until much later that the authors of those Christian books had much more marriage experience than I had. I am grateful that those first ten years are behind us and that our marriage grows sweeter and more precious every day. We've learned to work as a team even though we still see many issues differently.

There is really only one perfect person we can put our hope in at all times—the Lord Jesus Christ. He will never disappoint us.

Let our hopes be *high* in *Him*! Study more about hope that doesn't disappoint by reading Romans 5:5. Consider the difference between hoping for something and the certainty of our hope in God.

Itty Bitty Book Light

Your word is a lamp to guide my feet and a light for my path.

PSALM 119:105

When traveling and at bedtime, I'm lost without my Itty Bitty Book Light. Now that I'm aging gracefully (Lord willing) and my eyes are weakening, it has become even more of an essential item at my bedside. On those nights when I wake up and can't go back to sleep, I can turn on my small light and read, trying not to disturb Mark beside me.

After all these years, I still marvel at how that tiny light illuminates the whole page. But it doesn't come close to how much God's Word fascinates me. I am so grateful that God's Word doesn't need batteries and that I can carry it in my heart, no matter where I go. It illumines my heart and my path, and it never gets old.

The Bible is where I hear God's voice. It isn't audible, but that still, quiet voice booms from the Bible's pages right into my heart. I look forward to hearing Him in my daily reading. I don't want to miss anything the God of the entire universe has to say to me!

I also see myself in His Word—what I am really like and my need for Christ; how much Jesus Christ has done for me and how very personal He is. That personal aspect of Jesus is revealed in the Gospels as we see Him interact with people like us. He tells us how to live for Him.

I am thankful that His Word is a lamp to our feet and a light for our path. When we follow Him, He illumines our way.

Let's keep the true light and lamp, God's Word, handy! Buy a compact Bible or download an online version to your phone or other gadget. Keep the light of His Word accessible 24/7.

Confessions of a Leaner

Come close to God, and God will come close to you.

JAMES 4:8

As much as I'd like to, I can't hide it: I'm a leaner. I am always being caught in the act by my family and friends who are the embarrassed recipients of my natural inclination. I stopped counting the number of times my daughter has said in a public place, "Mom, you're leaning on me." I was oblivious! My "problem" is that I love to be close to people. Growing up, when I was walking anywhere with my friends—down the sidewalk, in the mall—they would be victims each and every time. I would just be brushing a shoulder!

Being in close proximity to people I love is how God made me. When I speak at churches or to women's groups, I ask if I can be as close to the women as possible. My husband, Mark, is the exact opposite. He needs some room, some sweet space! It's not just because he's tall; it's his reserved personality. Can you see why we're definitely a match made in heaven?

Naturally, I love leaning (pun intended!) toward the truth of today's verse. I can relate to it so well. It's comforting to know that our awesome God revels in our company. How amazing is that?

If you're thinking, *Kim, I'm too busy. I don't really have time to draw close to God*, here's what I would say: If you are reading this right now, you are actually being still for a moment. You are drawing close to God. Since God is the Word, we come close to Him by listening to what He has to say. As you meditate on His Word, you are leaning on Him.

Lean in, listen, and learn from God. Listen to others who love and lean on Him too. We can share this wonderful truth with those who do not know there is Someone they can lean on every day.

What has God taught you recently as you've leaned on Him? Find someone who needs to hear how God came close to you.

He's Got Us Covered

The eternal God is your refuge, and his everlasting arms are under you.

DEUTERONOMY 33:27

Have you ever been without heat in winter, where the only way to keep warm was to stay under a mountain of blankets? Or gone camping when it was so cold you had to burrow down in your sleeping bag?

But even a mound of blankets or a sleeping bag rated for extreme temperatures can't help when life seems to be out of control, our hearts are broken, or we feel completely alone. That's when we can count on God to meet our needs because, through Christ, God has us covered. It doesn't matter what difficult or unexpected circumstances we are experiencing in this journey called life. God has us covered—top to bottom, over and under, side to side.

That's why I want everyone I know to have a personal relationship with God through Christ. I want all of us to have a sure refuge where we can run to His everlasting arms. There is no better protection for whatever we're facing than a loving God who sent His only Son, Jesus Christ, to cover our sin with His shed blood on the cross. All we have to do is admit our sin and receive Christ by faith, and we are covered for all eternity.

It doesn't necessarily mean that this earthly life becomes a piece of cake. Any number of calamities could come our way. But we can endure them as we call on Jesus and wrap ourselves in His strength. "God is our refuge and strength, always ready to help in times of trouble" (Psalm 46:1).

When you make your bed today, think how God covers you with an everlasting love. His cover lasts when other, lesser covers—such as protection from natural disasters, financial stability, good reports from the doctor, or security in human relationships—are not sure things.

Truth

You will know the truth, and the truth will set you free.

JOHN 8:32

I am fascinated by the military and how they solve crimes on the television show *NCIS: Los Angeles.* I also enjoy watching how the main characters relate to one another. They look after each other in their personal quirky ways.

I have not seen every episode, but in a recent one the character G. Callen (played by actor Chris O'Donnell) and character Sam Hanna (played by actor LL Cool J) were having a conversation in the car before they went to get the bad guy. I found myself cheering over their words because secular media rarely presents God's Word in a positive way:

SAM: "What if the answers you find aren't the ones you are looking for?"

G: "Do you know the motto that's engraved at the CIA headquarters at Langley?"

SAM: "John 8:32. 'You shall know the truth and the truth shall set you free.'"

G: "Amen" (as they look each other straight in the eye).

Well, I just wanted to rise up on the sofa and scream, "Amen, too! *Wow!*" Whenever God and His Word are proclaimed anywhere in an honoring way in a world that mocks His name, sweet bells of truth start ringing in my ears! That was real truth on television!

The world may mock. The world may call us religious fanatics or penalize us for our beliefs. But we know that doesn't change God's truth or His desire for us to proclaim it.

"Lord, I want Your truth to ring out all over this hurting globe. Will You help believers to know Your truth and live it each day to Your glory and honor? Amen!"

Living by God's truth is the only way to be set free from sin and free to uphold the truth wherever we are! Pray today for God's truth to reign with fresh impact.

Where Are You Headed?

You are citizens along with all of God's holy people.
You are members of God's family.

EPHESIANS 2:19

I have a confession to make: I really don't enjoy exercising this side of heaven. I know that the Lord wants us to be good stewards of the bodies He has given us. It's not that I mind the actual physical exertion part. The problem is that I only like to get ready once per day! The thought of driving somewhere in workout wear, exercising, *then* showering and changing into regular clothes seems like too much of a rigmarole to me. Plus, if I were in a class with others I hadn't seen in a while, I'd want to know what God was doing in their lives, and I'd be more interested in reaching out to them than getting my heart rate up.

But guess what? In midlife, by God's grace, I've discovered that I am motivated to walk several miles if I have a destination. When a new sidewalk was put in near my neighborhood, I discovered that it conveniently led to the coffee shop a mile and a half away. I *sometimes* enjoy the three-mile round-trip trek for coffee and a quiet bench with my teeny Bible—the perfect size for a hand weight. Hallelujah! I think I may have found an exercise plan that works for me. It was all about the destination.

More crucial than a geographical destination is our eternal destination. When we die, we are all headed somewhere, whether we believe it or not. If we believe in Christ, we are already citizens of heaven while journeying here on earth. We are being made ready for our heavenly home through trusting in Him.

 Are you exercising your heavenly citizenship while here on earth? Remind yourself of your true home with Jesus and live your life right now as if you're homeward bound.

Don't Lose Hope

This hope will not lead to disappointment. For we
know how dearly God loves us, because he has given us
the Holy Spirit to fill our hearts with his love.

ROMANS 5:5

I love sweets, as if you haven't noticed already. But one childhood incident involving something sweet left a bitter taste in my mouth for a while. The fact that I can vividly remember it as an adult shows how much it affected me then!

I really loved being part of the junior-high choir at our church, and one of my favorite parts of choir practice was the sweet snacks afterward in the church fellowship hall. One particular late afternoon, we were served cupcakes that a choir mom had made. I scraped all the icing off my cupcake so I could savor that huge chunk of chocolate icing last! It was lying on the side of my paper plate when suddenly, the girl sitting beside me grabbed the hunk of chocolate icing right off my plate and stuck it in her mouth! To add insult to injury, the culprit was the preacher's daughter!

Well, I was shocked, mad, and devastated. And to make it worse, there weren't any leftover cupcakes to console me.

So many years later, I find myself getting that same feeling of disappointment at those times when something doesn't turn out the way I expected—my way! I feel like someone stole the icing off my cupcake and there is no hope of getting it back! When I start thinking that way, I talk with God about it because He cares about everything we care about! That's how much He loves us. He will use each letdown to remind us that He never fails us or disappoints us. He is our real hope.

Eat a sweet cupcake or other treat today, knowing that your hope in Christ is far sweeter!

God Never Exaggerates

I am with you always, even to the end of the age.
MATTHEW 28:20

We don't always mean to do it, but it happens: we tend to exaggerate. Have you ever caught yourself saying, "I'm starving"? How about "I'm dead on my feet"? Maybe someone has accused you of *never* doing something or *always* doing something else. These are pretty big statements to make.

According to Webster's dictionary, the word *exaggerate* means to overstate, or think or tell of something as greater than it is. Haven't we been taught that words like *always* and *never* hinder our communication with others, that many times using them fuels confrontations? I'm so encouraged by the fact that God never exaggerates.

All through Scripture, God communicates His unexaggerated but extravagant love for us through His Son, Jesus Christ, whom He sent to die on the cross for our sins. What loving earthly father would give the life of his only son or daughter for the life of another person? God did that for all of mankind. God gave His Son for you. God gave His Son for me!

The Word of God is full of claims that may seem like boasts or exaggerations, but they are really true statements.

> To *all* who did receive him, to those who believed in his name, he gave the right to become children of God. JOHN 1:12, NIV

> God is the King of *all* the earth. PSALM 47:7, NIV

> [Love] *always* protects, *always* trusts, *always* hopes, *always* perseveres.
> 1 CORINTHIANS 13:7, NIV

> He will *never* leave you nor forsake you. DEUTERONOMY 31:6, NIV
> (EMPHASIS ADDED IN ALL OF THE VERSES QUOTED)

God is the only One who can say these words honestly every single time.

Every time you read these words in Scripture—*all*, *always*, or *never*—highlight them in your Bible. And remember, God never exaggerates!

Logs in Our Eyes

Why worry about a speck in your friend's eye when you have a log in your own? How can you think of saying to your friend, "Let me help you get rid of that speck in your eye," when you can't see past the log in your own eye? Hypocrite! First get rid of the log in your own eye; then you will see well enough to deal with the speck in your friend's eye.

MATTHEW 7:3-5

Some of life's best lessons are learned at an early age. When I was five years old, I tattled to my Sunday school teacher that one of the boys in class had his eyes open during the prayer. "Kim, how would you know his eyes were open unless your eyes were open too?" the teacher kindly replied. Ugh, it embarrasses me all over again just telling you about it.

Unfortunately, this tendency to be critical of others isn't reserved only for kindergarteners. It follows us into adulthood. How many times have I jumped to critically point out things in my own family members that I am guilty of myself? In our household we remind each other of this by saying, "When you are pointing your finger at someone else, there are four fingers pointing back at you!" or "What are the five most important words? I'm sorry. I was wrong!" Hard to swallow, but true.

I am thankful that Jesus addressed this malady of "impaired vision." He shows us again and again how we need His help in our interactions with others. He wants us to stop and think before we rush to correct someone else. Let's face it: each one of us can use a generous dose of His grace and log-removing remedy on a regular basis.

Next time we are ready to say something critical, let's take a quick peek at our own tendencies first—it just may ax the comment.

Clean Conscience

I have the same hope in God that these men have, that he will raise both the righteous and the unrighteous. Because of this, I always try to maintain a clear conscience before God and all people.

ACTS 24:15-16

In this passage in Acts, Paul is defending and professing his faith to the higher-ups in prison. Years into our marriage, I told my husband, Mark, that I used to like myself better before I started reading God's Word regularly! My conscience did not seem to be pricked as much until I began to see God's holiness and kindness, which seemed to put a spotlight on my unholy, unkind attitudes! Still, the more I see what He is like and what I am really like, the more I see how much I need His grace, love, and mercy that are offered to me, and the more I want to please Him.

I had no idea what wonderful adventures were in store for me when I started hearing God's voice daily through the pages of His Word. Little did I know how often God would point out something He wanted to change in me, whether I liked it or not. I have settled this issue with God: His way is best! I want to do His will. Even though most days I feel like a slow learner, Jesus Christ is a loving, patient Teacher. I can "try to maintain a clear conscience before God and all people" in freedom because of Christ.

Practically speaking, this means that we may need to go to a family member and say, "I am sorry. I was wrong! Will you forgive me?" It may mean that we need to phone a friend ASAP and apologize for letting her down. It may mean we need to take back a receipt that shows we were undercharged and pay what we owe. Whatever God's Holy Spirit brings to our consciences, we want to address it in His power, by faith and not according to our feelings.

 Ask the Holy Spirit to reveal any thoughts, attitudes, or actions that need His conscientious, conscious cleansing!

Great Shout-Out to God

All the people gave a great shout of praise to the LORD, because the foundation of the house of the LORD was laid.

EZRA 3:11, NIV

God and the book of Ezra are getting a shout-out from me today! Tucked between 2 Chronicles and Nehemiah is the ten-chapter book of Ezra. Besides being one of the easiest book titles in the Bible to spell, it is so insightful about people—people just like us! We get glimpses of their responses to life's changing circumstances as they weathered a lot of delays and disappointments before finally being able to celebrate.

The book of Ezra came alive to me because my life is full of change too. This historical book records the story of God's people returning to Jerusalem from a seventy-year captivity with a goal in mind: to rebuild the Temple. When the foundation for the new Temple was completed, there was a huge, loud celebration!

A year ago I learned the term "shout-out" when my then twenty-year-old daughter commented that I got a shout-out about something I'd done well. When I read this verse, I smiled at the thought that God's people were giving Him a shout-out in joy and thanksgiving because the initial stages of the Temple were finished, but older men were shouting out with tears of disappointment because they knew it wasn't as magnificent as the original place of worship. No one could distinguish the sounds of joy from the sounds of weeping because the people made so much noise (verses 12-13).

Doesn't that sound like some of our interactions at times with other Christians who are different from us and have different ways of looking at things? Instead of getting snippy with each other for seeing things differently, let's focus together on who we're all praising.

Let's give a unified shout-out to the only true God! Next time we see someone in church worshiping a bit differently than we do, let's thank the Lord that He speaks uniquely to each of His own.

We Are Lavishly Loved!

See what great love the Father has lavished on us, that we
should be called children of God! And that is what we are!

1 JOHN 3:1, NIV

Wow! Two exclamation points in one verse. I love exclamation points! When I used to teach reading to children, it was always so fun to introduce them to exclamation points and hear them read aloud.

We are children of God if we have believed and received Jesus Christ. And as God's children, we are forever recipients of our Father's lavish loving on us! Isn't *lavish* a great word? According to Webster's, it comes from a French word I cannot pronounce that means "downpour, very generous, abundant, giving or spending liberally." Picture it. God just drenches us in a downpour of His love. I don't know about you, but I'd prefer being deluged with that kind of shower rather than being bone dry.

Not too long ago, I received a hint of this kind of love when my husband pulled out all the stops to celebrate a big birthday of mine. When I saw the results of all the time he put into it, I was touched beyond words. I didn't need a party after watching him so lavishly love me and seeing how he had worked to surprise me. The icing on the birthday cake had pink smiley faces. The pink tablecloths were laden with fresh, beautiful Ukrop's shrimp, appetizers, and cake! We ate leftovers for a week with our sweet neighbors. As well-loved as I felt that day, it is just a small taste of the abundant love we receive every minute from our heavenly Father here on earth. We have everything when we know Christ, and we have everything to offer others!

Let's live like lavishly loved children and celebrate by thanking our Great God, telling Him how much we love Him.

The Black Refrigerator

*Love is patient and kind. Love is not jealous or boastful
or proud or rude. It does not demand its own way.*

1 CORINTHIANS 13:4-5

Ouch! I am still living with the consequences of demanding my own way in the kitchen! Mark and I have been married for nearly thirty years, and for most of our marriage we had a refrigerator with the freezer on the bottom. My tall, athletic husband (a former University of Virginia basketball player) always loved the convenience of that extra space in the middle of the refrigerator for his tall drinks—milk, OJ, and soft drinks.

When our twentysomething refrigerator lost its vim and vigor—and handle— we went shopping for a new one. All my daughter, Kali, and I could talk about was a side-by-side refrigerator because we were wowed by the ice and water dispenser in the door. Mark wasn't so sure about that "fun" change. It was two strongly opinionated girls against one laid-back, kind man. Guess who won? Insisting on our own way, we eventually managed to wear Mark down. The side-by-side model was purchased and delivery arrangements made.

We didn't win, though! Soon after the fridge was squeezed into the kitchen, I discovered that one side door was so close to the wall that I couldn't open it enough to even slip a casserole dish inside. I'll admit it: I still miss our old refrigerator! So does Mark, but he's forgiven us for being stubbornly insistent and not thinking about his preference at all. It was a teachable moment for Kali and me.

In the same way, sin has consequences. But thanks be to God, He offers forgiveness to us too. He used a refrigerator to illustrate His truth to me.

Now, every time I walk into the kitchen, I'm reminded of the great grace of God and His forgiveness.

Do you need to apologize to someone because you demanded your own way? Try to do that soon and experience God's incredible forgiveness.

Bandages

He heals the brokenhearted and bandages their wounds.
PSALM 147:3

When I went to the drugstore recently, I couldn't believe the selection of bandages available! There were extreme lengths, pain and itch relief, quick stop (stops bleeding faster), advanced healing, antibiotic, gentle care, knuckle and fingertip, sheer, clear, transparent, waterproof, tattoo-designed, pop art, glitter, cartoon characters, even pink bandages! The decorated ones, especially with smiley faces on them, made me laugh!

Of course, I know that bandages are for minor cuts and scrapes, not for the deeper wounds made by a person's offhand remark or those we suffer when someone else receives credit for the hard work that we've put in.

Over the years, I have learned that no earthly bandage can heal my broken heart or cure my emotional wounds. Sometimes I resort to my own remedies, like SweetFrog frozen yogurt. But that's a momentary salve. Healing is God's job. He doesn't just apply a temporary bandage either; He is the surgeon who cuts to the core of my heart and brings sweet relief to my soul.

Of course, God uses His people as big bandages for other hurting people. The apostle Paul talked about that in 2 Corinthians 1:4: "He comforts us in all our troubles so that we can comfort others. When they are troubled, we will be able to give them the same comfort God has given us." You and I may be used by God to visit a sick person, sit by someone's hospice bed and hold his or her hand, write a note, provide a meal, read Scripture, sing hymns, or start an encouraging card ministry like my sweet friend Jayne did. We cannot change heartbreaking situations for people we love. Only one kind of procedure does it all, and it is no bandage. It is a full-blown heart transplant when you give your life to Jesus Christ.

Next time you're in the store aisle with all the bandages, think of your Soul Surgeon and your ultimate Healer, Jesus Christ!

Imperfect Vision

Now we see things imperfectly, like puzzling reflections in a mirror, but then we will see everything with perfect clarity. All that I know now is partial and incomplete, but then I will know everything completely, just as God now knows me completely.

1 CORINTHIANS 13:12

Have you ever been out doing errands in your car and been caught by a surprise rain shower? I certainly have! Once when that happened, I regretted the fact that I hadn't replaced my pitiful windshield wipers. I had meant to take care of that job, but I got busy with other things. Now, my windshield was so blurry that my vision was impaired. The people driving behind me probably wondered why I kept bobbing my head all around. "I'm so sorry, drivers! I'm just trying to find a clear spot on my windshield so I can see the highway!"

In today's verse from 1 Corinthians, the apostle Paul explains that our earthly vision is imperfect compared to the eternal vision we will receive when we see the Lord face to face. As a child, when someone much wiser than I would say she couldn't wait to go to heaven, I had to keep from rolling my eyes. I'd think, *What's wrong with her? That's the last thing I want to do right now.* I was having too much fun as a child, and there was so much more I hadn't experienced.

Thankfully, I have a different perspective now. As my responsibilities and heartaches have increased over the years, I understand what they were longing for. It will be wonderful to be in heaven one day and see Christ clearly—just as clearly as He sees us now.

Let's be encouraged and thankful that God sees us with perfect vision and loves us. Read Psalm 139 to see how well God knows each of us.

Sweet Kick in the Pants

Oh, the joys of those who do not follow the advice of the wicked. . . . But
they delight in the law of the LORD, meditating on it day and night.

PSALM 1:1-2

Could I give us all a sweet kick in the pants today?

I am trying to figure out how to say this without sounding bossy or legalistic. Okay, here goes: I think all of us believers in Christ need to prioritize our schedules so we spend time with God in His Word.

Listening to God's voice can be as regular as breathing. And if we check our phone messages, texts, e-mails, and hair every day, we can certainly check in with God Almighty in His Word for our marching orders and get our pink ducks in a row for the day ahead. We can put God and His Word at the top of our list, whether the time we carve out with Him is in the early morning, while we're having lunch, or just before bed at night. But if we do not plan our days wisely with the mind of Christ that God gave each of us, then our days will plan us.

I've been surprised at how God has delighted me with Himself in the nitty-gritty work of the day when I've committed to spend time with Him. He makes even the challenge of putting together this devotional book a joy because reading His Word is a delight! Thinking about what He says is pleasing, and talking to Him about it, which is called prayer, is too. His messages are so much more effective than mine. Nothing compares with Him.

You and I cannot settle for piggybacking off our favorite Bible teacher's or pastor's experiences with God. We need to have our own! We need wisdom and courage and strength of our own. We just don't have it in us—apart from Christ. We need to adopt the daily, life-changing habit of literally sitting still with open hearts, following a simple plan to read His Word, and in prayer offering to God ourselves and our days—which are really His days! We need to hear His voice above all others. I don't know any other way to say it.

Let's join forces and give each other a sweet kick in the pants to read His Word every day! Choose a daily study plan, such as reading the *One Year Bible* (or use the Bible you already have, following one of the schedules at www.oneyearbibleonline.com/readingplan.asp). Let's make the Lord's pink army stronger.

34

The Best Way of Life

*Let me show you a way of life that is best of all. . . . Love is patient
and kind. Love is not jealous or boastful or proud or rude. It does
not demand its own way. It is not irritable, and it keeps no record
of being wronged. It does not rejoice about injustice but rejoices
whenever the truth wins out. Love never gives up, never loses faith,
is always hopeful, and endures through every circumstance.*

1 CORINTHIANS 12:31; 13:4-7

I *love* this *love* passage, but not because it makes me feel like a loving person! In
fact, it reminds me of where I fall short in my relationships with people I really
love. That's especially true when I am struggling to forgive someone I feel has
wronged me in some way. I have to work hard to keep myself from holding a
grudge or fighting back.

I believe most of us have grown up thinking that the concept of love is pretty
simple and straightforward. You meet someone, fall in love, and live happily ever
after. First Corinthians 13 explains the many components of love, all characteristics of God, who loved us so much that "he gave his one and only Son, so that
everyone who believes in him will not perish but have eternal life" (John 3:16).
Love isn't as simple as it seems. It isn't as mushy as I always dreamed it would be.
There's a lot of work involved—but it's His best work.

God is the only One who demonstrates love perfectly. He keeps no record of
wrongs. He is always patient with us and kind to us. God is always loving toward
us, which means He never gives up on us, never loses faith in us, is always hopeful. He endures through every circumstance with us, and there have probably
been some tough ones. God *is love*! Reading 1 Corinthians 13 sheds light on how
much God has loved and forgiven us, and quickens our hearts to forgive others.
Love is the best way because it's His way!

Next time you are struggling to forgive someone, read 1 Corinthians
13:4-7 and ask God to give you the words you need to say.

Table Talk

Precious in the sight of the Lord is the death of his saints.

PSALM 116:15, KJV

Many times when we are sitting at our kitchen table, we enjoy drawing simple questions from a cute container to spark conversation and help us get to know family members or guests better.

I loved doing this when our daughter was young, hearing her form her first words, then phrases, then complete sentences. As any parent can attest, kids really do come up with unexpected observations. I'll never forget when Kali was five and drew this question from the box: "What are your favorite things to do?" Without hesitating she replied, "Busch Gardens, picnics, and burying people."

Her answer made Mark and me burst out laughing, which was a welcome relief at that moment. We were still grieving over the homegoing of Grandmommy Newlen, Mark's grandmother, from just a week before. She was a saint in Christ, so we knew we'd see her again on those heavenly streets of gold; death had taken her from this earth, but we would reunite again in the future.

That's why Kali added "burying people" to her list of favorite fun things. We had celebrated Grandmommy Newlen with other believing family members, music, flowers, food, and laughter mixed with tears—remembering her. We were thankful that she was in God's presence. It seemed like one big party to Kali, which I am grateful for.

When was the last time you looked in the mirror and said, "I am a saint"? If we have put our faith and trust in Jesus Christ as our Savior, we are saints who are precious in God's sight!

⚬━ Rejoice today if you are in Christ. There is no way to lose that precious gift. Ask God to comfort you with this truth when you grieve. And if you haven't done it already, write down how you came to faith so your family will know and can keep sharing your story.

Sweetwalking by Faith

*Faith is the confidence that what we hope for will actually happen;
it gives us assurance about things we cannot see. Through their
faith, the people in days of old earned a good reputation.*

HEBREWS 11:1-2

As a child, I was an occasional sleepwalker, wandering through the house with no awareness of my actions. I'm thankful that my midnight journeys never led to injury or trouble.

I wonder how many people in this world are sleepwalking through life with no awareness of God. They believe that life ends at death, that there's nothing more to our existence. Consequently, they try to do everything they can to achieve success on this earth. Many miss out on the most important fact: the Good News that there is a God and He has a plan for each and every spiritual sleepwalker. He is the only One who can really wake us up—for now and forever.

God wants to use His followers, those already awakened to Christ, to share His Good News. I know that when I get busy with my daily to-do list before hearing what God has to say through His Word, I never seem to get around to really listening to His voice above all the other voices that surround me.

I love the fact that King David "encouraged himself in the LORD his God" (1 Samuel 30:6, KJV), and we can certainly follow his example. God is the best Encourager we'll ever find, and we can use a lot of encouragement to do the things He wants us to do! It's great to have a divine Motivator giving us that extra reassuring boost.

Wouldn't you rather sweetwalk in the light than sleepwalk in the dark? Think of one verse from the Bible that awakens you to sweetwalk with Him. If you're having trouble remembering one, try Psalm 25:4; 27:11; or 57:7-9.

God Never Runs Empty

In him we live and move and exist.

ACTS 17:28

Although more than half of my life is probably over, I had never been to a gas station that didn't have gas—until recently! When we experienced a fuel shortage in our county, the gas station I frequent was out of gas. How can a gas station be out of gas? I thought they should have changed their sign to *No-Gas Station* or maybe *Ungas*. They didn't even have a fume! My car's fuel tank was almost on empty, which put my emotional fuel tank in a panic. I was afraid I was going to run out of gas trying to find another station that had some petrol. Thankfully, I didn't have to drive far to find one that did.

In those few minutes, it was like a lightbulb came on in my brain. God reminded me that it's impossible for Him to be empty—He is inexhaustible! God, spelled with a capital *G*—the one God, Creator of all things, and Master of the universe—is never out of little-*g* gas. Being His child in Christ, I never run out of gasoline either. He pumps His power into all His children through His Holy Spirit.

He fuels life with goodness, grace, and generosity. He replaces our weaknesses with His strength, which is stronger than any difficult set of circumstances we will ever face. It's only in Him that we can truly live and move and exist—and never be out of gas!

Is it time for a fill-up from the Holy Spirit? He helps us run and not grow weary, thanks to His ultimate premium power (Isaiah 40:31).

Let's stop running on earthly fumes, and let's step on the gas pedal of faith together, knowing we have everything in Christ. Right now, let's pray that the Holy Spirit will energize us.

Redeeming Your Free Gift

God saved you by his grace when you believed. And you can't take credit for this; it is a gift from God. Salvation is not a reward for the good things we have done, so none of us can boast about it.

EPHESIANS 2:8-9

Recently I was thrilled when I found a hefty gift certificate that had gone AWOL in the house. It was for a wonderful restaurant Mark and I had not tried, only because we couldn't find the gift certificate we had stashed away. Dining out is one of my favorite dates with Mark because I love to try new foods that I would never make at home. I also really enjoy how chefs make beautiful presentations with food. I'll admit that there have been times when my culinary experimentation was followed by a "No, thank you," when I didn't like what I ordered. I would then help Mark eat whatever he had ordered. He teasingly reminds me that I was the only girl he ever dated who seemed to always want the last piece of pizza!

Mostly, I enjoy a quiet dinner alone with my husband because I like his company, away from the distractions of phones or the television. And after enjoying a yummy dessert, the real icing on the sweet cake is not having to clean up!

As I held that gift certificate in my hand, I started thinking about our hurting world. Despite all our technological advancements, it seems many people are suffering loneliness and isolation on earth, never redeeming the free gift of salvation in Christ. We need to realize that everyone has been offered this gift. We only need to ask for it by faith.

Create a gift certificate from Jesus made out to you or someone else as a reminder of His free gift of eternal life.

Interest in Others

Don't be selfish; don't try to impress others. Be humble, thinking
of others as better than yourselves. Don't look out only for
your own interests, but take an interest in others, too.

PHILIPPIANS 2:3-4

Many times I learn God's life lessons the hard way, but I can say without exaggeration that every time I do things God's way instead of my selfish way, I feel better inside and end up having a lot more fun. Doing things God's unselfish way makes a big difference, especially in our relationships with other people.

Take marriage, for instance. When I compare our before-marriage dates with our after-marriage dates, I tease my husband that my pleasure truly seems to give him pain. You see, I want to experience all that an occasion has to offer. At dinner I want the appetizer, dessert and coffee, and everything in between. At a ball game I want the people, the weather, the hot dog, popcorn, drink, and then the event. On the other hand, my husband wisely wants to enjoy a dinner date without breaking our budget, and at a ball game he is interested only in the game.

Before marriage, these differences weren't even visible through my brand-new-in-love gaga eyes, but they shine bright and glaring during the after-marriage dates! Honestly, I usually have my own interests in mind, but when I consider his interests, that unselfishness proves to be a far more enjoyable relationship builder!

God made us all so different. He does not tell us that we are not to look after our own interests, but He exhorts us to take an interest in others, too. We're not to be selfish and try to impress people, but instead we ought to think of them as even better than ourselves!

Initiate a sweet date with your spouse or friend and do what he or she wants to do. Celebrate God-given relationships!

A Heart Set Free

I run in the path of your commands, for you have set my heart free.
PSALM 119:32, NIV

It's that time of year when we can't escape red and pink hearts—they're everywhere. What a great reminder for us to do a self-examination of our hearts. But beware, because instead of being red and pink, this examination is pretty black and white.

Sometimes it may be hard to describe what a heart set free feels like, but we sure know even at this minute if we are having heart problems. My heart feels locked up when it is overcrowded with the cares and distractions of life that are not discarded at the feet of Jesus.

Take a moment right now and read Psalm 119:32, which is found just about in the exact middle of the Bible. Then answer the question below by checking the appropriate box:

Is your heart set free?   Yes ☐   No ☐

How'd you do? Whichever box you checked, one thing is worth noting: you and I will never experience a heart set free if we are not in Christ. Because of Christ's indwelling by His Spirit, we receive His nudge when we're off track. We feel good inside when we do the right things, and we lack peace when we let our focus stray from Him. When we don't obey Him, we feel unsettled. That's the Holy Spirit convicting us that our hearts are not right with God.

There is no room in our hearts for contradictions! I told our daughter when she was growing up that good self-esteem comes from doing the right things. When we have right standing with God in Christ, we want to do the right things because His Holy Spirit resides in us. We're made in His image, to bring glory and honor to Him. That is true heart freedom!

Let's start living free, always tuning in to Christ's Spirit! Write down one thing you can do to help yourself tune in more consistently to the Holy Spirit's nudges and stay on course with Him.

View from the Balcony

Don't let your hearts be troubled. Trust in God, and trust also in me. There is more than enough room in my Father's home. If this were not so, would I have told you that I am going to prepare a place for you?

JOHN 14:1-2

Whenever our family goes on vacation and stays in a hotel, my biggest request is for a room with a balcony. My husband and daughter are night owls and love to sleep in the next morning, but no matter what time I've gone to bed, I am up early. I feel cheated out of the day if I miss the few fresh hours of morning. A balcony is a place where I can pop outside to greet the day, see God's handiwork, and enjoy the fresh air while my family is still sleeping.

As I write this, I am on vacation, enjoying the cool breeze from our twelfth-floor balcony—which overlooks a parking lot. I don't mind it. You see, if I train my eyes to look far beyond the parking lot, I actually see a harbor with ships, sailboats, and float planes, and beyond that, I see the mountains rising so firm and stately against the endless blue sky that it takes my breath away. "Thank You," I say to God aloud, "for giving us so much to enjoy in creation." All this beauty pales in comparison to what He has planned for us to enjoy in heaven.

It dawned on me (pun intended) that I could easily look down and focus on the parking lot below me. It's easy to live our lives in the parking lot and not in the eternal. But why would we want to miss God's best? Let's look beyond our crowded-parking-lot circumstances and see Jesus.

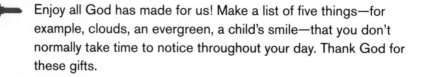

Enjoy all God has made for us! Make a list of five things—for example, clouds, an evergreen, a child's smile—that you don't normally take time to notice throughout your day. Thank God for these gifts.

"So Excited" Face

*Don't rejoice because evil spirits obey you; rejoice
because your names are registered in heaven.*

LUKE 10:20

Sometimes I get so excited about what God does that I just cannot seem to keep it in. My sweet friend Alison calls it my "so excited" face.

In Luke 10, Jesus sent out seventy-two of His followers ahead of Him to all the towns and places He planned to visit. In Luke 10:17 when they returned to report back to Jesus, it's not hard to imagine that they had on their "so excited" faces, too, because they eagerly told Him, "Lord, even the demons obey us when we use your name!"

But it is Jesus' response to His followers that really intrigues me. They were reveling in the successful ministry God had given them, a mission that had seen results. Jesus reminded His followers of the good things He had given them, like the authority to trample on snakes and scorpions and to overcome the power of the enemy so nothing would harm them. But then He said something unexpected: "But don't rejoice because evil spirits obey you; rejoice because your names are registered in heaven" (Luke 10:20).

This word *don't* gives us perspective when we have on our "so excited" faces for what God has done in our lives, our work, and our families. When we have experienced His power and cannot keep it in, we glory in Him and our position in Him for all eternity. Even when it seems that our mission has failed, we can truly be joyful because in Christ, our names are written in heaven—signed, sealed, and delivered by His sacrifice for you and me! Now that's something to have a "so excited" face about!

If we are not wearing our "so excited" faces, let's think of what Jesus did for us. Then write a thank-you note to Him.

Holding Back the Truth

If someone asks about your hope as a believer,
always be ready to explain it.

1 PETER 3:15

"Okay, Lord! I hear You now!"

I do not think I will ever forget coming home from college one particular weekend to see my sweet mama and daddy. It was so fun to eat my mother's good southern cooking and dawdle around town, visiting the new shops in our mini mall. Just as I was getting ready to leave the mall, a jewelry store beckoned to me.

While I was gazing into the sparkling glass cases, the clerk smiled and said something like, "You look so happy. You have a glow. What makes you so happy?" This question was so out of the blue and unexpected, I mumbled something like "Oh, I'm just happy" and exited the store as quickly as possible! I didn't like the feeling of being caught off guard, even though deep down I knew I should have answered honestly, that my joy came from knowing Jesus. But at that moment I felt embarrassed to admit it.

Outside the mall entrance, I leaned against the brick wall, devastated that I did not share the truth of my hope in Christ with the clerk. The words from Romans 1—"I am not ashamed of the gospel"—kept replaying in my mind. I felt as though I had broken God's heart.

"I am sorry, God, that I wasn't a bold witness for You. Please forgive me for not taking every opportunity to share what You have done for all of us. Jesus, You are the hope within me."

Life is so short. Do not hold back hope, the only hope, now and forever—Jesus Christ. If we in Christ don't tell others, who will? Be ready to seize every opportunity to share His truth, the simple Good News that you and I live forgiven in Christ.

Sweet Mail

*How precious are your thoughts about me, O God. They cannot be
numbered! I can't even count them; they outnumber the grains of sand!*

PSALM 139:17-18

Better than e-mail, bulk mail, junk mail, and bills is sweet mail! Sweet mail tells
you that someone is thinking of you. Think how you go through your mail.
Which letters do you always open first? The personal ones, I imagine. The ones
addressed in handwriting you recognize!

As delightful as it is to receive an unexpected note in the mailbox, there is
something even more wonderful I want to share with you. Someone is thinking
of you today. Someone who says His thoughts are so many toward you that they
would outnumber the grains of sand. Let that image soak into your spirit. That's
a whole lot of thoughts specifically about you. This Person perpetually thinking
of you is perfect and loving. How precious it is to have the only perfect, always
loving Person thinking about you and me *all the time*.

It's as if each one of our mailboxes is crammed full every day with personal
handwritten "I'm thinking of you today" cards. The sweet mail would be so abundant that we would be called by the post office because it would be impossible for
them to deliver it all; yet it would also be impossible for us to open them all in a
day. Each and every card is signed, "I'm yours, Jesus Christ."

Draw a heart on a sheet of white paper, color it pink, and place a
Band-Aid on it. Write a note to a hurting friend on the heart and
deliver it soon. And don't forget to write a sweet-mail letter to God.
He deserves one most of all.

The Fields Are (Pink) for Harvest

Lift up your eyes, and look on the fields; for
they are white already to harvest.

JOHN 4:35, KJV

Wake up and look around! Jesus is talking to us! If we have believed in Jesus Christ as Savior and have received Him by faith, then just as He told this to His disciples, He is telling this fact to us. When we see a sea of women around us, we know there is ripe, sweet fruit among them—women who are ready to be introduced to Christ. We are Jesus' branches, rooted in Him, and our job is to reach out to others.

Branches grow from the trunk of a tree, receiving nourishment from the tree and its roots. If the branches become separated from the tree, they die. We do not want to be those! We must stay connected to Jesus daily and grow spiritually in Him in order to bud and blossom.

When Jesus told His disciples that the fields were white for harvest, He was telling them that the fields were ready for picking! I think of it this way: the fields are [pink] for harvest with women who have never heard about Jesus' love, and we are His field-workers. As women who are following Jesus, we must lift up our eyes and be part of the harvest that He brings to our attention.

In Matthew 9:37, Jesus says, "The harvest is great, but the workers are few." Don't be discouraged by the task. We have the privilege of sowing broadly and nurturing as seed planters, waterers, or fertilizers by praying for people, inviting people to lunch or church, or simply befriending them. Now that's sow sweet!

We need to see ourselves as God does—as His dearly loved daughters with specific fieldwork to do!

The fields are [pink] for harvest! Let's choose a way to start sowing as we allow God to do all the hard work in the women we encounter!

Motivate One Another

*Let us think of ways to motivate one another
to acts of love and good works.*

HEBREWS 10:24

Besides God's Word, I learn the most from other women like you. I walk around our home and point to things I have been motivated to do because "sweet so-and-so" taught me. Not only does it bring a smile to my face, but it also benefits my family and friends who enjoy our home. More important, these special gifts of beauty and order, cooking and cleaning, and godly parenting all bring honor and glory to the Lord.

We all benefit from the suggestions of others encouraging us in specific ways to do things that show love. For example, my linen closet looked presentable only when the door was closed. But when a new Sweet Monday friend encouraged me to organize my closet and make it look pretty, I took it to heart. That week, I actually took the doors off my closet so I would have no secrets to hide. Little by little, I added attractive, sturdy baskets to house our sheets and toiletries. Now my family is sweetly served because they can easily locate items.

My friend Daphne taught me how to make easy, quick rolls after I had spent years throwing away yeast packs because they expired. My daughter loves bread, and she really appreciates it when I make Daphne's rolls. What a fun way to incorporate God's command in Hebrews to think of ways to motivate one another to acts of love as we share our lives with each other. That command provides endless opportunities for encouraging others.

Why not make a friend's recipe this week and let her know she motivated you? Then consider how a helpful sweet tweet or Facebook post could bless others when you pass it on. (Sweet Anne, you make a great chicken pot pie! Thank you!)

His Glorious Image

*All of us who have had that veil removed can see and reflect the
glory of the Lord. And the Lord—who is the Spirit—makes us more
and more like him as we are changed into his glorious image.*

2 CORINTHIANS 3:18

I don't know about you, but I like to think of ways to organize our home so it is simpler to manage. Disorder does not bring out the best in me! (Don't worry, someone else's mess doesn't bother me—just my own!) I am continually thinking of ways to use space wisely and "sweeten" our home so I can better focus on what is really going to last in this life—God, His Word, and people. I'll admit that sometimes it is easier to rearrange furniture than to allow God to rearrange me. But I am always up for change. Developing this threefold focus in priorities has definitely been a supernatural change that only God could make in me.

Sometimes only God can see this change. Maybe we need to quickly return a library book that we started to read but were troubled by its contents, or maybe we ought to throw away a cluttered stack of catalogs that particularly tempt us to overspend. Perhaps change can happen when we ask God to show us any attitudes that need to go right into the trash can, and maybe we need to take time to simply stop and ponder where God is moving in our lives so that we can move with Him by faith in the power of His Holy Spirit, even when we are afraid. Thank goodness the Lord is committed to conforming us to His image so He can shine brightly through us.

Celebrate God's Spirit making us more and more like Him! Let's ask God to show us one area of change that needs to happen in us; then let's be willing to step out in faith and make it happen.

Reaching a Lonely Heart

God places the lonely in families; he sets the
prisoners free and gives them joy.

PSALM 68:6

Over the years I've read the first two chapters of Genesis many times. Genesis means "beginning," and everything God created in the beginning as told in Genesis was good. The heavens, earth, plants, sun, moon, stars, animals, man—all we see and breathe—it was all good. And then God said in Genesis 2:18, "It is not good for the man to be alone." Wait—the first "not good"! Why the change? Because God made us for relationships with others and Himself.

When I stopped teaching school to be a stay-at-home mom, I was lonely for the very first time in my life. I missed interacting with other women. I spent consistent time with my sweet older friend across the street, whom we all called Grandma Hazel.

When I explained to Mark how I was feeling and asked if he thought there was something wrong with me, he assured me that I was just fine; I was adjusting to a different season in my life. Well, I do not know any woman who wants to be only just fine! I loved being a mom even though being on the baby's routine kept me at home. But during my months of isolation, God came near. He helped me see my need for a deeper relationship with Christ. I began to think that if I had such intense feelings of loneliness while knowing Christ, what about women in the same situation without Him? How would they be able to get through?

And then God stirred my heart almost twenty years ago to invite women to our home the first Monday of each month as a simple outreach of a new church plant we were part of. And over the past nineteen years, God has faithfully brought new women into my life each month. Once again, God created something extremely good when I needed it most.

This week, why not invite someone to do something with you that you have already scheduled?

The Importance of Salt

You are the salt of the earth. But what
good is salt if it has lost its flavor?

MATTHEW 5:13

Salt makes us thirsty, right? The Bible tells believers in Christ that we are the salt of the earth. Being around us should make other people thirsty for who we know. Salt is a preservative. When we point others to Christ, not only does He enhance our lives and theirs, but He is the only One who preserves us for eternity.

In fact, growing in my love for Christ was jump-started my first year at Erskine College when I met a true salt-of-the-earth friend. Sweet Cecilia seemed to know Him in a more personal way, and I wanted to know Him like she did. Because of her influence, I asked for God's help to know Him more directly, too, like Cecilia. In the days and years since, He has continued to answer my prayer by putting a lot of salty people (in the sweetest sense of the word) around me and speaking to my heart when I read His Word.

There are many simple, practical ways we can be salt and connect with people, thus connecting them to Christ. If we do not reach out to others in the name of Christ, who will?

If you don't feel important enough to make a difference, remember: you and I are salt! Christ used salt as an analogy because it was essential to life back then, and it still is a vital part of our health. We would die without salt. Only He can preserve this world, and He wants to use us as teaspoons and tablespoons of salt, more than we could even imagine!

Whether we feel salty or not, God wants to use you and me to draw others to Himself. He will do this hard work in others' hearts as we abide in Him. Ponder Matthew 5:13 and John 15:4, verses that tell us how we can be flavorful for Christ.

God's Power for God's Girls

By his divine power, God has given us everything we need for living a
godly life. We have received all of this by coming to know him, the one
who called us to himself by means of his marvelous glory and excellence.

2 PETER 1:3

It seems as though I am always encountering the slogan "Girl Power" written on
some fun knickknack wherever I go. With my years of ministering to women, I
certainly believe in unified girl power, but even more so I believe in God's power.
As a former schoolteacher, I want to cross out and change "girl power" to "God's
power" on every item I see.

God is clear that in His divine power He has given us everything we need for
a godly life. We spin our wheels and go nowhere by thinking we can be godly
apart from Him. We cannot grow in anything good without coming to know Him
in Christ. When I push through a too long to-do list in an unrealistic amount of
time, overcommit to opportunities (wonderful though they may be), and become
overly bossy with my family as a result, I get spiritually depleted! I am depending on my own puny girl-power strength instead of allowing God's power to flow
through me.

Whenever we feel like we're running out of His strength, we should express
our need through prayer for the Holy Spirit to take over. In addition to the gift
of His Spirit, God has given us each other in His big family! With God's power
at work in each of us who have received Christ, we are a stronger and sweeter
force that can be more effective for Him as we make an eternal difference in
our hurting world.

Next time you see the words *girl power*, thank God for His never-
ending supply of God power!

Need for Christ

Everyone has sinned; we all fall short of God's glorious standard.
ROMANS 3:23

I honestly did not fully realize I was a sinner until I got married! I had been a churchgoer all of my life and had accepted Christ at an early age. I tried to do the right things by following the Ten Commandments. I certainly hadn't murdered anyone or stolen anything!

I thought I was pretty clean. But the reality was that I actually looked better on the outside than I was on the inside. Literally, the week after our honeymoon ended, I had a fit when I didn't get my own way. I marched into my husband, Mark's, office, where he seemed to be hiding from my high expectations and pushed all the books off his top bookshelf, exclaiming, "You made me a mean person. I was not mean until I married you!" I wince every time I think about it; I still can't believe I said that.

I love Vance Havner's expression, "What's down in the well comes up in the bucket." My selfishness reared its ugly head that day. I was not aware that it was residing in my heart. It just took a few weeks of living with an "until death do us part" husband to bring it out in me. As hard as those early years were in our marriage, I am grateful for them because I was drawn to my need for Christ. To this day, no one can get my dander up like my husband, but he is the very one God has used the most to nurture me to grow in Christ!

If you have not recognized your need for Christ, reread "the love list" from 1 Corinthians 13, which I wrote about on February 4. These verses reveal our need for Christ and are a beautiful reminder that He is the only One who loves us perfectly!

Best Encourager!

This is my command—be strong and courageous! Do not be afraid or discouraged. For the LORD your God is with you wherever you go.

JOSHUA 1:9

God doesn't want us to be discouraged, but sometimes it happens. On those mornings when I wake up feeling discouraged, I ask Him to encourage me and to give me courage for that day. I know that my Father always knows best and He wants to lift my heavy heart.

Encourage simply means "to give courage to." God gives courage to my heart when I open His Word and hear Him speak. For the longest time I thought He spoke only to the important people in church—the pastors, the evangelists, the Sunday school teachers, and the Bible study leaders. I did not know that our *big God* would talk to *little me* straight from His Word. When I began going to Him every morning with my Bible in hand, I started to hear His voice resonate in my heart and soul.

Spending time in God's Word is no longer just a morning check-off on my to-do list. It is a way of life. I do not want to miss anything He has to say to me. If I take time to reflect on His words, an interesting thing happens—those words follow me around throughout the day. I find if I get dressed and get my shoes on before I meet with Him, I am out the door. But when I let the dishes soak a little longer and keep my bedroom slippers on, it forces me to slow down and park myself in His Word. He gives me courage by His Spirit, encouragement that will overflow to others. He is the best Encourager there is.

Let's park ourselves in His presence as much as we can. Even in the midst of our long to-do lists, we need to listen to God and be encouraged!

Pajama Morning Day

*You also must be ready all the time, for the Son
of Man will come when least expected.*

MATTHEW 24:44

I've come up with a new celebration day. We already have Administrative Professionals' Day and Boss Appreciation Day. I think there is actually a Friendship Day too. Well, I have officially added my own Pajama Morning Day.

The rest of my family likes to sleep in, but not me. I love the early morning when it feels like only God and I are up. To be honest, I complete more tasks in my pajamas than in any other clothes. (Let me clarify one thing: I'm not one of those people who will go out in public in my pajamas. I would be embarrassed to do that. But I think I may have run my daughter a mile to school on a busy morning in my robe, ducking down if I thought someone would see me.)

Inevitably, though, it seems that when I am comfortably attired, the doorbell will ring and I'll have to scramble to make myself presentable for the person at the front door. Of course, what I really want to do is stay in my pajamas and defend myself, making sure that the person at the door knows how early I got up and how much I accomplished in my pajamas.

In today's verse from Matthew, Jesus reminds us how important it is for us to be ready for His arrival. A surprise visitor at the front door is nothing compared to Jesus' unexpected return. He is coming at a time only He knows. Are we ready to meet Him? We're ready only if our hearts have been given to Him.

How grateful I am that if we have believed and received Jesus Christ, we are prepared, dressed in the clean clothes He provides us. We will never be caught unexpectedly.

Think of what you need to do to prepare for Jesus' return. Let's make it a daily prayer to ask God to focus our hearts and minds on Him.

Craving Simplicity

Seek the Kingdom of God above all else, and live righteously,
and he will give you everything you need.

MATTHEW 6:33

Wow! Nothing simplifies priorities more than what Jesus says in today's verse. Nothing motivates me to change more than God does through His Word. Why? A personal relationship with Jesus changes everything. It refocuses our commitments, our routines, our schedules, our relationships, and our bad habits. These things may not change overnight, but as we seek the Kingdom of God and live righteous lives by obedience to God's commands, He starts to change us from within.

Just think back. If you have known Christ for a while, have you been able to stop a bad habit that used to consume you a few years ago? Or are you doing something good now that you never would have seen yourself doing?

Even though I had my own dreams of what my "perfect" life should look like, God had greater plans. I never dreamed I would be the mother of an only child. I thought I would have enough children for at least a small parade, where I could dress them all alike. Instead of a long line of children, God has brought lots of sweet women in and out of our home on the first Monday of each month for Sweet Monday so I can be a tiny bridge between those who know Christ and those who need to know Him. This fun event is also a sweet and simple way to serve the Lord in my church as an outreach, a time when women can laugh a lot, learn from each other, and leave with an introduction to Jesus Christ. It's not anything like the family parade I imagined, but I know it's a movement that God gave me as He changed my priorities and showed me His vision for my life.

Today, initiate a conversation with a new person and invite her to your home for Sweet Monday or for a cup of coffee or tea.

Girl Hammer

The LORD will mediate between nations and will settle
international disputes. They will hammer their swords into
plowshares and their spears into pruning hooks. Nation will
no longer fight against nation, nor train for war anymore.

ISAIAH 2:4

Many of us have a small kitchen drawer that serves as a catchall. In a pinch, we can find paper clips, pens, matches, the key to our neighbor's house, or even a sticky piece of candy! This drawer is the most used one in my kitchen because it contains one of my most prized earthly treasures—a small, pink floral six-in-one hammer.

My "girl hammer" has both a standard and a Phillips head screwdriver, plus three other screwdrivers, right inside the handle. One is even tiny enough to tighten the screws in my sunglasses. I enjoy using my girl hammer regularly. I'm willing to share my hammer with my family on one condition—when they borrow my hammer, they need to put it back in the drawer or their privileges are revoked. You "don't mess with my hammer!"

In Isaiah 2:4 we see a picture of the Lord's future reign. The swords of war will be hammered into useful garden tools so there will be no more wars and terrorist activities. As you probably have guessed by now, I love everyday visual reminders of eternal truths. My girl hammer is a tiny tool that is as practical as it is pretty. It reminds me, as the prophet Isaiah said, that a better day is coming! Look what we have to look forward to: our Mediator, the Lord Jesus Christ, is coming back! When He reigns, nations will no longer fight with each other. His Kingdom will be governed in peace.

 Next time you pick up a gardening trowel or a hammer, stop and thank Jesus that He is coming back to reign on this earth! A better day is coming—with our Prince of Peace.

Wonder Woman?

Who can find a virtuous and capable wife? She is more precious than rubies. Her husband can trust her, and she will greatly enrich his life. She brings him good, not harm, all the days of her life. . . . Her children stand and bless her. Her husband praises her: "There are many virtuous and capable women in the world, but you surpass them all!"

PROVERBS 31:10-12, 28-29

Wow! What a wonder woman! I used to be discouraged when I read the description of this remarkable woman in Proverbs 31. I'd think, *How can I ever measure up to her?* But as I've read it and reread it, my perspective has changed. Now I see it as an encouragement to myself and all women. The writer celebrates everything we women do inside and outside of our homes.

We provide food for our families. We set about our work energetically. We make profitable transactions. We welcome and care for the poor. The list goes on and on. In a nutshell, with God's help, we mature to the point where all our energies fill and enrich others.

Proverbs 31 should be an encouragement to all of us, whether we're married or not. We are all brides of Christ if we have committed our lives to Him. We can all aspire to be women of noble character.

If you are married, think of one thing you can do that would greatly enrich your husband's life, and do it because it brings glory to God. If you are not married, enrich someone else's life today as unto the Lord! He sees and understands your heart—and He longs to fill it to overflowing!

Don't Forget Your Roots

You parents—if your children ask for a loaf of bread, do you give them a stone instead? Or if they ask for a fish, do you give them a snake? Of course not! So if you sinful people know how to give good gifts to your children, how much more will your heavenly Father give good gifts to those who ask him.

MATTHEW 7:9-11

For years after I got married and moved to my husband's native state of Virginia, my dad sent me annual gift subscriptions to *South Carolina Wildlife* magazine. My father had introduced me to South Carolina wildlife from the time I was a small girl by routinely taking me to feed the ducks and fish in the lake. Of course, I would fish only if Daddy baited the hook! So when he sent me the magazine, he told me that he did not want me to forget my roots!

Even though I inherited my tenderhearted daddy's love for animals and enjoyed his monthly reminder, I kept telling him I would rather have *Southern Living* magazine! In a letter home I paraphrased today's verses in Matthew 7. I wrote, "Daddy, if your daughter asks for a *Southern Living* magazine subscription, will you give her *South Carolina Wildlife*?" He got the message, laughed, and sent *South Carolina Wildlife* anyway. I loved it!

God sent us a fully paid gift subscription to eternal life in Jesus Christ. There are *no* substitutes! This free gift offer keeps coming this side of heaven but cannot be redeemed after we die.

As my gift subscription reminded me, we should never forget our roots. If we are believers in Christ, we are rooted in Him, and we can know that our perfect Father gives good gifts to those who ask Him. God is good! If you are not sure of your relationship to God, please open this free gift subscription in Jesus Christ by faith and receive Him today.

 Let's never forget that our real roots are in Jesus Christ! Share that offer with someone else soon.

Double Your Fun and Faithfulness

Two people are better off than one, for they can help each other succeed.
ECCLESIASTES 4:9

I need other women with fresh perspectives and different passions to inspire me when I am in a household rut. We had to replace our kitchen floor because of water damage, and I was cautious in choosing a new floor because I could not visualize how the finished floor would look based on just the small samples in the showroom. The samples I picked looked ugly when I got them home.

All it took was some honest Sweet Monday women saying to me, "You need a black-and-white checkerboard floor in your home." I never would have had the courage to pick that out on my own. They were exactly right, though, and the whole family was happy with it. "Two opinions are better than one!"

This outward example of the benefit of other perspectives can be applied to inward changes too. As we become more moldable to God changing us in every aspect of our lives, there's a good chance we will become less stuck on one particular way of doing things!

Oh, how I long to be a different woman—sweeter, kinder, more patient, not as easily angered, willing to change in every area—day after day, month after month, year after year, by the grace of God. I want to be like fresh Jell-O, taking on the form God has chosen for me—not conforming to the mold of the world.

It is exciting to invite people into our worlds who are gifted differently from you and me. We can learn so much from each other, and helping each other succeed is God's way of serving!

Call a friend to get you going in some area of your home that's been bugging you. (Thank you, Sweet Monica, for helping me hang those pictures just right.) And let's return the favors by being available to friends who may ask for our help. Now that's true double-time giving.

Man-He-Cures

Anyone who belongs to Christ has become a new person.
The old life is gone; a new life has begun!

2 CORINTHIANS 5:17

Getting a manicure is one of life's luxuries. I tell my husband it is physical therapy because it makes me feel particularly feminine for a week or more.

When I see that first chipped nail, it makes my heart sink. I learned recently that nail polish may not adhere as well if the nail is not cleaned first. Many times I have removed old color and rushed to apply a new coat before heading out the door. Little did I realize I was setting up my manicure to fail. Even when I'm in a hurry, I'd be wise to invest a little more time to do it right. The long-lasting results are worth the effort.

Sometimes I try to polish over my "small sins," thinking that a little debris in my heart won't matter. Surely one sassy response isn't so bad, right? And I really needed to speed to get to church on time. No biggie, right?

But that rationalizing approach to things we do wrong doesn't create an effective environment for God's character to "stick" in our hearts. He longs to create clean hearts in us so that we can sparkle in a world that needs His vibrancy, His complete makeover. When He cleans us up, He does a thorough job so that His grace and love can stick to us and shine to bless others!

Sometimes our humanness causes chips in our finish, but God still sees His children as clean, with an eternal topcoat that reflects His glory.

I am glad that our salvation doesn't need redos. But when we sin or get other chips in our faith, He commits to helping maintain us and repair those places. He is our daily Protector for our man-He-cured heart!

> Add some sparkle to your day. Talk to God as you apply a favorite color to your fingers or toes. Then pull out your Bible (careful, the color is still wet) and read while your nails are drying . . . physical and spiritual therapy!

Sticky Friendships

There are "friends" who destroy each other, but a
real friend sticks closer than a brother.

PROVERBS 18:24

Friendships are one of God's richest blessings in life, and I thank God for each of my friends. We've spilled out so much laughter and so many tears together over the years. Friends are true gifts, and I hope to bless them with faithful friendship as well.

Stop and think for a minute about why we love our earthly friends. Is it the ease with which we can call them anytime, day or night? Is it the fact that before we even mention a need, they have already taken care of it? Or maybe they are just plain fun to be with.

Yet in our darkest days of overwhelming circumstances with no easy solutions, even though friends offer welcome comfort, they can't always change our situation for the better. Sometimes other priorities require their attention; sometimes those we feel closest to move away, and we long for friends who stick around whenever we need them.

My sweet reader friend, each one of us has a Forever Friend. Whatever our distressing circumstances or heartaches, this Friend knows all about us and loves us unconditionally. He is never busy, always available, and always kind. He never moves away. He is the only Friend who promises (with power to follow through) that He will use all things for the good of His children in conforming us to Christ.

I hope and pray that you recognize Him as such a Friend and that you enjoy lots of time with Him. His name is Jesus, and He stays close forever. Our relationship with Him is one sticky friendship we cannot live without!

Let's remember that God longs for all of us to know Him as our very best Friend. Let's ask Him to help us offer a taste of His friendship to someone today.

Born-Again Birthday

Jesus replied, "I tell you the truth, unless you are born
again, you cannot see the Kingdom of God."

JOHN 3:3

Oh, I'll admit it. The term *born again* has caused some uncomfortable moments in my Christian experience. Some people get stuck trying to make a distinction between a Christian and a "born-again Christian." Maybe they're curious whether the born-again Christian has privileges not available to a regular Christian.

I was unsure where *born again* originated until I started studying God's Word. I was surprised to find it right there in the Bible! In John 3, Jesus said it first to Nicodemus, a biblical scholar who questioned the concept of being birthed again from his mother's womb. Jesus explained to Nicodemus that all people experience a physical birth, but in order to see the Kingdom of God, they must have a spiritual birth that happens when they accept His gift of salvation.

Jesus' words bring wonderful news to anyone wondering about being born again. A true Christian is a born-again Christian. Christians have been born physically and then are reborn spiritually when they accept Christ as Savior. And just as a physical birth happens only once, a spiritual birth is a onetime event as well.

This new spiritual life continues growing throughout eternity as long as a believer continues getting to know Jesus. Not only do we receive new life at the time of our salvation, but Jesus continues to re-create our hearts and minds to reflect His character and grace. When we stop to think about it, believers who actively seek Him are always experiencing new life.

Every day we make choices whether or not to live God's way and continue in this ever-new life. Godly choices keep us young at heart forever, and the celebration never ends!

Do you remember your spiritual birthday? If so, write the date here: _____. If not, pick a date that is meaningful to you. Then make a point to celebrate that day with a sweet prayer-and-praise time alone with Jesus. Thank Him now for simplifying the way to life eternal with Him, and enjoy your new life growth adventure.

Everyday Life Worries

I tell you, do not worry about your life, what you will eat
or drink; or about your body, what you will wear. Is not
life more than food, and the body more than clothes?

MATTHEW 6:25, NIV

The night before my very first television appearance, I wanted to look better on the outside than my fear made me feel on the inside! A precious friend came to my hotel room that night to analyze what I was going to wear. We discovered I had forgotten the shoes that coordinated with my outfit! I was going to have to wear my tea party *boots*, which did not match at all! I felt my confidence quickly waning, ready to plummet to the floor.

I did not sleep well because of my worries over my silly boots. The next morning I woke up weary and anxious, so I reached for my Bible for help to boost my spirit.

Wouldn't you know it? That day's reading was from Matthew 6. It was as if God highlighted its words pink just for me! The verses bear repeating for all women who worry: "Therefore I tell you, do not worry about your life. . . . Look at the birds of the air; they do not sow or reap or store away in barns, and yet your heavenly Father feeds them. Are you not much more valuable than they? Can any one of you by worrying add a single hour to your life?" (verses 25-27, NIV).

My heart leapt, and I had to praise Him: "Lord, we are so valuable to You that You echoed this 'Do not worry' today just for me when I was fretting about my boots."

Worrying does not add anything positive to our lives—it robs us of joy and sends God the message that we don't think He'll be enough for us. Instead, God wants us to expect Him to give us courage from His Word to face our challenges.

As for my shoe dilemma? God gave me the nerve, even in my inexperience, to ask the cameraman not to show my feet, and he so graciously obliged!

What worries you these days? Meditate on the fact that you are valuable to God. He tells you not to worry about everyday life— including your current challenges! Let your theme today be "I will trust instead of worry!"

No Returns Allowed on This Relationship

*I have written this to you who believe in the name of the Son
of God, so that you may know you have eternal life.*

1 JOHN 5:13

Sometimes in our Christian life, doubts set in, and we may feel that our faith isn't quite good enough. We may even think God wants to cancel His commitment to us because we have failed Him in a certain way or doubted or worried. Well, thank the Lord that we can relax about this one thing: faith in Christ is a done deal. There is no return policy, only opportunities for growth.

God wants each of us to trust Him to hold our lives and eternities securely. In His great love, grace, mercy, and kindness, He knows we will struggle and wonder if He is going to return us to the way we were, dead in our sin. Well, hallelujah, He will not!

In Christ, we are His and He is ours. The eternal deal He made for us lasts forever, which means that His presence and help are available to us every second.

Imagine living each moment trusting *fully* that He personally lavishes His grace and strength on you. He is a hands-on God, and He extends His grace to us when we sin and even when we fail to trust Him. He blesses faith that's as miniscule as a mustard seed (Luke 17:6), and He gives us more opportunities to grow in faith. He believes that we can learn to trust Him more, and instead of physically clobbering us over the head, He grows us.

He indwells us the moment we receive Him, and He wants us to live with the assurance that the exchange is complete and we have eternal life as well as His help during this earthly life.

How wonderful to celebrate every day knowing that God will not take back our relationship with Him.

Think about this truth of assurance the next time you are returning something at the store. Once you're God's, you're God's for good!

Help in a Hurry

*Please, God, rescue me! Come quickly, LORD, and help me. . . .
I am poor and needy; please hurry to my aid, O God. You
are my helper and my savior; O LORD, do not delay.*

PSALM 70:1, 5

Don't you just love those words from Psalm 70? I call it the "help in a hurry" psalm because in five short verses, David asks for help in a hurry three times!

I do not think I will ever forget when these words came alive to me. The Lord gave me a huge opportunity for a Sweet Monday Giant Purse Swap outreach. God provided the leader for the event on the front end, which was a blessing right off the bat, since the idea of planning a big event makes me want to faint. I do not have the spiritual gift of administration. And logistics? What are those?

However, a planning crisis hit when our sweet volunteer leader had to step down right before the event because of an emergency at home. She made the right decision, but we needed help in a hurry—and a week later God provided His huge help through Sweet Joyce. (Thank you forever, Sweet Joyceee!)

That was one of the most difficult waiting weeks I can remember. Over and over again I had to hand my concern over to God and trust that He would come through for the effectiveness of His outreach. God always provides for what He wants to accomplish. Even though the event is long past, I will never forget God's goodness to us in His great provision. He brought two thousand women to hear the Good News and see Sweet Katie Couric's donated purse being swapped! Fun! Fun!

We all benefit from reflecting on God's help to us, big or small, in our past, present, and future. Let's always call on Him first to rescue us! He's our Helper, whether we are in a hurry or not!

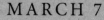

Marriage Woes and Wonders

If you do get married, it is not a sin. And if a young woman gets married, it is not a sin. However, those who get married at this time will have troubles, and I am trying to spare you those problems.

1 CORINTHIANS 7:28

This was one of the first verses I highlighted in my Bible as a newlywed, and it remains one of the most encouraging Scriptures to me. Back then I was an immature but growing Christian. I entered a Christian marriage unrealistically thinking we would never have problems because we were both Christians, and after all, Mark proposed to me at a real castle, dressed in a full suit of armor!

Paul's instructions on marriage encouraged me because, when I read that married people have troubles and problems, I suddenly felt normal. How could this princess with her knight in shining armor ever be in conflict? What was wrong with me?

If you're thinking, *Sin—that's what's wrong with her*, then you'd be right! My selfishness and desire to get my own way are normal parts of being human, married or single. Jesus is using marriage to refine those faults and conform me to His image.

This verse helped me learn to grab my "sword of the Spirit," which is the Word of God, to find strength and grace to walk through difficult times with my husband. God said through Paul that we would have problems in marriage, so I should not be surprised when Mark and I face conflict.

After nearly three decades and a lot more highlighted verses in my "sword of the Spirit," many newlywed battles have subsided. We still have troubles, but the whole armor of God in Ephesians 6:10-17 is a practical proposal for all of life's problems.

> Pull out your sword, the Word of God, to fight life's battles! One great way to begin today is by reading Ephesians 6:10-20.

Life: A Piece of Cake?

You will keep in perfect peace all who trust in you,
all whose thoughts are fixed on you!

ISAIAH 26:3

Sometimes my thoughts are fixed on chocolate when circumstances are particularly stressful. I crave the comfort of a big ole piece of chocolate cake with lots of icing. If my nerves are exceptionally frazzled, I can become convinced that such a sweet fix would bring peace to my troubled spirit. But sad to say, *peace* of mind does not come from a *piece* of chocolate cake or anything chocolate.

Peace is hard to define, but I certainly recognize when I *don't* have it! Matter of fact, I'm not feeling it right now because I just disagreed with my husband over a terribly important matter . . . where to put the computer in our home! My tendency is to blame him for my quick words, but the reality is that I rebel when I don't get my own way. My perfect peace is disrupted because my thoughts are not fixed on God.

I can feel the Holy Spirit working on me as James 4:1-2 comes to mind: "What is causing the quarrels and fights among you? Don't they come from the evil desires at war within you? You want what you don't have, so you scheme and kill to get it."

Conviction sets in, and as I begin to let go of my stubborn will, I feel something budding in my heart, a tiny seed growing bigger . . . It's the beginnings of peace, and it leads me to talk things over with God.

"Lord, I confess, sometimes I would rather sit down and eat a big piece of chocolate cake than acknowledge my sin and be restored to the peace that only You can bring. But I am always uncomfortable with this ineffective 'quick fix.' God, You are the answer. You are Prince of Peace (Isaiah 9:6), and I, like Paul, am the worst of sinners (1 Timothy 1:15). I was wrong, Lord, and I need You to restore my peace. Thank You that You will keep me in perfect peace when my mind is fixed on You."

 Next time that chocolate craving hits, or anything distracts you from the Source of real peace, remember that your peace comes from the Lord, and only He can give it to you.

God Will Do the Right Thing

The LORD is slow to get angry, but his power is great, and he never
lets the guilty go unpunished. He displays his power in the whirlwind
and the storm. The billowing clouds are the dust beneath his feet.

NAHUM 1:3

Recently two people told me they did not want to know a God who let criminals who committed horrible acts go free on a deathbed confession.

Whoa! I was surprised when this loaded statement came up two times in one week while I was out and about, and from people in different occupations and circumstances. But I loved that the subject of God came up! I think we talk about everything else in this world; why not talk about the One who really makes the world go round?

Although I always feel inadequate to handle deep questions, I know that God gives us everything we need to say. Breathing quick prayers, both times I said something like, "We can trust that God always does the right thing! He is the only One who can see anyone's heart, and we can trust Him to deal with each person in His ideal way. God cannot go against His perfectly just and perfectly gracious character."

In both instances, we were able to have refreshing conversations about real issues of life, and even though I feel so ineffective next to God's immeasurable greatness, I can defend His name as He empowers me! God is at work drawing people to Himself, and He does all the hard work in each person's heart.

As we go about the everyday details of life, we can rest in His answers while we dwell on the absolute fact that He makes everything right, in His way and in His time!

Let's meditate on the fact that God will make everything right for eternity. Consider an issue that needs to be made right in the world. Thank God now that He will fix it with His perfect methods and in His time.

Giving like God Does

*The generous will prosper; those who refresh
others will themselves be refreshed.*

PROVERBS 11:25

When we give—whether we offer gifts, time, encouragement, deeds of service, or hugs—our unselfish thoughtfulness refreshes others.

According to the book *The Language of Love* by Gary Smalley and John Trent, we all tend to give in the ways that we want to receive. They encourage us to learn the "love language" of those we care about and show love to them in the way they feel it most.

Great advice. But my problem is that I expect my husband to know all my love languages because I was raised by parents who knew all of them. I think the gift of prayer is one that I need to give to my husband: "Lord, please give Mark extra grace to live with me!"

One love language is gift giving. I would imagine some of the most treasured gifts we have received are handmade. (I'm not good at making gifts, but I sure appreciate those talents in others.) When a gift is handmade, it actually combines two gifts—time and the gift itself. Through homemade gifts, we offer part of ourselves to someone else. That is why a few words scribbled on a sticky note from Mark mean as much to me as any present.

When we abandon ourselves to God, the biggest Giver of all, we learn from His example to develop a habit of giving to others. When we are busy giving to others out of all God has given to us in Christ, we may not even notice if we ever receive a formal thank-you. We may be even more surprised to realize that we are refreshed in return when we share generously. This powerful, second-nature generosity comes as a result of experiencing and then sharing the depths of all we receive in Christ.

This poem I wrote years ago is still a prayer of my heart, and I'd like to give it to you as encouragement in your own giving too.

Lord, help me forget the things that I do.
  I pray they would only be reminders of You!

Give a gift of yourself today in any form and be refreshed. Meditate on Luke 12:48.

Conquering Clutter

Everything else is worthless when compared with the infinite value
of knowing Christ Jesus my Lord. For his sake I have discarded
everything else, counting it all as garbage, so that I could gain Christ.
PHILIPPIANS 3:8

I can easily lose focus when I am weighed down with garbage of the heart, mind, and home, with achievements and failures. I am sensitive and sentimental, and it is sometimes hard for me to release whatever triggers my emotions, whether it's a thing or a thought or a feeling. But I have learned that the more *lightly* I hold on to earthly treasures, the more *tightly* I hold to the eternal. I am not just talking about uncluttering my home, but uncluttering my mind, heart, and schedule as well.

In Philippians 3, Paul unclutters all his past achievements in an impressive worldly résumé. He points all of us ahead to what we need to focus on—knowing Christ. Knowing Christ is a journey that is always meant to move us forward. Our relationship with Him cannot be stagnant. When we give Him our focus, He invigorates us!

To follow Paul's lead, on a regular basis I try to get rid of something in our home that feels uncomfortable to let go of. I make this purge a household habit to lighten my heart. Whether it is a big undertaking or is accomplished little by little, discarding is a personal, outward step that reminds me of eternal gain instead of earthly loss.

As I discipline my heart this way, I typically find myself talking with the Lord about it all:

"Oh Lord, I do not want to miss anything You have for me, because I know it is the best. Why would I want to miss Your best? Help me to forget what is behind and strain toward what is ahead, as Philippians 3:13 says. Help me also not to hold too tightly to things."

Time to take out the garbage! Make a list of whatever thoughts, issues, habits, distractions, pastimes, attitudes, or actions end up looking like garbage in your life. Then throw the list in the trash can as you ask the Lord to help you leave those things there and, instead, prioritize Him and His desires for you.

Relationships Help Us Persevere

Let us not neglect our meeting together, as some people do, but encourage one another, especially now that the day of his return is drawing near.

HEBREWS 10:25

In this hectic, technological world, we are in danger of becoming more isolated. Surely you've noticed the number of people whose eyes stay riveted to their hand-held electronic devices. Think how much time children and adults spend alone watching television, texting, and sitting at computers doing work and homework. For all the benefits of advancement, I fear we're losing out on personal, face-to-face interaction.

The last half of Hebrews 10 is packed with a charge for believers to spend time in worship and persevere together in Christ. God made all of us for relationships—first with Him and also with others—and we help each other when we connect frequently.

During the ten years I was a teacher, I became concerned that relational skills were not being properly emphasized in the curriculum. Two vital skills that usually determine job success (and life success) are good communication and sensitivity to others. Because life continues moving faster, we have difficulty slowing down long enough to effectively teach these skills at home, school, church, work, and play.

As a body of believers, we can work together to reverse the trend of isolation that is bound to negatively impact future generations. Taking time for worship and fellowship, Bible study and prayer, milk and cookies, coffee and cake not only provides opportunities to teach manners, but it brings us out of our private worlds and helps us persevere together through life.

All people are precious, and really paying attention to others takes conscious effort and purposely unplugging to do life in real time, face to face. Patiently slowing down for the elderly person in front of us at the grocery store requires effort. Putting aside to-dos to give children the attention they need can feel unproductive. And it certainly takes time, even in the church community, to meet together and encourage one another. But God instructs us to do just that because we all benefit!

Unplug. Invite a friend to lunch. Or serve your children and their friends an after-school snack. Offer unhurried, personal attention and hear the highs and lows of their day.

God's Great Guidance

*The king's heart is like a stream of water directed by
the LORD; he guides it wherever he pleases.*

PROVERBS 21:1

Today's verse is one I committed to memory for a very personal reason that still means a great deal to me.

I discovered it many years ago in my own BC days (Before Committing to marry my Mark). I guess I could also call that season my AD (Always Dating) life, when I was immature and thought it was my job to find God's man for me!

While Mark and I were getting to know each other, God placed another young Christian man in my path when, for once, I was not even looking for one. My heart felt torn. I was so surprised by these new feelings for someone else. Now I am grateful I had already given my whole heart to the Lord, as much as I knew how, so I knew I did not have a "divided heart" toward God. For the first time, though, I had a divided heart about two great men! It was not fun. I was not flattered. It was a very upsetting time in my life, even though I had two great choices for a lifetime mate!

I needed help. I needed God's direction, so I turned to Him, knowing He saw everything. He knew my heart and that I wanted His choice for me.

I opened His Word and read this verse for the very first time. It was as if God's light was beaming into my heart. I felt like He was saying, "Kim, your heart is like a stream of water directed by Me. I guide it wherever I please."

With relief I responded to that still small voice, *Lord, I am reminding You that I gave You my heart. You guide it!*

I'm happy to say that He did guide me and has blessed my marriage with Mark through huge ups and downs. I'm confident now when I say He will lead His people if we allow Him.

Embrace God's great guidance. He will not let us miss it.

Smelling the Flowers

Be truly glad. There is wonderful joy ahead, even though you must endure many trials for a little while. These trials will show that your faith is genuine. It is being tested as fire tests and purifies gold—though your faith is far more precious than mere gold. So when your faith remains strong through many trials, it will bring you much praise and glory and honor on the day when Jesus Christ is revealed to the whole world.

1 PETER 1:6-7

Trials and flowers do not seem to have much in common, except that we sometimes send flowers to people experiencing trials, to bring cheer and to let them know we are thinking of them.

What is your favorite flower? Inside or outside your home, they add pizzazz and brighten your heart too.

But after a few days, how do they look? Flowers look cheerful when they're soaking up water in a vase or blooming in soil, but look sad when they turn brown and droopy. They provide tangible reminders of an encouraging truth: just as flowers bloom with the nourishment of water and soil, we can blossom during trials when Christ nourishes our faith.

God tells us in 1 Peter that our faith will be proved genuine in trials and there is wonderful joy ahead. We just can't see it yet! Only in Christ can we "be truly glad" when we get drenched by a trial or when tough times batter us like wind gusts against delicate flower petals.

Big, small, long, or short, trials are temporary. They actually work in our favor by motivating the roots of our faith to reach deeper for God's sustaining nourishment. When we grow this way, our faith is strengthened, we experience joy that only God can create, and our lives bring glory and honor to God.

I often wear big flower pins and decorate with floral pillows in our home to remind myself that something good is going on in the midst of my trials, even though it's hidden by the dirt. After all, a flower grows only when it rains.

Keep a small vase handy for flowers that little hands bring you from the yard, or treat yourself to a bunch of your favorite variety from the grocery store or florist. Thank God for His visual gift of joy and beauty.

Clothed in Christ

I am overwhelmed with joy in the LORD my God! For he has dressed me
with the clothing of salvation and draped me in a robe of righteousness.
I am like a bridegroom dressed for his wedding or a bride with her jewels.

ISAIAH 61:10

Now that my daughter is in college, I do not have instant access to her excellent fashion advice. She is much better at clothes than I am. She can choose an item off the rack and know if it will look good without even trying it on! Me? I am the chronic returner! I can't count the times I've brought home an item of clothing I'm excited about, only to sigh with disappointment when I stand in front of my bedroom mirror and see that it doesn't work on me. Back to the store it goes.

Aren't you glad that God will never return us to the store? He bought us with Christ's shed blood on the cross, and we are priceless! Knowing my value to Him overwhelms me with joy!

God sees you and me in the most gorgeous clothes imaginable, like a bridal gown complete with jewels—the clothing of salvation and the robe of righteousness. This lovely apparel symbolizes that we have right standing with God. As members of His royal family, we have an up-close and personal relationship with our Father and full access to Him. And we are clothed beautifully as the bride of the King of kings, who cherishes us.

These elaborate word pictures of our spiritual clothing paint a visual picture of being covered in Christ for all eternity, fitted to be welcomed by the Lord of the universe and the lover of our souls.

By dwelling on our royal lineage, we can experience overwhelming joy in the Lord, as Isaiah did when he pointed us to Christ in this magnificent Old Testament book. Imagine the joy in our countenance if we keep in mind 24/7 that we are dressed fit for our King, our heavenly Bridegroom. He loves to adorn our souls with His joy! Only then are we truly beautiful.

Let's wear a favorite earthly outfit today and be grateful to be spiritually clothed in Christ!

Lukewarm? No, Thank You

I know all the things you do, that you are neither hot nor cold. I wish that you were one or the other! But since you are like lukewarm water, neither hot nor cold, I will spit you out of my mouth!

REVELATION 3:15-16

For months the faucet on my kitchen sink would only dispense lukewarm water. No matter how far I turned it to the right or to the left, it was still lukewarm. It bugged me at first. But now that I look back, it is amazing how quickly I adapted, put off its repair, and decided to tackle bigger issues in our home.

All it took for a temperature change was a visit from my mother! The faucet just about drove her crazy. No lukewarm water for her—she needed hot or cold! I called the plumber.

Just as my mother didn't care for lukewarm water, God is not pleased with lukewarm believers. This was His message to the church in Laodicea, written in Revelation, the last book of the Bible. Even though there is much mystery about Revelation, even among godly Bible scholars, there is also much we can learn and take to heart from this book.

As faulty human beings, the faucet on our hearts begins to pump out only lukewarm faith when we don't keep going to God for maintenance. Oh, how we need to call upon Him, our Plumber, our Healer, our Provider, our Source of love, joy, peace, and comfort.

We do not want to be lukewarm Christians, but many times we cool off in our relationship with Him. This blasé temperature does not bring glory to God.

A lukewarm faucet may be tolerable, but lukewarm faith definitely must be dealt with. Let's not live with a lukewarm faith. No, thank you!

Ask God to help reset your love and zeal for Him. Then trust Him to help you pay attention to His perpetual maintenance plan.

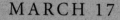

How Fun Is This?

Give as freely as you have received!

MATTHEW 10:8

Nothing sparks giving like receiving! What is the first thing we want to do when someone gives us something? We want to return the gesture, right after we say thank you! We often think about the sender and choose something that would be meaningful and special to that person.

The Lord inspires me by example more than anyone on this earth. If I am struggling in any way and I hear God's viewpoint from His Word, I am inspired by His Spirit to move closer to His way of thinking. The times I have been prompted in my spirit but failed to give are moments I regret. I can't think of one time I wished I hadn't given.

In today's verse the Lord is instructing us to give as freely as we have received. It's a practice that I have purposed in my heart to follow, especially since I get so much enjoyment out of the process. I look to God's immeasurable example. Two thousand years ago He gave us quite the inspiration to follow when He gave us His Son, Jesus, the ultimate gift.

As believers in Christ, we have received salvation—a gift that can't be topped. But He also has given us the power of His Holy Spirit and His provision of love, joy, peace, and comfort even in the midst of the difficulties and heartaches of life. Oh, how much we have received from His abundant love! There is no other response but to follow His example and make the choice to freely give to others our time, talents, and treasures.

Give something today that warrants nothing in return, ever, and do not tell anyone. That gift counts as giving directly to God. He sees, and His notice is all that matters! "When you give to someone in need, don't let your left hand know what your right hand is doing. Give your gifts in private, and your Father, who sees everything, will reward you" (Matthew 6:3-4).

Keep Watch!

So you, too, must keep watch! For you don't know what day your Lord is coming. Understand this: If a homeowner knew exactly when a burglar was coming, he would keep watch and not permit his house to be broken into. You also must be ready all the time, for the Son of Man will come when least expected.

MATTHEW 24:42-44

We keep watch over our children. We keep watch over our important papers and finances. We keep watch over our households and keep them in order so that trash doesn't overflow the can, laundry doesn't pile to the ceiling, food doesn't get moldy in the fridge, dust doesn't accumulate, and our loved ones and pets don't go hungry. And that's just being vigilant about everyday duties. We go into high gear when we're expecting guests, going to great lengths to ready our home for their arrival. Even though I'm not expecting guests right now, it still makes me tired just thinking about it!

But for all the preparation and care we give to our lives here on earth, how much greater the need to prepare ourselves for the Guest of honor, as well as for our trip to our ultimate destination—eternity. Do we keep watch for Jesus' coming? He is definitely coming back; He said so in lots of red-letter verses in Matthew 24. Jesus foretold the future and promises He will return, although we do not know the date or the time on the clock when it will happen.

When He arrives, He'll collect His believers and see us safely to our true, forever home in heaven with Him. Even more important than readying our homes and ourselves for earthly guests, we need to make sure we are prepared to greet Him whenever He comes back for us.

Being ready all the time for Him is a heart matter. He lives in our hearts; our hearts are His home. If we're creating an atmosphere of welcome for Him in our hearts on a consistent basis, we'll be unashamed by what He'll find in us when He returns.

Are you ready for Jesus to return tomorrow? How about fifteen minutes from now? Two seconds? One of these days He will arrive in a split second; ask Him to help you stay prepared to welcome Him.

Sweet T

*Don't copy the behavior and customs of this world, but let God transform
you into a new person by changing the way you think. Then you will
learn to know God's will for you, which is good and pleasing and perfect.*

ROMANS 12:2

Do you know offhand how many T-shirts you own? Could you make an educated
guess how many you've owned in your lifetime? Maybe you remember one or two
that had a logo or saying that really expressed what you felt.

T-shirts usually reveal some information about the wearer. My sweet friend
Brenda asked me if I had seen the one advertising a Functional Family Conference.
When I said no, she described it to me. It showed a picture of a large auditorium,
but there was only one person in attendance! Oh, I could have worn a Functional
Family Conference T-shirt for the first twenty-eight years of my life. My worst
memory was when I was twelve. My mom and I were shopping, and Mama asked
the sales clerk, "Where are the size-ten chubbies, please?" I was so embarrassed
that I wanted to run out of the mall.

But as I grew up and matured and started my own family, I soon realized that
there are no perfect families anywhere on this earth, not even in God's family.
When we trust in Christ, we become God's children forever. He shares His mind
and values and character with us (1 Corinthians 2:16) so we learn how to function as part of His healthy, holy family.

We all have some painful memories in our human families that we would like
to erase because God's children can make a mess of things here on earth. But
we will eventually enjoy an eternity of enriching, fulfilling family times together
beyond what we've ever longed for in this life.

There's no more uplifting way to live than as part of His growing family.

Let's sleep in our favorite sweet T-shirt tonight and rest in the fact
that, regardless of our past, we belong in God's good, pleasing, and
perfect family!

People Pleasing

I'm not trying to win the approval of people, but of God. If pleasing people were my goal, I would not be Christ's servant.

GALATIANS 1:10

I was born with people-pleasing DNA! I'm sure of it! I imagine you may share some of the same markers.

Why is it that we feel guilty saying no to an activity? For me it's because I want the person I'm declining to think highly of me. Deep down, I am afraid I won't look as unselfish or helpful if I answer with a gracious no instead of an enthusiastic yes.

One Sunday after church I was asked to make a meal for a precious God's girl who had just had a baby. I couldn't do it because of my traveling schedule, but I really wanted the person who asked me to know that I had gone to the baby shower and given her several gifts, and since I had just spoken at a weekend retreat, I needed to make a meal for my family! I was pooped.

That afternoon I was in a terrible mood and finally asked my husband what was wrong with me. He said, "I'll tell you what's wrong. You are too concerned about what so-and-so is thinking because you said no to making a meal this time." He was right!

Right then and there I asked God to forgive me. My desire to impress got in the way, and I turned a simple request for a meal into a struggle about my self-worth. I want to live daily to please the Lord more than live looking accomplished and capable to other people.

Whether your plate is full or not, next time someone asks you to commit to something, be slow to speak. If you're impulsive like me, ask him or her to give you time to check your schedule. Do a quick heart check—"Lord, am I doing this to please You in love and obedience, or just to be a people pleaser?"

Park 'N Go

Open my eyes to see the wonderful truths in your instructions.

PSALM 119:18

Every time I see the Park 'N Go sign near the airport, I think, *This is what we who are in Christ need to do every day: park in God's Word and go out and live in His power and strength.*

Unfortunately, many of us often miss out because we think we don't have time to spend with God. But honestly, I do not know how we can see the wonderful truths in God's instructions unless we make time to read and listen. We schedule time for everything else in life; let's encourage each other to plan time to read His wonderful truths.

I am not promoting a legalistic obligation to read a certain number of chapters per day in order to earn a star and please the Lord. My hope is simply to shine light on the blessings and benefits that come from prioritizing time with our personal, mighty God who longs to fellowship with us. *He* actually delights in being with *us*! When we communicate with Him, He imparts His character and Spirit to ours so we can experience the joy of knowing Him personally, as well as receiving His power to live for Him. When we still ourselves before Him, we start to understand in new ways what Psalm 46:10 says about knowing that He is God.

Begin by picking out a parking spot. It may be a place in your home or your car or your cubicle at work during your lunch break. Then literally self-park there. Some days you may have fifteen minutes; other days you may have five. The point is, there's a great deal of habit-building wisdom in disciplining ourselves daily in His Word. Pick a Bible reading plan, or start in the Gospel of John if you do not know where to begin.

Let's ask God to open our eyes to see His wonderful truths. Learning to listen to God, spending time alone with Him, is life-changing, motivating, and invigorating. As we seek Him, He does the hard work of speaking to our hearts and moving us in obedience to live His way.

Let's encourage each other to Park 'N Go!

Fragile Clay Jar

God, who said, "Let there be light in the darkness," has made this light shine in our hearts so we could know the glory of God that is seen in the face of Jesus Christ. We now have this light shining in our hearts, but we ourselves are like fragile clay jars containing this great treasure. This makes it clear that our great power is from God, not from ourselves. We are pressed on every side by troubles, but we are not crushed. We are perplexed, but not driven to despair. We are hunted down, but never abandoned by God. We get knocked down, but we are not destroyed.

2 CORINTHIANS 4:6-9

Do you ever feel hard-pressed? Perplexed? Persecuted? Sometimes it seems as though the world and everything in it are teamed up against us, ready to pound us, knock us down, and hurt us.

I felt knocked down when one of my smartphone app games declined me! I had not realized how many "Words With Friends" games I had going with my long-distance college daughter, but out of the blue a message popped up on that little screen declining me! Ouch! I had never been declined on my phone before. Of course, my daughter was not rejecting me; she was just being wise with her time. I took it personally, even though it was just one game out of nine that we were playing. But my clay jar cracked at the first sign of what felt like rejection.

The truth is, our hearts are all fragile like clay jars, and we can be hurt easily. But God still shines His light in us and infuses our souls with His Holy Spirit's healing power. We get knocked down but do not crumble to pieces even in the direst of circumstances. Because of His strength in us, all of us hard-pressed, weak vessels can be encouraged and effective.

And to our surprise, the very circumstances that make us feel crushed create the places in our lives where we see God at work, shining through the cracks as He mends them for even greater use.

Look up 2 Corinthians 12:9-10; write it down on an index card and place it where you can see it throughout your day.

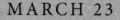

Frantic about Your Figure?

We never give up. Though our bodies are dying, our spirits are being renewed every day. For our present troubles are small and won't last very long. Yet they produce for us a glory that vastly outweighs them and will last forever! So we don't look at the troubles we can see now; rather, we fix our gaze on things that cannot be seen. For the things we see now will soon be gone, but the things we cannot see will last forever.

2 CORINTHIANS 4:16-18

I don't know about you, but I quickly lose heart when it comes to exercise. I know it is important because our bodies are the temple of the Holy Spirit (1 Corinthians 6:19), but fitting exercise into my schedule seems to require too much discipline. Right now what seems to work best is to plug in a twenty-minute video. I have accepted that I will never again have my cheerleader figure.

But more effective than any exercise regimen, fixing my eyes on Jesus instead of on what is seen—like my figure—has helped expand my very limited perspective of myself and my life into a broader, eternal one! When we fix our eyes on Jesus, we never need to lose heart with our limitations because He promises that our troubles are small and will not last long in view of the vast expanse of eternity. They will not even tip the scales when it comes to the eternal glory we will possess when we are out of earthly breath.

For now, as I continue to discipline myself to exercise for my physical well-being, I'm going to exercise my mind and heart to focus on His long-range plans for my good, too, so I don't become hung up on the temporary complaints about my figure or on any other longings of this passing life.

As we daily exercise our minds and bodies, let us fix our eyes on Jesus rather than on our figures. As we do, He will permeate every area of our lives and direct us in tangible ways to please Him—not only in our physically tired temples but in every area of life so we will not be weary in well-doing.

Look What He Did

*Come and listen, all you who fear God, and
I will tell you what he did for me.*

PSALM 66:16

It is difficult for me *not* to talk about God! I cannot seem to keep Him to myself. Rereading these simple devotions, I feel like I have blurted Him out on these pages.

But I am second-guessing myself right now because they are so personal and I am worried about what people will think. Is my concern because God's Word is on every page and He is so precious, true, right, good, instructive, and *perfect*? Or because His reputation is of much greater concern than my own and I'm not sure I can do it justice? Or is it because a few tiny words on paper cannot begin to describe Him adequately?

Telling what He did for me is a like a perpetual run-on sentence: God *is* grace, love, mercy, strength, love, redemption, ever-present, forgiving, glorious, honorable, perfect, complete, constant, assuring, kind, patient, personal, encouraging, enduring, peaceful, just, righteous, light, consistent, holy, powerful, friendly, true, comforting, caring, good, and on and on—forever and ever and ever and ever! When I think about God's character, I reaffirm to myself some of the reasons I love to talk about Him.

It is hard not to talk about such a great God, who is personal and who has saved me from sin so that I can wake up every day and face the future with hope and genuine gladness in my heart.

And you know what? Even in my feeble attempt just now to focus on Him, He has revealed the reason for my second-guessing: no words or expressions can touch His magnificence or how He deals with me with such love! I am accepting the fact that there are no words that truly glorify Him enough. But I'm going to spend my life offering Him my worship and praise and thanksgiving anyway! That is what He desires from each of us.

🔑 Brainstorm for five minutes and write a list of what God has done for you and how He shows you His love. Let's tell each other what God does! "Our heart's desire is to glorify your name" (Isaiah 26:8).

Great Expectation

All praise to God, the Father of our Lord Jesus Christ. It is
by his great mercy that we have been born again, because
God raised Jesus Christ from the dead. Now we live with
great expectation, and we have a priceless inheritance.

1 PETER 1:3-4

I grew up in a small southern town in South Carolina. I was a daddy's girl through and through and always wanted to dress like a princess. I imagined my grown-up family life being even better than my own childhood, which had very few sad memories.

Unrealistic expectations are not good.

Many days in the throes of being a new bride and later a new teacher and then a new mother with new responsibilities, I wondered, *Where's the sweet happily ever after this side of heaven? And where's my tiara?*

Growing up, I thought that real life would begin when my knight in shining armor not only found me and crowned me, but fought bravely for me, whisked me down the church aisle, and showered me with undying love and affection for the rest of my life! Our many children, dressed alike, flocking around our feet, and enjoying us at every stage of life, would just be icing on the cake. If I tried hard to do all the right things, life would be wonderful, wouldn't it? If only real life were picture perfect, like Cinderella's story was in the end!

Truth be told, I would not trade one of my unrealistic expectations now because God used them to show me, when I became a new person in Christ, that I could live happily ever after with one great expectation . . . knowing Jesus Christ better each day!

We can anticipate, dream of, long for, build up our hopes about heaven with Him all we want and still rest assured that our expectations will be met. Life forever with Him will be grander than our wildest dreams or greatest expectations.

What is one great expectation you grew up with? What is one you have as an adult? Has either one been met? Live with one great expectation! Thank Jesus now that He will never fail to measure up to your dreams—and in fact, He'll far exceed them.

Miraculous Mercy

Too much talk leads to sin. Be sensible and keep your mouth shut.

PROVERBS 10:19

Last night I did not keep my mouth shut when a Christlike response was warranted! It was late, I was tired and hungry, and I still had "piles to go" before I slept (thank you again, Robert Frost).

Well, I caved under the temptation to sin. No excuses. Too much talk that I did not mean rolled off my lazy lips. I continued in this sorry state by going to bed angry, which God instructs us not to do. Needless to say, I tossed and turned all night!

First thing in the morning, I ran to God and His Word, where I knew I would find mercy and grace. I plopped into my spot and said, "Lord, how can I write devotions when I sinned against You and my wonderful husband last night? Lord, forgive me."

I opened my *One Year Bible* and discovered that day's reading was Psalm 40:11-12. Just wait till you hear what God said through David that my heart echoed loud and clear: "LORD, don't hold back your tender mercies from me. Let your unfailing love and faithfulness always protect me. For troubles surround me—too many to count! My sins pile up so high I can't see my way out. They outnumber the hairs on my head. I have lost all courage."

The tears of repentance are falling, and the anticipation of restoration is awaiting. I can't see well right now as I write. But God sees me! He sees me and speaks clearly to my heart from His Word. He does not withhold His mercy. He does not treat me as my sins deserve. His love and His truth protect me. His love and truth protect you, too!

I can't wait for my gift-from-God husband to wake up so I can tell him that I'm sorry, too, and ask for his forgiveness and be restored.

"Thank You for Your mercy, Father, and for helping me see what I need to do to make things right. I'll take care of that, Lord, right away."

 No one else can ever love us perfectly like that—*no one!* Let's rejoice in God's great love and mercy for each of us today.

Start Making History

*You go before me and follow me. You place
your hand of blessing on my head.*

PSALM 139:5

Never have I been so grateful to have a history of walking with Jesus Christ than when I received that unexpected call from Dr. Rabhan the day after my routine mammogram. He told me an abnormality had shown up and that I needed to go right away to pick up my films and schedule an appointment with a surgeon before the end of the week.

The first thoughts racing through my mind were, *Lord, You knew it was there all along because You know everything! You know I'm hearing this news right now, and You are with me. You know the future, and You go before me. I can trust You to take care of my precious family and me. I am Yours and You are mine!* My second thought was, *How long will I live?*

What a comfort it was to me to have a personal relationship with the one true God when all the loose ends of cancer were looming—the unknowns of lumpectomy, mastectomy, chemotherapy, radiation, reconstruction, lymphedema, and future uncertainties.

A later thought that ran through my mind was, *Lord, there are a lot of other women today getting worse news than I am. Maybe their child has been killed. Maybe their husband just walked out. Maybe they have done something so bad that they fear they will never be forgiven. How in the world are they coping if they do not have a personal relationship with You through Jesus Christ? What fears are they passing on to their children who are so worried about their mother?*

I am thankful that I had a personal relationship with Christ, who gave me peace in the midst of my cancer chaos. And I want you to have one, too, for true comfort in any life crisis.

Start making new history with the Lord! If you're a child of God, know that your eternal destination is secure. Take comfort in His many promises to all of His children through His Word. Reread Psalm 139:15-16 to discover that you have always had a history with Him. Look forward to making history in your personal relationship with Him. Now that's sweet!

Need Illumination?

The teaching of your word gives light, so even the simple can understand.

PSALM 119:130

Sometimes it just sounds *so* simple—too good to be true—but God speaks to us through His Word.

Reading God's Word shows me what I am really like! Let me tell you, it's not always pretty. I need help because I cannot change myself, and neither can I fake my way past my need for grace! Something's got to give.

Well, Some*one* does! God knows our condition, and when we read His Word, we can see where we fall short. Seeing our own inadequacy is good when it leads us to seek His help to change us where we need it.

My gratefulness for God's sweet grace increases through the years as I experience more and more of my own faults and those of others. My husband and I have been married for nearly three decades, and those difficult early years of marriage forced me to my knees to hear what God had to say to grow me. I was focusing on my new husband meeting *all* my needs rather than focusing on Christ, the only One who can meet the deepest needs of my heart.

I'm grateful that I continue to hear God's voice through the pages of His Word. He speaks to me even though I'm not one of the people who know all the biblical words in the original Hebrew or Greek. Through regularly attending a Bible-believing, growing church, reading the Bible on my own, and spending time with people who lived their faith in Christ, the lights come on in my soul. God, through His Word, illumines my pink path and helps me understand my personal need for His big grace. Having His spotlight on my heart lessens my tendencies to focus on others' shortcomings because mine are so glaring.

Let's allow Him to illumine our hearts to understand why we need Him. Ask Him to enlighten our hearts about one specific character flaw He wants to change so we will look more like Christ. And thank Him for His discipline, which is meant to make us shine even brighter. It is all good.

Tear Collector

*You keep track of all my sorrows. You have
collected all my tears in your bottle.*

PSALM 56:8

Over the years, I've seen several movies and TV shows that portray a father buying his daughter a beautiful dress for a special occasion. Without fail, I cry every time. I don't know if I can ever communicate all the emotions behind the steady flow, but they are overwhelming and consistent.

Is my reaction a response to the sweet satisfaction over a father's tenderness or generosity? Or am I vicariously feeling the fullness in their hearts as they exchange loving expressions? Maybe the loss of my own wonderful dad or compassion for women who never knew fatherly love brings on my tears. Or quite possibly those scenes remind me of my empty nest now that my own daughter has moved into her first apartment. The tears trickle because I miss her even as I celebrate with her.

Tears. They ebb and flow throughout our days and years, and all along God is collecting them. Simply knowing He keeps track of my tears makes me tear up again with joy! Our big God is so personal to let us know that He is keeping track. He knew we would cry. He knew that sometimes we would not be able to explain the reasons for the overflow. But He sees and He knows. Even though our bottles are different sizes, He holds on to everyone's every tear.

I don't think I will figure out the exact explanation for all my tears over those particular movie scenes, but I know for sure I have tears of joy when I experience my heavenly Father's never-ending tender mercy toward me.

One day God, our Tear Collector, will wipe away our every tear (Revelation 21:4). Until then they are stored and we can know He sees our hurts, He feels our pain with us, and He loves us enough to heal us in His time. Ask Him to help you believe that He will be your Healer for any brokenness you are experiencing right now.

Purr-and-Praise Time

Not that I was ever in need, for I have learned how to be content
with whatever I have. I know how to live on almost nothing or with
everything. I have learned the secret of living in every situation,
whether it is with a full stomach or empty, with plenty or little.

PHILIPPIANS 4:11-12

Who would have thought we would have a kitty around our household? Both my husband and I had childhood pets, but they were *dogs*! We grew up as *dog people* and decided to wait on a pet until we had children. After six years of marriage and waiting for a child (not a pet!), we finally became a family of three with our beautiful daughter.

Not only do children change our lives, but God uses them (and pets) to facilitate change in us! Right? Oh, the things we all do for love in that changing process!

When new phrases started to roll off our toddler's tongue, we constantly heard, "Kitty! Kitty! Kitty! Kitty!" for at least two years. Then through providential circumstances, we adopted Fluffy from a friend, and I grew to be a slave to our new kitty! For fifteen years, Fluffy was a daily picture of contentment and a facilitator of our early-morning Purr-and-Praise time together.

Morning by morning, he plopped right down on my lap while I read my Bible.

I learned to appreciate Fluffy for many reasons, but most of all for the daily reminder to be content, no matter what is going on. During stressful times when I'd call out to God, Fluffy would be curled up on my lap, the picture of contentment. Seeing him there reminded me that I always have a place to curl up in God's lap, and I should plant myself there every day.

While my fur ball purred, I would pray, "Lord, help me be like Fluffy, content whatever my situation today. You tell us contentment is learned. I want to be a good student of Your amazing grace! You promise us strength for all things ahead, and I choose to rest contentedly in Your faithfulness."

Like Paul, we too can learn the secret of living contentedly in every situation. Whether or not you have a kitty, remember the lesson from Fluffy and start your Purr-and-Praise today.

Surprise! Surprise! Surprise!

*Very early on Sunday morning, just at sunrise, they went to
the tomb. On the way they were asking each other, "Who will
roll away the stone for us from the entrance to the tomb?"
But as they arrived, they looked up and saw that the stone,
which was very large, had already been rolled aside.*

MARK 16:2-4

Surprises are on my Life's Top Ten Favorites list, and Easter is a wonderful time
for them. Can you imagine with me for a minute the sheer surprise of seeing
Jesus after His resurrection?

I surprised myself one Easter when I decided, after a dozen years of marriage,
to attempt making yeast rolls one more time. In the early years of marriage, my
bread-making experiences ended up with dough and flour all over my kitchen
and me—but no bread! I got so exasperated that I ended up throwing all the
dough away. And I've thrown away many expired packets of fast-acting yeast
since that time.

God has a way of maturing us, though, and when Kali was five, I decided
yeast rolls would be a wonderful way to teach her about Jesus rising from the
dead. Last month I told you about my good friend Daphne, who is a kitchen
mentor and whose yeast-roll recipe is a favorite of Kali's. Well, that Easter
Daphne showed me how to make those rolls. It was a very hands-on experience,
and Daphne assured me I wouldn't fail.

Sure enough, on Easter morning I woke up my family, singing, "They arose!
They arose! Just like Jesus, they arose!" Needless to say, it was an Easter our family will never forget.

I love that Jesus' surprises for us did not end on Resurrection Day. In fact,
some of His best surprises are yet to come. I can only imagine that day in heaven
when we'll be celebrating an eternal resurrection day of our own, because Jesus
will have returned and taken all believers in Him to live with Him forever.

Together we'll rise up and shake the floors of heaven with praise for Him!

Let's "shake and bake" in joy and celebration that Jesus arose! Read
Revelation 22:1-5 for a glimpse of what's to come for believers.

Faith Is Not a Feeling

I did not even consider myself worthy to come to you.
But say the word, and my servant will be healed.

LUKE 7:7, NIV

In this Scripture, a Roman official, a centurion, remarked that he was not even worthy to come to Jesus to ask for his beloved servant's healing. Still, he was certain that if Jesus would "say the word," his servant would be healed.

Ney Bailey's book *Faith Is Not a Feeling* is based on this verse. It is a powerful story of God's faithfulness through tragedy. I read it right out of college, and its title alone had a practical and life-changing influence on me. Because I am an emotional creature, I need a constant reminder that my faith should not be based on my feelings but on what God says in His Word.

When He overheard the centurion express his unworthiness, Jesus wanted everyone around them to know that He had not found such great faith even in Israel. It was not the sick servant's faith He was commending, but the centurion's. This one man's faith was life-changing for his servant, and the miracle was confirmation to the centurion that Jesus was who he believed Him to be.

What an encouragement to me. What an encouragement to *all* of us. We need to choose faith over feeling every single time. There is nothing wrong with feelings, but they should not determine our choices. Whether we like it or not, God wants us to choose His way of faith and do what He says rather than what we feel like doing. Whatever God says through the pages of Scripture, we can take as Him "saying the word." God will never guide us to do something against His Word. We can believe and act on the fact that God said it, so it is true, regardless of how we feel. Faith is not a feeling. Thank you, Ney Bailey. "Thank You, Lord, that there is never an April Fool's Day with You."

Let's never base our faith on our feelings, but rather on what He says. Memorize Hebrews 11:1 (NASB): "Now faith is the assurance of things hoped for, the conviction of things not seen."

Dusty Frame

He knows how weak we are; he remembers we are only dust.

PSALM 103:14

I just failed as a mother *again*! I was impatient and short-tempered when my sweet child did not do something I asked her to do. Imagine that!

That innate rebelliousness, going astray like lost sheep and not following the Shepherd, is obvious even from an early age, and it travels with us as we grow older. Even as I scolded my daughter for disobeying me, I realized I have to be honest and ask myself how many times I have been disobedient toward my heavenly Father. There is probably no goal I want to achieve more in life than being an excellent wife and mother. So why are these the areas where my failures are most evident?

When I finally realized my own guilt, feeling overwhelmed that I had acted in such an unloving way that had displeased God, He kindly called to my mind 1 Corinthians 13 and its truth about love being patient and kind.

He knows how weak we are. He fashioned us from dust. No matter how many devotions I write or how many women I introduce to Christ, I still consist of dust. We all do.

But God is strong. He knows better than anyone else what we are made of, and He loves us unconditionally even though He understands that we will fail again. Remembering His patient love is so encouraging to my sorry emotions. God does not offer His forgiveness reluctantly. God loves to forgive us! And He renews a right spirit within us, right then and there, when we face up to our failures.

Next time you have a dust cloth in your hand, be reminded again that God knows what we are made of and loves us unconditionally!

What Weights Are You Carrying?

*Since we are surrounded by such a huge crowd of witnesses
to the life of faith, let us strip off every weight that slows us
down, especially the sin that so easily trips us up. And let us
run with endurance the race God has set before us.*

HEBREWS 12:1

What slows you down? Overcommitment? Too much stuff? Bad habits?
Unforgiveness? Pride? Lust? Lies? Fill in the blank: _____

God tells us to throw off anything that trips us up or slows us down in our
pursuit to know Him better. He wants us to lighten our heart loads as well as our
physical loads so we are free to be about His business without being weighed
down by guilt and regret, unconfessed sin and shame. If we deliberately do something we know is wrong, we are to simply stop, admit it, and turn away from it.
This workout will be different for each one of us. Right now I need to

- recycle or throw away a stack of catalogs and magazines that are becoming
  weights;
- clean out a closet that weighs my spirit down to even look in it;
- throw away several old lipsticks;
- talk less in public and listen more.

I'm sure there are other weights I carry, throw down, and pick up again. I can
trust the Lord to help me recognize and deal with them. I find that when I am
reading His Word, if He brings something to my mind that is confirmed by His
Word, I need to do it by faith.

We cannot fret over what weights other people are carrying because we have
enough of our own that God wants us to drop at His feet so we can carry on!
Obedience as spiritual exercise is the best kind of "weight loss." It frees us to run
forward in the race God has set before us and not get out of breath!

 Let's drop those weights of sin and opt for spiritual strength-building
that comes from obedience to God's Word.

Part 1: Argument with a Teenager

Do everything without complaining and arguing.

PHILIPPIANS 2:14

"Lord, I have never been a mother of a teenager until now! Are you sure you picked the right person for this? Where did my Christlike attitude go? How long have I been walking with You? Didn't I just spend time in Your Word? Who is supposed to be the wise, godly adult in this situation?"

That was my prayer after arguing with my daughter while she was home from college one spring break. I felt awful after she returned to school, so after I prayed I wrote her a two-page letter in an effort to clear the air between us.

Writing out my feelings and remorse was cleansing, but I still have much to learn about relationships and working through conflict. I'm thankful that at least I know *who* I want to learn from—the God who knows me inside and out!

After confessing to the Lord, I took responsibility for how I had wronged Kali. I wanted to make sure I did not miss an opportunity for the two of us to learn God's best restoration method together. I knew as I wrote it that the letter was much more for me than it was for her. I put my heart to paper, which I share with you as tomorrow's devotion.

In all honesty, part of me did not want to humble myself, but it was so uncomfortable to be stuck in my pride. Wouldn't you know, the wildest thing happened when I went to the *One Year Bible* reading for the very date I wrote my letter. The Old Testament reading included Numbers 20:12-13, the story of Moses' punishment for disobeying God by striking the rock.

I had no idea the story took place at the waters of Meribah, which means "arguing"! I wanted to shout, "Lord, You are so *personal*! You love me, and You see my disappointment in myself and my shame. Thank You that You have forgiven me and do not treat me as my sins deserve when I strike the rock."

> "Thank You, Lord, for Your good plan: 'Confess your sins to each other and pray for each other so that you may be healed' (James 5:16)." Is there something you need to confess to Him right now?

Part 2: Apology to a Teenager

Let the one who has never sinned throw the first stone!

JOHN 8:7

My dearest, sweetest Special K,

I just poured out my heart to God, which usually happens after I read His Word and I am reminded of what I am really like and how much I need Him. If He treated me as my sins deserve, I would not even be here. But in His mercy and great love for me, I am totally forgiven.

I must admit, my tendency to be easily angered is a true weakness and character flaw, and I am so sorry that I hurt you with my shortcoming. It seems like I should be further along in modeling a Christlike attitude, but I am not. However, I am meditating on these Scriptures to help me grow:

Short-tempered people do foolish things.   PROVERBS 14:17

A gentle answer deflects anger, but harsh words make tempers flare.
PROVERBS 15:1

A hot-tempered person starts fights; a cool-tempered person stops them.
PROVERBS 15:18

Sensible people control their temper; they earn respect by overlooking
wrongs.   PROVERBS 19:11

I am thankful that my sins do not surprise Jesus. In the history of humanity, no one has been perfect except Him. All my Bible heroes had weaknesses too. Good old Moses never even saw the Promised Land, because in his anger he struck the rock instead of speaking to it as God commanded.

I'm so ashamed of my failures. Please know my great love for you and the fact that I love the woman you are becoming. . . .

[To be continued tomorrow.]

I cannot hear 1 John 1:9 enough: "If we confess our sins to him, he is faithful and just to forgive us our sins and to cleanse us from all wickedness." My friend, what does this verse mean to you today?

Part 3: Restoration with a Teenager

Make allowance for each other's faults, and forgive anyone who offends
you. Remember, the Lord forgave you, so you must forgive others.
COLOSSIANS 3:13

Sweetest Special K,

I want to always point you to Christ and the love, mercy, kindness, and great
favor He bestows on you. I don't ever want to discourage you with my words,
tone, expectations, or the quality of the example I set for you.

I am asking God to change me as only He can—to help me be more patient
with an offense and to overlook those I should. Oh, being detailed and creative
(you are the same way!) can feel a bit like a curse. But with every strength
comes a weakness. Mine is very evident, and I wish it was more hidden! (I tell
Daddy his flaws are more hidden, while mine are more "out there" for all the
world to see.)

I could not be more grateful to the Giver of all life for giving you to me. You
fill my heart every day, and I long for God's best for you in every way. I am so
proud of you, and by the time you get this, your full week will be over!

An "Aware of My Many Shortcomings" Mommy
BSSYP
XXXOXXX

SP (Sweet Pea): I take my actions seriously, knowing that I am not in sweet
fellowship with God until I do my part to set my relationships with others right.

Kali responded,

You are the best mom in the whole wide world! I just got your precious and
heartfelt note. Thank you so much. And don't worry, I have a lot of work to do,
too, when it comes to improving my actions. I love you and BSSYP.

"Lord, thank You! Sweet restoration comes only from You!" Let's
choose one of our favorite Scriptures from the past three days and
pray through it today.

My Way or God's Way

*"My thoughts are nothing like your thoughts," says the LORD. "And
my ways are far beyond anything you could imagine. For just
as the heavens are higher than the earth, so my ways are higher
than your ways and my thoughts higher than your thoughts."*

ISAIAH 55:8-9

I want to soak in this encouragement from God for a minute with you. We each have a lot of our own thoughts and our own ways, don't we? Our minds process countless ideas every day—some we speak and, thankfully, many we leave unspoken.

I have no idea how many thoughts on average run through an individual's mind each day. We definitely have our individual ways of processing concepts and accomplishing things. In the simplest duties of daily life—from squeezing the toothpaste tube from the bottom, the top, or the middle to washing our hair every day or a couple of times a week—our idiosyncrasies are many and varied. And those examples don't even begin to touch on the deeper issues of life!

It is mind boggling that God not only knows my every thought and my every way, but He knows yours, too, and those of every living creature. Yet He is so personal to each of His children. He knows before we do everything that will pass through our minds and how our choices will affect us. He wants the very best for each of us and understands each of our unique dreams—and in every way His are higher.

The more I read about God and His thoughts and ways in His Word, the more *He gets bigger* and I grow smaller. How thrilling! Let's take another peek at some of His ways that we know for sure.

God's way is perfect. All the LORD's promises prove true. PSALM 18:30

The way of the LORD is a stronghold to those with integrity. PROVERBS 10:29

Accept the way God does things, for who can straighten what he has made crooked? ECCLESIASTES 7:13

Knowing the Lord's unfathomable ways, why would we settle for less? Today let any confusion and questions fade as His higher ways become your desire!

Choose God's Word

People do not live by bread alone, but by every
word that comes from the mouth of God.

MATTHEW 4:4

There is an old saying that goes, "When faith goes to market, it always takes a basket." I like that. Faith moves. It requires action, even if it means we must wait.

There is nothing complicated about the Christian life—unless we let our human perspectives and weaknesses clutter our hearts and edge out the space rightfully reserved for God. Through the power of Jesus Christ, faith in Him is the simplest, least burdensome way to live! His Word, the Bible, tells us what that looks like.

In Deuteronomy 32:46-47, Moses said to God's children, the Israelites, "Take to heart all the words of warning I have given you today. Pass them on as a command to your children so they will obey every word of these instructions. These instructions are not empty words—they are your life! By obeying them you will enjoy a long life in the land you will occupy when you cross the Jordan River."

I'll take the liberty of modernizing the quote that began this devotion: "When faith goes to the grocery store, it always gets a cart." Before I go to the grocery store, I always make a list of the things I need to pick up for our weekly meals. I drive to the store, select a grocery cart, choose my items, and place them in the cart. I have never been grocery shopping without putting something in my cart.

Living by faith requires that we pick up the Word of God and actually put His promises in our personal grocery carts. When we practice this habit on a daily basis, our appetites will grow to want more of Him. When we want more of Him, we'll be motivated to do things His way and act in faith to move in His direction and not our own.

🔑 Remember that God's Word is *nonperishable*, and His words are as life-sustaining as the food we eat. Feasting on His goodness sharpens our craving for more of Him.

Swinging

All Scripture is inspired by God and is useful to teach us what is true and to make us realize what is wrong in our lives. It corrects us when we are wrong and teaches us to do what is right. God uses it to prepare and equip his people to do every good work.

2 TIMOTHY 3:16-17

Relationships are a two-way street. A relationship cannot exist with fewer than two people, and healthy communication is a back-and-forth endeavor, like a swing. The nature of a swing is that it goes back and forth. Talking to God and listening to His Word—going back and forth with Him—is the sweetest swinging of all.

As I go back and forth (literally) through the pages of His Word, I find He prepares me for every circumstance I face. All of us can make this investment. It makes sense that reading His Word helps us learn more about who we are swinging with. We can find related truths spaced hundreds of pages apart, with hundreds of years spanning the dates they were written, and they apply to everyday life no matter the century.

For example, in 1 Corinthians 13, God not only tells us through the apostle Paul what love is—patient and kind—He also tells us what love is not—jealous, boastful, proud, or rude. Love does not demand its own way, is not irritable, and keeps no record of wrongs. *Whew!* If I'm unloving, especially to the two people on earth I love the most—my family—I go *forth* to 1 Corinthians 13 and see how wrong I was. Then I turn *back* to Psalm 51, and I am reminded of God's great love for me and that He forgives.

The most wonderful thing happens in this process. God brings *forth* my many shortcomings and I see my lack of love, so I flip *back* to be reminded of His great love for me. I am washed clean of my guilt. Better yet, this back-and-forth process keeps me so busy that I am less likely to spend time focusing on the faults in others!

In our communication with God through Scripture, let's go back and forth so often that our pages are worn but our relationship with Him and with others is strong—two-way, honest communication. And if reading the Bible through seems overwhelming, no worries. Start with a psalm or proverb.

Do You Need to Rest?

Come to me, all of you who are weary and carry
heavy burdens, and I will give you rest.

MATTHEW 11:28

"Come to me," Jesus says.

"Okay! I'm coming!" I answer when I am weary and am carrying heavy burdens. It is such a relief to drop them at His feet!

Where do you and I get rest? I am talking about real rest—rest that doesn't seem possible when we look at all the things we need to do. Rest in the midst of marriage and motherhood, work and play, and all the people we love and need to love.

Where do we get rest when we've been up all night with a sick child? When cancer treatments and medication keep us awake? When grief from losing a loved one causes pain so deep that we wonder if we can make it through another day? Where do we get rest when we find out we have a terminal illness, or have been in an accident or lost a limb, or cannot fulfill a responsibility because of circumstances in our lives? Where do we get rest when our cups seem to overflow with stuff that should not be in them in the first place and we feel like we are going to crack?

We find rest in Jesus! He is our rest. He is the only One who can give us all we need in order to accomplish what He has given us to do. And He gives with abundance, so that not only will we not crack, but we will overflow with His goodness into the lives of others, flavoring this hurting, isolated world so much that others will find rest in God alone too!

Treat yourself to a few restful moments today. Curl up on the couch with a favorite warm beverage and read through some psalms. Talk with Jesus, and thank Him for providing perfect rest fit for your present circumstances.

Hymnlines

*Praise the LORD! How good to sing praises to our
God! How delightful and how fitting!*

PSALM 147:1

One thing I love about the old hymns I learned as a child is that they are based on Scripture. When I am alone in the car, I try to recall as many hymn lines as I can. This is good discipline, not only for my busy brain but also for my soul. When I sing them, I'm declaring the living Word of God that moves us and changes us and offers life to all who pay attention.

No one can hear me singing in the car, and driving keeps my eyes focused forward, where I can see the big sky all around and imagine the vast heavens beyond my view. Driving alone is an ideal private place to practice praising. Singing hymns helps me stay focused on God's priorities.

I call my hymn memory game "hymnlines." Whereas hemlines on our skirts and pants change as fast as fashion trends (think maxi, mini, midi, capri, or cropped), God's Word never changes! The hymnlines help me belt out the truth in praise to the Lord. Here are just a few of my favorites:

Amazing grace, how sweet the sound.

'Tis so sweet to trust in Jesus, just to take him at his Word.

Onward, Christian soldiers . . .

This is my story, this is my song, praising my Savior all the day long.

And one last line from "Jesus! What a Friend for Sinners": "I am His and He is mine" explains why I sign most of my correspondence "His." How grateful I am for this hymn heritage!

Read a psalm or sing a hymn you can remember right now. I would imagine you already have started humming! Do a Google search to find out whether any of your hymnlines are drawn directly from Scripture.

Smiley Faith

The faith and love . . . spring from the hope
that is stored up for you in heaven.

COLOSSIANS 1:5, NIV

Since sixth grade, I've been putting a smiley-face sun beside my name (see my signature on p. xii). You see, my teacher, Mrs. Medlock, used to put two dots and a smile by her name when she signed our papers. This simple gesture delighted me, so I just added a circle and a few sun rays, and adopted a new signature at eleven years of age. Oh, the influence of a teacher!

Over the years, my sweet family and friends have supplied me with quite a collection of smiley faces. When our daughter was three and on a shopping trip with my mom, they came home with a sunglasses case covered with smiley faces. Mama told me that Kali insisted on getting it for me, saying, "My mommy will *love* it!" What a treasure—my first tangible gift from my toddler.

One day years later, I was glancing through a notebook that had a big smiley face on the front, but I did not feel like smiling. It was rare that seeing a smiley face didn't prompt a smile in my heart, if not on my face as well. But life was hard and felt hopeless at that time, and I was down in the dumps.

These were just feelings, of course. Fortunately, we have the Holy Spirit, who helps us rise above our circumstances. By His prompting, right then and there I changed *smiley face* to *smiley faith*, based on Colossians 1:5: "The faith and love . . . spring from the hope that is stored up for you in heaven."

Regardless of my feelings, I knew my troubles were temporary. A home in heaven awaits believers in Christ. As believers in Him, we can truly smile about the future while we're waiting here on earth!

⚷ Next time you see a smiley face at a Wal-Mart or a gas station or wherever, think of *smiley faith* that springs from the hope that is stored up for you in heaven.

The Mediator

There is one God and one mediator between
God and men, the man Christ Jesus.

1 TIMOTHY 2:5, KJV

A few years ago a meteor shower was forecast in our area for the wee hours of the morning. Our family—complete with my sweet widowed mother, who was visiting—piled into the truck, drove out to the country, and watched the glorious sight in our sleeping bags, laid out in the bed of the pink truck.

It was quite a sight, but what I will remember most is heading for church the next morning. I usually keep candy in my pocketbook, in a dish in my foyer, or in my pink truck. I'm sure this habit is a result of my sweet dad's huge influence. He used to tuck candy in his pocket for my siblings and me when he arrived home from work. I carried this habit into our family, and we hardly ever got into my late daddy's truck that I inherited without having cute candy mints (with verses on them) handy. They were my daughter's favorite!

Well, as we sleepily drove to church the morning after the meteor shower, I pulled out a mint at my daughter's request, and she read, "There is one 'meteor' between God and men." What a wonderful opportunity to laugh and share about our only way to God—our Mediator—Jesus Christ.

Jesus being our Mediator is the sweetest Good News we will ever hear! We know God personally through the man Jesus Christ, who makes possible our relationship with the Creator and Ruler of everything. His Spirit in us guides us through life and helps us reflect Jesus' character to people all around us who need Him to mediate on their behalf too.

Thank God today for *the Man—our Mediator, Jesus!* Write a note of gratitude to Him today; tell Him what His love means to you and how you value His role as Mediator to connect you with your heavenly Father.

Cleaning Out

*Those who use the things of the world should not become attached
to them. For this world as we know it will soon pass away.*

1 CORINTHIANS 7:31

"Those who use the things of the world." Hmm . . . that would be sweet you and me! God advises us through Paul's pen not to become attached to the things of the world.

God's Word inspires and motivates me to apply His truths to every area of life, including my daily household duties. By now you've probably caught on that I am very sentimental, so sometimes I have a hard time spring cleaning! We do not have an attic, basement, or garage in our home, but I am not complaining. The lack of storage space has helped me become less attached to the things of the world. I am attached enough, all right, but God keeps cleaning me out, and change is happening!

Every time I read in Scripture about the brevity of life, I am personally encouraged to remove things from my home that I am not using and that would help someone else. Sometimes, even though it is hard, I try to remove things that are really hard to give away. This discipline adds oil to my tight grip. I think the only thing I have ever really missed is a red "prairie" dress with a fun, fancy ruffle on the bottom!

I smile because God sees this futile tendency to concern myself with the things of this world, and He lovingly reminds me not to worry about whether I will have enough clothes to wear. And He does not want me to worry about *which* of those clothes to wear either! When I spend unnecessary time letting earthly things occupy my thoughts, I'm thankful that God's Word gently steers my mind and heart back to Him. In Him I can rest assured that my cares and I are in the best hands possible.

Let's tell the Lord now that we want our hearts to attach to His ways, not to things that will not last. Then let's ask Him for gentle reminders today to help keep our focus and priorities in line with His. (I think I'll go and get rid of one earthly pile right now!)

Undone

I said, "Woe is me, for I am undone! Because I am a man of
unclean lips, and I dwell in the midst of a people of unclean
lips; for my eyes have seen the King, the LORD of hosts."

ISAIAH 6:5, NKJV

Isaiah was known as the messianic prophet because he saw the future and spoke of the Messiah's glory (John 12:41). He is the Old Testament prophet who is most often quoted in the New Testament.

Does it surprise you to hear that a prophet is a sinner, too? Isaiah was well aware of his sin, but he was chosen by God even though he had "unclean lips." And God used Isaiah to convey His message of Christ's coming and of His future glory. Isaiah's "undone" state highlights God's holiness and our shabbiness, and we can marvel and worship the Lord of hosts along with Isaiah.

Undone. I have not heard that word in a while, but here it is in God's Word, making me pause to contemplate its meaning. It packs a lot of imagery, and it describes the way I feel when I start pushing for my own way in our home, thinking *my way* is best. I start to get irritated and bossy, and pretty soon I am a woman of unclean lips because I have self-righteously pointed out the sins of other members of my family. (Self-righteousness is not in the Lord's wife-and-mother job description! Neither are irritability and bossiness.)

The undone state comes as the Holy Spirit convicts me of my unclean lips, because nothing about that kind of communication resembles the way Jesus modeled leading, guiding, and inspiring others to follow Him. I love Jesus Christ and want to please Him, yet I fail. This undone state brings brokenness to my spirit, which brings me back to Jesus and then leads me to praise Him for how He extends real love, forgiveness, and restoration to me.

What circumstances cause you to know you are undone spiritually? How does your "undoneness" impact your life and others around you? Thank Jesus that He restores you and doesn't leave you undone.

Lay Your Burdens Down

My yoke is easy to bear, and the burden I give you is light.
MATTHEW 11:30

Every now and then I catch myself singing the lyrics of an old song: "Lay your burdens down, lay your burdens down." Perhaps these words mean something to me because I have a tendency to carry my burdens.

There are endless types of burdens we can carry on this earth, whether they are the weights of sin we hang on to, or the heartache we feel caring for sick loved ones, or the burden of trying too hard to fix ourselves or our family members and make everyone happy.

But burdens are not my department, and they are not yours, either. God did not design our frail frames to bear them. In fact, He instructed us in Hebrews 12:1 to "lay aside every weight, and the sin which so easily ensnares us" (NKJV).

Because of past surgeries, I have purposefully laid aside every physical weight, even changed my pocketbook size and decreased the number of coins I carry in it. Disciplining myself this way has been a necessary nuisance, but it has also been a very visible reminder of God's command to lay aside what weighs me down. When I am overloaded from taking on too many to-dos or want-to-dos, I grow impatient with myself and others, especially with my sweet family, whom I love most.

This weight becomes a barometer for Holy Spirit air pressure. It is so easy to fall short of God's standards, and sometimes it feels good for a second to "let it all out." But sin always has consequences, just like decreasing barometric pressure indicates that a storm is on the way. God's Holy Spirit zeroes in on the fact that I am operating in my own weak state and reminds me I am as frail as dust and not designed to carry heavy loads. Let's drop the physical burdens and the spiritual weights we're carrying and give them to Jesus. He will restore our hearts by lightening them.

Think about what weighs you down. Pick one burden right now and imagine yourself laying it at Jesus' feet. Leave it for Him to handle. Then commit to walk in His lightness the rest of the day.

Loose-End Living

Let us fix our eyes on Jesus, the author and perfecter of our faith,
who for the joy set before him endured the cross, scorning its
shame, and sat down at the right hand of the throne of God.

HEBREWS 12:2, NIV

In this busy, fast-paced world, sometimes I long for an official home holiday designated as a Loose-End-Living Day. A day to deal with

- the big water mark on the ceiling that needs painting . . .
- the hanging hem in my dress . . .
- the full gutters . . .
- the photos that need to be put in albums . . .
- the phone that's beeping for a battery . . .
- the unmailed wedding gift.

Whew! Have I inspired you to make your own Loose-End-Living list right now? These are small-potatoes loose ends. We may be able to list some big-potatoes loose ends, too, that cannot be dealt with in a day, a month, a year, or even this side of heaven:

- a debilitating disease . . .
- a depleted bank account . . .
- an unworn wedding dress . . .
- a rebellious child.

Sometimes thinking about handling these two kinds of lists forces me to focus on what is *fixed* and will not change—namely, Jesus! When loose ends hang over my head, He is the only One who can really tie them up.

When I fix my eyes on all the loose ends in my life, I start to unravel. However, when I fix my eyes on Jesus, He enables me to prioritize my schedule, activities, time, talents, and treasures toward the eternal. I am grateful that His Spirit helps me organize and accomplish what He knows needs my attention.

Think of a small loose end. If you can, go ahead and take a few minutes to tie it up now. As you work, ask Jesus to help you trust Him with the big loose ends too.

Part 1: You Have One Job!

Worry weighs a person down; an encouraging word cheers a person up.

PROVERBS 12:25

When I received the unexpected bad news of breast cancer on Good Friday almost ten years ago, my main heartache was my impressionable twelve-year-old daughter watching the ordeal of cancer from the sidelines. I did *not* want her to worry, and I did not want to miss being there for her wedding day someday in the future. I did not want to be away from home and unavailable to greet her as she came home from middle school.

I will never forget hugging Kali in the foyer before my mastectomy. In fact, God has continually used this particular mother-daughter interaction in both our lives. Many years have passed since that day, yet it still seems as fresh as yesterday. As we were saying our good-byes in the foyer, I looked at her and said, "You have one job while Mommy is away."

She looked at me with those beautiful, almost-teenager eyes and rolled them as if to ask, "Do I have to empty the dishwasher, vacuum, and blow the leaves off the back porch?"

Catching her nonverbal response, I said, "No, your only job is *not to worry*! You see, Mommy is in the best hands possible—the Lord's. So are you and Daddy. And I am not afraid because I will not be alone, and God loves me and you and Daddy more than we can imagine. As a mother with 'crazy love' for her beautiful daughter, my biggest fear is that you will be worried about me! I want you to enjoy your school and friends and your dad while I am in the hospital. I want to *not worry* about you because that will be much harder for me than the mastectomy!"

She got the biggest smile on her face. Every now and then in the days that followed I would ask her how she was doing with her job. It became our thing—*no worries*! God gave both of us courage in cancer *not to worry*!

There's more to the story in tomorrow's devotion.

⚷   Can you name the biggest worry of your life? Write it down, then write the words of Proverbs 12:25 over it. God does not want His children to worry.

Part 2: Falling Down on the Job

Worry weighs a person down; an encouraging word cheers a person up.

PROVERBS 12:25

We women don't need any extra weight, but worry can sure pile it on to our tender spirits. I'm using the same verse two days in a row because it perfectly fits the rest of the story.

On Mastectomy Day, I told Kali that pretty soon I was going to look funny with no hair, but she and I were going to celebrate because *no hair* meant the chemotherapy was killing the bad cells as well as the good ones. I would have to look worse before I got better! I also made wig shopping a fun affair and let her pick out one for me. (She chose one totally opposite of my short hair, and I looked like a plain Shania Twain!) In summer, the wigs were hot, so bandanas ended up being my pretty personal headgear choice.

I told Kali she had *one job*: not to worry! Months later, during my rigorous chemo schedule, God gave me an opportunity to take a special trip with my husband, but it meant Kali would fly by herself to be with my sweet sister, Shawn, in New Mexico. I was going back and forth about taking the trip because I worried about getting sick on the plane and worried about Kali flying alone for the first time.

I did decide to go, although I was still reluctant. Then God used a set of circumstances to confirm this was the right thing to do. I literally had my chemotherapy, then drove straight to the airport with my daughter. (Mark was already at our destination, waiting for my arrival.) When Kali had to proceed to concourse B and I had to go to concourse A, I fell apart in the airport! I started to panic—my heart was racing and tears began welling up!

"Mommy, what's wrong?"

"I'm having a harder time trusting God with you getting on that plane than I ever did having cancer!"

She looked me square in the eye and said, "Mommy, you have *one job*—not to worry!" I had fallen down on the job, but the wisdom of God was ringing in my ears. It was the closest I have ever come to audibly hearing the voice of God. He boomed His "no worries" message through Kali's unexpected reminder.

🔑 Do not worry! Live this precious life lesson daily.

Dreams I Wanted to Keep

I lie awake thinking of you, meditating on you through the night.
PSALM 63:6

I agree with David's words in this psalm. There have been many nights when my restless mind has been calmed by thinking about God. It seems fitting to spend time thinking of our Creator as often as we can.

One middle-school morning, my daughter was really hard to awaken from sweet slumber. I tried my usual wake-up song (which is a slight variation from the original)—"Good morning, good morning, you slept the whole night through; good morning, good morning to you"—but it wasn't doing the trick.

When she finally opened her eyes, I asked her why she was a real sleepyhead this particular morning. Her answer melted my heart. "I was having dreams I wanted to keep."

Dreams I Wanted to Keep sounded like a great book title to me! Later in the day, I pondered the words. A personal relationship with the God of the whole universe is not a dream. It is a reality. When we awaken every morning surrounded by the Lord's presence in this earthly life, our connection with Him is "for keeps"—now and for all eternity.

Jesus Christ's Holy Spirit is our constant companion who lives inside every believer. We can live in hopeful anticipation of seeing His face when He calls us home to heaven. In the meantime, we must carry His truths close to our hearts and meditate on them always, day and night.

To be honest, Jesus is the greatest dream come true and the most precious One we can keep and offer to others.

When we wake up in the morning, let's thank the Lord Jesus Christ that He is not a dream! He is "for keeps" now and forever!

Most High Expectations

When you came down long ago, you did awesome deeds beyond
our highest expectations. And oh, how the mountains quaked!
For since the world began, no ear has heard and no eye has
seen a God like you, who works for those who wait for him!

ISAIAH 64:3-4

I was disappointed when I arrived home with the wrong size sweater in my shopping bag. I went back to the store to exchange it with an expectation that when I returned "their mistake" to the store, they would say, "Oh, we are so sorry. Please enjoy a 10-percent discount on your next purchase." I was shocked when this did not happen!

Recently I read an article about customer service. The article contained an invitation to a public meeting to share thoughts about customer service and answer questions such as "Who treats you well and poorly?" and "What are your expectations, and have they changed?" We all long for good customer service, and most of us know some sweet companies that have flourished based on this marketable commodity.

You and I have expectations of people as well as of retail stores. There is no perfect company this side of heaven because there are no perfect people. But we have an expert model to follow in customer service, and that expert is Jesus Christ. He will always exceed our highest expectation. Everything He does is right. He does not tire of serving His children.

The list goes on and on of what we can expect from Him. He is true to His name: Most High. We can have the most high expectations from the Most High God.

Thank God, we can have the highest expectations of Him and His wonderful work on our behalf! For more about all we can expect from the Lord, read Ephesians 1:3. How can having a Most High perspective instead of our own help us live free from unrealistic expectations of others? How can we learn from His example of service and develop a heart that lives to serve Him and others?

Christ: Our Common Denominator

You are all children of God through faith in Christ Jesus. And all who have been united with Christ in baptism have put on Christ, like putting on new clothes. There is no longer Jew or Gentile, slave or free, male and female. For you are all one in Christ Jesus.

GALATIANS 3:26-28

No matter where we are in God's big world, when we meet another believer in Christ, we automatically connect! Why wouldn't we? We have the greatest relationship in common—a relationship with Jesus!

Jesus affects our relationships with others and the choices we make for the rest of our lives. When each of us is following Him in obedience to His Word, we are of one heart and mind. We may be total opposites in personality, height, weight, and interests. We may live on different continents. We may go years without meeting again; but if we do, we pick up where life left off because of Christ, our Common Denominator.

Apart from Christ, this kind of unity does not happen. Believers effectively serve each other and reach out together as we truly are in the "Lord's army" together.

What a privilege to be on the same team—no matter what. We are able to instantly connect because we are one in Christ. Our connection in Him transcends denominational differences, history, geography, and hardship. To me, caring connections provide some of the most refreshing pick-me-ups in our difficult lives. Wherever we go, Christ is the Common Denominator linking His followers forever!

Second Timothy 2:3-4 explains more about the army of God we are part of. Thank the Lord today that you have the power of His Spirit, His entire heavenly army, and His entire earthly army to support you through life.

Eternal Perspective . . . Where's Mine?

God has made everything beautiful for its own time. He has
planted eternity in the human heart, but even so, people cannot
see the whole scope of God's work from beginning to end.

ECCLESIASTES 3:11

"Eternal perspective? Eternity planted in my heart? Lord, I am not sure I have it! How do you get it? It sounds very important."

Have you ever wondered these things too?

When I finished my education with absolutely no training in sharing my faith or talking about God, and without ever going to Campus Crusade for Christ (Cru) meetings as a college student, I ended up on staff with this wonderful evangelical organization immediately out of graduate school.

You see, a cute boy named Leon told me that he could see me working on staff. God kept this notion on my heart, so I did what any normal person would do. I looked up Campus Crusade for Christ in the Yellow Pages and called the local director and his wife. After new staff training in San Bernardino, California, I was assigned to the University of Virginia to work with college students.

But instead of jumping for joy, I cried. I wanted to go where I could hide behind a lot of other staff members who knew what they were doing! I was the only single girl on staff with a married couple. Once the director asked me to give a message on "eternal perspective," and I had to tell him I couldn't do it because I simply didn't have an eternal perspective at the time!

God used pain and loss to cultivate eternity in my heart, and I am grateful to know that I have an eternal perspective now. It just took some time to grow! You and I have an eternal perspective planted in us since we are created by God, but we must do our part to cultivate it by getting to know Him through His Word, worshiping Him with growing believers in the body of Christ, and learning from godly leaders.

God plants eternity in our hearts and can fertilize our souls even in loss, when we cannot see the whole picture. Consider how you are cultivating an eternal perspective in the daily circumstances of your life. Ask Him to help your perspective grow as He reveals Himself to you.

Sin Awareness

The woman was convinced. She saw that the tree was beautiful and its fruit looked delicious, and she wanted the wisdom it would give her. So she took some of the fruit and ate it. Then she gave some to her husband, who was with her, and he ate it, too. At that moment their eyes were opened, and they suddenly felt shame at their nakedness. So they sewed fig leaves together to cover themselves. When the cool evening breezes were blowing, the man and his wife heard the LORD God walking about in the garden. So they hid from the LORD God among the trees.

GENESIS 3:6-8

Sin is a *big problem* we all have in common. I have wondered why this deadly problem never bothered me very much when I was younger. I think it's because when I was a child, I thought of sin as things that landed people in jail, like murder and stealing. The truth is that choosing our selfish way over God's way at any time is sin! It's sobering to think how often we make those choices every day.

I was not consistently in God's Word as a young adult, but after I started reading the Bible daily at age twenty-eight, I began hearing His voice in my heart. Not only did I start to fall in love with a personal God who revealed His love and mercy throughout its pages, but I started to grow and mature as His child. His Word really is powerful and sharper than a two-edged sword, capable of getting to the heart of our sin problem and cleaning us up (Hebrews 4:12).

When I sin, I want to hide from God and cover up like Adam and Eve did. I feel the shame they felt over having their underlying nature exposed as unfit for God's presence, but the exposure leads me to Christ, where I find His forgiveness, grace, and mercy.

🔑 Sin is an earthly and eternal destroyer. Have you admitted yours to Him and asked for forgiveness? When we believe in Him by faith, God is ready to offer pardon to us and to remove the shame that sin brings.

Set Your Affairs in Order

Hezekiah became deathly ill, and the prophet Isaiah son of
Amoz went to visit him. He gave the king this message: "This
is what the LORD says: 'Set your affairs in order, for you are
going to die. You will not recover from this illness.'"

ISAIAH 38:1

I'll admit that I'm sort of a stickler for having the dinner table set properly for meals. But don't worry—I don't notice it when I'm in other people's homes! In case you need a refresher course, the knife goes on the right with the blade pointing inward for safety. The spoon is to the right of the knife, and the fork is on the left with a napkin beside it to the outside. If you look at your place setting from left to right you'll see napkin, fork, plate, knife, and spoon.

In today's verse, this instruction from God for King Hezekiah was delivered just as matter-of-factly as when I ask Kali to help set the table.

Something that we need to set in order that is far more important than how to set a proper table is our eternal destinies. We can hobble our way through life, crippled by the things that separate us from truly connecting with God. Or we can get right with Him through Christ and enjoy intimate friendship each moment of every day.

It's true that these physical bodies of ours are going to die one day. Setting our spiritual affairs in order involves first of all knowing that we can become children of God by believing and receiving Jesus Christ into our lives. Growing in our relationship with Him means putting Him first in our lives, getting to know Him through His Word, communicating with Him through prayer, and trusting Him to help us grow to become more like Him.

Next time we set the table, let's reflect on the time when we made sure we had set our spiritual affairs in order and thank God for setting a place for us at His future banquet table.

Little Hairy

The grass withers and the flowers fade beneath the breath of the LORD. And so it is with people. The grass withers and the flowers fade, but the word of our God stands forever.

ISAIAH 40:7-8

This passage always reminds me of a certain gift from a very sweet and funny friend named Lee. We have decorated the Sweet Monday office with all the fun packages she sends! I am always tickled pink whenever I receive one of her surprise gifts.

One particular package contained what our family fondly named "Little Hairy." He was a bald, potato head–looking contraption that we put in our kitchen window and watered every day. Pretty soon, green grass sprouted from Little Hairy's scalp, and before long he had enough green-sprout hair to make ponytails, which our daughter enjoyed creating.

But then we went away for a family vacation and did not bother asking our sweet neighbor Robin to water Little Hairy. When we arrived home, Little Hairy had turned completely gray, dry, and brittle, and he showed no signs of life.

His sorry condition reminded me of this verse in the Bible about grass withering but God's Word standing forever.

The prophet Isaiah was comforting God's people, Israel, by telling them that the Word of the Lord is always alive and never fades. God's Word is self-watering, and He never takes a vacation from us! He is always ready to nourish us with His truth. As we grow older and our physical bodies fade like the temporary flowers and grass on earth, our spirits can grow richer and more fertile if we spend time filling ourselves with His nourishment that never runs dry.

Let's water ourselves daily with God's Word! Compare today's verse with the message of Psalm 1:3 and John 15:4. Let's think about the fact that healthy things grow, then make sure we're doing our part to feed ourselves with God's Word so our spiritual health doesn't fade like our hair color but grows stronger.

What Diet Are You On?

*I have rejoiced in your laws as much as in riches. I will
study your commandments and reflect on your ways. I will
delight in your decrees and not forget your word.*

PSALM 119:14-16

I used to wonder why Mama would ask my younger sister, Shawn, so many questions when we were growing up because she didn't seem to ask me very many. I felt like I was put on a "no question diet," and I did not like it! Years later, I finally asked Mama, and she told me that I always told her everything, while my sister needed prompting!

God made us all different, didn't He? The Bible is where God tells us everything He wants us to know. He does not have us on a "no question diet." He wants us to know about Him. He reveals His never-ending love, grace, justice, and mercy over and over in Psalm 119, the longest psalm in the Bible and one of my all-time favorites! In 176 verses, it lists the benefits of God's Word. For starters, God's Word

- revives us (verse 25)
- encourages us (verse 28)
- expands our understanding (verse 32)
- gives us an eagerness for His laws (verse 36)
- reassures us of His promises (verse 38)
- helps us abandon our shameful ways (verse 39)
- renews our life with His goodness (verse 40).

God tells us what He is like, what we are like, and how much we need Him. His Word is a nourishing feast for our souls and healing balm to our hurts and vulnerabilities. Reading His Word increases our appetite for living His way. It is one diet that we can never overindulge on.

Let's go ahead and eat up today. We never need to diet when it comes to God's Word! It shows us what He is like, what we are like, and how much we need Him. Indulge in Psalm 119 today.

Tongue Scraper

*Do not let any unwholesome talk come out of your mouths,
but only what is helpful for building others up according
to their needs, that it may benefit those who listen.*

EPHESIANS 4:29, NIV

I had never heard of a tongue scraper until a sweet and very funny woman brought one to my home and shared it as a beauty tip. I laughed so hard, and the next day I went right to the drugstore to buy one!

Often I think women would benefit from tying a piece of dental floss around the tongue scraper and wearing it as a necklace as a reminder to speak "only what is helpful for building others up according to their needs." We know unwholesome talk does not glorify God, and we sometimes forget about speaking the timely word that does glorify Him, which is alluded to in Proverbs 15:23 (NIV).

James also provides insight about controlling the tongue. James 3:2 says, "If we could control our tongues, we would be perfect and could also control ourselves in every other way." The power in a tongue for good or for harm pushes me to want more and more of Jesus. James goes on to say, "And a small rudder makes a huge ship turn wherever the pilot chooses to go, even though the winds are strong. In the same way, the tongue is a small thing that makes grand speeches" (James 3:4-5).

Each day we have dozens of opportunities to speak. As women, we love to communicate, but the more we talk, the more opportunities we have for letting less-than-constructive words come out of our mouths. On the other hand, we can take a positive approach and see just as many opportunities to speak words that glorify God and benefit others.

Let's ask the Lord to keep our tongues useful to Him to build others up and not harm them in any way! We can be reminded about the good, the bad, and the ugly about our lips by reading James 3.

We Have an Advocate

My dear children, I am writing this to you so that you will not sin.
But if anyone does sin, we have an advocate who pleads our case
before the Father. He is Jesus Christ, the one who is truly righteous.

1 JOHN 2:1

Don't you love it when someone stands up for you and watches your back? We are so appreciative of the people God puts in our lives who go the extra mile to defend and encourage us—people who really step up for us in difficult situations.

There is no escaping trouble in this wounded world. Even for those who have walked wholeheartedly with the Lord for many years, sin is not a stranger. The fact that everyone in Christ has an advocate—Jesus Christ Himself, the One who is truly righteous—is worth celebrating today and every day. His presence provides a sweet place of grace where we can go when we sin.

God sees our case through the cross of Christ. We no longer face a prosecutor because the defense team of Jesus has won every case of the accused who have chosen Him by faith. It's the only way to stand before our righteous Judge—God Almighty! But sometimes we forget our Advocate.

All of us have a go-between, Someone who literally steps in and always goes to bat for us. His name is Jesus. He is the go-between who reconciles a holy God and our sinful selves. He makes the way for us to have a personal relationship with God.

Our personal Advocate—our way to God—is always interceding on our behalf. No perfect person on earth can do this for us—only Jesus!

Take heart. You have a personal Advocate who is always right and always pulling for you. Praise Him for personally handling the accusations against you for sin. And when that grace gavel is pounded on God's desk of mercy, He will proclaim, "Not guilty!"

Lipstick Miracle

"God loves a person who gives cheerfully." And God will generously provide all you need. Then you will always have everything you need and plenty left over to share with others.

2 CORINTHIANS 9:7-8

How many times has the Lord refreshed you and me through the generosity of others? We could make a very long list!

One day, my sweet friend Christy told me she was getting ready to go to the beach and needed lipstick. (When you say "lipstick," my ears perk up.) I immediately went to my lipstick stash and pulled out several tubes. The one she really needed was my brand-new, most favorite lipstick with SPF 15 sunscreen.

It occurred to me that if Jesus needed lipstick, I would give Him my best one, so I should give her that lipstick. But I did not want to because it was new. I quickly, by faith and not feelings, put it in a bag of goodies and delivered it to her before I could change my mind! The next morning, I missed it and felt guilty that I struggled with such a stingy heart. I did not tell a soul at the time, but now you all know!

That very afternoon when I walked in my front door, I saw a cute little bag hanging on my doorknob with a note from Sweet Faye. The note said, "Just thought you'd enjoy this." Guess what was inside? A brand-new tube of lipstick— the exact same color with sunscreen that I had given to Christy! *Faye had no idea about my struggle to give my best, but God did!* I stood at the door and cried. It was a special delivery from God Himself through Sweet Faye! It was a true hug from heaven, a good and perfect gift that told me He saw what I gave and blessed me abundantly in return.

Our generous God hugs even reluctant hearts! Let's be generous too! What can you give today in secret, leaving the results up to God?

Remember When?

He causes us to remember his wonderful works.
How gracious and merciful is our LORD!
PSALM 111:4

In Henry Blackaby's wonderful devotional *Experiencing God Day-By-Day*, he says, "Spiritual memory is crucial in the Christian life." As you and I face life head-on with its many ups and downs, it is so encouraging to remember our gracious and merciful Lord! Recalling times when He came through for us bolsters our faith to trust Him again.

When I feel small and insignificant in this big, isolated world, God reminds me from His Word that He has been caring for me all along. I love to read stories in the Bible of His faithfulness. They show that He sees all, knows all, and truly directs the paths of His people, like when He parted the Red Sea so the Israelites could escape from the Egyptians. Every time I see the word *remember* in the Bible, I try to mark it.

I'll never forget His specific faithfulness to my family when we traveled south one summer to visit my relatives. We had a great time at my widowed mama's home, along with my sister Shawn's seven-year-old son, Elias. As the time neared to head home, the plan was to meet my sister at the halfway point to drop off Elias. But the day before we left, we decided to completely change plans and take all the cousins to see Aunt Doris and Uncle Eddie in Hickory, North Carolina, and meet Shawn there.

Mama had remarked the previous day that she was anxious to hear from my brother, Ryan, who was traveling a lot and hadn't been able to see her very much. We all missed him on this visit.

Well, just two hours before we left for Hickory, Ryan (I call him my smart Bubba) called and said he was driving through the area. Mama told him our change in plans. "I'll be near Hickory at about the very same time," Ryan replied.

Only God could have organized all three siblings who live in different states to be on the interstate simultaneously. He surprised us with an extended family visit that we'll remember always as His special faithfulness to us.

Remember God's personal faithfulness and know He doesn't need a GPS to find us.

May Mother Madness Month

Be still, and know that I am God!

PSALM 46:10

I think it would be fitting during the month of May for every mother to stamp "May Mother Madness Month" across her forehead. It would possibly help explain her frazzled, stressed-out countenance to everyone she encounters!

In May, the school year draws to an end, as do Bible studies and extracurricular activities, which warrant end-of-year special events. Moms are helping their children gear up for school exams, summer weddings, graduations, piano recitals, Johnny's and Sweet Susie's athletic tournaments, plus other numerous activities squeezed in.

No wonder the powers that be decided to make Mother's Day a May celebration! A special day for her is deserved more than ever this month. I feel overwhelmed handling our schedule with one child; I can only imagine how busy moms with several kids must be, trying to coordinate their whereabouts here, there, and everywhere. I get tired just thinking about it!

When I pause to catch my breath, I'm strengthened by remembering that Jesus is still in the craziness of May. He is smack-dab in the midst of every minute of every day, in every hour of every month—yesterday, today, and forever, unchanging and fully aware. "Be still, and know that I am God" is not just for May! *It is for every day!*

I know I can be far from nice when I am overscheduled. I know I get bossy with my family when I don't use His good judgment in making commitments and forget to first make room for Him in my day. He gives me what I need to accomplish what He wants me to do. It's only when I don't use my time wisely or add tasks He never intended for me that I get grumpy and frazzled.

As sisters in Christ, we can encourage each other—not just in May Mother Madness Month, but every day—to be still with the Lord, to know He empowers us with what we need, and then to *go* calmly and truly carry on, armed with His kindness and strength each day!

⚷ What's on your day's to-do list? Take a deep breath now, then say a prayer for wisdom to use your time as God desires. Be still and know . . . then go in the power of His Holy Spirit!

A Cushioning Rock

Let all that I am wait quietly before God, for my hope is in him. He alone is my rock and my salvation, my fortress where I will not be shaken.

PSALM 62:5-6

I read about a traveling man who always packed his breakable bottles inside his socks and then put them into a plastic bag inside his suitcase before going on a trip. In case the bottles broke, the socks would provide cushioning, and the bag would contain the mess. What a great idea!

You and I really love the cushions and protections in our lives, and not just for travel. Just think how many pillow styles we can choose from to cushion our heads at bedtime, or stadium seats to make the hard bleachers at ball games more comfortable to sit on. Add a warm blanket to wrap around us as a cozy shield, and we're ready to handle any of the elements. And think how theater seats and church pews have changed over the years—bigger, softer, more luxurious. We're all about comfort, aren't we?

Don't you wish you could wear an invisible sock or a cushion around you on difficult days? Or maybe you'd prefer having a rock wall around you for protection. Sometimes life seems to deal blow after blow, and we all need protection and comfort when our heart is breaking. We long for the people we love to have that too.

It's a great security to know that believers in Christ have both a Comforter and a Cushioner! The Lord is a cushion to absorb life's heartaches, a blanket to shield us, and a rock of protection and security. Psalm 62:6 and 1 Corinthians 10:4 refer to Christ as a rock, and Psalm 91 is loaded with symbolism of our security in Christ. In the first four verses alone, the psalmist calls God a shelter, refuge, place of safety, armor, and protection. Like a shield, "He will cover you with his feathers. He will shelter you with his wings. His faithful promises are your armor and protection" (Psalm 91:4).

Jesus Christ is the most versatile cushion of all because He is strong, immovable, constant, and comforting all in one.

Treat yourself to a decorative pillow or a new pair of socks. Every time you use your cushion, remember that your constant cushion is Jesus, the Solid Rock!

Sweet Rest

He lets me rest in green meadows; he leads me beside
peaceful streams. He renews my strength.

PSALM 23:2-3

I don't know about you, but sometimes I feel as though a stressed-out state is the norm. Feeling rested and peaceful seems to be a rarity for our culture. Many of us experience sleep deprivation, but when we add the stresses and troubles of everyday life or full-fledged suffering, we've got the recipe for physical, emotional, mental, spiritual, and relational exhaustion.

I'm guessing you can relate. Just because we live in an age where things have become easier for us doesn't mean we won't feel worn out. Glance at Psalms and you'll see that weariness has always had the power to catch up with anyone, no matter when or where they lived. People often talk of the past in nostalgic terms, calling them simpler times ("those were the days"), but actually we humans have been wearing ourselves out since the Fall in the Garden of Eden.

Kings are no exception. David surely felt worn out repeatedly. His words in Psalm 23 are like balm to the spent spirit. When we feel like we have to keep running at a frenetic pace just to meet the demands placed on us, it is freeing to read that God "lets" us rest in green meadows.

Quiet yourself right now. What do you hear? Can you feel the soft breeze of that calm meadow? God gives us permission to rest! Then He leads us by peaceful streams, and in the process He renews our strength.

No matter how busy life is, God gives us permission to get away with Him and enjoy His rest. That may happen in five minutes or fifty, but He is capable of giving all of us the rest we need today.

 Read Psalm 23. Thank Jesus Christ for giving us permission to rest in Him. He knows we need it, so go ahead and take a break today— with no guilt!

BFF

"Abraham believed God, and God counted him as righteous because of his faith." He was even called the friend of God.

JAMES 2:23

"Father Abraham had many sons." Remember that song from Sunday school? If we have trusted in Christ as our Savior and become children of God, then we are spiritual descendants of Abraham too. And we're God's friends forever. "So let's just praise the Lord!" In Jesus Christ we have a BFF—Best Friend Forever—beginning now, on this temporal earth.

Friendships are one of God's richest blessings. Laughter, tears, and fun are all a part of life with friends. And sometimes on dark days, when circumstances overwhelm us and no easy solutions are in sight, friends are welcome comfort. Even so, no human friend can make everything all better and fix our difficult situations.

You and I must put our faith and trust in our Best Friend Forever, who can and will make everything perfect in His time. He knows all about us and loves us unconditionally. He understands our strengths and weaknesses, our areas of pride and fear and heartache. He accepts us even when we don't feel acceptable to anyone.

To top all that, the Lord is never busy. He is always available. He is always kind. He knows what is around the corner in our future, and He has big plans for us. His name is Jesus, and we all need Him.

Jesus' type of friendship is hugely unselfish, too. He is always for us, and He will not compete for first place in our hearts. It's our choice to learn from Him and become the type of friend He is, choosing to place His priorities above our own. In the process, we learn to love to the point that the friendship we offer to others looks like the friendship He embodies. And the best part is that we get to enjoy His friendship for all eternity. BFFs—Best Friends Forever for sure!

Make sure that today, in Christ, you have a BFF—a Best Friend Forever! Ask Him to show you how to offer His type of unselfish friendship to someone else so that person can understand what it means to also have Christ as a BFF.

Daily Dose of God's Word

People do not live by bread alone, but by every
word that comes from the mouth of God.

MATTHEW 4:4

These days there seems to be a vitamin for anyone whose body needs a boost! Vitamin D, omega-3, B_3, B_6, B_{12}—the variety of vitamins and nutrients available can be mind-boggling. Manufacturers promise they'll help heal the heart, the kidneys, the immune system, and the gut, for starters. There are even vitamins for stronger nails.

Jesus is very clear in today's verse that bread and water are not really enough for the kind of living that makes for real health—physically, mentally, socially, and spiritually. Just as vitamin supplements add healthy components to our physical diet, God's Word adds vitality to our spiritual diet: "People do not live by bread alone, but by every word that comes from the mouth of God."

This truth should encourage us not only today, but every day. God is our Sustainer, the sustenance for our souls. He offers us full access to Himself, and He speaks to us through His Word, knowing His Word will serve as spiritual nourishment.

I don't know about you, but when I forget to eat or do not eat the right kinds of food, I get a headache and start to feel sluggish. Just get me an iced tea, cheese and crackers, nuts, beef jerky, and chocolate for my antioxidants, and I perk up.

Jesus tells us in Matthew 4:4 that Scripture sustains us; more than just a quick snack, it offers us lasting satisfaction and strength. The Lord used Scripture to battle temptation against Satan when He was physically famished. If Jesus—God Himself—used Scripture, we need to be digesting what He has to say in daily portions!

His power and obedience to His Word are exactly what we need to survive the onslaught from the enemy and from our own weaknesses. His Word leaves us satisfied, strong, and ready for battle!

 Let's read 1 Peter 2:2-3 as a reminder of our need for daily nourishment and put it into practice in the power of the Holy Spirit. It's how we hear His voice!

All Must Go?

*Don't store up treasures here on earth, where moths eat them
and rust destroys them, and where thieves break in and steal.
Store your treasures in heaven, where moths and rust cannot
destroy, and thieves do not break in and steal. Wherever your
treasure is, there the desires of your heart will also be.*

MATTHEW 6:19-21

My yard-sale sign reads, "All Must Go. Husband Says So." I put it up whenever
the time comes to purge. Yard sales are just one practical way to release my
earthly treasures and loosen my attachment to things that won't last.

Moths proved to be another way, as my sweet friend Daphne learned. She once
left a prayer request on my answering machine, saying, "Please continue to pray
about my moths. Evidently there are still some around here in the house, but I can't
find them. I came back from my two-week trip, and both of my traps were loaded.
It has me torn up, because they are flying everywhere. So it's all in God's hands. I
have torn this house apart, and He is the only one who can lead me to the source."

God did lead her to the surprising source. A handyman told her that all the
traps she had bought were actually attracting the moths. As soon as she got rid
of the powerful traps, the moths left!

Now, there is a lesson to all of us from this handyman! Who but a professional
would have suspected that the traps were causing the problem? His insight helped
free Sweet Daphne from her panic about the creatures that were cluttering her
mind and heart.

God is our professional handyman, spiritually speaking. He helps us learn
that we need to loosen our grip on things by the power He gives us through His
Spirit, so we are released to spend our time investing in things that will last: God,
His Word, and people. If we pay close attention to Him, He sometimes reveals
surprising culprits that are distracting us from His best and wreaking mothlike
havoc on our hearts.

It's as simple as this. God will show each of us specifically how we can clear
out our hearts as we yield to Him—moths, yard sales, and all.

⚷ Yard sale or not, let go of something that you don't need anymore.

Distracted

Martha was distracted by all the preparations that had to be made.
She came to him and asked, "Lord, don't you care that my sister
has left me to do the work by myself? Tell her to help me!"

LUKE 10:40, NIV

Can you feel Martha's intensity in this scene? Some of us may want to hand her a chill pill, but I have a hunch that most of us can identify with her anxiety. Her to-do list loomed, and she was stressfully distracted.

"Tell her to help me!" The exclamation point makes Martha's point difficult to miss. I feel her pain, and I cannot help but laugh every time I read this because I see myself in her. I see my sin. I see my own distractions in life and how much I wish that someone would help me!

I'm not laughing about my sin. I'm laughing in gladness that God put this story in His Word. He reminds me *again* that He knows me so well. He knows my weaknesses and my strengths and how my driven personality can be both a weakness and a strength in my life. My laughter results from pure joy that our big God, Creator of the universe, would be so kind to reveal this propensity we women have to be "worried and upset about many things." After calling Martha's name not just once but twice, Jesus reminded her plainly, "Only one thing is needed. Mary has chosen what is better, and it will not be taken away from her" (verses 41-42).

I call Mary and Martha the sweet M&Ms. They have different personalities, but both are infinitely loved and valued by the Lord. I'm touched that He calls Martha's name twice. I hear Him say to me, "Kimmie, Kimmie, you are worried and upset about many things, but only one thing is needed—it's Me!"

 Let the Lord speak to you right now. "_____, _____, you are worried and upset about many things, but only one thing is needed—it's Me!"

Read the Directions

*Trust in the LORD with all your heart; do not depend
on your own understanding. Seek his will in all you
do, and he will show you which path to take.*

PROVERBS 3:5-6

I didn't develop a taste for coffee until I was an adult visiting my sweet mama. She and my younger sister would drink it together in the mornings, and since I didn't want to miss anything, I joined in. The more coffee I had from my mother's favorite china cups with the thin rims she loved, the more I liked it.

When I returned home after that first trip, I knew I had to learn to make coffee myself. After making the rounds at various coffee shops, I decided on my favorite brand and was delighted that I could also purchase it at the grocery store.

But for some reason when I made it at our home, it never came close to how it tasted in the coffee shops or at my mother's! I changed coffee pots, changed filters, and even changed creamers. I tried adding more boiling water. Nothing worked.

I finally figured out where my brewing skills went wrong (although I am almost too embarrassed to admit it). I never read the directions on the side of the package that gave the proper measurements for the water and the coffee. I completely skipped them and foolishly wasted a lot of coffee and filters.

When I finally came to my senses, I said to the Lord at my kitchen counter, "I do not want to do this kind of thing with You, Lord. Not ever. I want to follow Your directions laid out in Your Word, day by day, moment by moment."

Let's all be sure we read God's directions in His Word—with or without a cup of coffee—keeping His instructions handy for living faithfully. That's really something to sip on.

Grace Missing

You must grow in the grace and knowledge of
our Lord and Savior Jesus Christ.

2 PETER 3:18

I'll never forget the night I spoiled our family's downtime and bedtime prayer.

Mark came home around 8:30 p.m., exhausted with back pain after leading four sports camps that day with young children. He could not wait to recline! It was a big day for our daughter as well. She found out who her teacher for sixth grade would be, which we celebrated only briefly because it was past her bedtime.

Unfortunately for them, my physical battery had been depleted an hour earlier. I was not even thinking about who I belonged to. I was preoccupied with trying to please everyone and, most of all, my mama self! You may know the one: the mama who has cooked, cleaned, chauffeured, washed laundry, ironed laundry, folded laundry, put away laundry, mailed the wedding gift, decorated the birthday cake, and delivered a meal to the neighbor, maybe while holding down a full-time job!

Dinner had been served and the dishes were cleared by 9:00 p.m. My work wasn't finished yet. I still had camp certificates to complete for my husband before morning. I was frustrated and ungracious when Kali didn't want to go to bed. She just wanted to talk, and I was too tired to listen.

My grace battery had run down too! Instead of exercising God's supernatural grace, strength, and power, we all missed a sweet catch-up time as a family because of my rigid routine and wanting my own way, which is sin. Thank God that He is committed to revealing our need for Him and growing us in the grace and knowledge of Him, even in our failings.

God reminds me most of His sweet grace when I fail to extend it. His grace prompts me to confess my lack of it, receive forgiveness, and be restored to those I have been short with. Grace *always* feels so good when it is received from family members and the Lord!

 "There's no other place to grow in grace, Lord, than with you." Read Hebrews 4:16 and take the message to heart.

Fish and Bait

Jesus called out to them, "Come, follow me, and
I will show you how to fish for people!"
MATTHEW 4:19

Did you ever go fishing in your elementary school classroom? You may think I'm telling you a fish tale, but I really did fish in my classroom.

We all looked forward to a learning game our teacher played with us. She put different-colored construction paper fish in a bowl. Each "fish" had a word or math problem written on one side, with a paper clip attached. Our fishing poles were straws with magnets tied to the end of strings. Of course, we all fished for the ones with easy problems on them!

My brother, Bubba, is an avid fisherman of real fish—he's even designed a special lure. I also enjoy being on the water and would probably like fishing if I didn't have to bait the hook or take the fish off when I caught it.

In order to fish successfully, you need fish and bait. The same is true in this scene from Jesus' life. People are the fish, and Jesus is the bait! Several of Christ's disciples were fishermen by trade, so I think Jesus in His wisdom knew just the right analogy to use to make that important connection for them.

Jesus is calling all of us in Christ to do the same: follow Him and fish for people! Oh, how I love that Jesus says "follow" first. Our first focus is to stay connected and close to Him so we can learn His methods for reaching out to people. He is the one who actually "catches" the hearts of people who have become hungry for Him. We just get to go fishing! With Jesus, it is always fun—and the net results are all His.

Follow Jesus and watch for opportunities to go fishing with Him.

Hiding the Sweets

Turn my eyes from worthless things, and give me life through your word.
PSALM 119:37

My husband enjoys going to the grocery store, but it is not on my list of favorite things to do, although I do love to eat the food goodies we buy there. And sometimes the treats are big temptations.

I teasingly call Mark "My Snack Man." When he goes to the grocery store, he stocks up on the sweet and salty snacks we both love. I recently asked him to hide them from me in a place where I could not readily see them. He has more self-control than I do. We don't nag each other about dieting at all, but since I am trying to eat healthier, I don't want the sweets staring me in the face.

I've never been tempted by lima beans, chicken livers, or any piece of meat that is an appendage. But put a cookie near me, and a little voice inside of me says that if I eat them all, there won't be any left to be tempted by. I confess that, in a weak moment, I have succumbed to eating half a pack of Girl Scout Thin Mints cookies.

To try to avoid junk food, I tell myself that sweets are worthless to me. Of course, cookies are not totally worthless, but when I mentally place them in that category, it helps me maintain my focus on what's best for me to eat. My lack of self-control makes it clear that I need God's guidance in all parts of my life.

In the context of this psalm, the worthless things could be anything that distracts us from the Lord and His Word.

Through His Word, God not only instructs me but motivates me by His Spirit to make better choices in all things, not just food, and to minimize the distractions. We all struggle and are tempted by "worthless things." God knows our weaknesses and tendency to depend on things for comfort and satisfaction. He will guide us by His Spirit to implement changes in areas of our lives when we submit ourselves to Him.

Let's not be afraid to ask our family and friends for help, too, in turning our eyes from "worthless things."

Citizenship in Heaven

We are citizens of heaven, where the Lord Jesus Christ lives.

PHILIPPIANS 3:20

"Kim, how did you *not* know passports expire?"

"God knows everything, and He knew that I didn't know that," I replied to my husband, Mark.

Granted, the timing was less than perfect. I had made the discovery less than twenty-four hours before boarding a flight to Germany.

My true citizenship is in heaven, and I wasn't thinking much about my earthly citizenship, since it is temporary! Still, God had given us this reunion trip from Sweet Aunt Gladys, and He could make a way for me to get there when there seemed to be no possible way it could happen.

I phoned a friend whose husband had worked in DC and then, at her suggestion, phoned the congressional office that handled expedited passport requests. I was told I would need to drive two hours to the passport office in DC the next morning with my expired passport to get in line and wait. In order for me to make the flight, I had to be back in Richmond by 1:00 p.m. There was no wiggle room.

I am a girl who grew up in a one-stoplight town. I had *never* driven in DC traffic before. Mark was in charge of basketball camp that morning, so it was God and me—or no Germany! My friend gave me detailed instructions of what to do, including hailing a taxi (another first step of faith). I left our home at 5:00 a.m., drove to DC, parked, got a taxi to the passport office, waited in line, and explained my dilemma.

They expedited my passport at 10:00 a.m., and when I got back to my car I screamed at the top of my lungs, "Thank You, God!" When I beat Mark home from work, I yelled, "I became a woman today! I drove to DC all by myself . . . only because my citizenship really is in heaven!" I am still in awe of God's personal care.

 Do something out of your comfort zone today to celebrate your citizenship in heaven that never expires. This passport is issued by our personal God in Christ Jesus.

Release It to God

Love is patient and kind. . . . It is not irritable,
and it keeps no record of being wronged.
1 CORINTHIANS 13:4-5

God has used my wonderful husband more than anyone, not only to cheer for me, but to steer me to do things I don't have confidence doing. "Thank You, Lord!" God also uses Mark to sharpen me. If love did not cover a multitude of sins, I'd be sunk.

Mark and I lost three precious parents in three years. When he and his brother were settling their parents' estate much later, the only thing Mark said that he would like to have from his family's home was the old pool table in the basement.

When he told me, I blurted out, "Where in the world are we going to put a pool table?" Inside I was thinking, *That massive, worn table?* I couldn't imagine it being in our home. My remark must have sounded unkind to Mark.

The next morning when I was reading my Bible, my heart became convicted. It was almost as though I heard God saying audibly to me, *If you really love your husband, you will care about the things he cares about. You will not insist on your own way.*

I immediately decided to sell all our dining-room furniture, which included a table, eight of my grandmother's chairs, a sideboard, and a china cabinet, to make room for that pool table! (I did have to let his brother know right away so the pool table wouldn't be sold.) Months later, I was delighted with the look on Mark's face when he saw the pool table—refelted and polished—moved in for the first time. His reaction was priceless. Mark and I both experienced joy that came from loving obedience! I haven't missed the dining-room table at all. When we have people over, we just pull out the Ping-Pong tabletop from behind the piano, put it on top of the pool table, and cover it with a nice tablecloth, and it becomes God's huge table!

Ask God how He wants to love others through your kindness and obedience. We all need lots of practice!

Blameless!

To him who is able to keep you from stumbling and to present you before his glorious presence without fault and with great joy—to the only God our Savior be glory, majesty, power and authority, through Jesus Christ our Lord, before all ages, now and forevermore! Amen.

JUDE 1:24-25, NIV

I can't imagine a better way to start the day or say "sweet dreams" than by praising God! Because of one person—Jesus Christ—we can wake up every day and place our heads on the pillow each night with an overflowing cup, no matter what we've done or what troubles we encounter.

If we have placed our faith and trust in Christ as our Deliverer from sin and death, our future is taken care of. The most important matter for you and me—where we will spend eternity—is a done deal.

Because of Him, we can face anything with boundless amounts of joy! Because of Christ's sacrifice, when our time comes to stand before God, He will declare us blameless for all the wrong things we've done, all of our mistakes, weaknesses, shame, and regrets that cripple us in this life. They will all vanish in the presence of our glorious Lord.

In the small book of Jude, God reminds us of what Jesus Christ did for us. Most likely the book was written by Judas, Jesus' half brother (Matthew 13:55), not the disciple Judas, who betrayed Him. What an amazing proclamation he makes. Before all time, God has set in place this wonderful plan for our salvation. It applies to us in the present and extends into the future, beyond all time!

🔑 Read Jude 1:24-25 out loud in praise to our great God and take courage for the future.

God Threw His Own Tea Party . . .

Is anything too hard for the LORD?

GENESIS 18:14

On sweet May 16, 2005, the tenth anniversary of Sweet Monday, 7,250 pink-clad people broke a Guinness World Record for the world's largest tea party. Our cups were truly overflowing! It was as though God threw His own tea party and let us attend! Only He could do so much with so little. He certainly multiplied our five cupcakes and two pieces of candy with Ukrop's butterstar cookies with pink dollop and sweet tea.

We would have missed the joy that comes from obedience if we had not stepped out in faith. Personally, I really did not want to do it at first. I told God that not even a pinkie fingernail of mine felt like hosting a tea party while going through chemotherapy, but if He wanted me to do it, I was willing. I begged Him to please let me know for sure!

Jesus says in John 15:5 that we can do nothing apart from Him. I did not want to invest a lot of time if my efforts did not count in God's eternal economy. If He was not in it, I did not want to move forward.

The next morning when I opened my Bible, the first verse I read for that day's passage was today's verse: "Is anything too hard for the LORD?" A tear ran down my cheek and I said, "Lord, is that You? Are You telling me to take the next baby step of faith?"

I made one phone call to a volunteer, and three days later the University of Richmond in Virginia called and offered their basketball arena—the Robins Center—for this *big* step of faith. As it turned out, we still didn't have enough parking or policemen for all the traffic, and our community was tickled pink by our *big God*!

What issue in your life seems too hard to accomplish, fix, or heal? Ask yourself, *Is anything too hard for the Lord?* Answer out loud with a resounding *no*! Then ask Him to show you His power and guidance in your situation, whether it be a tea party or trouble.

... and He Let Us Come!

Anyone whose name was not found recorded in the
Book of Life was thrown into the lake of fire.

REVELATION 20:15

Whoa! You might be thinking, *Kim, that is not a very sweet verse.*

You're right. It isn't sweet news for those who reject the Lord. But God's sweet and loving invitation is offered to everyone. He wants all of our names to be there in the Book of Life.

Yesterday I wrote about celebrating God's faithfulness on the tenth anniversary of Sweet Monday, Women's Socials on a Shoestring . . . Tied to a Generous God. At that party, we raised our teacups to Him and broke a world record at the same time. To comply with Guinness rules, we had to get a signature from every person who attended. It was amazing how many people shared that they were coming to write down their name and be counted. It was a wonderful opportunity to see our community celebrate together the cause of Christ.

As much as we enjoyed all the laughter and fun, we were challenged to share the Good News of Christ that day. That was why we were there. It was far more important for everyone's name to be in God's Book of Life than in a world record book.

"Lord, we all count to You. You know the exact number of people who are in the world right now because You created each one of us. There is no one like You! Thank You for loving us and letting us come to You and be counted, now and for eternity."

Spend a few fun minutes considering what record you would like to set or break. Then think about a few of the records the Lord has set (i.e., created the universe in six days, rose from the grave, works countless miracles every day).

God's Guiding Light

Your word is a lamp to guide my feet and a light for my path.

PSALM 119:105

Unexpectedly, writing daily devotions has brought joy to my spirit because it has helped me remember God's never-ending faithfulness. It is one simple way I can cheer for God and His Word! On the other hand, writing devotions with my heart on my sleeve seems to bring out things about myself that I do not like, might not want others to know, or are just plain silly. Yet those ordinary, everyday aspects of life are the very things that God uses to remind me about Himself.

For example, I have some pet peeves. (Don't we all?) One day when I have time, I would like to list every one of mine just to see how many I have. Topping the list are dim lightbulbs.

My first summer out of college, five friends and I worked at the beach as waitresses in various seafood restaurants. Four of us lived together in one trailer. It was tight quarters, but since it was temporary and we were saving a lot of money for school, we managed to make it work. I clearly remember that my first purchase for our trailer was several 100-watt bulbs! I can't live in a place with dim lighting. Forty-watt bulbs would never be found in my home. I have actually sold low-wattage bulbs at a yard sale!

One of the reasons I love God's Word is because it acts as a bright lamp for our feet and a light for our path. Its truths are 100-watt sure, and God's promises found in its pages never dim over time. If we need light shed on any situation, we can look to God through His Word!

 Turn on God's bright light in your life with the truths in His Word. Two good verses to plug in to your heart and mind are Psalm 139:23-24.

God's Glow

*[Moses] wasn't aware that his face had become
radiant because he had spoken to the LORD.*

EXODUS 34:29

Have you ever tried self-tanner to give yourself a more radiant glow without damaging your skin with UV rays? Some people think it's the best product ever made, while others haven't had positive results. Self-tanners may seem simple enough to use. After all, you just have to apply them. But sometimes even that simple step can be a bit tricky.

First you have to get past the smell because some brands leave a lingering scent you may not like. Then applying it correctly takes practice in order to avoid telltale streaks. Finally, you might have an allergic reaction, and with some inferior brands, you risk waking up with an orange glow that resembles the University of Virginia, Clemson, or Tennessee orange.

Before self-tanners were ever formulated, Moses found the best way to get a lasting radiance that goes deeper than just the skin. When Moses walked closely with God and talked to Him personally, he glowed! He had to cover his face because God's anointing was so powerful it could have blinded anyone who saw him.

We can experience that same glow when we spend time with God. In addition, we always have access to the Holy Spirit. As well as His presence, we have the Bible for wisdom and encouragement for all the trials we encounter between here and heaven! His Word is the map for our rocky roads as well as for life's cliffhangers and mountaintop experiences.

We glow with Him when we hear His voice through His Word, and we do what He says by the power of His Spirit.

Let's face it: Only in Him can our faces, hearts, and lives radiate His love. Ask Him to work in and through you today . . . reflecting God's glow.

Are You Weak and Burdened?

Come to me, all of you who are weary and carry
heavy burdens, and I will give you rest.

MATTHEW 11:28

"Come to me," Jesus says.

"Okay!" I answer. "I'm coming!" I say it right back when I am weary and am carrying heavy burdens. It feels so good to drop them and run to Him!

Where do you and I find rest? I am talking about real rest—rest in the midst of a full schedule; rest in the midst of mourning a loved one's death or enduring the weariness of a lingering illness; rest in the midst of good things, too, like work and marriage and motherhood and looking after our households.

How do we find rest when our schedule is packed? When we've been up all night with a sick child? When cancer treatments and medication keep us awake? Or when personal grief causes us pain so deep that we wonder if we can make it through the next day?

Rest can seem elusive when we have been in an accident or circumstances prevent us from fulfilling a responsibility. Where's the hope of rest then?

For each of those situations, as well as for everything else that comes up, we find rest in Jesus. Only He can give us all the resources we need to accomplish what He has given us to do. He gives abundantly of His Spirit. Living refreshed by Him, we can flavor this hurting world and whet the appetites of others so they can find rest in God alone too!

○━ Our rest is in Him! Say, "Okay, Lord. I'm coming!" Treat yourself to a few physically restful moments today. Curl up on the couch with a warm drink and read through a few psalms. Talk with Jesus and thank Him for providing perfect rest, even in the midst of any unrestful present circumstances.

Lost in the Kitchen Drawer

If you look for me wholeheartedly, you will find me.

JEREMIAH 29:13

When I lose something, I become a bit of a crazy woman until I find it. I pride myself on trying to have a place for everything and everything in its place. Even if a drawer may look messy at first glance, I know that what I'm looking for is in there . . . somewhere!

Has this ever happened to you? You distinctly remember putting something in a drawer, but the moment you really need it and go to retrieve it, it seems to be missing. Regardless of how long you scramble around looking for it, it is nowhere to be found. Then a few weeks later, when you are looking for something else, *voilà!* You find the thing you had searched so hard for before!

It was there all along, but it was lost in the clutter of that catchall kitchen drawer.

I think sometimes we cram our lives so full with things and activities that our relationship with God suffers. He gets lost in our clutter, and we wonder why we're so disagreeable. We feel easily overwhelmed, and we start to worry. When anxiety sets in, we miss out on the abundant life found in Him and become weary in well-doing. We need to stop and recognize that His peace is missing but readily available to us.

God promises we will find Him when we seek Him with all our heart. He wants to ease the heart of that "crazy woman" mentality and replace any frazzled spirit with His peaceful one. Isn't that wonderful and mentally freeing? Let's allow Him to clean up the cluttered kitchen drawer of our souls. Seek Him in His Word and talk to Him in prayer, whether with eyes open or closed, while driving or lying in bed. He will always be found!

Read Jeremiah 29:12-13 and seek Him through His Word today. He isn't hiding from us! His peace passes all understanding.

No Failed Promises

*Deep in your hearts you know that every promise of the LORD
your God has come true. Not a single one has failed!*

JOSHUA 23:14

When Mark and I were first married, we fell more than once for the lure of advertisements that promised free gifts or trips if we would visit a campground or condo. We still laugh about one place we were strongly encouraged to buy so we could enjoy it for years to come. There was only one problem. Because Mark is so tall and the ceiling in the cabin was so low, he couldn't stand up straight without hitting his head! Once the tour was over, there was no way he ever wanted to step foot in that place again. We had to hold back our giggles the entire time.

A few years later, we sat through another presentation where we were lured by a selection of wonderful prizes—a trip to Florida, a diamond necklace, and luggage. I could do without the trip or the necklace, but I had my heart set on the luggage.

When the presentation was finally done, I hurried over to pick up my promised suitcases. I encouraged Mark to help the sales clerk, since I knew the luggage would be too heavy for the tiny lady. Mark looked at me like I was crazy. "Oh, no," the woman assured me. "I can handle them myself." She disappeared into a back room for a couple of minutes, then returned with a flat, letter-sized package.

I couldn't believe it. The small package contained three pieces of plastic luggage that unfolded like sheets of paper. Talk about a major letdown! And the alternative prizes weren't that great either. The trip to Florida required purchasing a round-trip ticket, and I could not even see the "diamond" in the necklace!

Once again, it's a laughable memory for Mark and me. And a great reminder to always be thankful to God that His promises never disappoint. He always proves true to His Word.

 Know that every promise of the Lord our God has come true or will come true in His perfect way and time. Not a single one has failed, and He's not about to fail you or me!

Sweet Things Come from Hard Places

I would satisfy you with wild honey from the rock.

PSALM 81:16

I love this image—honey from the rock. Some of life's sweetest experiences come from hard places, just like sweet honey can flow from a hard rock. Only God can produce this kind of abundance from barrenness. I know you have some great stories of God's provision, like rocks oozing with honey. I would love to hear all of them! I will share a few quick examples from my own life.

Sweet Monday. It was a ministry birthed by God out of my loneliness and isolation. Nearly twenty years later, women still come to our home the first Monday night of the month to laugh a lot, learn from other women, and leave with an introduction to Jesus.

My cancer. This physical disease helped me grow bolder as I got balder. I never imagined that it could be a pathway to greater spiritual effectiveness, but that's what happened.

Fluffy, the kitty, goes missing. Our dear kitty has been part of our family for more than fifteen years. From the time Kali was three until she was five, all she talked about was *kitty, kitty, kitty.* Fluffy and I ended up having Purr-and-Praise time every morning. He sat in my lap as I read my Bible. Most days Fluffy never veered much from his routine, but one day when he went outside, he did not come home. We were all heartsick. I cried every day because I missed him! We posted "Lost Fluffy" signs and a newspaper ad and unabashedly yelled his name from car windows in hopes that he'd hear us. On the twelfth day, he miraculously appeared in God's answer to our prayers. He was skinny and dirty, but alive. This recovery mission was not successful because of our puny prayers but because of the power of God.

Sweet things from hard places—honey from the rock. They are surprising life lessons of God's love for His children. God has a way of awing us with His ways when things seem hopeless. *He will go to all extremes* for one of His own!

Let's keep looking for honey from the rocks we encounter! Expect God to bless you with signs of His presence and provision, even when circumstances tempt you to lose hope. How does Joel 2:25 promise similar hope?

Sweet Feet

How will anyone go and tell them without being sent?
That is why the Scriptures say, "How beautiful are
the feet of messengers who bring good news!"

ROMANS 10:15

When I was growing up, my sweet southern mama always told me not to call attention to my feet because they were not my best feature! I usually listened to her, but this was one piece of advice I haven't followed as an adult. You see, I really love shoes! Since I am such a visually creative person, my eye tends to go to the wild, colorful ones. High heels and wedges are my favorites. I have an eclectic selection in my closet to complement my wardrobe. I enjoy variety and lots of color.

Far more important than what my feet look like is who they belong to and where He wants them to go! I'm grateful for this perspective-building truth in Romans 10:15 (above) and am reminded of His purposes for me when I read Jeremiah 17, too. This serious chapter reminds God's people of their sin and the punishment for worshiping idols instead of God Himself. The idol worship took place on every "high hill" (verse 2), which, when I read it aloud, sounds like "high heels." I can't seem to avoid thinking about shoes!

But God stops my mind's wandering tracks, and I begin to meditate on what He says about our feet. They are beautiful feet when they bring the Good News about His hope and grace and salvation to other people. It does not matter what kind of shoes we have on—high heels or orthopedics, designer or clearance bin—as long as they are on feet that follow the Lord Jesus Christ.

Let's use our sweet feet to follow Him on His mission! Wear a favorite pair of shoes today and think about the eternal journey you're walking with God. What steps of faith and surrender do you think He wants you to take?

Cracked Boots

The LORD is close to the brokenhearted; he
rescues those whose spirits are crushed.

PSALM 34:18

I turn into "Miss Tea Party" when I don an old pink hat that I hand decorated with candles on top to resemble a birthday cake. My sweet neighbor Audrey in Charlottesville, Virginia, gave me the floral hat years ago when she saw my third "greaters" parade into my home for a tea party.

Not too long ago, "Miss Tea Party" and my daughter, now "Miss Tea Cup," were invited to take part in a fashion show. In a moment of last-minute desperation for my black ankle-top boots to match our mother/daughter white May dresses, I spray painted my only pair of laced boots with leftover glossy white paint. I was pleased with the result. They looked shiny, beautiful, and perfect.

That is, until I arrived at the party. With every step I took, the white paint cracked and peeled to the floor, leaving a nice little trail behind me! After the party was over, I took my boots to a shoe repair shop to see if they could be salvaged. The man just shook his head and said there was nothing he could do—I had used the wrong kind of paint! I was crushed by disappointment, but I wasn't crushed in spirit.

Sometimes the circumstances of life leave us crushed and cracked, and we try all kinds of things to "paint" over how we really feel, in hopes of soothing the pain. Death, disease, divorce, hurricanes, and many other real personal tragedies can be found all around us. You may be going through your own personal 9/11 right now or may need to make a 911 call to God. He has promised to rescue us when we're crushed and revive our spirits.

Jesus Christ was not defeated when He died for our sins on the cross. He was victoriously resurrected. When you feel like your life is falling through the cracks, call on Him.

Failure

If we confess our sins to him, he is faithful and just to forgive us our sins and to cleanse us from all wickedness.

1 JOHN 1:9

I am a Christian wife and mother. I love the Lord now more than I ever have! But I am still human. Even though I did not do something as destructive as cutting off a soldier's ear like Peter did in the garden of Gethsemane (John 18:10), I did call my husband a name! I was *so* mad at him, and it just popped out.

I can't believe it slipped, but it did. I feel ashamed, and I don't know what to do.

Then again . . . yes, I do! The truth settles in my mind, and I know I need to call my sin what it is. I need to admit my wrong and ask God and Mark to forgive me. "I am sorry. I was wrong." I begin by praying.

"I love You, Lord. I have believed in You since age nine. I gave You my whole heart in college and turned my life over to You. I have been walking with You for years, but I have failed today!

"I need You to 'restore to me the joy of your salvation' (Psalm 51:12) because I sinned against my wonderful husband and against You.

"What if I could not go to You, Lord? What if I had to carry my sin forever? 'Who will free me from this life that is dominated by sin and death? Thank God! The answer is in Jesus Christ our Lord' (Romans 7:24-25). You will free me, Lord. You will forgive me!"

Once I take care of heart business with my God who loves me, I am ready to sit down with Mark and ask for his forgiveness, thankful that he loves me too.

As I teach young children and adults at tea parties, it's good manners to say five important words: "I'm sorry. I was wrong." Let's own up to our sins sooner rather than later. Jesus can set our hearts and relationships back on track. He offers grace and forgiveness when we fail.

Got Hope?

Even Christ didn't live to please himself. As the Scriptures say,
"The insults of those who insult you, O God, have fallen on
me." Such things were written in the Scriptures long ago to
teach us. And the Scriptures give us hope and encouragement
as we wait patiently for God's promises to be fulfilled.

ROMANS 15:3-4

Got hope? If only having hope were as easy as getting a milk mustache—one taste and we'd be branded with it.

Sometimes it feels as if hope is hard to come by. But hope in Christ is readily available every minute. God wants us to drink deeply of it, believing that hope can never be wiped away! He tells us that the Scriptures, such as today's verses written by the apostle Paul, give us hope and encouragement. Since the Scriptures are God's actual words to us, it is His personal encouragement and hope that we are receiving.

This hope is designed to permeate our souls so that even under the most dire circumstances, it strengthens us and the glory of God shines through us so others will see that He is the Source of our hope.

If we can't seem to find hope right now, we need to ask ourselves how long it's been since we last opened the Scriptures. I'm not talking about looking up something for an assignment or to prepare for a Bible study—just purposely being still, ready to listen to God's voice.

God tells us plainly through the Scriptures that we can have hope! He knows how much we need it in our anxiety-filled lives. He assures us over and over again that every promise He makes will come true.

You and I have probably spent a lot of time in the "waiting room" of life, hoping for greater hope, waiting to hear a word from Him. When hope is our companion in the waiting room, those moments can be a joy, privilege, comfort, and exciting adventure while we thrive in His presence!

Remind yourself that hope is always available. Write "I will hope in Christ alone" on a card or sticky note and put it someplace where you can see it often.

Former Things

God will wipe away every tear . . . there shall be no more death,
nor sorrow. . . . For the former things have passed away.

REVELATION 21:4, NKJV

"Great has been the blessing from consecutive, diligent, daily study. I look upon it as a lost day when I have not had a good time over the Word of God."

Me, too! Me, too! That's what I want to shout when I read George Müller's words. When I read God's Word, sometimes I cry, sometimes I groan, but sometimes I burst out laughing, even during a trying time. I do believe God laughs with us!

I recall an especially good time with God in His Word one particular morning after receiving bad news the previous night. I was home alone that evening when Dr. Melzig called. "Kim, I am so sorry. You are looking at a mastectomy. I know tomorrow is Saturday, but since Mark is not home, will you bring a friend? My wife will come with me since the office is closed. I want to put you on the ultrasound table and see how we missed it."

Needless to say, I was crazy about my kind surgeon. From that day forward, Dr. Melzig went the extra mile just for me and was so thorough. I remember hanging up the phone in shock but not feeling alone because I knew the Lord knew everything that was happening to me. I actually slept that night.

What I remember *most* is pulling out my Bible the next morning and reading that the former things have passed away (Revelation 21:4, NKJV). For some reason the verse struck me so funny that I laughed out loud. I felt as if our *Lord Himself* was sitting in the upholstered chair across from me, laughing and crying with me. I was reassured that He knew and understood that I was going to lose a breast, but He comforted me. I was held tightly in His grip. What a faithful Friend we have, who even helps us laugh in heartache!

God is Someone who knows exactly what will cheer us or encourage us. He knows our deepest needs right now as well as what we will need to get us through. Cry with Him over the bad news, celebrate the good news with Him, and cherish the fact that He knows you personally.

Simple and Steady Diet

This is love for God: to obey his commands. And
his commands are not burdensome.

1 JOHN 5:3, NIV

When I pick up a women's magazine and find any tip that helps simplify my household chores, I think it is worth my time. Many times the word *simplify* even appears on the covers of those magazines because they specialize in that kind of advice.

Following their tips, I have cleaned out a kitchen drawer and have pared down my knives (pun intended) to simplify cooking preparation. I have followed their recipes to streamline my meals and save time because life is short.

However, two areas that I continue to struggle with are my closet and cooking organization. Those areas in my home don't always look like the pretty pictures in the magazines because even if I'm inspired by clever ideas, I am overwhelmed thinking what it would take to carry them out. I can't seem to stick to the plan for very long, like pulling everything out of my closet at one time. It is burdensome to wade through a long list of directions in a recipe, too, only to complete a task and then see it still fall short.

Fortunately God's instructions are created for us to succeed, not fail; they are simple for us to understand and heed when we stay connected to Him as our source for ongoing inspiration.

God's commandments are not burdensome when we desire to follow them out of love for Him. If we are walking around troubled, encumbered, and oppressed, then we probably are not walking obediently on God's path, because His path leads to joy! The only way to enjoy a simple, unburdened life is by following Jesus' commands.

Let's follow God's plan and let Him unburden us. When we love Him, we'll obey Him, and we'll experience joy in following Him. Doing so is possible only through His Holy Spirit's power.

Reminders

And now, O LORD, God of Israel, carry out the additional promise you made to your servant David, my father. For you said to him, "If your descendants guard their behavior and faithfully follow my Law as you have done, one of them will always sit on the throne of Israel." Now, O LORD, God of Israel, fulfill this promise to your servant David.

2 CHRONICLES 6:16-17

How do you remind yourself of things you don't want to forget? Maybe you're a list maker, and you keep a pad of paper close by at all times. Maybe you've grown attached to the calendar on your favorite handheld device. Or maybe you're one of those rare people who keeps all details carefully sorted in your head—if so, I am truly impressed.

This passage serves as a timeless reminder about God's promises. Solomon, David's son, had completed his appointed task of building the Temple of the Lord, furnishing it, and placing the Ark of the Lord's Covenant in the sanctuary. The people offered songs of praise and many sacrifices in thanksgiving to God. The whole nation of Israel was there, and Solomon prayed for all the people. King Solomon praised God for keeping His promise that He made to Solomon's father, David.

I'm glad that God never needs reminders, but we can reaffirm our own faith by reminding *ourselves* in front of God of what He promises throughout His Word. Repeating His promises as we pray and worship Him can rally our faith.

God's promises in Scripture give us courage to live with vibrant faith. Like Solomon, we can boldly "remind God" that we are counting on His continued faithfulness to us. We will see God proven true over and over again!

We need a daily review of God's faithfulness to us. Choose a couple of your favorite promises and review them with God. Tell Him you believe His promises and you know they'll be proven true!

Ultimate Redemption

Fear not, for I have redeemed you.

ISAIAH 43:1, NKJV

Redeem is a big word in the Bible. I looked it up in my *Scholastic Children's Dictionary*, where the definition read, "to exchange something for money or merchandise."

When I was a little girl, my father worked for a company called Sperry & Hutchinson (S&H), which gave out green stamps at the grocery store based on the amount of money you spent. We always supported the store that gave out green stamps because it supported Daddy's company, and we loved the rewards.

After shopping, Bubba and I would run home to lick and stick our stamps into little paper books, excited to watch the books pile up. We were saving up for something pictured in the prize catalog, or better yet, we'd go to the actual store where the merchandise was displayed and redeem our green stamp–filled books for some toy, game, or vacuum cleaner. (Please, Mama, not the vacuum!) It was so much fun to collect and save for *free stuff*.

As a child, I had a hard time understanding that there was a cost involved. That childlike mind-set is what I believe the Lord would like us to have when He says, "Fear not, Kim. Fear not, Sweet (insert your name). I have redeemed you." Jesus Christ has purchased our freedom from the bondage of sin, at the ultimate cost to Himself, His blood shed on the cross.

We can't begin to really understand all it cost Him, but because of what Jesus did, we can enjoy freedom from fear. He redeemed us for eternity, and He looks out for us perfectly and practically in this life.

What do you fear? Offer it back to God as a step of faith, thanking Him for buying your freedom and allowing you to enjoy living with childlike trust in Him.

Thank God today for removing our fears. If you need to release a fear to Him right now, please do so. He has redeemed you as His own at great cost.

The Celebration of All Celebrations

Blessed are those who are invited to the wedding feast of the Lamb.

REVELATION 19:9

Here is one invitation we do not want to miss! No matter how young or old, heavy-laden or carefree we are, this invitation is ours for the taking. Because Jesus was always saying, "Come" (Matthew 11:28), we can extend the same invitation to others and introduce them to Jesus, the Lamb of God. This is worth spreading the news about! The invitation list is all-inclusive—no one is left out.

Remember what it was like when someone at school was having a birthday party but not every child in the class was invited? If you didn't receive an invitation, it felt awful to know that something was going on and you were not included.

The invitation to the wedding feast referred to in today's verse is an invitation to everyone! It isn't just any old gathering either. It's the premier event of all time and beyond—the wedding feast that will finally celebrate the reunion of Jesus, the Lamb, with His bride, the church—believers in Christ.

The invitation is open until Jesus returns to gather His own for the journey home. He desires everyone to give an RSVP of "Yes!" and then spread the word about His coming back. Although we cannot RSVP for other guests, Jesus is delighted when they respond to Him with their own personal RSVP of believing faith.

We need to tell others that they have been invited personally by Jesus! If they only check their hearts carefully, they will see His personal welcome waiting there.

We are blessed by this invitation, and we can do our part to encourage others to join us when we share with them the meaning of the wedding feast.

Let's share the excitement about the feast Jesus is preparing for His wedding party! Help others realize they're invited, and they can't afford to miss it. Read Revelation 19:6-9 for a glimpse of the best of all wedding celebrations.

Remember the Sabbath

Remember to observe the Sabbath day by keeping it holy. You have six days each week for your ordinary work. . . . For in six days the LORD made the heavens, the earth, the sea, and everything in them; but on the seventh day he rested. That is why the LORD blessed the Sabbath day and set it apart as holy.

EXODUS 20:8-9, 11

This fourth commandment is often overlooked. I have been contemplating this commandment recently because there seems to be very little distinction between the six days we do our work and the one day each week that is holy—the Sabbath dedicated to the Lord our God.

Holy means "set apart." Whether we feel holy or not, we are set apart in Christ when we receive Him. One day in our week is to be set apart and made different from all the rest. If we are in Christ, let's ask ourselves, *Do I keep the Sabbath day holy? Is it different from other days in my heart and in my home? How?*

It's easy to fall into the habit of letting work consume us. After all, God gives us work to do, and we can honor Him with our work. But God created us to rest, too. Rest refuels us inside and out. We read in Genesis that God the Father rested after He finished creating the world, which was a big job! In the Gospels, Jesus often withdrew alone to rest and talk to His Father.

My mama's best friend, Dorcas, is a firm believer in rest. Sometimes I would hear my mama ask her what she was doing, and without hesitation Dorcas would reply, "I was taking a little rest." Dorcas has become my friend, too, and I have spent a lot of time with her over the years. I have never seen her impatient or in a hurry. God's rest helps her.

God knows what we need better than we do, so let's heed Him when He tells us to make the Sabbath a day given wholly to Him.

God gave His commands to benefit us. Think about what changes you need to make in order to set aside the Sabbath for God.

Lock In Those Wraps

I am the way, the truth, and the life. No one can
come to the Father except through me.

JOHN 14:6

I love simple household tips that save me time and energy. Two former house-mates, Sweet Meg and Mimi, gave me a real gem that I couldn't believe I didn't already know.

Did you know that the boxes that aluminum foil and plastic wrap come in have tabs on the ends to lock in the wraps? After years of wrangling with tangled foil and plastic, I finally learned to lock the rolls in place by pressing in the tabs. Name brands and generic wrap boxes both have them—such a wonder!

This small addition to the box has turned out to be a giant stress reliever for me. Now my rolls of foil and plastic wrap don't tumble out of their boxes, and I'm not fumbling around, trying to find where the wrap starts. And it's safer, too—I am less likely to cut my hand on the serrated edge.

Of course, obstinate wrap is not a life-changing issue, but it does make me think about faith. Is my faith locked up tight when life gets tangled and threatens to twist, unravel, and tear me up? We lock in our faith by taking our troubles to God and staying close to Him through conversation—listening to Him by reading His Word and talking to Him in prayer. When we do that, He reaffirms our security in Him. He holds us firm to keep us from becoming undone and protects our souls from the jagged edges of our difficult circumstances.

Being locked into God by faith means we will never run out of love, joy, peace, and comfort in this life because He locks in His promises for all His children—even in the midst of torn and tangled lives.

 Lock in your faith with Psalm 18:35 (MSG): "You protect me with salvation-armor; you hold me up with a firm hand, caress me with your gentle ways."

The Power of His Word

The word of God is alive and powerful. It is sharper than the sharpest two-edged sword, cutting between soul and spirit, between joint and marrow. It exposes our innermost thoughts and desires. Nothing in all creation is hidden from God. Everything is naked and exposed before his eyes, and he is the one to whom we are accountable.

HEBREWS 4:12-13

One of my God-given roles as a wife is to be my husband's helper. While I heartily embrace this, there are times when I don't find it easy to live up to that role, especially when it requires me to do something I don't feel like doing.

Recently Mark asked me to help him by making a phone call early in the morning. I was reluctant to do it because I was in the middle of my Bible study and I knew it would mean spending a lot of time waiting through endless prompts. (I'm sure the day's study had to do with putting others' needs above our own.)

As I sat there, the Holy Spirit nudged my reluctant heart and cut through my bad attitude while I was reading God's Word. Here are a few thoughts He brought to my mind:

Where did that selfish, sinful attitude come from? (Answer: Mark 7:21-23)

I forget so quickly there is a war going on in my soul! (Galatians 5:17)

But Lord, I want to be like You. (Colossians 3:12-13)

God's Word shows me what I am really like, and I am eternally grateful for that. Talk about "cutting between soul and spirit, between joint and marrow"! It sounds like an amputation, and it feels like one, too, when our "innermost thoughts and desires" are exposed! No wonder I hurt when I sin against God. The best part of this problem? Jesus! He died on the cross and paid the price for all of our sins forever.

"Lord, thank You that I am not alone and completely undone in this struggle. Even Paul, your faithful servant, struggled with sin, but he also reminded us of our Rescuer!"

Thank God for His vital and powerful Word! Read about the apostle Paul's struggle with sin in Romans 7:21–8:2.

155

We Will Get Up

*It is my Father's will that all who see his Son and believe in him
should have eternal life. I will raise them up at the last day.*

JOHN 6:40

I enjoy going to zoos because I am fascinated with animals, especially the wild ones. I see God's artistry in the black and white stripes of a zebra as well as the gorgeous spots on a leopard and the varied patterns on a giraffe. Is it any wonder that animal print fabrics never seem to go out of fashion?

A baby giraffe has a rough introduction to the world. When the calf drops from his mother (some eight feet), you'd think the fall would kill it. And then the mother giraffe shows her "love" by kicking the calf repeatedly until it gets up. As soon as the calf gets up on its spindly legs, mom giraffe kicks her baby down again because she wants her offspring to remember how it got up. Talk about a rough set of circumstances early in life. Sounds like something I would like to forget! But her actions are all for her calf's good; she's instilling strength for survival.

Throughout our lives, you and I face rough times. I'm sure you wouldn't have to think very long to recall situations when you've felt kicked down, when it was a struggle to even think of getting back up on your feet. Sometimes we feel as though we have nothing left inside to help ourselves get up.

But be assured that God is the One who will raise us up permanently. He doesn't leave us down forever. Jesus lovingly tells His followers that He will raise them up to be with Him forever. When we reflect on His eternal perspective, we realize it instills strength for survival through the ups and downs of this life.

No matter how many times in this short life we fall down or are weighed down or even face death, we will be raised up forever, never to go down again!

 Up and at 'em! Let's adopt Jesus' eternal perspective in John 6:40, asking Him to instill His strength in us today.

Our Help

We put our hope in the LORD. He is our help and our shield.

PSALM 33:20

In 2011, the movie called *The Help* brought to life the stories of several African American maids in Mississippi during the 1960s. Many of those women brought a great deal of wisdom with them into the affluent—but needy—homes of their employers.

When I first heard the title of the movie, I kept thinking, *I know the Help—the real Help. I have needed His help in the past. I need it now, and I know I will need it in the future.*

Our Help is the Lord, and He is on duty 24/7. It's not a matter of His being submissive to our every beck and call; it's that He is available to guide, lead, and direct us in His wisdom.

We have help even when we do not feel like we have help, even when we do not welcome it. There will never be a time on this earth when we will not have His expertise and power at our disposal. When you and I have put our faith in Christ, we have all the Help we could ever need.

Do you ever need His assistance with

your children?	your disappointments?
your husband?	your depression?
your aging parents?	your anger?
your dreams?	your commitments and responsibilities?

We have His help for everything! His Holy Spirit indwells and guides us, as well as letting us know when we need to get back on track. He gives us the mind of Christ for direction about everyday living. And He gives us His Father's protection, limitless power, and constant love. We are His dependants. Never underestimate what the *real* Help can provide.

Let's help ourselves to the genuine Help! Bring a current need to Him in prayer and thank Him that He's already providing solutions His way, in His time.

God's Word Is Always in Style

*You must love the LORD your God with all your heart, all your soul,
and all your strength. And you must commit yourselves wholeheartedly
to these commands that I am giving you today. Repeat them again and
again to your children. Talk about them when you are at home and
when you are on the road, when you are going to bed and when you are
getting up. Tie them to your hands and wear them on your forehead as
reminders. Write them on the doorposts of your house and on your gates.*

DEUTERONOMY 6:5-9

God's Word is always fresh and never goes out of style. But did you ever think
about decorating your home or wardrobe with it?

I have read today's verses many times, but until now I hadn't pondered the
reason that Moses instructed God's people to actually style themselves and their
homes with God's Word. They did not have their own copies of the Scriptures
in their homes, much less multiple versions like we do today. The only way they
could pass down God's promises and directions was by making these important
truths such a part of their daily lives that they stored them in their hearts and
were able to recite them in their homes.

In the world, fashion continually changes, and society keeps adapting to keep
up with the times. God's truth never changes because it doesn't need to! His Word
is always relevant and is available to us in countless versions of the Bible as well as
being accessible online. His truth will be evident in our homes and in our hearts
when we practice it by faith. He doesn't want His truth to remain closed in a
book; He wants to use it by His Spirit to style us more like Him.

You and I cannot give out what we do not have. Wherever we are, we cannot
talk about the Lord and what He says through Scripture unless we know what it
says. God asks us to commit ourselves wholeheartedly to His Word because He is
the Word.

 Let's dress for the day with His Word in our heart! Choose a verse
to memorize today. How about the first sentence in today's verses
from Deuteronomy above?

Daily Exercise

"Not by might nor by power, but by my Spirit," says the LORD Almighty.
ZECHARIAH 4:6, NIV

Because our bodies are the temple of the Holy Spirit, I attempt to exercise regularly. But I don't have to like it. (I have a sweet friend, Katherine, who always says, "I love to exercise!" I wish I had her enthusiasm.)

Since I'm being honest, I admit that I do not feel mighty and powerful after I attend a fitness class where we use weights; in fact, while I'm there, it reminds me how weak I am! Still, I do my best to keep at it, even though in today's verse I'm reassured that physical exercise doesn't need to be my primary priority in life. Exercising daily through reading and obeying God's Word is a far more important discipline! Whenever I feel inadequate for the responsibilities God has given me, it energizes me to know that ultimately, my life happens by the power of God's Spirit . . . not by my own might.

If something significant happens in my life, I know it didn't result because of my puny hand but because of the powerful hand of the Lord Almighty. I long for a David heart in a Goliath world.

I desire to rally sweet Christian women across our hurting land and remind all of us that we have incredible power because we have Jesus Christ. We are His chosen ones who can offer His love to everyone He places in our path, and He provides the necessary resources. Our job is to be obedient by faith. The more we know about God's character, the more we fall in love with Him and desire to do His will. The more we are following His path, the more of Him will be reflected, and our influence will be greater.

Zechariah 4:6 is God's encouragement to us to live beyond the limitations of our weakness.

The pressure is off of you and me! God, through His might and power, works through us. "'Not by might nor by power, but by my Spirit,' says the LORD Almighty."

What do you need strength to accomplish today? Ask God to show you in a specific way that He will handle your need in His power.

He Has Your Back

*Joshua conquered all these kings and their land in a single campaign,
for the LORD, the God of Israel, was fighting for his people.*

JOSHUA 10:42

Most of us have heard it said on television or in a movie battle scene. One soldier says to another, "Don't worry. I've got your back." It's a statement meant to dispel fear and boost courage in crisis or danger. Kali said this to me before I stepped off a mountain for a *very* high-ropes mother/daughter adventure.

How blessed the Lord's people are that our Heavenly Commander has our backs. And just so we'll be absolutely secure, He also goes before us into every battle. He knows the winning tactics, and He leads us through the fight, no matter how difficult the terrain or the depth of darkness we find ourselves in.

Isn't it comforting to know that we have an invincible Father who is also our Warrior and our Protector? He always has our best interests at heart. He knows we are weak soldiers made of dust, and He even understands that sometimes in our panic or confusion we push against Him instead of leaning into Him. Even then, He still loves us. When we submit to His strategies and authority, we can march throughout life's circumstances empowered by His Spirit in ways we may never even see to fight life's battles.

And to top it off, *He always wins.* Not only is He undefeated, but He is *undefeatable.* No matter what, we are always on the winning side. When we take our marching orders from the true Commander in Chief and we stay on His path, follow His orders, and allow Him to fight for us, we are assured of ultimate victory. That's a battle plan worth defending!

Let's commit today to fight our battles with God, not against Him, leaning into Him for support. When we say, "Yes Sir, Lord" to everything, we are assured of ultimate sweet victory!

We Belong—No Cuts

If we live, it's to honor the Lord. And if we die, it's to honor the
Lord. So whether we live or die, we belong to the Lord.

ROMANS 14:8

My husband, Mark, is a knowledgeable, kind, funny, inspiring teacher and coach of middle-school students. For over twenty-five years, he has invested his days in the lives of young teenagers, teaching them how to play a variety of sports. Through his wonderful wit, sense of humor, and laid-back style, he encourages children at that awkward age to learn new skills and the rules of the game. Every summer I fall in love with him all over again when he dons his whistle at his private basketball camps and teaches not only the fundamentals but the joy of the game.

Every school year Mark has to cut players from the girls' tennis team. It is always an agonizing experience for him, one that gives him many sleepless nights. I melt like butter, witnessing the level of love he has for the students in his care. Cutting players who yearn to belong is the last thing he wants to do, but he has to make the hard choices because there can only be so many players on a team with a limited number of practice courts to hone their skills. When it's time to travel to a match, there is only so much space in the vans and so many days available in a season to fit in all the games.

"I could never do what you do, Mark," I told him. "I could never be a coach because I would not be able to tell someone he or she couldn't be on the team!" I so admire the grace with which Mark handles this process.

Thankfully, once we are on the Lord's team, we cannot be cut. Because of Christ, our spot on His team is secure. Let's give a cheer for being part of God's eternal squad! We belong—no cuts!

⚷ Read Romans 8:38-39 aloud. We cannot be separated from Him.

Changed

*This same Good News that came to you is going out all over
the world. It is bearing fruit everywhere by changing lives,
just as it changed your lives from the day you first heard and
understood the truth about God's wonderful grace.*

COLOSSIANS 1:6

Over the years I have appreciated what I've learned from reading women's magazines—skills such as how to arrange furniture, pick out a paint color, make a fruit smoothie, or apply brow powder. But honestly, nothing major in my life was ever really changed by reading a women's magazine.

On the other hand, *I* am changed as I grow to know Christ better each day through His Word. He promises that His infallible Word always produces fruit and accomplishes all He wants. It prospers everywhere He sends it (Isaiah 55:11). When I get a daily dose of what God has to say and walk by faith in His strength, He works His life-changing transformation in me.

I love to try new products and change things around from time to time. Getting a new chair for the living room adds a fresh look to our home. A new lipstick color rejuvenates me. But there are other changes that unsettle me, especially if they are unexpected and take me through tough times or require me to step far out of my comfort zone.

But God created us with His heart for greater purposes beyond our own plans. Living for Him means having an openness to let Him do things differently in us. If He knows our current path doesn't lead to His best for us, He may reroute us another way. We can trust that His changes are always for our best as He leads us on an adventure that will glorify Him.

When we allow Him in His wonderful grace to have His way in us, we are assured of a life that fits who He created us to be.

Let's thank the Lord today for changing us and making us ready for His greater purpose for us. We can trust Him to be there when we are steered out of our comfort zones.

Trouble Listening

Spouting off before listening to the facts is both shameful and foolish.
PROVERBS 18:13

I have been keeping a list of Bible verses that mention our mouths because, frankly, sometimes my mouth needs to be buttoned up.

At times I am as impulsive as the disciple Peter, who got so excited that he practically jumped out of a boat to walk on the water to Jesus, only to begin to falter and sink when he let his attention be diverted from the Lord.

Yes, my impulsiveness is often expressed verbally. I may interrupt someone out of excitement or fear that I am going to forget something important if I don't blurt it out immediately. In fact, my early-morning phone friend, Daphne, and I are working on not interrupting each other, but it's hard because we have a lot to cover in such a short amount of time!

Being talkative isn't a bad thing, but the more talkative we are, the more we open ourselves up to can't-take-back words flowing from our lips. Our family friend Skip used to say he did not enjoy being around BMWs (Big-Mouth Women). Abrupt, intrusive talk is not becoming to a godly woman *or* man.

"Lord, how many times have I answered a family member or a coworker or a friend without listening?"

When others speak, I want to listen because I really do care about them. Today's verse reminds me to pause before letting every thought become verbal. The book of Proverbs is practical because it reveals so many of our weaknesses and our sin, but in such a positive way. Solomon tells us how to reflect more of Christ through these wise sayings.

God is the only perfect talker and listener. He hears everything, and He is always available. He never does or says anything wrong. He does not react impulsively, but instead responds thoughtfully for our good, even though the truth is sometimes difficult for us to hear. Because He wants us to reflect His gracious truth more fully, if we need help in this area, we only need to ask and listen.

Today let's be wise women who listen for His wisdom. Let's work on really listening to people without interrupting or thinking of the clever comebacks we have ready.

Falling in Love

The LORD helps the fallen and lifts those bent beneath their loads.

PSALM 145:14

It hurts to fall. Most of the time, falling hurts on the inside even if it doesn't really hurt on the outside. I have had my share of falls. I've tripped over my tall husband's basketball player–sized feet, and I have fallen in a hole or two or three. In each instance, my pride feels wounded every bit as much as my bruised muscles or scraped skin.

If I had a choice, I would choose physical pain over emotional pain. I have an extremely high pain threshold, so I'm able to deal with physical pain pretty well. But emotional pain is another story. It can cause excruciating pain that no anti-inflammatory medicine can touch. No matter what the origin of our emotional pain or the level of our pain threshold, our heart needs healing!

You may be hurting from emotional pain today. Maybe you are struggling to put one foot in front of the other. Possibly the circumstances in your life have changed drastically overnight and you feel battered to the point that you can't even seem to stand on your own.

I'm so thankful that there is one type of fall that feels wonderful! Falling in love can't be beat, especially when it comes to falling in love with the Lord. I have definitely fallen in love with Him through His Word. If my heart is heavy and I feel bent beneath my load, I run to the Lord in the Psalms. There I am reminded of His strong help and kind care.

Jesus lifts up all those who are burdened with heartache. As we look to the Lord in hope, we can trust that the Great Physician's timing is always best. When we fall down—and we all do—the Lord Almighty is upholding us and will lift us up in His way and time.

Read all of Psalm 145. Then spend time falling in love again with the Lord. Praise Him for all His "awe-inspiring deeds" (verse 6) of love that have already taken place in your life as well as those yet to come.

Got Joy?

I have told you these things so that you will be filled
with my joy. Yes, your joy will overflow!

JOHN 15:11

This wonderful promise that Jesus shares with His disciples was among His last words to them before His death on the cross. He reminds His best friends of the keys to joy, which are still true for us today.

Jesus identifies Himself as the Vine, and we are the branches. When we remain in the Vine and stay connected to Christ, we'll experience overflowing joy. Drawing vitality from Him, our lives will bless others and produce much fruit. And fruit is naturally sweet!

In our sad, cynical world, it's not possible to capture this genuine joy apart from Jesus Christ. Even when we are going through extremely difficult times, the Vine continues to pump His life into us.

You and I cannot manufacture joy apart from the Vine, just as a branch does not grow—in fact, *cannot* grow—when it is disconnected from its life source. If that happens, the chances of surviving and producing fruit are severely jeopardized. Although believers do not lose the security of eternity with God once they have made the step of faith, we can lose the Holy Spirit's power that He offers us to rally on His behalf in this world.

I know a faithful coworker in Christ who exudes genuine joy. Joyful Jamie (JJ for short) is a walking, breathing branch reaching out to others from her True Vine—Jesus Christ. She loves Christ and is obedient to Him, and her joy can't help but overflow. People love to be around her because they are naturally drawn to the treasure of joy inside her. It's a treasure that is available to all of us.

🔑 I wish you God's joy today. Read John 15:1-17 and stay connected to Christ.

Traveling Light

We brought nothing with us when we came into the world,
and we can't take anything with us when we leave it.

1 TIMOTHY 6:7

As Sweet Monday has grown as a ministry, my travel schedule has grown. I used to lug a heavy bag with numerous outfits in a variety of colors, along with separate jewelry and shoes to match each ensemble. Needless to say, I grew weary of the backaches caused by lugging so much gear.

Over the years I have improved my packing strategy a little. I've implemented travel tips from other women like you. I've learned to wear my heaviest items, such as jeans and a coat, instead of putting them in my carry-on. I try to choose one color scheme (like black, white, and pink) for my outfits, and I make sure every item matches at least one or two other things in my case.

And shoes? If I can get away with taking only the ones I wear, then my suitcase is a lot lighter. Can you believe one pair of brown boots carried me all the way through my speaking responsibilities at a sweet retreat in Hershey, Pennsylvania? I looked like a Hershey bar all weekend, but having lighter luggage was worth the monochromatic wardrobe.

In addition to enjoying a lighter suitcase, I simply feel good changing bad habits. The lighter luggage also reminds me that I can't carry anything with me into heaven, so I'd better make room for Jesus in my life. I want my heart to be full of everything that only He can give me—His Spirit, His love, truth, grace, and all the sweet spiritual fruit.

There will be no heavy suitcases in heaven! Isn't it wonderful that we don't have to check luggage to enter? This eternal trip means privileged travel for all believers; it requires no packing, no porters, no suitcases, no standing in security lines. I get excited just thinking about it!

As believers in Christ, we can travel through this life knowing the hope of our ultimate destination is in sight. If the burdens of this life are weighing us down, we can give them to God to carry for us. Now that's traveling light!

No more packing those burdens, either here or for eternity. Let's drop them on Him and pack His presence and His promises of a glorious future into our bags.

Abba, Daddy

*Now we call him, "Abba, Father." For his Spirit joins with
our spirit to affirm that we are God's children.*

ROMANS 8:15-16

My daddy has been in heaven many years now, but I still miss him. Some of my best memories with Daddy were in his car or truck. Getting the chance to sit in the front seat was exciting because that was where he stored the Lifesavers, breath mints, and chewing gum! If it was just the two of us together, we were most often going fishing, to the pond to feed the ducks, or to the grocery store for Mama.

I regularly drive my daddy's 1986 Ford F-150 pickup truck around town. It was once a man's big blue truck until I surprised my husband, Mark, and painted it sweet candy pink with a back bumper inscribed, "Only a real man can drive his wife's pink truck!"

The truth is that I still have a father—a heavenly Father—in the truck with me, and not just in the truck, but everywhere I go. Because of Christ's death on the cross, I can call God my Abba Father, which is an affectionate name for Him, like calling Him "Daddy." It is exciting to think about my heavenly Father giving me the rights and privileges of a loved daughter. This perfect God and heavenly Father can do no wrong. It's hard for me not to feel overwhelmed by my Creator not only noticing me but cherishing me as His child, His very loved daughter.

I realize this mention of fathers may bring sadness for you if you did not have a good relationship with your earthly father. God takes your feelings seriously and grieves that loss with you. But most of all, He wants you to be encouraged to know that if you are in Christ, you have a perfect Father, too, all your own. He promises to protect and provide for you and never to leave you. You are truly a son or a daughter, too, with a King for a daddy.

Call on your Abba Daddy today for every single heartache, confusion, and concern. He will never leave your side, and the inheritance you will receive from Him is infinitely greater than a pink '86 pickup!

Getting Rid of Junk

Anyone who belongs to Christ has become a new person.
The old life is gone; a new life has begun!

2 CORINTHIANS 5:17

A few years ago, I was gazing out my kitchen window at the worn secondhand swing set and the neighbor's discarded tree house that had landed in our backyard as a playhouse years earlier. Many sweet memories were made on those play things. But our tall teenage daughter could barely fit on the small swings anymore. She had outgrown them years before, so it was time to put nostalgia aside and get rid of this "junk" taking up room in our backyard. But who would I call to haul it away?

Then I remembered a postcard advertising 1-800-GOTJUNK. I called immediately, before I had time to chicken out. They said they could come out and give me an estimate for tearing the items down, packing them on their truck, and disposing of them. The cost would be based on how much space the debris took up on their truck. What was there to lose?

Their estimate was reasonable, and within an hour's time they had dismantled everything and completely removed all debris from our yard. I was ecstatic, and Mark was spared wrestling with a big to-do item that was now erased from his list. It saved a lot of sore backs and necks, and precious time.

This experience prompted me to think about Jesus. On a spiritual level we can always make a free call to 1-800-GOTJESUS. The sin junking up our hearts is more damaging than any earthly junk we may accumulate. Our sin mess is why Jesus Christ came to this earth—to die for our sins and clean us up so that we could enjoy a personal relationship with God now and forever. He created us as His masterpieces, *not junk*, and He wants us to spend eternity with Him where there won't be any sliver of junk around!

Celebrate in Christ if the "old you" is gone and the "new you" has come! And if you have never called 1-800-GOTJESUS, call Him now in prayer and ask Him to take your sin away.

Sweet Tooth for God's Word

How sweet your words taste to me; they are sweeter than honey.

PSALM 119:103

I have a confession to make. I have a big sweet tooth. If I had to point a finger at the culprit, I'd have a doughnut hanging there. Yes, it's true. Doughnuts are to blame.

When I was growing up, our family went to the beach every summer, and in the mornings my early-bird dad would go to the local doughnut shop and buy fresh ones hot off the conveyor belt for us. It was really a sweet "special delivery."

When we'd get home from vacation, we would beg Mama to make homemade doughnuts. She obliged us on a regular basis by deep-frying canned biscuits. She used a plastic bottle cap as her doughnut-hole cutter. We could choose chocolate or vanilla icing for her homemade delicacies, and she would slather it on and we would scarf them down! My mom fried the doughnut holes, too, which were my favorite because I could dip them in icing, covering the entire pastry.

I'm not a doughnut-a-day person anymore, but every now and then I buy the little powdered-sugar doughnuts to go with my coffee and Bible in the morning. In the same way I developed a craving for doughnuts, my sweet tooth for God's Word developed by repetition. When I actually began to read the Bible on a daily basis, His words became sweeter and sweeter as I interacted with Him each day through its pages.

As humans, we long for food that tastes good to us. We crave things that are pleasing to the taste, flavors we can savor for a while. And we love our sweets! In Bible times honey was the sweetest substance on earth.

In today's verse from Psalm 119, the psalmist craved the sweetness of the Lord's promises and instructions. In fact, for 176 verses, he cannot say enough about the value of God's Word. Do I hear an amen to that?

Enjoy your sweet time with the Lord, indulging daily. His Word provides a sweet sustenance you and I cannot live without.

⚬━ Let's encourage each other to have a sweet tooth for God's Word. Dessert first! We read Psalm 119 back in April. Skim it again and choose a verse or two that have become even more precious to you in the last few months.

Backdoor Mercies

Joyful are those you discipline, LORD, those
you teach with your instructions.

PSALM 94:12

Have you ever gone through a difficult season—whether through God's discipline or because of heartache—only to be surprised by the amount of growth and blessing you gained through perseverance? During the struggle, we often feel miserable and can't wait for the circumstances to ease. In our minds, nothing good seems to be happening.

You've heard the saying that when God closes a door, He opens a window. Hard times seem to drive us through a door that slams shut behind us, and sometimes we feel like turning around and banging on it, begging to be allowed back in. We believe we'd be safer in a place that was at least familiar.

I've been surprised in my own life to discover how good comes in those tough times. It's because God specializes in "backdoor mercies" that are on the other side of the door we're being pushed through. In most cases, they are hidden blessings that see us through and help us grow, only to be discovered later.

As I've shared already, the struggles during my early years of marriage not only drove me to question if I had made a mistake, but they drove me to my knees and to God when I needed Him most.

When I said my wedding vows, I didn't realize I was entering a lifetime training program to spotlight my selfishness. I felt as if I'd been pushed out a door into a world of heartache and frustration. But because of God's growth in me, I can now look back and say that I would not trade those years for anything. Through them He revealed my need for Him and my powerlessness to change myself. I learned that I needed the Lord's help, not just in marriage but in every area of my life.

Let's thank the Lord today that Christian living is not trouble-free; rather, it's a daily opportunity to experience Christ's mercies in changing us to be more like Him. Right now, think of one specific way God has changed you in the last few years. Be encouraged.

Real Power Source

I am the light of the world. If you follow me, you won't have to walk in darkness, because you will have the light that leads to life.

JOHN 8:12

Rushing around in my kitchen one morning, I could not determine why the refrigerator light was not coming on when I opened the door. Because I was in a hurry, I didn't think much about it at the time. However, when I returned home late in the afternoon and flipped the switch on the electric teakettle to make a cup of tea, the red light didn't go on. *What's going on here?* It was time to investigate.

When I checked the plug on the kettle, I was even more perplexed. It wasn't in the same outlet as the refrigerator. By this time, evening was setting in, and my kitchen was growing darker. My favorite white lights that stay on year-round in my kitchen window weren't working either. The food in the fridge wasn't cold anymore. It was time to really take action! I was momentarily clueless until I put two and two together and *finally* realized that all three outlets were on the same side of the kitchen.

Duh! The fuse box! (You probably knew the answer before I did.) With a few quick steps, I located the fuse box and found the breaker switch for the kitchen.

Ahh . . . I heard the blessed rumble of our refrigerator kicking in. I knew that God could see my "so excited" face shining in the dark kitchen. I had fixed something on my own—without having to call Mark! All I had to do was flip a switch for power to be restored from the main source.

How many precious people in this world are walking around in darkness and without power because they have not flipped the switch in their hearts to welcome the only true Power Source in this dark world—the King of kings and Lord of lords? Jesus Christ dispels all of our darkness. The Light of the World came to enlighten people, and He still does today. He makes everything work. Faith in Him flips on a switch in us that will make us shine forever.

Next time you lose your power, remember the only true Power Source. First John 1:5-7 tells us about the Light that never grows dim.

Come Boldly

Since we have a great High Priest who has entered heaven, Jesus the Son of God, let us hold firmly to what we believe. . . . So let us come boldly to the throne of our gracious God. There we will receive his mercy, and we will find grace to help us when we need it most.

HEBREWS 4:14, 16

When I was in college preparing to be a teacher, I was fascinated by different learning styles. The way our brains process information and how we communicate is very complex. I am someone who processes information verbally, which explains why I tend to leave long phone messages.

Yes, I am an out-loud processor who sometimes gets overly excited and says too much. It can be embarrassing. Most men do not like hearing all the details, so I am horrified if I leave a fun message for a friend whose husband happens to hear it. Unlike me, Mark processes and summarizes information very logically. He figures out what he is going to say before he says a word, while I think out loud.

When I read today's verses from Hebrews, I was so relieved. God clearly wants us to come boldly to Him, whether we blurt out all our thoughts or present them logically. He does not care how we express them. He simply wants us to come to Him. It is better to get things out with God than to hold back, because He knows our hearts either way. Not only is it cleansing to confess, rant, and rave to Him about someone hurting you or decisions you must make, but talking with God first can prevent us from gossiping about an issue with a friend. Spending time with Him gives Him the opportunity to work on our hearts and show us if our feelings and rantings are misguided, and He sends His calming Spirit to settle us.

God will always have the right response to us. He wants us to come to Him as we are, no matter what our communication style may be. How freeing is that!

Because of Christ and our faith in Him, we can come boldly and confidently into God's presence. Write down Ephesians 3:12 as a reminder to share with Him whatever is on your heart today.

Pursue Christ

Whoever pursues righteousness and unfailing love will find life, righteousness, and honor.

PROVERBS 21:21

I wish I had known this verse during my college dating years. I pursued boyfriends and a husband instead of righteousness and love! I used to call home and tell my mother that I thought this guy or maybe that guy must be "the one"! We laughed together many years later when we were reminiscing about the time I said, "He must be the one. He is the most like Jesus of any man I have dated."

One of the best pieces of advice I ever received as a young adult came from Melanie Alquist in a talk she gave to college students on dating relationships. She said, "Flee the physical. Pursue Christlike love as you would in any friendship. Do not pursue marriage!" She encouraged us to focus on our own personal relationships with Christ and let Him lead us toward the life and love He knows would be best for us.

To pursue means "to chase, seek, hound, track, or stalk." *Wow.* Those words are loaded with action. Whether we are married or single, dating or going solo, we are wise to ask ourselves how assertively we are pursuing righteousness and unfailing love. If we're looking for wholeness from any other source than Christ, then we are using up vital time and emotions pursuing less than God's best for our life.

Sure, we all need love. Many women desire marriage, and God created that relationship of oneness to be a beautiful reflection of His abiding, sacrificial love for His church. But pursuing Him and His heart of righteousness and unfailing love needs to take priority. Those blessings can be found only in Christ. He is our source of wholeness; we are incomplete without Him.

It's an astounding revelation that Jesus pursued us first. Let that truth settle in your spirit for a few minutes. Bask in the knowledge that you are His cherished treasure and He is committed to you for eternity.

Let's pursue Jesus because He is Righteousness and Love! He is the perfect Pursuer of our hearts. Choose a quiet place to spend a few minutes meditating on today's verse.

Redeemed

He redeems me from death and crowns me with love and tender mercies.
PSALM 103:4

I broke my foot. I wish I could tell you that I tripped running a marathon or performing some other athletic feat, but instead I tripped over my tall, athletic husband's foot! And to add insult to injury, I did it in front of other people. My husband and I were making our way through the convention center to cheer for our daughter's volleyball game. On the way to our seats in the bleachers, I went to hug another mother, and to my chagrin, I did not step gracefully.

For the first time in my life, I received an unsolicited signed note from the foot surgeon permitting me to apply for a blue handicapped-parking tag. At least my embarrassment earned me two months' legitimate use of a prime parking spot.

However, I balked at getting the tag because it required a trip to the DMV. I imagined an unbearably long line and kept putting it off. Three weeks of hefting my big black boot on my foot still didn't get me there to take care of the handicapped-parking tag. The doctor's crumpled order was somewhere in my purse. When my mom visited me and expressed regret that I had not redeemed it, I realized how silly I had been. I had missed out on a great deal of help that had been offered to me.

"Lord, that is the way it is with anyone who knows You personally! In addition to Your gift of salvation, You offer us all the benefits and privileges of being Your child. But it's up to us to take advantage of all the love and help You offer us."

When my faith feels faint or I fight selfishness in showing His love to others, I remind myself of my days spent hobbling around in the big black boot. His grace and strength are mine to claim as my own if only I take the hobbling step to accept them.

Surrender yourself to Christ right now and receive your eternal parking tag; it not only assures your place in heaven, but it also guarantees you the Holy Spirit's power today!

Heroes among Us

Be happy with those who are happy, and weep with those who weep.
ROMANS 12:15

We all need Christian heroes this side of heaven to model Jesus Christ. Being surrounded by so many heroes in my life has helped me grow in my love for Christ.

Most of my close heroes have been women, simply because I have only two
men in my life whom I spend time with: Jesus and my husband. But over the
years I have certainly learned much from people who have shared God's wisdom
through their books, sermons, and occupations. The great men and women of
faith in the Bible are also heroes to me because God recorded His words to us
through them and they helped grow the early church. We are all a part of that
early church today if we have trusted in Christ.

Anyone can be a hero of faith simply by living God's way day by day. Often-
times the ongoing stresses of the mundane can try our faith more than a more
intense but short-lived trial. Everyday heroes is what Romans 12 is about—
practical ways God's people live the Christian life as a living sacrifice to God.

As Christian brothers and sisters, we are recipients of God's great love and
mercy for us through each other. Right now, think of someone who has sacri-
ficed his or her time, spiritual gifts, or earthly treasures for you. In Romans 12:15
we are instructed by Paul to "be happy with those who are happy, and weep
with those who weep." Being a faithful and available servant who ministers to
others takes heroic strength, patience, unselfishness, and courage. Getting in the
trenches and sharing someone's hardship shines Jesus' light and love over someone who needs Him.

My sweet friend Jayne has a card ministry. It is something God has given her
to do. I am always amazed by her thoughtfulness toward others in the good times
as well as the sad situations. You and I may not have this particular hero quality,
but we can find our own style of reaching out. That's what branches do (John 15)!

Have you ever considered your potential to be a hero? You don't
need a fancy costume or superpowers. Your power comes from God
Himself. Think of a way to give of yourself today and be a hero in the
little things. God makes your effort big.

Hurt Heart, Need Comfort

*"Comfort, comfort my people," says your God. . . . Have you never
heard? Have you never understood? The LORD is the everlasting God,
the Creator of all the earth. He never grows weak or weary. No one
can measure the depths of his understanding. He gives power to the
weak and strength to the powerless. Even youths will become weak and
tired, and young men will fall in exhaustion. But those who trust in the
LORD will find new strength. They will soar high on wings like eagles.
They will run and not grow weary. They will walk and not faint.*

ISAIAH 40:1, 28-31

My heart hurts. Last night I went to bed upset about something, and this morning
I awakened with the same splinter lodged in my heart. I'm sure you know what a
hurt heart feels like! I think I'd trade this ache for a broken bone any day. At least
then I could go to a clinic and get medical attention. Being assured that the healing process was in motion would ease my anxiety, knowing how and when that
bone would be restored.

We can look at a physical injury and assess what it will take to mend it, and we
can use X-rays or other diagnostic imagery to figure out what's wrong. But hurts
of the heart are often invisible and difficult to diagnose, much less to heal. Even
counseling has its limitations for healing.

Only God can reach down into a person's heart and bathe it with cleansing
balm that cleans out the cut—whether it's small or gaping—to bring comfort. No
human therapy can thoroughly remove emotional pain and replace it with wholeness like God can.

Every emotion that we can ever feel and every hurt we can ever imagine has
been experienced by Jesus. He comforts us throughout His Word by reminding
us of His presence and plan for restoring us.

Isaiah 40 is packed with Jesus' healing balm for our wounds. Go to the everlasting God, the Creator of the earth and of every human heart, for comfort that
only He can give.

 Hurt heart, need comfort? Open your Bible to Isaiah 40 and read
about God's comfort for hurting hearts.

H-O-P-E

Why am I discouraged? (Why am I discouraged?) Why is my heart so sad? (Why is my heart so sad?) I will put my hope in God! (I will put my hope in God!) I will praise him again—my Savior and my God! (I will praise him again—my Savior and my God!)

PSALM 42:11 (PSALM 43:5)

It's okay. You don't need to get your eyes checked after reading today's verses. It's really not an error. Both of these psalms end with the same chorus. In fact, in many Hebrew manuscripts these two psalms are combined as one, a single song.

Are you discouraged today? Did you wake up with a "so sad" heart? I mentioned to Mark that I have been writing some of these devotions during one of the saddest times in my life, after I lost my precious mother to cancer. Mama taught me everything I know about creating a warm and welcoming home. Do you know what Mark said? "A lot of the psalms were written during sad, difficult times too." He's right. It must be why I relish reading a psalm every day! God gets me! I'm not alone! He understands how heavy my heart is.

These two psalms (along with Psalms 44–49) are attributed to the descendants of Korah, a choir of temple singers who had been appointed by King David. Here they may be lamenting a time when they were in exile. Discouragement and sadness are universal problems, even for men and women of faith. But then comes the answer to the cries of lament: "I will put my hope in God!"

I remember being just out of college, visiting a church in Tennessee where I heard a pastor use this acrostic for hope:

Happy
Optimism of
Promises
Expected!

Whenever I am struggling with sadness that seems to sap all my energy or discouragement that is difficult even to express at times, I will focus on God. When I dwell on His Word, praise just naturally follows—and so does HOPE . . . Happy Optimism of Promises Expected!

 Choose hope in Christ. Read Romans 15:13.

Gifts That Connect Us

To all who did receive him, to those who believed in his
name, he gave the right to become children of God.

JOHN 1:12, NIV

Teaching elementary school gave me so many opportunities to do fun things with children. To this day, I often have a grab bag hanging on the back of my front doorknob so children who visit can reach in without peeking and retrieve a tiny inedible "sweet something." From a rubber ball to a slap bracelet, each one has a "Smiley Faith" on it!

When Kali was growing up, I also created a "Smiley Faith" box for her by covering a box and lid with smiley face wrapping paper. Every day I was away, she could grab a "sweet something" from it—sometimes edible, sometimes not. I didn't travel often, but I wanted her to know that she was always in my heart, whether I was near or far.

Spending time with children, particularly my own child, pushes me to God. I want only God's best for my daughter, but I understand that I, as an imperfect parent, cannot begin to fathom God's perfect parenting with me.

For instance, I have a strong desire to stay connected with my daughter when we cannot be together. But it cannot begin to compare with how strongly God wants to stay close to me, even while we are physically apart in this lifetime. He gives gifts to me along the way to let me know He still cares and thinks of me constantly. Gifts like peace, grace, hope, His Word, the relief of just talking to God in prayer, worship, fellowship with other believers, a role in His Kingdom work, and so much more—each gift lets me know He is there.

God in His great mercy and love is the Giver of all good gifts. His commitment to stay connected with us through Christ is His ultimate gift.

God yearns for us to receive what He has given us! Open your heart today and look for the "sweet somethings" He sends your way to let you know His Perfect Parent heart is always filled with love for you.

Help Yourself to Me, Lord!

*My old self has been crucified with Christ. It is no longer I who
live, but Christ lives in me. So I live in this earthly body by trusting
in the Son of God, who loved me and gave himself for me.*

GALATIANS 2:20

I love what Oswald Chambers says about this verse in his classic devotional book, *My Utmost for His Highest*. During a lecture to his students at Bible Training College in Clapham Common, London, he said, "This college is an organization that is not worth anything. It is not academic; it is for nothing else but for God to help Himself to lives. Is He going to help Himself to us, or are we taken up with our conception of what we are going to be?"

Wow! My heart replies back: *Lord, help Yourself to me! Take seconds, thirds, fourths, and fifths!*

Isn't it wonderful that we will never be sent back to the kitchen, banned from sitting at God's banquet table to feast on His perpetual potluck dinner prepared just for us in Christ Jesus? It's a perfect dinner spread out on white linen tablecloths, with real silver and gorgeous china plates—all God's best He has offered to us. He wants us to help ourselves to His presence, too!

We may bring a fancy dish or a simple one because we all have faith of different sizes, and we have different styles of expressing our faith and worshiping Him. He delights in variety because it is evident throughout His creation. Just as no two people are alike and each snowflake is different, so it is with our unique places and contributions at His banquet table.

Yes, He loves variety, but He wants the same wholehearted devotion from each one of us. He wants all of us to hear and respond, "Help Yourself to our lives, Lord!"

In what way can we say, "Lord, help Yourself! Help Yourself, Lord, to us"? Perhaps we can demonstrate His love to someone this week. Maybe we could commit to letting His character shine brightly in the ways we respond to others. Or maybe we could ask Him whether He has a new direction for our lives.

JUNE 29

Holy Housekeeping

*[Jesus Christ] gave his life to free us from every kind
of sin, to cleanse us, and to make us his very own
people, totally committed to doing good deeds.*

TITUS 2:14

Imagine this happening to you: You've been traveling all day and finally arrive at your destination. You are so weary that you can't wait to check in to your room and get a much-needed rest in a cozy bed. And then you open the door to your hotel room. The room hasn't been cleaned! The beds are unmade, the used towels are lying on the bathroom floor, the wastebaskets are overflowing—you get the picture. You make a beeline to the front desk. There is no way you want to stay another minute in that room.

That is what an unbelieving heart full of sin looks like to God. He is holy and cannot reside in such a mess. But thankfully Jesus Christ came to earth to offer His life for our sins. His gift of salvation cleans up our sin so God can abide in us. His Spirit remains to do the maintenance work of holy housekeeping so that others are drawn to the comfort of His presence in our lives. We still need His regular dusting and polishing to bring His glory and honor to this dying world.

Being clean in Christ gives God something to work with to bring His refreshment and rest to this sin-filled world. We represent the Lord's beautiful home, and we can offer a taste of heaven on earth to souls who are weary for true rest. How clean are our hearts? Are they ready for God to move in?

Remember today that you are white-glove clean in Christ! Let's be sure to allow the Holy Spirit to do His ongoing holy housekeeping.

Seeking Shelter

The godly will rejoice in the LORD and find shelter in him.
And those who do what is right will praise him.

PSALM 64:10

Years ago, while camping with five other girls in the Tetons of Wyoming, I went for a horseback ride and was caught in a surprise storm, with hail as large as golf balls falling fast and furious.

We were about a mile from the stable, and my horse, spooked by the hail pelting us, was racing at full speed. I feared for my life. *I don't want to die young. I want to get married and be a mother!* I vividly remember crouching down as low as I could, and praying that God would help me hold on to the horse and spare my life. Thankfully, we made it back—shaken, sore, but safe.

Later I noticed that I had red welts all over my back, arms, and neck—the places where the hail had hit me. When I had calmed down from that welt-raising ride, I realized the welts were nothing compared to what could have happened if I had been tossed off the horse at full speed.

Now, when I cross paths with that beautiful word *shelter*, this incident comes to mind. A shelter is a refuge, a haven, a protection. Who doesn't want to find shelter during a huge hailstorm?

I think we often forget that the Lord Jesus Christ is our Shelter. He has provided a way of salvation so that we will be sheltered from the consequences of dying in our sin and living apart from God forever, in an actual place called hell. He also acts as our Shelter in the lightning, thunder, and hailstorms of life. Even in the little showers that are more frustrating than dangerous, He provides a shelter for our minds and emotions. We are completely covered in Christ's protection and care always.

Take cover in His shelter today—every day—forever and ever! Check out the way Jesus, the righteous King, is described in Isaiah 32:1-2.

Lightest Way to Live

*Come to me, all of you who are weary and carry heavy burdens, and
I will give you rest. Take my yoke upon you. Let me teach you, because
I am humble and gentle at heart, and you will find rest for your souls.
For my yoke is easy to bear, and the burden I give you is light.*

MATTHEW 11:28-30

I don't know about you, but whenever I hear the word *yoke*, I immediately think
of egg *yolk*. Of course, that isn't what Jesus is talking about in these verses from
Matthew. Those who heard His words understood the reference. A yoke, according to *The Scholastic Children's Dictionary*, is "a wooden frame attached to the
necks of work animals, such as oxen, to connect them so they can plow or pull a
heavy load." Although we rarely see them used on animals in the Western world,
yokes would have been common in Jesus' time and are still widely found in third-
world countries today.

How often have you rubbed your neck when you're feeling stressed? Many of
us carry the loads of life on our necks like yokes, which causes not only physical
problems but mental, emotional, and spiritual burdens as well!

God did not design us for heavy loads. I like to imagine that the wooden
yokes of Jesus' day were made of the same wood as the cross He died upon. We
are connected to God through Jesus' death, and that connection—or yoke—isn't
burdensome. It feels light to us because it offers us freedom from sin instead of
oppression.

In Matthew 11, those sweet words from our Savior are an invitation to align
ourselves with Him. If we are weary and burdened, He lovingly wants us to come
to Him for rest!

Wear a favorite scarf today to remind yourself that Jesus' yoke
is light and beautiful. Throughout the day, release to Jesus any
emotional load that threatens to weigh you down.

Everlasting Life

I tell you the truth, anyone who believes has eternal life.
JOHN 6:47

The Lord is my only company this very quiet but very sad morning. I feel as though I'm the only one up in the whole world! This time of day is when I miss my mother the most, because I remember so many early-morning phone conversations as we caught up with each other over a cup of coffee.

This particular morning God has painted the sky pink just for me, and I am wondering what my mama is doing right now in heaven. Is there coffee there? Is she rearranging her mansion? Is she making pimento cheese? I can only imagine her joy. It is still a mystery to me here on earth, but the one thing I know for sure that fills a part of this big hole in my heart is the fact that my mama is in the Lord's presence!

His Kingdom is the most beautiful home and garden she has ever seen! When she arrived, He called her by name: "Maxine Kiziah 'Honey' Bowman." He removed her cancer; she never has to battle it again. She has no more pain, no more tears, no more sorrow (Revelation 21:4).

As salty tears of loss and grief start to run down my cheeks, the joy and gratefulness I feel for the hope of heaven and everlasting life found only in Jesus Christ makes the bitterness sweet.

Jesus promised, "I tell you the truth, anyone who believes has eternal life" (John 6:47). My heart is uplifted with the understanding that one day He'll reunite all His believers with Himself. Our separation on earth is temporary, but the sweet heavenly reunion will never end.

Are you suffering a loss too? Be comforted by the God of all comfort. He is a personal God who sees your sorrow and feels it with you. But He also wants to revive your spirit today with His hope of eternity.

Wake-up Call

I was sad, as though they were my friends or family,
as if I were grieving for my own mother.

PSALM 35:14

Sometimes my emotions overwhelm me. Today, for instance, my sadness over missing my mother still lingers. After spending time talking with the Lord in prayer and listening for His messages to me, I opened His Word to today's verse. When I saw that it was Psalm 35:14, I felt like I had been followed . . . followed by God through His Word.

God sees me and He pursues me! He understands the emotional weights I carry, and He wants to let me know that He is always with me. That verse felt like a big holy hug. In fact, it felt as close to a physical hug as I could experience from Him this side of heaven.

I love it when God surprises me with gifts of truth, like this verse was for me today. It came straight from God's heart to let me know He sees my heart. His surprises are why I want to greet Him first thing in the morning. I don't want to go the whole day without hearing Him and miss something because I get preoccupied with so many other things.

For over a quarter century, I have rearranged my day to "hear" Him first through the pages of the Bible. Because I listened this morning, I enjoyed His gift throughout the day. My heart gained courage and I felt genuine joy instead of feeling weighed down by grief all day.

God is so personal, so real, and He will speak to us any time of day. But there is something precious and extra helpful about committing our early minutes to Him before everything else begins to pull us in different directions. When we go to Him first, He asks that we trade in our emotions for a confident faith in Him to deal with whatever we will face.

Let's not miss Him or anything He has for us! Take to heart Psalm 5:3 (NKJV): "My voice You shall hear in the morning, O LORD; in the morning I will direct it to You, and I will look up." Treat yourself to an earlier bedtime tonight so you can wake up a little earlier to begin the day with Him.

Splashes of Glory

The heavens declare the glory of God; the skies
proclaim the work of his hands.

PSALM 19:1, NIV

Soon after our family completed the onslaught of my cancer treatments, Mark took us on a gift trip to Hawaii. We had a wonderful time, and before we left the island to return home, he asked me if there was anything I really wanted to do before I left.

"Yes," I replied. "I want an adventure. I want to swim with the dolphins in the deep blue ocean, their natural habitat in the wild." I had seen an advertisement for this excursion in the touristy paraphernalia at the airport. Kali thought it was an exciting way to end our celebratory trip. So with a few pink butterflies fluttering in our stomachs, I called and signed us up.

The boat was big enough to hold six people, but our family was the only one that showed up that day. (Mark was with us, too, staying dry and watching us from the boat.) It was like having our own private adventure. The guide stopped the boat near a pod of at least two hundred spinner dolphins, which he admitted was an unusually large number and sighting.

As Kali and I glided in the warm water with face masks and snorkels, we felt as if we were the only two land mammals in the entire ocean. It was like God arranged it for just the two of us! We were having so much fun in Awe Land that we stayed in the ocean three hours. We did not break for lunch and did not care that our sunscreen wore out long before we did.

The experience was worth every second and every inch of sunburn because it gave us a chance to see a fascinating part of God's beautiful creation up close and personal. We couldn't help but worship Him alongside His aquatic creatures.

The dolphins declare the glory of God! kept running through my mind. I saw the glory of God through my face mask as He let me experience one of His top ten wonders on my personal worship list!

 "The heavens declare the glory of God." The dolphins do too! If you need a fresh dose of God's glory, go to a zoo, walk on a nature trail, spend a day at the beach, or simply eat lunch outside. And by all means, look up!

Exit to Freedom

Because God's children are human beings—made of flesh and blood—the Son also became flesh and blood. For only as a human being could he die, and only by dying could he break the power of the devil, who had the power of death. Only in this way could he set free all who have lived their lives as slaves to the fear of dying.

HEBREWS 2:14-15

These two verses in Hebrews 2 are rich with meaning. Jesus set us free from being enslaved by the fear of death. Here, through the mention of slavery, the writer offers a reminder of how God repeatedly set His people free from earthly captivity. Throughout time, God has proven that He is an expert in freedom and in bringing life out of what appears to be dead.

In Exodus, the second book of the Bible, we see God's creativity in freeing His people from Egyptian slavery. I admit that I was a little hesitant about reading this book, thinking it would be pretty hard to understand. But Exodus is thrilling! In this historical account written by Moses, God's people *exit* Egypt after four hundred years of bondage. Generation after generation had held on to hope that God would finally free them—and then one day He did free His people, all at once. The word *exodus* actually means a departure of a large number of people at one time.

Just as God ended the bondage that characterized the Israelites' lives, His Son's sacrifice for our sins meant the exodus of death's power, the end of spiritual slavery for all who turn to Him for salvation.

Everywhere we go, we see exit signs, which can be visible reminders of how God loves to free us from whatever threatens to bind us. Just as surely as God freed His people from slavery, He has freed us from our sins and our fear of death. Jesus is our exodus from this world's failings as we enter into an abundant relationship with Him. He is our exit from hopelessness and our entrance to life—now and for eternity.

🔑 Next time you steer onto the "exodus" ramp, be encouraged! Thank Jesus that His exits always mean something good is up ahead.

Pay It Upward

These righteous ones will reply, "Lord, when did we ever see you
hungry and feed you? Or thirsty and give you something to drink?
Or a stranger and show you hospitality? Or naked and give you
clothing? When did we ever see you sick or in prison and visit you?"
And the King will say, "I tell you the truth, when you did it to one of
the least of these my brothers and sisters, you were doing it to me!"

MATTHEW 25:37-40

You've heard the term "pay it forward." But today's verses make me want to "pay it upward"!

When we feed hungry people, give thirsty people something to drink, show hospitality to a stranger, provide clothing, or visit sick people or prisoners, we're ministering to Jesus as well as to those in need.

Throughout the Gospels, Jesus tells us how to live. *Gospel* means "good news," and Jesus Himself is Good News! In some Bibles, the words of Jesus are printed in red ink (it always looks pink to me). Every word in Matthew 25 is red! When we read this chapter, it's like we are sitting with the followers who were hearing Jesus in person.

These verses are truly an invitation to love. Those who know Jesus understand that His love for the downtrodden is so great that He identifies Himself with them in order to impress on His listeners the value of serving them.

Jesus' way of service is not burdensome to us. It truly is a joy to reach out to others with the love of Christ, particularly those who suffer in this life. We can imagine His smile of compassion and hope each time we share His mercy and thoughtfulness, each time we purposefully open our eyes to look for those who need His love.

When we live to give, we not only pay it forward on a horizontal, earthly level, but we also pay it upward to Jesus. Do for Him by doing for others because He has done so much for us.

Choose one simple way to share God's blessing with someone today. Don't tell anyone—just do it and pay it upward.

One Dose

Christ suffered for our sins once for all time. He never sinned,
but he died for sinners to bring you safely home to God. He
suffered physical death, but he was raised to life in the Spirit.

1 PETER 3:18

For many years, I took my calcium supplements all at once each day just to get it over with. I recently learned from a nutritionist that our bodies cannot absorb that much calcium in one large dose. After I got over the initial shock of having wasted all those big, white calcium tablets, I followed her instructions and began taking them in smaller quantities at each meal. And now I have it down to two times a day.

I needed the calcium to do its job because my bones have been compromised by chemotherapy. So I have been doing my best to replenish what my body needs. But I have to admit that I was not happy to add another detail to my routine. Ugh! I was afraid that I would forget since it wasn't something I had been doing regularly over the years. But I listened and changed my regimen.

One good thing comes from this new routine: I have more than one reminder each day to thank Jesus that our salvation is a one-time deal. Let's absorb 1 Peter 3:18 again, as this Good News always bears repeating! Christ suffered for our sins once for all time. He never sinned, but He died for sinners to bring us safely home to God. He suffered physical death, but He was raised to life in the Spirit.

First Peter 3:18 is the gospel in one sentence. Christ makes getting up each morning, no matter what life's circumstances, a lot easier to swallow than a big, fat calcium tablet! I don't have to believe and receive Jesus into my heart three times a day over and over again or feel burdened by a strict routine to be accepted by Him. It is a done deal, once for all time. Every minute of every day, His Spirit is working greater eternal health and healing in me than any vitamin or supplement ever could.

Good News! Along with whatever nutritional supplements you may take today, treat yourself to a favorite dessert or activity to celebrate, knowing it will never supplement Jesus' one-dose victory for us.

Shoulda, Woulda, Coulda

I do not treat the grace of God as meaningless. For if keeping the law could make us right with God, then there was no need for Christ to die. . . . Christ has truly set us free. Now make sure that you stay free, and don't get tied up again in slavery to the law.

GALATIANS 2:21; 5:1

Shoulda, woulda, coulda. Do you ever get trapped by those heavy words? They lurk in the crevices of our minds, always ready and willing to pounce on us with guilt trips and loads of self-recrimination. They tell us we have let others down, we have failed to measure up, we ought to have done more. They can be so convincing and condemning. Combined, they may make a fun rhyme, but they're not so fun when we allow them to bombard us!

These three words especially enjoy attacking our faith by telling us we need to do all kinds of extras to ensure we have right standing with God. They're masters of confusion, and they are capable of muddling our thoughts to the point that we forget that our first priority is knowing Jesus—actually *enjoying* Jesus and His salvation and other blessings, instead of always trying to impress Him with the good things we do.

The *shoulda, woulda, coulda*s were happening to the believers in the Galatian church. They were forgetting their freedom in Christ, so Paul wrote this letter to remind them that religious practices like circumcision do not guarantee a personal relationship with the Lord. Paul even called Peter out on the false and destructive behavior of trying to add to salvation. If Peter—someone who knew Jesus intimately—could be so blinded, do any of us have hope of conquering *shoulda, woulda, coulda?*

Yes! We have hope if we can take the message of Galatians to heart. Let's enjoy Jesus with grateful hearts today. We can release ourselves from thinking His acceptance of us depends on *how much* time we volunteer, *how much* money we give, *how many* hungry people we feed, or *how many* Bible studies we attend.

Jesus wants our hearts open to Him, thankfully rejoicing that He conquered *shoulda, woulda, coulda* for us forever.

Let's thank Him for setting us all free from striving to earn His acceptance—we already have it!

We Can Do This

Trust in the LORD and do good. Then you will live safely in the land and prosper. Take delight in the LORD, and he will give you your heart's desires. Commit everything you do to the LORD. Trust him, and he will help you. . . . Be still in the presence of the LORD, and wait patiently for him to act. Don't worry about evil people who prosper or fret about their wicked schemes. Stop being angry! Turn from your rage! Do not lose your temper—it only leads to harm.

PSALM 37:3-5, 7-8

I'm a list maker. A list helps me remember things and feel productive throughout the day. There's something about checking things off a list that floats my pink boat! When I make a list, I love putting a little box like this ☐ in front of the task or item so that I can check it off *and* cross a big line through it!

The beginning of Psalm 37 lists wonderful practical wisdom that I like to check off in my head as a reminder and help in submitting to God's ways instead of going with my natural tendencies. I don't rush through it; instead, I pray and ask God to help me stick to what He says. I'm so thankful that in His power, His list is possible to accomplish. For example,

☐ I *can* trust in the Lord and commit everything I do to Him
☐ I *can* be still in the presence of the Lord and wait patiently for Him to act
☐ I *can* refuse to worry about the wicked or their schemes
☐ I *can* stop being angry and losing my temper

The instructions work together. For instance, when we wait patiently for the Lord to act and trust in Him, we have an easier time avoiding worry about evil people who prosper in their wicked schemes. When we still ourselves in the Lord, we take delight in Him and naturally want to commit our ways to Him, to do good, and to hold our temper.

In the Spirit's power, we can cross off all of these instructions daily. Then we can enjoy the blessings God offers each of us, including peace and joy.

⚷ Pray through the Psalm 37 list today and ask the Lord for His strength to help you live His way.

190

Tick Removal

*If we claim we have no sin, we are only fooling
ourselves and not living in the truth.*

1 JOHN 1:8

There are at least two things all people have in common—sin and stress. A basic definition of sin is simply being selfish, desiring to go our own way. Chuck Swindoll, in his book *Laugh Again*, defines stress as more severe than worry. "Stress is intense strain over a situation we cannot change or control—something out of our control."

I was extremely stressed when my then six-year-old daughter was changing her clothes and I noticed a new "mole" on her back. When I touched it, it wiggled. A tick! I experienced a real-life case of the heebie-jeebies, and since I am a pitiful faker, I know I passed my fear on to my precious Kali.

I didn't know what to do. Mark kills all the bugs, but he wasn't home. So I grabbed my *Taking Care of Your Child* book and ran across the street to my neighbor, Grandma Hazel. After a pep talk to calm me down and some simple instructions, I reluctantly returned home to take charge and remove the tick. Grandma Hazel didn't have what I needed to complete the "surgery," but her advice helped. Back in those days, most people held a lit match near a tick, causing it to retract its head and making it easier to pluck the insect off the skin. (This method has long been discarded because of many other risks involved. In other words, don't try this at home!) Grandma Hazel recommended cutting a tiny hole in a bandage to leave the tick exposed, which would also protect Kali's skin from being burned by the match's flame.

I was more nervous than Kali, so we prayed out loud with our eyes open as I applied heat to the tick and gently pulled it with tweezers. After several attempts, the tick loosened and I managed to pull it off. I could not believe how strongly the small insect had burrowed itself into my daughter's skin!

When the tick had been disposed of, I reflected on how sin is a lot like that tick. When given the chance, it becomes deeply embedded in all of us. But because of Christ's loving sacrifice, for every single time we have sinned because someone ticked us off, our sin will be removed.

Thank Jesus Christ for being our deeply embedded sin remover. His blood shed on the cross releases and heals you and me!

Grace on the Interstate

God saved you by his grace when you believed. And you can't take
credit for this; it is a gift from God. Salvation is not a reward for
the good things we have done, so none of us can boast about it.

EPHESIANS 2:8-9

I can certainly boast in Christ, but I cannot boast about my driving. There are times when my foot on the pedal wants to go as fast as my hurried heart on the highway. (And I've already explained in a previous story that none of us should ever apply lipstick while driving!)

One day while I was on the interstate heading home, I realized I was in the wrong lane and was about to miss my exit. I did what good drivers are *not* supposed to do: I slowed down in the middle lane, almost to a complete stop, to get over into the right lane. (I did put my turn signal on, but it was at the very last minute!) My action was definitely the wrong thing to do, but the precious driver behind me responded with grace and slowed down so I could get over. When he passed me, I waved a thank-you. When he waved in response, my heart could have floated right up to heaven in relief. I momentarily looked up, my eyes welling up with tears. That simple act of grace caused me to worship and thank God for His protection for all involved and for His amazing grace—undeserved, unsolicited, and free.

God is like that man in the car every second of every day. Jesus gives us total access to God. He doesn't just squeeze us in when He has a spare second, but instead He opens up His treasure and time and power to guide us on our journey home. He does not require a perfect-living record either, and we can't lose our license! He helps us to successfully maneuver the daily traffic called life. He's our lifetime Driving Instructor.

 The next time you're out on the road, thank God for His grace. Be a courteous driver and model grace to others. It just may be the only kind thing that happens to someone all day.

Separation Deadly!

*God in all his fullness was pleased to live in Christ, and through him
God reconciled everything to himself. He made peace with everything
in heaven and on earth by means of Christ's blood on the cross.
This includes you who were once far away from God. You were his
enemies, separated from him by your evil thoughts and actions.*

COLOSSIANS 1:19-21

My favorite kind of physical therapy is a pedicure! Like most women, I favor certain features that God gave me more than others. Some women love the hair God gave them. I happen to like my toes!

My sweet friend Cynthia gave me a new pair of socks with the toes cut out. They made me grin from ear to ear. Because the socks separate my toes, I can leave the salon in socks and shoes with my painted toes exposed to dry! Not only are the socks necessary to avoid smudging the newly applied polish, but I love the fact that they keep the lotion in to do its work and keep my "new feet" clean for a while!

Separation is beneficial to protect fresh pedicures, but separation from God is a very serious matter. Paul clearly says in Colossians that without Christ, we are totally separated from God. Apart from Christ, we would be God's enemies. Our evil thoughts and actions, our sin nature as humans, separates us from Him. That separation is deadly.

But even believers can live with divided loyalty. If we allow ungodly habits to draw us from Jesus, we separate ourselves from the full power of the Holy Spirit working in and through us.

In order to sparkle with the true, fresh colors of Christ, we must remain or abide in Christ just like we did when we first gave our hearts to Him.

Let's remove any barriers that separate us from true fellowship with Jesus Christ. Read John 15, one of my favorite chapters in the Bible.

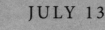

Have Bible, Will Travel

Your commands make me wiser than my enemies,
for they are my constant guide.

PSALM 119:98

Constant guide? I take this verse quite literally! When I travel for speaking engagements, I carry with me pages from my paperback *One Year Bible*, one of two matching paperback copies that I own. This copy that I call my "Have Bible, Will Travel" edition is held together with a shoestring because its pages have been taken out and put back in.

I keep my first copy of this Bible in my "go to" spot at home and my travel copy near my suitcase. I've been reading the *One Year Bible* for years. I love that each day's reading is dated and that I get Old Testament and New Testament portions, as well as readings from Psalms and Proverbs every day!

When a sweet friend named Kathy gave me my second *One Year Bible*—my traveling Bible—I began this new practice of tearing out pages whose dates matched the days I was away. The pages are lightweight, and when I get home, I stick them back in the Bible and tie it all together to keep the loose pages from falling out! At first, I was a little hesitant to take my Bible apart, but then I remembered reading that Billy Graham once tore out a page of the Bible to use in his sermon notes, so I exercised my freedom in Christ, knowing God knew my heart.

This well-worn *One Year Bible* looks like I have literally been chewing on God's Word. Not only does it keep my suitcase from exceeding the weight limit, but more important, it helps me stick with my three simple, sweet, and salty personal priorities of spending time with God, His Word, and people.

Wherever I am, God's Word is a constant guide at my fingertips.

Let's keep God's Word handy wherever we go. We can get creative to ensure that His Word is constantly close at hand. Consider putting a compact Bible in the glove box of your car or in your purse. Download an electronic version to your smartphone or tablet, or buy a small box of Scripture cards to keep on your windowsill or desk. Commit to a Scripture memory plan so that His Word is hidden in your heart and mind—then you can practice your style of "Have Bible, Will Travel."

Meals That Minister

They brought sleeping mats, cooking pots, serving bowls, wheat and barley, flour and roasted grain, beans, lentils, honey, butter, sheep, goats, and cheese for David and those who were with him. For they said, "You must all be very hungry and tired and thirsty after your long march through the wilderness."

2 SAMUEL 17:28-29

In this story in 2 Samuel, King David was camping in the land of Gilead with some of his men, fleeing from his traitorous son, Absalom, who was trying to kill him. I imagine they were exhausted, and then, seemingly out of nowhere, God fed them by way of some kind people. It is a biblical example of how food can really minister to people.

Thousands of years have passed since King David's day, but we can still minister to others by providing the sustenance of a meal, whether someone is stranded in the desert of distress and grief or has a reason to celebrate!

Even if we haven't been camping or fleeing danger, we have all experienced hunger and thirst. I wonder sometimes if we women hold back ministering to people with food because we think we have to prepare a five-course meal.

As I read today's verses, God brought to mind women who have ministered to me and my family in this unique way, by providing their own special food: Sweet Sue's cinnamon bread, Sweet Debbie's soup, carrot juice from Joyful Jamie . . . what a wonderful way to try new things! Even a peanut butter sandwich tastes better to me if someone else has spread the peanut butter across the bread!

Sometimes I go to a popular pizza place and buy gift certificates. I ask for small delivery boxes and four napkins for each box to use as "tissue" paper. I wrap a gift certificate in each cardboard box and enclose a menu, a love note, or a card, then mail it to a family so they can enjoy a pizza night together. Each time I send one, I pretend I am delivering it to Jesus!

Let's feed this thought as God prompts us. Providing a meal or a sweet surprise is one tried-and-true way to minister to others, whether it's a home-cooked dish, a take-out special, a bag of fresh fruit from the local farmer's market, or sweet candy.

God's Green Thumb

I am the true grapevine, and my Father is the gardener. He cuts
off every branch of mine that doesn't produce fruit, and he prunes
the branches that do bear fruit so they will produce even more.

JOHN 15:1-2

A green thumb? I don't have one. In fact, mine is perpetually pink.

I did not inherit either of my sweet mama's green thumbs—she had two of them! She was a gardening gal through and through. Mom would run out of land to work on in the front and back yards, so she would just extend our backyard into the woods behind our house.

Because I do not know one plant from another, I have great respect, admiration, and awe for precious people who do—God's gardeners! You just may be one of those people who take what God has given them in nature and tend to it lovingly, carefully, and consistently.

In John 15, Jesus says that God is a gardener. How thrilling to have the Gardener who created the first garden tend us lovingly, carefully, and consistently as His children. Even when the landscapes of our lives seem plowed up, God is at work. And when it seems our branches are being lopped off, it's because God is pruning us for greater growth.

When I went through the literal pruning of a mastectomy, I was encouraged to know that good growth comes after pruning. And though the "pruning" was painful, I can honestly say I have grown and even blossomed in the ugly process.

Let's not settle for small, pitiful plots in our hearts. We need to allow God to control our living landscapes. He knows just the right amount of pruning or fertilizer or weed killer needed. He is ever tender and always on hand to offer shade and shelter and nourishment as we grow.

"Lord, let my garden grow!" Ask the expert Gardener to prune you as He knows best; thank Him that He doesn't leave your growth to a lesser gardener to handle. Only in Him can we sow sweet.

Meltdown!

Create in me a clean heart, O God. Renew a loyal spirit within me.
PSALM 51:10

If it were not for the unrelenting grace, love, and sweet mercy of God, my heart would be a constant disaster zone. I love the Lord. I have been walking with Him wholeheartedly for more than twenty-five years, but I just had a major meltdown of my own creation! Have you ever had one of those?

It was late in the day and hot outside. I was hungry and tired, and before I knew it, I rattled off my complaints to the two people I love the most—my husband and daughter. After my tirade, my husband said, "Now, do you want to tell me what you really think?"

In my sorry state, I tried not to smile at his attempt at humor, even though he is the funniest person I know. Sin is not funny, though, and I felt true remorse for spouting off like I did. Even though I confessed my sin, I'm sure they were still shocked. It speaks well of Mark and Kali that they did not fire back at me. I knew my spirit needed a cleanup, the kind only God can handle.

James 4:1-2 (NIV) says, "What causes fights and quarrels among you? Don't they come from your desires that battle within you? You want something but don't get it." Ugh! I acted like a child, a real two-year-old! I wanted something and did not get it.

Even though my husband playfully pointed out the verbal mess I had made, neither he nor my daughter could fix my heart. No human person can give us a clean conscience; no human can take away our guilt. No one living and breathing beside us, whom we can visibly see, can restore our joy and peace and totally change our spirit.

I am grateful that God is capable of renewing me with His Spirit—grateful for myself and my family.

God creates the clean heart and renews our loyal spirit in Jesus Christ. Buy yourself some special bath salts or a new loofah. Enjoy a cleansing, renewing soak as you ask the Lord to cleanse your spirit with His own.

Soaking Up as Much as I Can

Anyone who believes in me may come and drink! For the Scriptures declare, "Rivers of living water will flow from his heart."

JOHN 7:38

When I read today's verse, my heart cries out, "Thank you, Jesus, for this invitation to be refreshed and brought to life by You, our *Living Water*." Christ is our *never-ending* Spring that will never run dry.

More than anything, I long to be a sponge that soaks Him all in. I want to absorb everything about the Living God of the universe through Jesus Christ. For many years I've asked God to please show me everything He has for me; I don't want to miss out on anything in my relationship with Him. His plans for me are perfect. When my spirit is dry, I can count on Him to bring me back to life. I desire to be so full of Him that when I'm squeezed, I will help water this parched world in the power of His Spirit. We all need to be full of the Living Water so that when the painful circumstances of life squeeze in on us, we have much sweet water to pour out on others.

Let's not squeeze the Lord out of our schedules. Dip into His Word daily. If you haven't read the Bible on your own before, just read a few verses on a regular basis. I think you'll discover how thirsty you'll become to get to know Jesus.

If we drink deeply, before too long, streams of Living Water will flow from us!

Let's soak up God's Word daily like a sponge, then look for opportunities to offer others the Living Water. Take to heart Isaiah 55:11. How will God's Word affect you today?

Believe

Anyone who believes and is baptized will be saved. But
anyone who refuses to believe will be condemned.

MARK 16:16

I live close to a city where the word *believe* appears all over town! It seems that every department store I go into has the word imprinted on some item. It gives new meaning to the saying, "Paint the town red!"—I see "Paint the town *believe!*"

But every time I see the word *believe* by itself, I think, *Believe what?* I am hoping it is Jesus! It really matters what we believe. Our beliefs affect our choices. The daily choices we make affect our own circumstances and those of others. Some choices have serious consequences, such as whether we believe Jesus is our only Savior. That choice will determine where we spend eternity—with Him or in the very real place of hell.

There are also other choices each day that we make regarding our faith. Salvation faith is secure forever, but the extent to which we choose to believe in Jesus' power for our every need on earth goes a long way toward how much we thrive in His Spirit.

If we believe that His mercy is essential to our growth, then we will spread His mercy to others as well. If we believe that our words matter—as we're told repeatedly in His Word—then we will see more clearly our need for His help to restrain our tongues. And if we believe His Word when it says that our heartaches on earth are nothing compared to the restoration we will have when we focus on Jesus, we're able to have hope when things are hard.

Choosing belief over unbelief affects eternity. It also affects today. If we are granted this whole day to live, will we live it in His Spirit, believing He is with us all the way? We can answer yes only if we *believe!*

How will your belief in Jesus impact your joy today? How about your hope and peace and the grace you offer to others? Memorize John 20:29.

Sleep Peace

I have told you all this so that you may have peace in me.
Here on earth you will have many trials and sorrows. But
take heart, because I have overcome the world.

JOHN 16:33

Whenever I see a heart I think of Sweet Sherry, because she loves hearts so much she has one in every room in her home. Recently she showed me a surprise outside in her rock garden. A tree had been cut down and the stump was shaped like a heart. She has plans to put a marker in her garden that says, "Love the LORD your God with all your heart" (Matthew 22:37). One Christmas she gave me a two-inch silver heart bookmark that never falls out of my bedside book and has been a reminder of God's peace countless times during the night.

When I wake up in the middle of the night and want to quickly fall back asleep, I turn on my teeny book light in an attempt not to disturb Mark and begin reading where I left off. Usually within a page or two, my eyes grow tired and I fall back to sleep.

One night, I was especially troubled by certain trials and sorrows that were swirling in my head. I tried to read to take my mind off everything, but it wasn't helping. Then, in the darkness, I noticed the shadow of that little silver heart from my bookmark on the ceiling above our bed.

The sight was so precious I had to resist waking up Mark to say, "Look! Look!" If I could have jumped out of bed to physically hug God, I would have! If God can put a heart on the ceiling in the middle of a troubled night just for me, He can do immeasurably more than all you and I could ever imagine (Ephesians 3:20). We really can feel His peace in the midst of struggles and dark times, knowing His heart for His children is tender and kind.

Let's take heart! We will have trouble in this world, but Jesus has overcome the problems we face.

Clinging to Him

I cling to you; your strong right hand holds me securely.

PSALM 63:8

I have already confessed that I suffer from an incurable habit of space invasion in my devotion "Confessions of a Leaner" (see page 21). I have always liked to sit close to people—shoulder-to-shoulder, elbow-to-elbow. Even when walking down the street while shopping with my daughter or girlfriends, I tend to move into their personal space without realizing that I am sometimes too close for their comfort! But thankfully, we always end up laughing about this habit of mine!

Isn't it wonderful that God wants us to sit close to Him? We can never get too close for His comfort. Not only does He want us to stay close whether we're sitting or walking or running through life together, but He tells us to cling to Him— to tailgate, hang on, piggyback, however you want to express it—to never let go, *ever*! He does not want us to drop His hand.

I love to visualize sticking so close to Him that no one can squeeze between us—because *we are tight*! What an absolutely fabulous ride to live life clinging to a strong and loving Father who never shrugs us off or nudges us out of His way. I long to cling to Him so I will not skip off the path or take a detour; I don't want to miss a stop on His personal journey for me, not even for a second. His way is the best way. He is always in the lead, and He ensures that the stops He makes are only for my good. Even if the stop does not appear inviting to me, He is still there, helping me see that He will bring good from the experience. Clinging to Him, I will never be lost or alone.

If you are unsure whether you are connected to God, He is ready and willing to take your hand and pull you close. It's your move to put yourself in His big hand every day and never let go.

Let's cling to Christ! We can start by making James 4:8 (NIV) our verse today: "Come near to God and he will come near to you."

Just Sayin' . . .

God has spoken plainly, and I have heard it many times: Power, O God, belongs to you.

PSALM 62:11

Almost every day I seem to hear someone make a point with the words, "Just sayin'." And every time it makes me smile.

At the end of Psalm 62, King David was just sayin' that power belongs to God, and so does unfailing love! David knew who loved him and where to find his strength. He knew it as a shepherd boy when he faced the giant Goliath, and he knew it as a king facing enemies from all sides. He knew the only place to safely hide was in the shelter of the almighty God. And he knew that when the fortress of his palace came tumbling down, his *real fortress, God Himself,* would stand unharmed (verse 6)!

Whenever we hear "just sayin'," we can be reminded to reread the wonderful Bible stories where we see God's love and power in action. These true accounts help us know God's unchanging character and give us the Christ-confidence we need to trust that God will be powerful and loving in our situations too!

When you have time, go back and read all of Psalm 62 and mark David's repeated phrases where he reminds himself that God alone is his rock and salvation. We can take this timely tip from David by daily remembering that God is strong and loving even when we feel weak and unloved. With Christ in us and our strong Father's loving presence holding us up, we can believe and trust that He will make all things well, even if they are not right now.

So next time we're working out with our five-pound weights, we can visualize ourselves building up our spiritual muscles:

"My God is strong!" (right arm curl).

"My God is loving!" (left arm curl).

God said it. So be it. Just sayin' it's true.

 Read through a couple of Psalms or turn to a favorite Bible story and write down three more truths that God is just sayin', words that you can take comfort from today. Just sayin'.

Affecting Future Generations

*I lavish unfailing love for a thousand generations on
those who love me and obey my commands.*

EXODUS 20:6

I love this verse. I love its truth for my family and, Lord willing, future generations of descendants. It gives me hope that my life of faith will bless them, despite
my mistakes and flaws.

Another reason I love today's verse is because God is explaining that His merciful love toward His own extends to hundreds of generations. Therefore, when I
don't hold my tongue but allow my words to hurt the people I love the most, I can
rest in the knowledge that God loves to forgive and renew. His mercy to me will
resound for decades to come.

God's desire to lavish His forgiveness on so many reveals the depth of His
love for us. I think it is easier to recognize God's steadfast, forgiving Spirit when
I do not have a steadfast spirit. In my humbled state, I long for what the Forgiver
offers.

I was less than loving last night when I got home from a long, fruitful day. I
was tired, and it didn't take long for my steadfast spirit to go right out the window. (You should know by now that I'm not a night owl but an early-morning
girl.) I said some harsh words; in short, I was not sweet! I know that when my
mood deteriorates like it did, the first people I unload on are my husband and
daughter.

Naturally, I regret my attitude at home with my family, perhaps even more
than I regret other sin. My family takes priority. I want to serve them in a way
that pleases God. I take seriously the fact that more is "caught" than "taught"
about faith by those around me as well as my descendants. I'm especially grateful
that God's love covers a multitude of sins (1 Peter 4:8). Because I am His, His love
to my family outweighs my shortcomings.

Let's commit to pray for those who come after us, whether they
are in our families or are people we mentor or tell about our faith
in Christ.

You Look Fine

*The LORD doesn't see things the way you see them. People judge
by outward appearance, but the LORD looks at the heart.*

1 SAMUEL 16:7

Whenever I ask my daughter or husband how I look and they reply, "You look
just fine," I want to head right back to my closet and start over! Of course, I usually do not have enough time for that, so I leave the house looking "just fine."

What is meant by "fine" anyway? My children's dictionary, which I prefer
to use for simplicity, defines *fine* as "very well or healthy." All I can think of is
that I don't look sick and that because I look "healthy," people think I've gained
weight!

Our loving God tells us plainly that although we see outward appearances and
do not see the heart, He does see the heart, and that's what really matters. What a
beautiful truth! He sees the good, the bad, and the ugly in our hearts, regardless
of the state of our outward appearance. Beautiful to Him is quite different from
the world's definition of beauty.

He sees my heart when it isn't so fine because I've failed, yet He knows I want
to please Him. He knows my weak heart is made of dust but it still beats for Him.
He knows I love Him and want to be obedient until my heart stops beating on
this earth, when I finally will see Him face to face. That happens not because I
look fine, but because I *am* very fine—perfect, actually—in Jesus Christ. You, too,
are very fine—perfect, actually—in Jesus Christ, whether you feel or look "just
fine" or not.

It is encouraging to know that even though God sees and knows everything
about us, He still has plans for us that are a lot more than just fine!

🔑 Thank God He made our hearts forever perfect in Jesus Christ.
"Just fine" will hardly do!

Hanging with Him

*The LORD said to Samuel, "I am sorry that I ever made
Saul king, for he has not been loyal to me and has refused
to obey my command." Samuel was so deeply moved when
he heard this that he cried out to the LORD all night.*

1 SAMUEL 15:10-11

I read this portion from God's Word, and a big road sign flashes across my mind: a circle with the words "Disloyal to God" in black letters with a big red diagonal line running through them.

I don't ever want to be disloyal to God. I am hanging with Him no matter what. King Saul was sinfully disloyal to God, insisting on his own battle plan against the Amalekites instead of what God had asked him to do. When King Saul made an excuse for his actions, the prophet Samuel, God's mouthpiece to the people, rebuked him with a question (15:22): "What is more pleasing to the LORD: your burnt offerings and sacrifices or your obedience to his voice? Listen! Obedience is better than sacrifice, and submission is better than offering the fat of rams."

There is so much practical application in these Bible stories for everyone. Not only can we recognize ourselves in them and repent for our disobedience, but most of all, we can see God's heart. His heart cares about our heart's loyalty to Him. His heart wants to grow ours to beat like His, to love His ways. We can sacrifice our bodies, time, and treasures to all kinds of good causes, but God delights in us when we "hang with Him," obeying His commands. I have never had a fun, good time when I wasn't following His commands. The life of Saul serves as an example of how God wants us to learn about the value of obeying Him.

He gave us everything we need to live by in Christ. Like one of my favorite hymns says, "Trust and obey, for there's no other way to be happy in Jesus, but to trust and obey."

Christ never leaves us, so hang with Him in loyal obedience. Believers in Christ should always be the ones who exude the most joy and have the most fun! If not, we should evaluate who we're hanging with.

Wise Advice

Your laws please me; they give me wise advice.

PSALM 119:24

Who doesn't need wise advice at some point in life? I need it all the time. Bad advice is easy to come by in our world; the difficult part is recognizing when it's faulty.

In order for believers in Christ to grow, it is essential that we go to the right place for wise advice. Because God embodies wisdom, His Word holds all the answers we need to live faithful lives that reflect Him in a world that often mocks Him.

I did not always understand the gold mine of practical wisdom found in the Bible. But when I began to dig into it daily, I prayed that God would teach me through His Word, and His Spirit revealed to my heart the things I needed to know and change in order to grow more like Him. And He still does. Luke 10:21 tells us that He shows us what we need to know in ways that are understandable to children, yet those same things remain hidden from adults who think they are wise on their own.

We can know we are moving in His direction, according to His laws, when we allow His words to be our counselors. We can also seek out people who follow His Word to direct us according to biblical truth, which is more true than our feelings or ideas.

His laws are a delight, and therefore we can experience that delight when we follow Him. I never feel good inside when I do the wrong things. As I mentioned previously, I used to tell Kali that good self-esteem comes from doing the right things that God says to do—simple obedience. Obedience is not a prerequisite to knowing God; rather, it is a thing I "want to do" after becoming a child of God through Christ Jesus.

o━ Let's continue to let Him speak to us through His Word. Choose a chapter in Proverbs to read and soak up the Lord's wise advice through Solomon.

Always Connected

I am convinced that nothing can ever separate us from God's love.
Neither death nor life, neither angels nor demons, neither our fears for
today nor our worries about tomorrow—not even the powers of hell
can separate us from God's love. No power in the sky above or in the
earth below—indeed, nothing in all creation will ever be able to separate
us from the love of God that is revealed in Christ Jesus our Lord.

ROMANS 8:38-39

Before my beautiful, naturally curly-haired, redheaded mother (her hair reminded me of Lucille Ball's) went to be with the Lord, she told me she got exasperated with long phone-recording prompts. One time she had tried several times to reach a real person to take care of essential business. After hearing "This call may be monitored for quality assurance," she left her own message: "I sure hope so, because I have something to tell you!" I wish I could hear her say those words now so I could laugh out loud again in her actual presence.

Meditating on the verses from Romans 8 that are quoted above feels like God is pulling us close and saying, "I have something to tell you: Nothing can separate you from My love!" You and I can be encouraged, no matter who or what we are separated from, that *absolutely nothing* can separate us from God through Christ Jesus.

His quality assurance is so reliable that we never get a recording when we call on Him. We never have a dropped call with Him, and His signal strength is amazing—it's everywhere! He promises His constant presence and immediate attention. He even knows before we do when and in what way we'll need Him.

You know what else? Staying connected is even more important to Him than it is to us. He chose long ago to rescue us, and He's not willing to ever give us up. Our connection with Him is as secure as He is—perfectly so.

Talk about great service. God can't be beat!

You know that concern that's been sounding a busy signal in your thoughts? Call on God and tell Him about it. There's no need to leave a message; He's available and He always answers, His way, His time. He got the message for sure, and oh, He has no need for caller ID, either—He already knew you'd be calling.

Whatever!

And whatever you do, whether in word or deed, do it all in the name of the Lord Jesus, giving thanks to God the Father through him.

COLOSSIANS 3:17, NIV (EMPHASIS MINE)

This verse gives new meaning to the word *whatever* that is often used as an exasperated response from a teenager's lips! The apostle Paul isn't using the word here with a begrudging tone. Instead, this *whatever* embraces all the potential joy it can pass on. Whatever you and I do as God's children, we can do with a thankful heart in Jesus' name. It brings to my mind the song that the seven dwarfs sang in *Snow White*, "Whistle While You Work." (Wouldn't that make Walt Disney proud?)

A believer's every action points to Christ! Lest those actions reflect negatively on our Savior, Paul encourages us to keep in mind that we have countless opportunities each day to uphold Christ's name. *Whatever* we do or say in Jesus' name, giving thanks, happens only through His Spirit living in us.

The book of Colossians was written to believers in the church in Colosse, people who had already put their faith and trust in Christ. But some of those believers were thinking their salvation depended on "doing the commandments." Paul was reminding all of them (and us) that Christ alone is sufficient, and His sufficiency makes it possible to get our eyes off of ourselves and our human goals, and focus on Jesus. Reflecting Him will draw others to want to know Him too.

Colossians begins with C, as in "Christ first." As believers in Christ, we need to heed Paul's reminder, too, and not confuse the truth of today's verse as a way to earn merit with God. When we focus on Him, we grow to love Him more. As we love Him more, our *whatevers* become opportunities to experience and express His joy as we represent Him in this hurting world which is so quickly moving toward isolation.

⚷ As we go through the day, let's be mindful of *whatever* ways we can represent Him well in a world that needs to know the real Jesus.

No Condemnation

*There is no condemnation for those who belong to Christ Jesus.
And because you belong to him, the power of the life-giving Spirit
has freed you from the power of sin that leads to death.*

ROMANS 8:1-2

The buckets and beach towels are out, but we are not going to the beach! Containers litter the floor of my husband's office, collecting water. A storm swept through and uncovered a major unforeseen leak in our roof.

I have to laugh to keep from crying since it has been years since we have done any fun home improvement project. This was our summer to reorganize the utility room, but now it looks like we'll be tackling a roof repair and an office redo instead.

Things always look worse before they look better when you start a home repair. When I looked at the big brown water stains and huge crack in the ceiling, I cringed. Who knew? It was a slow, hidden leak that ended up being damaging and costly. It was ugly—and I do not like ugly. I like pretty, and I do not like a mess because it brings out the worst in me. I wanted order! I felt that the ceiling ought to be condemned. (Okay, maybe I'm exaggerating a little, but you sense my frustration, right?)

"Lord, I need You to reorder my heart by the power of Your Holy Spirit so I will not crack. Lord, my ugly brown spots are poking out too—and I don't mean freckles or age spots! Lord, where would we be without You?"

Suddenly I sense something—or rather Someone—moving my heart. Now the ugly ceiling that I was ready to demolish moments ago is reminding me of my complaining attitude. I think it needs as much renovation as the ceiling—maybe more. And this isn't a do-it-yourself job.

What a relief that God is the master Renovator of our hearts. He does a top-notch job and is all about the details and finishes. His cleanup of our sin is thorough, making us look more like Him. With God, our hearts become welcoming spaces for Him to dwell in. No condemnation, just splendid renovation. And now for that ceiling . . .

What home project lingers on your to-do list? It might loom over you, but you can always thank the Lord that He is already on the job in your heart—no condemnation, just beautiful renovation.

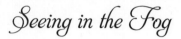

Seeing in the Fog

We live by faith, not by sight.
2 CORINTHIANS 5:7, NIV

I am almost breathless. God's creation is spectacular! My "so excited face" is on right now as I am literally sitting in a cloud! No, I am not in an airplane. I am outside early in the morning, sitting on a balcony surrounded by mountains.

Just a minute ago I was gazing at the valley and small town below, getting ready to read my Bible while anticipating a slow and restful week with my family on summer vacation. I was gazing at the tops of the mountains and pieces of blue sky peeking between the clouds, wondering if it was going to rain. Then all of a sudden, I couldn't see a thing! I was totally enveloped by a cloudy fog.

I cannot see the church steeple, cannot see the forest, cannot see one mountain peak because of the clouds surrounding me. But I can still hear. I hear the sound of a gushing waterfall. A few more seconds pass before it dawns on me that I cannot see God, either! But I know He is here just as sure as that mountain is sitting behind the cloud. Paradoxically, it is probably one of the clearest visual pictures I have had personally of what it means to walk by faith and not by sight!

"Lord, right now, my circumstances are a bit cloudy, and I do not know what is ahead, but I do know that You do. And as sure as those mountains are still behind the clouds, You are behind every cloudy circumstance in my life. You never leave, Lord."

Our circumstances can change abruptly, without warning, and leave us feeling blinded about what to do next. Many times we cannot see what is behind our situation or what unknowns lie in front of us, but we can still hear God in His Word. I hear Him in this Bible beside me. I hear Him saying right now that one day my faith will become sight.

It's okay that we cannot see God. We can hear Him and know that He is present with us because He says so over and over in His Word. Let's pray now that He will help us trust Him so much that we find peace in the fog.

God Watches Over Us

He will not let you stumble; the one who watches over you will not slumber. Indeed, he who watches over Israel never slumbers or sleeps. The LORD himself watches over you! The LORD stands beside you as your protective shade. The sun will not harm you by day, nor the moon at night. The LORD keeps you from all harm and watches over your life. The LORD keeps watch over you as you come and go, both now and forever.

PSALM 121:3-8

How many times have you and I told young children to look both ways before they cross the street? And how many times have we told a teenager in the driver's seat to be sure to check in both directions before pulling out into an intersection?

We'd like to be able to always watch over those we love, but we have to trust that when it matters most, they will act on the wisdom they've been taught. Fortunately, we can trust God to be on guard over them at all times, even when we cannot be with them. Sometimes we feel even more peace knowing that He is caring for those we love than we feel knowing that He's watching over us!

Psalm 121 is a short and sweet reminder that God is at attention in our lives 24/7, wherever we are, whatever we are doing, in and out of our households, from the mundane to the exciting, the ordinary to the extraordinary—whatever, wherever, God is watching over you and me!

If you have your Bible handy, turn to Psalm 121 and notice that in eight verses the psalmist declares six times that God helps, watches over, protects, and stands beside you and me. At the beginning of the psalm we are on the lookout for God: "I look up to the mountains—does my help come from there? My help comes from the LORD" (verses 1-2). One of life's most abiding comforts comes from knowing that even if *we* are not on the lookout moment by moment, God is always watching over us!

 Join me in watching and waiting on Him daily! Thank God for His hedge of protection around you in Christ.

Never Ever Die

Jesus told [Sweet Martha], "I am the resurrection and the life. Anyone who believes in me will live, even after dying. Everyone who lives in me and believes in me will never ever die. Do you believe this, Martha?"

JOHN 11:25-26

"Do you believe this, _____?" (Put your name in the blank.)

"Do you believe this, Kim?"

"Yes! I believe it, Lord, even though it seems that death is all around me these days!" Death is a sad loss for us on earth, whether we physically lose someone we love, or someone we care about is grieving a loss.

This past summer I hired an older gentleman to paint a room in my home. The advertisement on his van read "Airless Jordan, Airless Spray Painting—High Quality Paint Job with a Down-to-Earth Price." When I mentioned how clever his sign was, Ron Jordan explained, "I wanted some words to attract people's attention." He certainly had mine.

"How long have you been in the painting business?" I asked.

"Not long."

His explanation surprised me. He had been a funeral director in a small town for a long time. He was always on call, 365 days a year, even having to cut a family vacation short once to come home and ready someone for burial. "You were a mortician and arranger, responsible for everything?" I could not even imagine! He said he had to do it all because there was no one else to do it, and death happens. But after many years, he decided to switch careers. Needless to say, I was a bit fascinated to have a "mortician turned painter" in my home!

Those who know the Lord as Savior can view death with hope and eternal anticipation because we have the promise of eternal life. It's true that our mortal bodies will die, but our souls will not miss a beat. One day we'll be "airless" on earth but forever with the Lord if we have trusted in Christ.

Spend some time considering your relationship with God in Christ. Is it settled? Think about the first seconds after your physical body dies. Sure, there are unknowns about how and when that will happen. But purposefully choose to anticipate meeting Jesus in person, hearing His heartbeat when He pulls you close.

Sheer Delight

He led me to a place of safety; he rescued me because he delights in me.

2 SAMUEL 22:20

When I was in third or fourth grade, I remember a particularly delightful surprise at my first sleepover birthday party. I invited a group of girls to bring their own pillows and sleeping bags and spend the night. Little did I know when we awoke the next morning that my mom and dad would scoop us all into the car *with our pajamas on* and drive us twenty minutes away for ice-cream sundaes for breakfast. Now that was a delight!

When I turn once again to my trusty children's dictionary, I learn that the word *delight* means "great pleasure." Did you know that God delights in His children? Because He is the same yesterday, today, tomorrow, and for all eternity, God has always delighted in each one of us and always will. Wow! Put your name in the blank and see how meaningful that is: God delighted in _____ before she was born, and God delights in _____ now. God will delight in _____ forever! I don't know about you, but that almost makes me squeal aloud.

When we delight in someone, we long for that person. This longing creates a desire to spend time together. That describes God's desire toward us.

Dwell on this truth today and every day: God takes great pleasure in you and me. Jesus took great pleasure in saving us, despite His pain and separation from His heavenly Father while on the cross. He still takes great pleasure in being with us, in growing and restoring and healing and loving us and offering us grace and truth, no matter what our past, our present, or our future. His delight toward us is steadfast. It bubbles up in our souls and helps us delight in Him right back.

Treat a friend to something sweet, whether it's edible or not.
Be delighted today that God delights in you and me!

Crawling through Chronicles

In everything that he undertook in the service of God's
temple and in obedience to the law and the commands,
he sought his God and worked wholeheartedly.

2 CHRONICLES 31:21, NIV

I am nearing the end of the two books of Chronicles in my *One Year Bible* reading, and I think I am going to miss them! I used to crawl through those books because of the seemingly never-ending genealogy, along with the repeated history from Genesis through 2 Samuel. But then I thought that God must have had a good reason to repeat certain things for you and me, so we're wise not to skip over them. The books of 1 and 2 Chronicles also contain the rich stories of King David and his son Solomon, as well as telling us about the Temple and how God deals with His people.

I am glad I stuck with these two books, otherwise I wouldn't have learned so much from the life of King Hezekiah, whose story is found in 2 Chronicles 31–32 as well as 2 Kings 18–20. Tucked in with accounts of many bad kings and a few good ones, we find the report of Hezekiah's rule. He was a rare leader who did it right. We may miss the lessons of his life if we skip over these chapters. Although Hezekiah's father, Ahaz, had betrayed the Lord, Hezekiah called people back to worshiping the one and true God instead of idols; he followed God wholeheartedly and promoted that singular devotion among his people. Although he wasn't perfect, he repented when God showed him what he'd done wrong (see 2 Chronicles 32:24-26).

Years ago I wrote in my Bible near chapter 31 of 2 Chronicles, "Lord, I want to be like Hezekiah. I want to show wholehearted devotion to You in cooking, cleaning, carpooling, working, playing, discipling, laughing, loving—life!" Honestly, some days my heart feels like the good, the bad, and the ugly instead of the good, the right, and the faithful. On those days, God reminds me with mercy and grace that because of Jesus in me, He sees my heart as good, right, and faithful because Jesus dealt with the good, the bad, and the ugly on the cross. I'm free to live in wholehearted and obedient devotion because my heart is His.

Pray with me: "Here are our hearts, Lord! Help us. We want to seek You wholeheartedly too!"

Where Did My Guilt Go?

When I refused to confess my sin, my body wasted away, and I groaned all day long. Day and night your hand of discipline was heavy on me. My strength evaporated like water in the summer heat. Finally, I confessed all my sins to you and stopped trying to hide my guilt. . . . And you forgave me! All my guilt is gone.

PSALM 32:3-5

Summer heat in Richmond, Virginia—got that! Groaning all day—got that! Heart of discipline heavy on me—yes, yes, I've got that, too! I sure struggle with my attitude when I'm uncomfortable, but I don't help myself when I gripe and groan and take out my frustrations on those around me.

Oh my, I can wear myself out with guilt over things I shouldn't have said or done that I said or did anyway. I have a heavy heart when I have not made things right with another person and the Lord. This spiritual drain seems to zap me of physical energy as well. I want to hurry and confess—to be guiltless, to be free, and to have my strength and joy and peace back!

King David felt the drain of sin, too, and he also got excited when he confessed and asked forgiveness. Only then did he feel guilt's grip loosen and his strength return. Repentance is vital to our health.

Many years after his ancestor King David lived, Jesus said, "So if you are presenting a sacrifice at the altar in the Temple and you suddenly remember that someone has something against you, leave your sacrifice there at the altar. Go and be reconciled to that person. Then come and offer your sacrifice to God" (Matthew 5:23-24). You and I need to get things right with others and with God. Jesus' advice is very clear and practical. We cannot separate our relationships with others from our relationship with God.

"Lord, when I am guilty and do not confess, I feel like I just dropped Your hand when we were walking side by side. I know You never leave me, but to have our fellowship restored I need to confess and turn back to You. There's no other way for that joy and peace to return!"

If you need to deal with unconfessed sin, confess it now. Ask God's forgiveness and also be restored to the person you have wronged.

Son Rays and Sonscreen

*Jesus spoke to the people once more and said, "I am the light
of the world. If you follow me, you won't have to walk in
darkness, because you will have the light that leads to life."*

JOHN 8:12

You would be laughing if you could see me right now. It is early morning, I am in my favorite lightweight long robe, and I just sat down to read my Bible. It's too cold to go outside for devotions, so I am doing the next best thing—sitting near the window. What's so funny is that I had to get up and put on my sun visor to read my Bible in the house! I could have moved from my sunny spot, but I did not want to because the sun's warmth makes me realize that God's Son, Jesus Christ, is sending His rays in my direction.

Shine on me, Lord. I need Your Sonshine!

Christ is comfort. Christ is light. As I am soaking in physical warmth and light from the sun, I long to soak in the One who created these necessities. I long to allow the Son to illumine His way for me this day, this hour—all day and night and the next until I reach heaven, where there is no darkness!

The rays really are bright, and I briefly consider whether I need to get sunscreen. I'm so glad that when it comes to getting burned by the heat of my sins, I have the 100++ percent protection of *Sonscreen.*

Lord, You are my shield from sin. You see me without sin's damage, made perfect through the death of Christ, Your Son, on the cross.

I probably should get out of the sun before it burns me, but I never need to limit my time in the direct presence of the Son, and neither do you. In fact, the more we soak Him up, the more we'll glow with His Sonshine lighting us from the inside out. Jesus is our SPF 100++ (Son Protection Forever).

> You and I may be facing some dark situations, so let's reread today's verse and let Jesus' words shine into our hearts. When we follow Him, we have the protection of Sonscreen and the Son rays. His Spirit produces the glow!

Fear the Lord?

*Come, my children, and listen to me, and I
will teach you to fear the LORD.*

PSALM 34:11

When my daughter was little and fearful of something, my mother-heart longed to *make* things safe for her. Actually, I longed to help her *feel* safe as well, in the only real security I could offer. Childlike faith is so precious. Children often have an easier time trusting Jesus than adults. I admit to my own set of fears, which prompts me to talk to God. Whether a child or an adult, once we talk to God about whatever scares us, it is easier to rest, knowing that God's got it covered and things will be okay.

I wanted to raise my daughter to not only fear the Lord but trust Him with her fears. As adults, we can have a more difficult time trying to grasp the concept of what it means to fear the Lord. Although we almost always associate fear with something scary, that isn't what is meant here. The concept of fearing the Lord can be confusing, but I like to clarify it in my mind by imagining Jesus reacting two different ways to two different situations.

First, He is altogether kind and loving and gentle with those who belong to Him. But on the other hand, He can be fearsome and fierce and intimidating to His enemies who hate His holiness or who threaten those He loves.

When you have a healthy fear of the Lord, you realize that He is a loving Father who is also the King of kings. He is all-powerful, a characteristic to be feared by His enemies and respected by all. He is also all-loving, a quality that brings security to those who love Him and call Him Savior.

When we see Jesus in every aspect, we not only gain a deeper respect and fear for Him, but we begin to approach our worship time with Him differently too. We become closer to Him, and we feel free to give Him our fears.

Let's live with a healthy, respectful, worshipful fear of the Lord. We can do that by going to Him with our worship, praise, thanksgiving, needs, questions, and fears—acknowledging that He is sovereign over our lives.

Learning Contentment

True godliness with contentment is itself great wealth. After
all, we brought nothing with us when we came into the world,
and we can't take anything with us when we leave it. So if
we have enough food and clothing, let us be content.

1 TIMOTHY 6:6-8

Can you think of five people right now who you know are truly content? How about four? Three? Two? One? Is contentment becoming a lost virtue?

From Philippians 4:11 we know that contentment can be learned. But does our saturated society hinder us from living in true contentment when it sends the message that things we want are really things we need, whether or not it's true? Are we really failing or passing in this "learning contentment" education? Are we doing any homework in this area?

When we read daily what God has to say in His Word, we hear His voice and understand more clearly what He is like. We also allow Him to fill us with more of His Spirit, which gives us true fulfillment. Being with the Lord grows contentment.

Reading today's verses, let's ask ourselves if we are growing in godliness and contentment. Aside from spending time with God, we can avoid areas that bring us discontentment. Personally, sometimes I look at too many catalogs and then buy things I don't need. I am more content when I am budget conscious and keep my innate "need to shop" tendencies under control.

Comparing ourselves with others is a surefire route to being discontented, so let's avoid doing that. Discontentment will look different on each one of us, but godliness looks the same for all of us. God's Spirit will zero in where He wants each of us to take a step of faith in obedience to Him.

⚷ Jump-start learning contentment. What is causing discontentment in your life today? Right now, rest in your present circumstances as a child of a perfect God.

A Constant Struggle

I want to do what is right, but I can't. I want to do what is good,
but I don't. I don't want to do what is wrong, but I do it anyway.
But if I do what I don't want to do, I am not really the one doing wrong;
it is sin living in me that does it. I have discovered this principle of life—
that when I want to do what is right, I inevitably do what is wrong.
I love God's law with all my heart. But there is another power within me
that is at war with my mind. This power makes me a slave to
the sin that is still within me. Oh, what a miserable person I am!
Who will free me from this life that is dominated by sin and death?
Thank God! The answer is in Jesus Christ our Lord.

ROMANS 7:18-25

If I were to post these verses on Facebook, I believe they would invite the most likes and dislikes of any status update this year! We can like the fact that we're not alone in our struggle to live right; our sin nature is common among everyone. However, we dislike how these verses make us squirm with the stark reality of our condition.

The apostle Paul bares his soul about his personal struggle with sin and reminds us all of the dilemma of the war within that we all wage. As God's children, we are not alone in this struggle. You and I have probably said something similar to Paul's words: "Oh, what a miserable person I am! Who will free me from this life that is dominated by sin and death? Thank God! The answer is in Jesus Christ our Lord" (verses 24-25). They bear repeating!

Jesus' Spirit frees us from being enslaved to our human nature. Yes, we still sin, but His power in us gives us the choice to live in freedom from sin's hold; we don't need to remain trapped by its bondage. Not only that, but the Holy Spirit empowers us to live in greater obedience when we consistently invite Him to take charge in our hearts. When we do, Paul gives us the good news: "Now there is no condemnation for those who belong to Christ Jesus" (Romans 8:1).

Let's thank God every day that we are free from condemnation. That ought to garner countless "likes."

Fresh, Bubbling Spring

Those who drink the water I give will never be thirsty again. It becomes a fresh, bubbling spring within them, giving them eternal life.

JOHN 4:14

Over the years, I've learned the benefits of drinking water. Not only does it decrease my appetite, it keeps me from being thirsty at the end of a long day. And it really does hydrate my dry skin, too. The only downside is that drinking sixty-four ounces of water daily is not an easy thing for me to do, but I'll keep trying!

When it comes to Jesus, the Living Water, I'm not a sipper; I'm a guzzler, and I want to guzzle all day long! Jesus makes it clear to us in Scripture that when we receive Him, He will produce a fresh, bubbling spring in us.

The story in John 4:1-42 is one of my favorites. Jesus is weary and thirsty after journeying all day, and while His disciples go into town to buy food, He sits down at Jacob's well. A woman comes to get water, and Jesus asks her for a drink. She is startled because she knows that a Jewish man normally wouldn't talk to an outcast like her. But not so with Jesus. He knows everything about her, but He still offers Himself to her as the Living Water. The woman accepts Jesus' gift, goes back to town, and tells everyone she meets what happened. Because of her testimony, many others believe and receive Jesus too.

Wow! I can't imagine the excitement in town that day or the life changes that her newfound joy and salvation prompted in her.

The Lord loves us so! He is the only one who can keep our spirit fresh and bubbling with His life in us, regardless of how the world's troubles threaten to dry us up and scorch our tender souls.

Doesn't it sound more appealing to have a fresh spring in our hearts than a stagnant pool? Life often leaves us spiritually thirsty, but when we are hydrated by Him, we can thrive even in desert situations. When we drink daily from our Living Water supply, hearing His voice above all others, we can pour out His freshness to a thirsty world.

Fresh and bubbling? Life-quenching? I'll take it! Won't you?

Pleasant Words

Pleasant words are a honeycomb, sweet to
the soul and healing to the bones.

PROVERBS 16:24, NASB

The Bible's proverbs are so practical! This was the proverb I read during my
"Be still and know that I am God" quiet time today.

I had to laugh when I read the phrase "healing to the bones" in Proverbs
16:24 because my annual bone-density exam was this very same day too! A bone-
density test is an easy screening. You lie still while a magnetic shield passes over
your body and records your bone density. Just like that, a lot of information about
your bones gets recorded, printed out, and sent to the doctor, who goes over it
later with you.

While this test is effective in providing helpful information, it has no healing
power and is not nearly as fun as pleasant words. We all know what they feel like:
gracious . . . kind . . . uncondemning. God can use pleasant words to lift the spirit
of even the most critically ill patient. As destructive as the tongue can be, pleasant
words are much more powerful!

Recently my family members (including me) slipped into a habit of not carefully filtering our tone or editing the words we were saying to each other. We all
fell into the pattern of letting less-than-gracious words slide off our tongues—
words that did not feel sweet to the soul or healing to the bones.

Words are so powerful. That's why reading God's Word is so life changing. We receive genuine encouragement through these holy and God-breathed
words. In the Bible we learn how to develop speech patterns that honor God
and others.

As we listen to God's pleasant words, let's consider what genuine,
pleasant words we can use to encourage others!

Christ in Common

All the believers were united in heart and mind. And they felt that what
they owned was not their own, so they shared everything they had.
ACTS 4:32

Today I'm mulling over the extraordinary reality found in this verse and feeling thankful for you, my sweet reading friend. Although we may not have met in person, we can look forward to meeting in heaven someday. I love that hope!

It is extraordinary to me that no matter where we go or how many people we meet, when we discover another believer in Jesus Christ, we feel like we've found a sweet BBFF (Big Best Friend Forever). I already feel a kinship with you, even if we never meet on earth. If Christ is our common denominator, then *we already have the greatest thing in common*: Him!

Have you ever met someone and discovered that he or she is a believer? If so, then surely you remember feeling a sense of camaraderie, of belonging to the same family, a connection that is understandable only to those who share true faith in Christ. That unity grows from God's promise of spending eternity together with Him.

When each of us is following Him in obedience to His Word, we are of one heart and mind. We may be total opposites in personality, height, weight, and interests. We may live across the country from each other. (Right, Sweet Dawn? Angie? Debbie? Marj?) We may go years without meeting again, but if we do, because of our Christ Common Denominator, we can pick up where life left off as believers with one heart and mind. It's a heart that beats with Christ's heart for God and others, and a mind that thinks about Christ's priorities (1 Corinthians 2:16). Apart from Christ this kind of unity does not happen.

Is there someone you haven't been in touch with for a while that you now feel compelled to reconnect with? Send that person a note or an e-mail, or if you don't know where the person is, take a moment and pray for this one who shares your BBFF.

Sweet Songs in the Night

I am deeply discouraged, but I will remember you . . . I hear the
tumult of the raging seas as your waves and surging tides sweep over
me. But each day the LORD pours his unfailing love upon me, and
through each night I sing his songs, praying to God who gives me life.

PSALM 42:6-8

Who feels like singing in the middle of the night, when you can't sleep and are thinking about another full day ahead? Maybe you find it difficult to sing because you're hurting.

I wonder if we are learning to sing anyway, in the most inconvenient circumstances. Did Job, who had everything taken away from him, sing to God in his deepest suffering? I am certain he yearned for God's nearness and His songs during the darkest hours.

Of course, if we live with others, we cannot belt out songs at midnight or even start loudly humming. But we can acknowledge God, our Maker, the very One who sees through the dark and never sleeps or slumbers (Psalm 121:3-4).

Recently, I was wide awake at 3 a.m. because I had a lot on my mind. I lay there thinking, *Lord, You see me not able to sleep. You see my mind racing about details of the days to come. You care about me, and You see me struggling to sleep.*

Then my phone beeped at 3:55 a.m. because I forgot to turn off the ringer. I laughed in my heart that someone else was wide awake and, Lord willing, singing in the night. A sweet friend, Allison, had been taken by ambulance to the hospital, where she was admitted and waiting for surgery! She was asking for prayer and praying through Psalm 13 because her pastor had read it to her that day. I prayed for her, then finally fell asleep for another hour or so. "Thank You, Lord!" When I woke up, I looked up the psalm.

Guess how Psalm 13 ends? "I will sing to the LORD because he is good to me." Only by knowing Christ can we receive such songs in the night and truly sing them together!

Before you close your eyes in bed tonight, "sing" yourself to sleep by reading a psalm, repeating the words to a praise song, or singing it out loud. May you have sweet dreams of praise!

Paul's Medical Chart

*I have worked harder, been put in prison more often, been whipped
times without number, and faced death again and again.*

2 CORINTHIANS 11:23

When we visit a doctor's office, we often have to fill out a medical history, answering either yes or no to questions regarding whether or not we have had a seemingly endless list of ailments. Reading 2 Corinthians reminded me of that medical history questionnaire. I began putting a check mark by each of the things Paul endured, as well as noting the frequency of those "symptoms"! It also made me thankful that if I were going down the same list, my answers would have been no in most every case.

☑ beaten with a whip (thirty-nine lashes each time!) . . . . 5 times
☑ beaten with rods . . . . 3 times
☑ stoned . . . . .1 time
☑ shipwrecked . . . . 3 times
☑ spent night and day in the open sea . . . . 1 time
☑ faced danger from various sources . . . . constantly
☑ hungry and without food . . . . .often
☑ in pain . . . . .often
☑ thirsty . . . . .often

After getting this far on the list, I am feeling thankful that I have been spared many of Paul's hardships. I have no desire to suffer like he did.

Surely Paul did not enjoy suffering either. But through his hardships, he enjoyed a deeper relationship with the Lord because he trusted that God was using the trials for good. This former enemy of Jesus' followers was re-created and reformed to become a relentless warrior *for* Jesus, even under much opposition and criticism. In his missionary travels to the early churches, Paul is a real-life example to us of how to remain faithful in extremely difficult situations. As the progress reports of the various believers got back to him, he rejoiced and passed on the encouragement to others. "We proudly tell God's other churches about your endurance and faithfulness in all the persecutions and hardships you are suffering" (2 Thessalonians 1:4).

 Let's ask God for endurance and faithfulness too, no matter what is on our medical chart.

Call on God

I will call on God, and the LORD will rescue me.

PSALM 55:16

In an earlier devotion I told you that I inherited my dad's 1986 Ford pickup and repainted it from man-blue to girl-pink. It still runs well for neighborhood errands—women going to the consignment store or men friends frequently borrowing it to haul large items. Mark teases me that he tries to use it only at night. If you live near me and need to get a sofa or refrigerator home, I'm your girl. My pink truck is available.

Recently, I needed to pick up a large wardrobe with the help of two other women, and transport it home until I could drop it off at a consignment shop. It was not easy for three women to load, but a kind man gave us the extra boost we needed and then shut the tailgate. Unbeknownst to me, the tailgate was not completely latched. On a busy road on my way home, the huge piece of furniture fell out of the big pink truck into traffic! I could not believe it!

I was so relieved that the wardrobe had not fallen onto another car, caused an accident, or hurt anyone and that it landed near the side of the road instead of in the middle of the street. "Emotional me" remained supernaturally calm—embarrassed, but calm. All I said aloud was "Lord!" Thinking about it now, I love that He gave me the instinctive reaction to call His name immediately when I needed help and needed to know I wasn't alone. I was so happy to have Him to talk to—to literally call out to!

After sitting through a long stoplight, I maneuvered to a spot where several helpful men from a nearby store could haul the heavy, bruised and broken piece back to the bed of my pink truck!

Later I wondered how many people go merrily on their way every day, following their own path, unaware that God is a very present help to whom they can call out, "Lord!" when they are in trouble (Psalm 46:1, NKJV).

Hide Psalm 46:1 in your heart right now so the next time you're in trouble, His Spirit living in you can urge you to call out, "Lord!" too.

Our Father Always Knows Best

[Jesus] never sinned, nor ever deceived anyone.

1 PETER 2:22

Have you ever gotten something in the mail that says you have won a prize? My first "free prize" experience was in high school. Several days after a big fair came to our small hometown, I received a letter saying I had won a trip to Florida.

I couldn't contain my excitement. My dad came into the kitchen to find out what was causing all the commotion. When I showed him the letter, he said quietly, "Kim, this is a gimmick. There's a catch."

"No, Dad, I'm sure this is real." I didn't want to think that I had been tricked. Dad advised me to call some of my friends who had gone to the fair with me and had entered their names into the drawing for free prizes. I was ready to prove my dad wrong, so I got on the phone. Of course, Dad was right. All of my friends had "won" too! I was extremely disappointed.

My wise earthly father knew best about that so-called "free" prize. What's more, our heavenly Father knows and sees everything, more than we can imagine. All the more reason to trust Him.

We can know for sure that in all things, in all circumstances, and in all situations our heavenly Father speaks truth. He always knows best and never tricks us. We don't have to enter a raffle or a drawing to receive the greatest prize ever—eternal life with Him. God arranged for all of us to receive that free gift through His Son, Jesus Christ. All we need to do is ask and receive. It's the best thing we could ever hope to possess.

What a daily comfort it is that our Father knows best. What question do you need clear truth about today? He answers in His Word.

God Does What He Says

There was always enough flour and olive oil left in the containers, just as the LORD had promised through Elijah.

1 KINGS 17:16

In this wonderful story from 1 Kings, God blesses a poor widow because she is obedient. She becomes a firsthand witness of how God keeps His promise to His people. The prophet Elijah is hungry and asks this widow to share her pitiful portion of oil and flour with him. It is all she has to feed herself and her son, but she is willing to give up their last meal. God honors her faithfulness and provides a never-ending supply of oil and flour thereafter. In the same way, God is trustworthy to keep His promises to us today.

I'm sure most of us have been in a situation where we said we were going to do something but did not do it. We may have had the best intentions, but either we ran out of resources or we got distracted and ended up not keeping our word. In everything, I want to be a woman of my word and a woman of His Word, but the reality is that I don't always get it right. God can always be trusted to follow through on His promises. He never gets distracted and never runs out of resources. He can be counted on to keep His Word to us.

I like to imagine how the poor widow's faith grew more each day as she saw God providing for her and her son. He wants to build our faith, too, provision by provision, as we pay attention to His working in our lives.

Let's nibble on this great truth today and trust God to keep all His promises to us. Stop by a bakery to pick up your favorite rolls or cookies, or bake them yourself with the flour of your choice. As you share and deliver them to someone who could use some "sweet bread," thank God for His faithful sustenance and that He *always* delivers on every promise.

The Lights Are Off but Somebody's Home

Jesus spoke to the people once more and said, "I am the light of the world. If you follow me, you won't have to walk in darkness, because you will have the light that leads to life."

JOHN 8:12

I don't know about you, but I take electricity for granted—until it's dark! We have lost power in our home many times due to bad storms whose winds broke off huge branches from our beautiful trees and downed power lines. One time, my husband and I were both working on projects in different parts of the house. All of a sudden, it was so dark that we could not see our hands in front of our faces.

We stumbled around looking for flashlights and candles, hoping that the lights would come on quickly so we could finish what we were doing. Mark walked outdoors to see if our side of the street was the only one to lose power. Sure enough, the houses across the street had power, so our kind neighbor stretched a long extension cord across the road. We connected our cords to his, giving us a temporary power source for our lights that night.

God is our constant Light. He never goes out! Our connection is never breached unless we unplug from His power and choose to continue stumbling through the dark. What a reminder to us about the importance of living close to Him. Our connection with Him is our lifeline and our light. Just as my husband and I couldn't function well in our darkened home, we need Jesus' floodlight to illuminate our way through life.

  My earnest plug: connect to Christ today in His Word by reading John 1:1-5. When we walk in His light, we will all shine brighter and be more effective for Him in this dark world!

First Find Out . . .

Jehoshaphat added, "But first let's find out what the LORD says."
1 KINGS 22:5

Jehoshaphat had a good idea. When I read these true accounts of kings and battles, of victories and defeats throughout God's Word, I feel like putting on my pink army boots. I am reminded that even though I don't have a chariot and a sword, I am fighting some personal battles, just as you probably are. It doesn't matter if the battles are big or small; they all require us to make decisions.

This fascinating chapter begins with a three-year blessing of peace between the nation of Israel and its neighbors. During this time Jehoshaphat, the king of Judah, visited King Ahab of Israel. Ahab was readying plans to lay siege to Ramoth-gilead, which he believed rightfully belonged to Israel. Ahab asked Jehoshaphat if he would go into battle with him against the king of Aram.

As I read it, I started thinking, *Good idea. "Two people are better off than one, for they can help each other succeed"* (Ecclesiastes 4:9). But then I cheered for Jehoshaphat because I *loved* his reply to Ahab: "First let's find out what the LORD says." Jehoshaphat had a much better idea than Ahab!

When you and I have decisions to make, it's important for us to first find out what God says. We need to lay our own hearts and plans on the table, more for our benefit than God's, because He already knows we need help and He sees what is on the other side of our decision. More true is that He sees all sides of the decision.

We need to be sure we are listening to His wise commands in Scripture. God will never go against His Word or tell us to do something contrary to it. With the Holy Spirit's power, we are never alone in battle. Our assignment is to surrender to His strategy and obey whatever practical steps He shows us, realizing that the fight is under His control. When we listen to His battle plan, we can be confident that the victory is not on our shoulders—it's on His, and He always wins!

When you need to make a decision, first find out what the Lord says! Keep in step with Him as He leads you from battle to battle. Review Ephesians 6:10-17 to become familiar with how God equips you for all the big and small skirmishes in life.

Go God!

The LORD is faithful to all his promises and loving
toward all he has made. . . . The LORD is righteous in
all his ways and loving toward all he has made.

PSALM 145:13, 17, NIV

Let's celebrate today whether we feel up to it or not! God wants to lift our hearts now.

Perhaps today you're feeling sad or unloved or discouraged. Maybe you are wondering if anyone really cares about you. Well, look with me at Psalm 145 and celebrate the Lord's greatness, just like His child David did!

God's methods might seem a little unusual. He could remove all of our troubles in an instant. But more often He calls us to draw near to Him, and He lifts our spirits as we celebrate Him.

Reading this psalm makes me feel like God's cheerleader. By the time I finish verse 21, I'm practically shouting, "Go God!" No matter how I feel when I begin, my heart is lifted as I echo David's words.

We have reason to praise the Lord because:

- He is the only One who knows us inside and out!
- He can be nothing but loving toward us.
- What He says goes. And we need to be glad it does because He is always right!
- He is faithful to all His promises!

We are reminded in this psalm that God is righteous and faithful in all His ways. No matter what you and I are facing or feeling right now, He is loving on us! We need to harness our faulty feelings and by faith remind ourselves of what we know is true.

God created us with feelings, but we don't want to make decisions based on feelings or have our feelings determine the outcome of our day. Let's base our emotions on what God says, knowing He always has our backs!

He is loving toward all He has made, which includes sweet you and me!

Continue celebrating God's greatness. Spend five minutes listing the ways God has acted faithfully and lovingly toward you and your family.

Something Good Is Going On

We know that God causes everything to work together for the good of those who love God and are called according to his purpose for them.

ROMANS 8:28

Romans 8:28 definitely makes the top ten in my Precious Personal Promise list. I memorized this verse as a young Christian, and it has truly given me courage in every difficult situation. I know for a fact that even if I can't see any good in my circumstances when I am in the midst of them, God is working behind the scenes for my good.

I love going to stage productions. Part of my fascination is how quickly the stage crew can change scenes. Everything grows dark for a few moments, and then—all of a sudden—the curtain opens, the lights come on, and the audience sees a whole new world!

Whatever scene God's children are in, change is coming. We can find hope not only in that, but even more so in His promise that the final scene change will be phenomenal! Isn't this encouraging? No matter what happens to us on earth, we will come out ahead in the end as His children.

Who else can promise gain in loss? Who else can promise beauty in ugliness? Who else can promise joy in sorrow? Only God!

By dwelling daily on the promise of Romans 8:28, we can encourage ourselves in the Lord, no matter what. Something good is always going on with God.

SP (Sweet Pea): In this wild world we live in, many of us are in tight spots. You and I may be in one right now. We must pull together and refuse to let the enemy discourage us. I am sending a tight, holy hug to you today. If you belong to God in Christ, your biggest battle is won. Something good is going on in your life! Ask Him to give you hope to believe today.

Sweet Scars

Through suffering, our bodies continue to share in the death
of Jesus so that the life of Jesus may also be seen in our bodies.

2 CORINTHIANS 4:10

I'm going to guess that many of us have a few scars. It's impossible to survive many years in this world without bearing emotional or physical scars from the hurts we inevitably experience. While they may not look pretty to us, they remind us of a great truth: our scars can be signs of growth and can mirror the scars Jesus bore for us.

In *My Utmost for His Highest,* Oswald Chambers says, "It is better to enter into life maimed and lovely in God's sight than to appear lovely to man's eyes but lame to God's." I so want my "ugly" scars to reveal Jesus' beautiful character.

The difficult times in my life, along with the scars I still carry from walking through them, really did draw me closer to the Lord and fertilize the desire in me to live for Him. I can recognize some of the beauty that has already emerged from those scars.

No one feels good right after surgery, but with each suffering situation, we can gain patience and courage as we submit to the Lord. We always need patience and courage when we give our whole selves to the Lord—for His plans and not our own. It is easier to accept physical and emotional suffering when we know it has been filtered through His hands that were nailed to the cross for us. He took on the surgery of the whole sinful world.

As we allow Jesus' love to glow through our scars, He beautifies those symbols of pain and glorifies Himself to a wounded world in need of His healing.

We have suffering in common with Jesus. Ask Him to glow beautifully through your scars today.

SP (Sweet Pea): If you know of some product that diminishes actual physical scars, I would love to know about it. I love sweet tips.

Good Medicine

A cheerful heart is good medicine,
but a broken spirit saps a person's strength.

PROVERBS 17:22

When I was going through chemotherapy, I wanted to reassure my daughter of God's kind care for me even when I looked different—without any hair, eyelashes, or eyebrows. (Boy, did I ever learn some new makeup skills!)

I explained to her that the chemotherapy was "good medicine," and losing my hair was a sign that the good medicine was working, killing the good cells as well as the bad cancer cells. Also, I assured her of my gratefulness to God for all the doctors and nurses that He had provided to give me the medicine.

But just as surely as there is good medicine, there is also bad medicine. Some medicines can immediately offer lifesaving benefits. Others, if used incorrectly, can cause death. As important as it is to have the correct medicine for our physical bodies, it's more critical to know what we need for our spiritual health.

How in the world can we call in a prescription for a joyful heart? By obediently remaining in Jesus' love (John 15:9-11) and taking our needs to God in Jesus' name (John 16:24). Now, *that's* good medicine! I have never had a cheerful heart when I've disobeyed God's Word. I have never had a cheerful heart if I have refused to forgive someone or if I have lost my temper and failed to make it right. However, I have experienced joy when I have lived by God's Word and entrusted my needs to Him.

True joy comes from living in close fellowship with the Lord, which includes obeying and trusting Him. We cannot manufacture this "good medicine" on our own. It comes from a personal relationship with Jesus Christ.

We can keep a cheerful, joyful heart in our "good medicine" cabinets by being obedient to Christ's commands and trusting Him with our needs.

Good News Girl

[Jesus] said to his disciples, "The harvest is great, but the workers are few."
MATTHEW 9:37

Right now I have on my "so excited" face, thankful to be a worker in God's fields with all believers. No matter what field or occupation, we are all full-time Christian workers as children of God. He says His fields are ripe for harvest and we're His workers, His "God girls."

We are God's girls who know the Good News, that God loved us so much that His Son gave His life for us. There is a lot of sweet work involved in sharing His love. But guess what? God does all the truly hard work—the "heart" work—in people's lives. It is clear that the Lord is in charge of the harvest. We get to go along for the sweet ride, praying and working wholeheartedly together for the Lord.

What does this work look like? Some workers plant the seeds of the Good News by sharing about their hope in Jesus, then more workers come and water these seeds with the truth of salvation. As these seeds sprout and interest in Jesus grows, other workers provide support and answer questions. When hearts are ready to accept the Good News of salvation in Jesus, some workers help guide them toward this life-changing decision. Unless we are willing to go out into the fields and work together, we may miss the opportunity to share God's love by planting tiny sweet seeds, watering them, or fertilizing them for growth.

As God's girls, our first joyful job is to pray for more workers in the fields God has given us and start sowing. Sow sweet!

Let's not forget that God is in charge of the harvest. We have the joy of being God's girls with Good News! Who will you cross paths with today out in the literal field where He has planted you? Remember, He can use you for His Kingdom work.

Power to Share, Power to Trust

Jesus told him, "Because you have seen me, you have believed;
blessed are those who have not seen and yet have believed."

JOHN 20:29, NIV

One summer when our family was traveling overseas, we had an especially trying day. We had been stuck in the airport and then the car for nearly the entire day. We couldn't wait to arrive at our hotel. Needless to say, sharing the gospel was not the first thing on my mind.

When we arrived hot, tired, and dirty at our hotel, we were greeted by two older men at the front desk. We checked in and then asked them for recommendations on what to see in the area. "Our city isn't known for anything," one man replied. Since he seemed to be apologizing for it, I tried to encourage him. "Well, I saw a beautiful old church not far from here."

"Yes, but I'm not interested in church and faith. I believe in only what I can see."

My husband, Mark, said to the man that he sounded like Thomas, one of Jesus' disciples, who expressed similar doubts. With my heart thumping, I trusted God to help me communicate the Good News to the hotel clerk in a sentence or two. It wasn't perfect or fancy, but I proceeded to share the hope within me. John 20:29 seemed to be a verse written with him in mind.

I don't know how God used my weak efforts, but I trust that He used His Word that I offered to nudge the man one step closer to Himself. God promises His Word will never return void.

I'm amazed that God is always ready to use us to share His love with others. It does not matter if we are weary and our thoughts aren't connecting as clearly as when we are fully rested. God empowers us to offer His truth and trust Him to work—and to trust Him still today with the results, even though we may not ever see them.

Let's pay attention to God's divine appointments to share Him with others—even late at night in strange places. Trust that it isn't up to us; we just need to be willing for Him to work through us. "'Not by might nor by power, but by My Spirit,' says the LORD" (Zechariah 4:6, NKJV).

I've Had Enough

[Elijah] came to a broom tree, sat down under it and prayed
that he might die. "I have had enough, LORD," he said.

1 KINGS 19:4, NIV

I must admit that sometimes I laugh out loud when I am reading God's Word.
I had that reaction when I pondered today's verse.

How many times have I said those exact words to God? "I have had enough,
Lord!" I laugh when I see myself in Bible stories, even when God uses the examples
to pierce my heart, exposing my sin and my need to ask for His forgiveness. But
I also see how personal God is and how much He loves me!

Elijah was afraid and running for his life when he just plopped down under
a tree and prayed to die. I've shared about the difficulties and discouragement
I dealt with during our early years of marriage. Mark and I were both believers in
Christ but total opposites, and my expectations were off the charts. I remember
thinking we committed ourselves out loud to God and in front of a lot of people,
and we committed for better or worse, for richer or poorer, in sickness and in
health, till death do us part. Well, that very year we had the poorer, the sickness,
and the worse, so the death part looked good! Seriously!

I really felt like I'd had enough. But what happened to Elijah happened to me.
God came through then, and He hasn't stopped yet! In the rest of 1 Kings 19 we
see specifically the kindness of God toward Elijah. God fed him, talked with him,
listened to his complaint, gave him courage, and provided assistance. God can do
all those things and more for us.

God is always enough! If you're feeling weary today, ask God
to surprise you with His provision.

Makeover Takeover: Cleansing and Hydrating

*You were cleansed; you were made holy; you were
made right with God by calling on the name of the
Lord Jesus Christ and by the Spirit of our God.*

1 CORINTHIANS 6:11

It's spa day! Our beauty treatment today is not just a makeover, but a *takeover* of
the heart. We are going to apply these cleansing and hydrating tips together as a
whimsical way to put God's Word into our hearts. These tips really are a beautifying treatment of the heart that only God in Christ can do. We can always use
some freshening up to the glory of God!

Together we are going to discover how to look better with a few practical
beauty tips and how to be sweeter on the inside to the glory of our great God.
This beautifying from the inside out explains why I call this a takeover instead
of merely a makeover.

Jesus wants to take over every area of our life as we submit to Him by faith.
When He does, His beauty shines through and glows on our face, even changing
the way we carry ourselves.

The takeover starts with a good cleansing. Each morning when we pull out
our washcloths or makeup-remover cloths, let's greet God and thank Him that He
has cleansed us and made us holy. As we apply toner, let's thank Him for gently
removing any dry layers of sin that block His glow. Finally, as we smooth on
moisturizing cream, let's be reminded to apply the hydrating power of His Word
on a daily basis.

Jesus is our Takeover. He is the only makeover we need for eternity. We can
wear our heart's glow on our faces now!

⚷ Makeover? Who needs it? Jesus is our Takeover! Buy yourself some
new moisturizing cream (with sunscreen) and make sure to apply
God's hydrating Word to your heart as well.

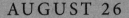
Makeover Takeover: Foundation

Whoever is building on this foundation must be very careful. For no one can lay any foundation other than the one we already have—Jesus Christ.

1 CORINTHIANS 3:10-11

I had so much fun at spa day yesterday that I think we ought to continue it today with some help about our foundation.

It is amazing how many foundation formulas are available today. There are liquid and gel foundations, mineral powder foundations, mousse-like foam foundations, foundations with sunscreen, and anti-aging formulas. And the colors—such variety!

I need help from an expert to choose the right foundation. Thinking about all the varieties makes my head spin. In fact, most days I am lazy about applying foundation and just don't do it because I have not taken the time to ask a professional for help to select the right color and formula.

There is only one Foundation that we all need. Jesus Christ is the Foundation that fits everyone! He is the only Person capable of creating the right Foundation for life. He shields us from the winds and weather that storm around us and ensures that our beauty will last. He keeps us from absorbing the dirt and debris we are certain to encounter.

As our Foundation, He stays on forever, which is wonderful news to wake up to every morning. Our Foundation is sure—a perfect match—a covering for our sin and a smoothing out of our rough spots.

Practical tip: if you are applying foundation this morning, always check under your nose in the mirror because foundation has a tendency to clog there. Now smile in the mirror because Jesus is your true Foundation! With Him you can literally face whatever comes your way, trusting that He will not fade in power.

Makeover Takeover: Concealers

Have mercy on me, O God, because of your unfailing love.
Because of your great compassion, blot out the stain of my sins.
Wash me clean from my guilt. Purify me from my sin.

PSALM 51:1-2

Concealers come in all shapes and sizes, and unlike foundation, I really enjoy wearing concealer because it hides more of my imperfections. Also unlike foundation, which is created for overall coverage, a concealer will cover the spots we don't like, hide our blemishes, and diminish the dark circles under our eyes or other signs of fatigue, giving us a refreshed look.

I love the way the right concealer seems to erase those pesky spots and imperfections that I have memorized on my face. They really bug me. However, after I apply concealer, it's as if they don't exist. They certainly lose their power to frustrate me and detract from my best look, but the imperfections are back the next day.

When we look in the mirror, let's thank God that He is not only our Foundation but our Concealer, too, covering our sin. His Holy Spirit continues the beautification work day by day by focusing on the stubborn spots in our hearts and minds. How's that for a makeover takeover?

Psalm 51:1-2 says that God blots out the stain of our sin. He erases it completely. Isn't that wonderful? The Lord doesn't just cover up our imperfections as our Concealer. He keeps us pure, spotless, and radiant as we live in love and obedience before God.

Memorize Psalm 51:1-2: "Have mercy on me, O God, because of your unfailing love. Because of your great compassion, blot out the stain of my sins. Wash me clean from my guilt. Purify me from my sin." Let's thank God as we apply concealer today that our sin was blotted out permanently when Jesus died on the cross for all our sin spots.

Makeover Takeover: Eyes

The eyes of the LORD are on the righteous, and
his ears are attentive to their cry.

PSALM 34:15, NIV

Today the eyes have it!

I think the application of eye makeup is the most time-consuming part of our makeover because it involves several stages. In fact, I just discovered one more step I need to add to my regimen. A friend just told me about using eye shadow primer to prevent eye shadow creases. Oh great, what else do I need to add to this already cumbersome routine?

After the primer comes the shadow and possibly liner. My sweet sister, Shawn, recommends brown shadow for liner, which she applies with a small paintbrush from a craft store. Apparently it doesn't smudge like the pencils! Mascara is next, and to top it all off, we can't forget our brows because they frame the eyes. Oops— I forgot the eyelash curler! Did you know that you can lightly heat your eyelash curler with your blow-dryer before curling lashes? It works great, as long as you test it first to make sure it's not too hot, or you'll burn your eyelid like I did!

Whether you're getting ready for the day or heading to bed, look straight in the mirror, child of God, and know that "the eyes of the LORD are on the righteous, and his ears are attentive to their cry."

Those of us who are in Christ are the righteous, in right standing with God. His eyes are zeroed in on you and me, and He hears every cry of our heart, silent or sobbing! He sees when our eyes sparkle with His love and joy. He sees when they fill with tears of sorrow.

When we "put on our eyes," let's remember that God's eyes are on us. Let's keep our eyes open to see how we can love others with His love.

God's eyes are always on you and me! Who will you see today who needs someone like you to notice and care?

Makeover Takeover: Cheeks

If someone slaps you on one cheek, offer the other cheek also.
If someone demands your coat, offer your shirt also.

LUKE 6:29

A makeover takeover would not be complete without blush. When applying blush, it's important that we turn the other cheek . . . so that it will be the same color!

Of course, we know that Jesus is not giving us a beauty tip about blush in this verse from Luke. He commands us to turn the other cheek in Luke 6:29 as part of His Sermon on the Mount.

When Jesus takes over our hearts, He asks us to do something that's possible only with His help. He says, "Love your enemies! Do good to those who hate you. Bless those who curse you. Pray for those who hurt you" (Luke 6:27-28).

I can see some of us saying to ourselves in the mirror, "Say what? Really? Love our enemies? Lord, that is hard!" Yes, it is. But Jesus doesn't ask us to do anything He hasn't done for us. He loved us when we didn't love Him, and He still shows us incredible grace and patience and forgiveness.

Not only does Jesus ask us to turn the other cheek, He says that we are to go the extra mile, too. "Give to anyone who asks; and when things are taken away from you, don't try to get them back. Do to others as you would like them to do to you" (verses 30-31). Right in the middle of Jesus' sermon, He mentions what we now call the Golden Rule.

Turning the other cheek is easy when it comes to makeup, but we definitely need the Holy Spirit's power in our hearts to love our enemies. That's when we say, "Jesus, take over!"

🔑 We share the same makeup bag in Christ! Turn the other cheek . . . without blushing. We'll be amazed at how Jesus can work for good when we follow His example, even when it's very difficult.

Makeover Takeover: Lips

My lips will praise You.

PSALM 63:3, NASB

"Lord, please take over my lips!"

Throughout each day I find myself saying that to God. Oh, if I could just conquer this area of my life once and for all, I'd never say anything regrettable. How lovely that would be!

But every day I wake up to find that I am still human, and I will continue to make mistakes and sin with my lips, even though I sincerely want lips of praise that bring glory and honor to the Lord at all times. That will happen one day in heaven.

The Bible contains quite a few references about our lips, our mouths, and our tongues. That's because they can get us in a lot of trouble and hurt people. But no human being can tame the tongue. James 3:8-9 says, "It is restless and evil, full of deadly poison. Sometimes it praises our Lord and Father, and sometimes it curses those who have been made in the image of God."

I have presented this "BeautyFull Makeover Takeover" message many times to groups of women, and when I ask them what one beauty item they would not leave home without, lipstick usually wins hands down. (I have a lot of tubes of lipstick, but I am still searching for that one that *really* stays on for twenty-four hours. Thanks for your recommendations, Sweet Debbie and Kat!)

Each day we need to continually apply praise for God on our lips. We can be encouraged that when Jesus comes into our life by faith, He stays with us 24/7 and helps us control what we say. When we're busy praising Him, it's much harder for negative words to slip out of our mouths. I look forward to nonstop praise someday in God's presence!

 Pull out your lipstick and praise God! As you apply color, ask Him to apply His Spirit's guard over your mouth as well so that only sweet words of grace are spoken.

Makeover Takeover: Sweet Perfume

*Thank God! He has made us his captives and continues to lead us
along in Christ's triumphal procession. Now he uses us to spread
the knowledge of Christ everywhere, like a sweet perfume.*

2 CORINTHIANS 2:14

Last but not least in our makeover takeover is sweet perfume. We all want to
smell good, and we associate certain scents with memorable experiences, much
like we do with food. In fact, one Sunday at church, our pastor Steve started his
sermon something like this: "I love food! Food is very important to me, and the
reason I know it is important to me is because I can remember certain meals."
I was thinking, *I love smells—good ones—and I know fragrances are important
because I associate certain fragrances with sweet experiences.*

As a child, when I would visit Aunt Doris and Uncle Eddie in Hickory, North
Carolina, I would anticipate going into their powder room because Aunt Doris
redecorated it every year. She changed the color scheme, coordinating the towels
and candles with the wall color. What I remember most is that it always smelled
so good. It was the scent of Dove soap. To this day, every time I smell her brand
of soap, I recall special memories.

Fragrances are important to us, and they are to God, too. Perfumes should not
be so overpowering that they give people headaches; when properly used, they
gently invite others toward the source.

God actually uses us to spread the knowledge of Him everywhere as a sweet
perfume. We are to have a Christlike fragrance (2 Corinthians 2:15) that invites
others to the Source of our joy, peace, hope, acceptance, truth, grace, and love.
Whenever we dab on perfume, let's remember that our lives can disperse the love
of Christ into this world that craves His freshness.

> We always smell beautiful to God in Christ, so let's spread His
> fragrance to others who need His sweet love! Spray lightly (don't
> splash) your favorite scent on a small piece of paper and put it
> in your car or in your desk drawer as a reminder to smell sweetly
> of Christ.

Sweet Invitation

Come, follow me, and I will show you how to fish for people!
MATTHEW 4:19

I love receiving personal invitations to events. When I see words like "Please join us," I want to respond immediately. Whenever possible, I try to honor the person who invited me and attend.

In this verse from Matthew, Jesus was recruiting His disciples with an invitation to "come." God has never stopped inviting people to follow Him. His followers are asked to carry His invitation with them and extend it to others—first to believe in Him and then to grow in Him. Did anyone's invitation initiate your faith journey?

Recently my friend Donna told me that she did not realize the significance of receiving an invitation until a friend personally invited her to a Bible study with some other moms whose children attended the same school as her young children. She said, "I had heard about it, but I never would have just walked in. It was only because she personally invited me that I decided to go." It was so surprising to me to hear someone like her—one of those "very beautiful people"—say how grateful she was to receive an invitation. The Bible study has been such a blessing in her life, and she is growing in her love for the Lord.

Jesus is our model and our guide. He modeled the gift of offering an invitation by saying, "Come," and He invites us to follow Him and fish for people. We really do need each other, not only to accomplish His work but for relationship too. Someone may need an invitation today, and you may be the ideal person to offer it.

Follow Jesus and fish for people! Always be ready to extend an invitation to someone who needs to hear about Him. That's why I started Sweet Monday in my home. I always have something sweet, simple, and fun to invite women to, no shoestrings attached. They do not have to do one thing—just come.

Stepping over the Setbacks

Then as I looked over the situation, I called together the nobles and the rest of the people and said to them, "Don't be afraid of the enemy! Remember the Lord, who is great and glorious, and fight for your brothers, your sons, your daughters, your wives, and your homes!"

NEHEMIAH 4:14

Have you ever headed up a project where things seem to be going smoothly, and then suddenly everything comes apart at the seams? When I am in those situations and am ready to throw up my hands in defeat and physically want to throw up from stress, I take a cue from Nehemiah.

What a crisis call Nehemiah gave to rally his "God troops"! Nehemiah is a good example of strong leadership and perseverance, and I am fascinated to watch him organize those under him. The way he communicated with his team makes me want to be on the front lines with him. Nehemiah was a leader who prayed and acted with great courage, even when he faced great opposition.

Nehemiah pointed people toward God to reinforce their courage: "Remember the Lord, who is great and glorious." (That would make a sweet tweet!) First Nehemiah prayed, and then he evaluated the situation for rebuilding the Temple, knowing full well that God's people would continue to be targeted by their enemies. So he prepared his workers by reminding them who was really in control of their work and their future!

Even though I am not a contractor, I really enjoyed reading Nehemiah's "business plan and blueprints." He persevered even when things slowed down. When troubles fell at his feet, he helped the people learn to step over the barricades of opposition and continue moving forward in faith.

God's people can always expect opposition—it's part of our faith journey as well as life in general. Because we live in a broken and hurting world, we face a spiritual battle every day, being waged outside our personal walls as well as right smack within our walls. We need to remember not to be discouraged when things don't go exactly as planned, but instead, to live with the courage and perseverance of Nehemiah.

Remember that the Lord fights for you and me, and do not be afraid.

Can't Trust Technology

Those who know your name trust in you,
for you, O Lord, do not abandon those who search for you.

PSALM 9:10

Oh my, the time I have wasted double-checking technology. I can't be the only person in the world who checks the "Sent" file to see if an important e-mail went through or who scrolls through the list of text messages to see if the text really did go where it was supposed to go. It is mind boggling to think about how typewritten words can travel to distant places in a matter of seconds! *How do they do that?*

As much as I appreciate technology for quickly and efficiently sending communications, the truth is that if I'm always checking up on it, it means I really don't trust it completely. Maybe being a little skeptical is a good thing, because technology is not always trustworthy.

Only Jesus Christ is completely trustworthy. Only He is 100 percent reliable all the time! When we pray, which is simply talking to Him, we don't ever have to wonder if our prayers arrived, if He heard us, or if He will misread the messages of our hearts. His signal is always strong, and He always replies in the way and time He knows is best for us.

I am very thankful that when we confess our sins, He deletes them from memory. The God we trust doesn't merely put them in the trash file, where He can retrieve them later. He totally erases them, and there are no archived copies!

No matter how impressive human technology appears, it changes constantly and forces us to update and relearn its ways. God, on the other hand, is constant and always cutting edge—He simply cannot be improved on. His Holy Spirit is our personal Instructor and Troubleshooter who never crashes when we bring our issues to Him.

Let's thank the Lord for all the wonderful ways technology allows us to communicate about Him, and then ask Him to remind us daily to put our wholehearted trust in Him alone.

The Three Rs

I tell you the truth, unless you are born again,
you cannot see the Kingdom of God.

JOHN 3:3

Even though September is back-to-school time for most students, I am not referring to the well-known three Rs associated with education: *r*eading, *w*riting, and *a*rithmetic. I am thinking about a different set of three Rs: *R*eborn and *R*econstructed because of the *R*esurrection!

Once we are reborn spiritually through Christ, we spend the rest of our lives on this earth being reconstructed to look more like Him. It's only because of His resurrection that we are able to be reborn and receive resurrected bodies when our earthly ones die.

The actual resurrection of Jesus from the grave is the most important fact in history. At first, even Jesus' disciples, His closest friends, didn't believe what had happened. But when they were convinced that He was alive again, they began to experience His spiritual reconstruction that molded their character and strengthened their faith. They became rock-solid followers of Jesus who shared with individuals and crowds the good news of salvation and eternal life. Thousands believed and died to defend that belief. Because of the three Rs, we have

- *Assurance of eternal life.* Disease and death can't take it away from us.
- *Hope.* What we are experiencing now isn't all there is to life. There is so much more to look forward to in our eternal home in heaven with the Lord.
- *Protection and provision.* God protects and meets the needs of His children.
- *Abundant life.* No matter what difficulties we are dealing with, God provides joy and peace smack-dab in the middle of them all!
- *Companionship.* We are His and He is ours!

These promises are ours, given to us by the world's greatest Teacher, who still lives—Jesus.

Remember the three Rs. We are being Reborn and Reconstructed, and we will one day be Resurrected!

Picking Priorities: Simple, Sweet, and Salty

Seek the Kingdom of God above all else, and live righteously.
MATTHEW 6:33

How in the world do I wisely arrange my days, hours, and minutes—coordinating schedules and responsibilities—and still find time to rest? There's much to accomplish. As I find myself daily being attentive to both my family's needs and my work schedule, I must stop and ask myself whether my days are reflecting my priorities.

Years ago when I was a student, my ears perked up during a sermon in church when the pastor said, "There are only three things that are going to last in this world: God, His Word, and people."

Right then I decided my life's priorities. Little did that pastor know how much God would use him to help me make daily decisions and choices for the rest of my life. Why would I want to invest my time in anything that doesn't matter? His words come back to me frequently and prompt me to consider my everyday priorities:

- Am I seeking the things of God above all else?
- Why would I want to invest my time and resources in anything that isn't going to last?
- Are the things that are important to God important to me, no matter what my occupation, and do I work with God's eternal mind-set?
- Do I crave God's Word, knowing it truly is sweeter than anything else?
- Do I live as salt among the people in my life, looking for ways God can use me to help create a thirst for Him in them?

This list helps me apply that pastor's wisdom from the Bible to keep God, His Word, and people as top priorities. When we filter our schedules through this checklist of the heart, we can adjust our time according to God's priorities for us.

 Pick eternal priorities with simple, sweet, and salty lives for Jesus Christ.

Fresh and Flourishing

Even in old age they will still produce fruit;
they will remain vital and green.

PSALM 92:14

When I read this verse I think of Sweet Fannie Lou! She is eightysomething, and still fresh and flourishing in her faith, still giving her best for God to use.

She once told me, "I do not cook. I do not clean. But I sew!" And sew she does! She makes the most gorgeous slipcovers you have ever seen and gives the profits from her sales to God. She loves the Lord, and she serves so many women. She is my "Dorcas." (You can read about the biblical Dorcas in Acts 9:36-41.) Dorcas was one of those followers of Christ in the early church who remained vital and green, still producing fruit in old age.

God is so good to enrich our lives with older friends who are fresh and flourishing. What gifts they are to us! As much as I want to be like them, I must admit that I have had some minibattles with the aging process. I have ordered a few beauty creams when I have been in a physically weakened state. After my surgery, at a very weak moment, I did a little shopping off the hospital-room television in the middle of the night after seeing before-and-after pictures of women reflecting great results from those creams. Out came the credit card! Suffice it to say, the cream to reduce dimples did not work. The product for under your eyes to "hold them up" did not work either.

But sweet friend, I take courage in the fact that, far more than beauty creams, Christ Himself keeps us fresh and flourishing as we follow Him. My friend Fannie Lou is living proof of His beautifying power in a willing life.

We have everything to look forward to as we grow older in Him but remain vital and green. He wants to continue to bless others through us to our last day on this earth!

Fresh and flourishing—I'll take it! Write a note to a fresh and flourishing older woman in your life, thanking her for the wonderful example she has been of giving God all.

Caught and Dismissed

Jesus stood up again and said to the woman, "Where are your accusers? Didn't even one of them condemn you?" "No, Lord," she said. And Jesus said, "Neither do I. Go and sin no more."

JOHN 8:10-11

Have you ever been caught "accidentally" speeding? Maybe you missed the sign and were unaware that the speed limit had changed. Maybe no other cars were around and you were preoccupied. Maybe your foot was a little heavier because you were closer to home, and your speed picked up just like a horse's does when he can see his home barn ahead. (Is that why they call it horsepower in cars?)

Even when my car is on cruise control, my heart drops when I hear a police car's siren or catch a glimpse of flashing lights in my rearview mirror. As I quickly double-check my speedometer, I think, *Lord, please don't let it be me!* None of us wants to be caught, but if we are, we hold our breath until the officer either writes us a ticket or just gives us a warning. It's always a sweet relief when neither happens and he whizzes by me, with another agenda in mind. (I hope it's not sweet you!)

In John 8, a woman caught in adultery was brought before Jesus to be killed by stoning. Jesus' response? "Let the one who has never sinned throw the first stone!" (verse 7). Talk about a reality check! The accusers silently slinked away. When Jesus asked the woman—the only person left—if anyone accused her, she could honestly say no. "Neither do I," replied Jesus. "Go and sin no more" (verse 11).

No matter the sin, God's grace, mercy, and kindness is extended to us equally. We still need Him to forgive and dismiss our sin instead of condemning us. Just as He told the woman in John 8, we must "go and sin no more."

Being eternally released from the penalty of our sin is worth celebrating. Although we may still face consequences in this life for the wrong things we do, we can trust that God forgives us when we repent. He is ready to help us change our course and make decisions that please Him.

Choose Thankfulness

*Give thanks for everything to God the Father in
the name of our Lord Jesus Christ.*

EPHESIANS 5:20

I am literally sitting in a corner, all boxed in, on a writing deadline. There are tarps covering the furniture around me, except for the small sofa I am sitting on. Roofers are hammering away on our twenty-year-old roof that came with a thirty-five-year warranty that is now null and void—the company is no longer in business!

All the estimates that we received from other roofing companies confirmed that, yes, we needed a new roof. Apparently it was not put on correctly the first time. Who knew that important information but God and the original roofers? I am writing while waiting for the drywall installers to arrive and repair the damage inside our home caused by the leaky roof.

I'm having trouble finding a quiet place where I can think. Mark's day began when his sleep was interrupted by the sounds of the workmen, and he walked in here and found me hidden behind all the tarps. There was so much noise we both burst out laughing to keep from crying.

Lord, what can I learn in all this mess about You? About me? About my response? This is not a catastrophe but an inconvenience in a world where I take conveniences for granted!

What is a God's girl supposed to do in such a physical mess? His answer? Choose thankfulness!

Thank You, Lord, that we have a home to fix!

Thank You, Lord, that You see me in the corner, and You understand and care about the details in my life. You aren't distant. You're right here with me!

Thank You, Lord, that You are constructing me to look more like Christ. My life can be in a mess, but in Your grace and mercy, You are the only One who makes good out of ugly (Romans 8:28).

And thank You, Lord, that You always make good on Your eternal lifetime warranty in Jesus Christ!

Let's choose thankfulness! Jot down your own thanksgiving list today!

I'm In!

*Jesus said to the people who believed in him, "You are truly
my disciples if you remain faithful to my teachings. And you
will know the truth, and the truth will set you free."*

JOHN 8:31-32

*I'm in, Lord, I'm in, I'm in! I believe You are talking to me. I want to remain faithful
to Your teaching and, more important, faithful to You!*

No half-pint living for me! I want to be a gallon jug of sweet tea, filled to overflowing, that is fresh every day and perpetually full so it can be continually poured
out to others. I would call that kind of living about as abundant as it can be!

To experience this abundance requires that we grow to be faithful, but what
does being faithful look like? *Faithful* is an adjective, a part of speech that describes
another word. A faithful person is one who is reliable, dependable, firm, sure,
unswerving, conscientious, and steadfast—all qualities that describe Jesus. I love
being around God's faithful people, don't you? They look like Christ, and He is
beautifully apparent in those who are faithfully His.

Living in complete faithfulness is a choice. Choosing God's way over our own
requires multiple decisions every day, but they are the best decisions you and I
can make!

The Holy Spirit inside of us is the One who gives us this desire to remain completely faithful. The only way you and I can stay true to Christ is to stay attached
to Him, our faithful Vine, as He pours Himself into us. He is 100 percent dependable, firm, sure, unswerving, conscientious, and steadfast. When we let Him have
His way in us, we will grow in faithfulness.

Consider for a few moments what your life—and this whole world, for
that matter—would be like if God were less than 100 percent faithful.
Thank Him that because He is all in, through Him we can be all in
too!

God Delights in You and Me

He rescued me because he delights in me.

PSALM 18:19

Psalm 18:19 reminds me of a day when God showed my daughter and me how much He delights in us as His children and loves to hear from us.

One afternoon Kali and I were window-shopping in a sleepy town with many meandering streets. We wanted to revisit a secondhand shop we had discovered by car, but when we tried to find it again on foot after parking far from the store, we couldn't remember quite where it was. We had lost our bearings.

Knowing that God knew right where we were at that very minute, I just asked Him in a whispered prayer to show us the way if He wanted to. I told Him it wasn't a problem if He didn't, but I at least wanted to ask since He knows everything. Imagine our excitement when we "just happened" to stumble across the shop a few minutes later!

My daughter congratulated me on finding it, but guess who really deserved the credit? Maybe God tells us to pray about everything so we can witness Him providing and feel His delight toward us. We didn't *need* to find the store, but He knew it would be special to us if we did.

It was like our big God of the whole messy world led us there for no other reason than because He delighted in us! Even if He hadn't helped us find the shop, He still delighted in us and heard my prayer.

God delights in sweet you, too. He cannot help it. His pleasure in us is another characteristic of a perfect Father who loves each of His children in the most lavish way possible. His love never fails. His love is a constant for those who belong to Him.

We can pray about everything, since prayer is simply talking to God. He's right here. God loves when we run things by Him that are important to us. He loves us, and He should always get the credit for His answers, whether it is *yes*, *no*, or *wait*. Revel in the fact that He delights in you right now!

Words Tucked in My Heart

I have hidden your word in my heart.

PSALM 119:11

As a family, we all learned Scripture in the car when Kali was a toddler by listening to Steve Green's *Hide 'Em in Your Heart* tapes. I have trouble remembering Bible verses, especially the references, so those lively songs were as profitable for me as they were for our daughter. I still find myself humming them in my mind or singing them when I'm alone in the car. Those words came in handy for me on a tragic day we all remember.

My daughter was in fourth grade at the time, and I had the parent privilege of going with her class on their long-awaited field trip to George Washington's home in Mount Vernon, Virginia. It was the morning of September 11, 2001.

Kali, several friends, and I were seated in the very back of the bus. When we got to Mount Vernon, which is only thirteen miles from the Pentagon, the bus driver parked outside the entrance, and we all waited to get off the bus. As the minutes passed, we started wondering why we weren't getting off the bus. Finally, we heard the news about what had happened in New York City and at the Pentagon.

As the shock started to seep in, the words tucked in my heart from one of the songs came to mind: "When I am afraid, I will trust in you" (based on Psalm 56:3). By God's grace, I was able to comfort my daughter and tell her God's truth. It didn't change the tragic circumstances or reverse what had happened. But it reminded us that God is in control! We could recall His promises and comfort because these words were hidden in both of our hearts.

We didn't see Mount Vernon that day. Our bus driver immediately turned around and took us back to school, and the children were given the rest of the day off. What a comfort we have in God's Word. We can take it anywhere in our hearts and know we can trust the One who gave it to us. He's a loving God in an unpredictable world, and He has given us not only eternal salvation but earthly peace as well through Christ Jesus, His only Son.

Put Psalm 56:3 in your heart: "When I am afraid, I will put my trust in You." On this anniversary of 9/11, ask God to comfort those families who are still mourning their great loss as God grieves with them too.

Parting the Red Sea

When Pharaoh finally let the people go, God did not lead them along the main road that runs through Philistine territory, even though that was the shortest route to the Promised Land. God said, "If the people are faced with a battle, they might change their minds and return to Egypt." So God led them in a roundabout way through the wilderness toward the Red Sea. Thus the Israelites left Egypt like an army ready for battle.

EXODUS 13:17-18

This story of God delivering His people from the oppressive Egyptians is very encouraging. God gave Moses instructions, and the Israelites followed Moses the long way around via a desert road toward the Red Sea!

I have a quirky attraction to this passage because I have my own Red Sea parting in the back of my scalp, created by a very determined cowlick! When Kali was younger, I'd frequently ask her, "Is my Red Sea showing?" Every hairdresser I went to heard the same mantra: "Will you please cut my hair to hide the Red Sea?"

Like my own Red Sea, this passage can be a visual reminder to us that we can trust God's route, whatever it is. Maybe we feel as if we are on a desert road heading toward the unknown, or maybe we've reached the Red Sea, and we are trapped in front of extremely rough waters with no place to go.

Rest assured that God always sees what is ahead. For Moses and the Israelites, there was a shorter route out of Egypt, but it meant they would have to travel through enemy territory. God directed them to the desert for their protection. The shorter, easier way is not always better for us, either. If we belong to God and desire His direction, we can be sure no matter what His route, He is guiding us safely toward His best for us!

Only God can part the Red Sea and lead us on the right route, roundabout or not. If you are struggling with an important decision, ask Him to show you the next faith step He wants you to take. Even if you can't see what's ahead, He can.

God Is Rich!

God is so rich in mercy, and he loved us so much, that even though we were dead because of our sins, he gave us life when he raised Christ from the dead. (It is only by God's grace that you have been saved!)

EPHESIANS 2:4-5

God is rich in everything! And if you're His child, then so are you! How's that for good news in our struggling economy?

It's true. God's riches are vast and uncountable, and they all belong to His children. Those who love Him as Savior and Lord have all the benefits as heirs, and we can claim many parts of our inheritance today.

He makes His children rich in mercy, loaded with His kindness, wealthy in compassion, overflowing in grace, abundantly forgiven, and invested with hope. His affluence cannot be measured. We cannot fathom the lavishness of His love for us.

God is so magnificent and infinite, and we are so puny and poor. In His richness, He became poor for our sakes. He did not have to. Right now we can lay hold of all the riches He is pouring out upon us and trust that He will forever overflow those to us because He is inexhaustible. His wealth of wisdom, mercy, grace, love, and truth—everything good and right and pure and lovely—is ours through Christ. Because He loves us, He cannot help but give us His best.

Even though shoestring budgets are becoming the norm in our economy, God never operates on one. He doesn't skimp and never shortchanges us or withholds Himself from us. He never has to pinch and scrape and save to keep His resources from running out.

As I list His riches off the top of my head, my heart starts racing with joy. My heart can hardly hold His wealth, but I can be thankful that every day He's growing my heart larger to hold more of Himself.

Bank on being the richest girl in the world in Jesus Christ. No matter what your bank account holds today, you are wealthy by God's Kingdom standards if you are His child. Ask Him for more of Himself today. Now take that to the bank!

God Does All the Hard Work

We don't know what God wants us to pray for. But the Holy Spirit prays for us with groanings that cannot be expressed in words. And the Father who knows all hearts knows what the Spirit is saying, for the Spirit pleads for us believers in harmony with God's own will.

ROMANS 8:26-27

When my daughter was applying to colleges, she asked me where I thought she should go. I told her I honestly did not know what God had in mind for her, but I knew His choice was best for her, and that if she asked Him for wisdom, He certainly would give it. I prayed God's best for her and that He would direct her steps as she trusted in Him. I also pointed her to Proverbs 3:5-6: "Trust in the LORD with all your heart; do not depend on your own understanding. Seek his will in all you do, and he will show you which path to take." What Christian mother doesn't want God's good, pleasing, and perfect will for her children (Romans 12:2)?

When all we can do is ask God to be Himself, He will be true and guide us as He knows best. God does all the hard work, even in prayer! This passage is comforting to me because I can relate to what Paul said in Romans 8. Like him, I don't always know what God wants me to pray for. The power in prayer comes from God. He always knows what good, pleasing, and perfect thing is needed in every single situation, and He knows that my heart wants His best.

I know He is sovereign over all that happens and He will always do the right thing. He cares about me and the people I love, about our country and our world. You and I can truly bring everything to Him in prayer, whether our requests are spoken out loud or silently, under our breath or in our minds. The Spirit of God does all the hard work and pleads for us believers in sync with God's own will.

When life's direction looks unclear, keep praying and trusting God to show you His will, which will never veer from His Word! Then wait for His peace and expect His answer as you move forward in faith.

Paralyzed by Fear

*The LORD is my light and my salvation—so why
should I be afraid? The LORD is my fortress, protecting
me from danger, so why should I tremble?*

PSALM 27:1

One of our family's best friends, Skip Wilkins, was paralyzed in a waterskiing accident just after graduating from high school. A gifted athlete, he had been offered many college football scholarships, which could never be realized. He would never walk again, but Skip remained extremely active. Once when Skip and his sweet wife, Daphne, visited our home, I asked him to walk over and look at something. He said in his charming way, "Kim, I can't walk. Remember?" (God gave Skip such a wonderful perspective on life and a great sense of humor. Now he is walking on the streets of gold.)

Although I have the use of my legs, I faced many situations in my childhood and early adulthood when I was literally paralyzed by fear. At times I have been so immobilized by the fear of failure and what others think of me that I have been unable to walk by faith. I could not take the next step to follow through, make the phone call, or complete a responsibility.

People who know me now cannot believe that I walked off the stage at a piano recital without playing a note, or called the church's choir director days before the Christmas pageant and said, "I cannot sing Mary's part," or burst into tears before giving a speech to only fifteen people in my senior year of college!

The Lord changed me when I gave Him my whole heart and told Him I did not want to miss anything He had for me. Being available to Him required faith. He does not want us to be afraid. He promises to be our light and salvation, a stronghold we can count on.

When I think back to how fear used to control me, I have a hard time believing that in 2005 I shared the Good News in front of 7,250 people at a Sweet Monday Guinness World Record event—the world's largest tea party! God does amazing miracles when we give our hearts fully to Him.

Life is not a tea party, but we can encourage each other to fight fear with faith! Pray Psalm 27:1 until you feel the Lord's peace work through your fear.

Rescued from the Pit

He lifted me out of the pit of despair, out of the mud and the mire.
He set my feet on solid ground and steadied me as I walked along.

PSALM 40:2

I am convinced that opposites attract. When I married an extreme opposite, I felt like Mark truly was from Mars and I was from Venus. No wonder there seemed to be so much *space* between us. Our different ways of communicating and handling conflict were enough to land me in an emotional pit. He wanted to stay home, and I wanted to go out. He wanted a hamburger, and I wanted steak. He wanted to be quiet, and I wanted to talk. Imagine that. As more and more of our differences surfaced, I felt that I was falling into a pit that I couldn't escape. My pit was a rough start to marriage, followed by years of infertility.

I could identify with the story of Joseph. At the age of seventeen, Joseph was thrown into a pit or deep hole by his brothers. In the Bible, the word *pit* also is a reference to the actual place of hell, but more often, *pit* is used metaphorically to mean deep trouble, with no way out. That's how I felt those early years of marriage.

When my world collapsed, I camped in the book of Psalms because that's where I heard God speaking to me the most. I would read, cry, and laugh. It is also where many pit references are found, in the Psalms and Proverbs.

I searched the Bible, hoping God would show me a way of escape from my personal pit that would please Him. But there was no escape that would bring glory and honor to Him! As I struggled with my circumstances, it became clear to me that I was selfish. Only He could lift me out of this deep hole, set my feet on solid ground, and steady me. I'm so grateful that He did. No one else is able to do that kind of heavy lifting other than God!

Are you feeling that you are in a pit right now, in deep trouble with no way out? God will lift you out if you call on Him—in His way and His time! His way out of the pit is always the best way.

Practice Hospitality

Always be eager to practice hospitality.

ROMANS 12:13

Practice requires repetition. Romans 12:13 clearly says that we should always be eager to show hospitality, over and over again.

As I mentioned in other devotions, the past several weeks my house has been filled with workmen who are replacing our leaky roof. Because of the noise and inconvenience I'm dealing with, I'm not feeling as hospitable as I should. It seems like one more thing to cope with, and I'm physically tired.

Being a firm believer in God and the truthfulness of His Word, I want my faith to triumph over my feelings every time! When you and I step out in faith in practical ways, like doing something God tells us to do—even when we do not feel like it—joy always follows. Joy and obedience go hand in hand. I have never been joyful when I have not been obedient. God wired us to thrive only when we remain in Him (John 15:1-4).

Therefore, I am purposing to practice God's hospitable grace even in this situation that is stretching my patience. I'm thankful for the stash of cold canned drinks and water we keep available for whomever God may bring to our door. This week, all day long, convenient or not, I've been offering beverages to the roofers, the postal worker, and the trash collectors.

I am amazed at how many workmen have said a hearty yes! You know what? It was good for me to serve, even with deadlines and responsibilities and many interruptions. I needed the practice of living out what I believe. You may not be a soda girl, candy girl, or cookie queen, but you may bake a mean cinnamon bread like Sweet Sue or have a scrumptious store-bought snack available. Purpose to practice hospitality.

 Find your handy "signature snack," and be ready to practice hospitality, no matter how small the effort may seem.

God's Taste

Don't just pretend to love others. Really love them.
Hate what is wrong. Hold tightly to what is good.

ROMANS 12:9

Good taste is something I always want to have. However, sometimes when my creative juices are flowing, I can veer toward tacky, like using way too many "sweets" in my writing or too much pink in one place. There is nothing wrong with sweet pink, but there's something to be said for tasteful moderation. I appreciate the good taste of others so much—Sweet Faye's thoughtful gifts, Sweet Debbie's web smarts, and my sweet daughter's fashion sense.

When it comes to bigger issues of life, I want to strive for God's taste because His is always very good. In Romans 12:9, we see that God's taste is to love others, hate what is wrong, and hold tightly to what is good.

Over time, God develops our taste for what pleases Him as we conform to the image of Christ. Early in my faith journey, I had a lot to learn about discernment. Through the years, as I've gotten to know God personally through His Word, my conscience is pricked more about what is His taste and what is not.

If you are thinking now about whether or not some things in your own life reflect God's taste, that means the Holy Spirit is at work in you. That's a very, very good thing!

If we want God's taste reflected in our lives, we need to love people, hate what is wrong, and hold tightly to what is good.

Try this "good" word game with me: If we remove one little "o" from the word *good,* we get *God.* God and good are inseparable because God is always good and there is no real good apart from God! Reflect God's taste today.

God's Children

See how very much our Father loves us, for he calls us his children,
and that is what we are! But the people who belong to this world don't
recognize that we are God's children because they don't know him.

1 JOHN 3:1

Do you ever get stuck in a rut, feeling like you're nothing special? Like no one would miss you if you disappeared or that life would be better for others if you actually did? It's easy to feel dragged down by wounded self-esteem. My heart goes out to any and all of us who have had even fleeting feelings like that. Many people who don't feel special at all would do whatever they could to feel even moderately special. Imagine how much richer our lives would be if we understood how *incredibly* special we are to God!

Losing an earthly father or never knowing one does not mean we are no longer cherished by anyone. If we are God's children through our faith in Jesus, then we are 100 percent adopted into the family of Almighty God. God, our heavenly Father, treasures His children. When we dwell on the fact that we are very precious to God, our self-worth increases simply because we know we belong to Him.

And oh, how God wants us to belong to Him! He is the perfect Father for all His children, each son and daughter designed differently. And yet we all look the same to God, perfect in Christ Jesus.

He knows us inside and out because He uniquely designed us in His own image, for the extraordinary purpose of bringing Him glory.

 Rejoice today that in Christ we are part of God's family, His dearly loved children.

Sweet Ps

> *I will study your commandments and reflect on your ways.*
> *I will delight in your decrees and not forget your word.*
>
> PSALM 119:15-16

Psalm 119 is the longest psalm in the Bible, and as much as I would like to include it in its entirety here, there isn't enough room! These two verses from the psalm are great motivators—I don't want to miss a day of hearing God's voice through the pages of Scripture. How in the world can I delight in His decrees if I don't know them? How can I reflect on His ways if I do not know what God is like? How can I hear God's voice above all others if I don't recognize it?

In all honesty, I can't delight in something I don't understand or value simply because I'm told to do so. Our delight for something or someone is a gut-level response, a natural overflow of the heart. When I read God's Word daily, I come to know and love Him, which leads me to delight in what He says—just as today's Scripture says.

I don't ever want to forget His Word. But because I have an imperfect memory and a tendency to question and wonder, I need reminders of all the reasons why He's so worthy of my delight. Here are five Sweet P tips to cheer us all along in God's ways:

1. Prioritize. Let's make knowing God a priority. Knowing God is the purpose of reading His Word, which is accessible to everyone.
2. Pick a comfy spot in your home where you do not see the dishes and the laundry. Face a window or go outside. Have your Bible and a mug of coffee or tea handy.
3. Pray. Prayer is just talking to God: "Lord, will You teach me about Yourself when I open Your Word? Will You teach me about myself, and show me ways to put what You say into practice?"
4. Plunge in. Do not be afraid. He talks to all His people through His Word.
5. Put some sticky notes near your Bible to mark places that you want to return to as you flip back and forth through His truths.

🔑 Please join me in delighting daily in the Lord's decrees.

Pretty Out of Ugly

[God] has made everything beautiful in its time.

ECCLESIASTES 3:11, NIV

When I was growing up, my mother created a beautiful home and yard. Her organization and attention to detail inspired other people.

She told me before she died that sometimes Daddy couldn't find her when he came home from work. He would walk back to where our property ran into the woods and call out, "Honey, are you decorating the woods again?" One time I came home from middle school and was surprised by one of her creations—she had erected a floor-to-ceiling bookshelf between my younger sister's bed and mine so each of us would have our own space! Needless to say, we were delighted with the change and loved the new bedspreads and matching curtains she had added as well.

At Mom's funeral my sweet sister, Shawn, said, "Mama made pretty out of ugly." She said our mother was the only person she knew who could turn anything ugly into something of beauty. To my grieving ears, that skill sounded just like what God does! He makes pretty out of ugly too.

As wise Solomon tells us in today's verse, somehow in all the causes and effects of life, God—in His time, in His way, in His sweet providence—works out everything for beauty and good. In the many messes we find ourselves in, He is the only One who can make pretty out of ugly. Whether we are in a hospital bed awaiting a biopsy, estranged from a child, lonely, or grieving, God can bring beauty from it.

One of my wise mentor friends, Sweet Sherry, has a wonderful husband, Richard, going through early-onset Alzheimer's. She concludes all her e-mails with today's verse from Ecclesiastes, and my heart is encouraged every time we correspond.

Only God makes beautiful out of ugly. Only His people can model joy, hope, and trust through whatever challenges come their way.

Trust today that God makes everything beautiful in its time! Thank Him for His plan to create beauty from your pain and for His lovely presence with you today and always.

Holy Heat

For I, the LORD, am the one who brought you up from the land of Egypt, that I might be your God. Therefore, you must be holy because I am holy.

LEVITICUS 11:45

Have you ever taken a few shortcuts in completing a task to save precious time? To this day, my beautiful daughter has a little scar from trying to iron her clothes while they were still on! I wonder who she got that creative idea from!

I thought about this episode recently because I was ready to tackle a project—replacing the fabric lining in the special Lane cedar hope chest that my parents gave to me when I graduated from high school. Grabbing my staple gun, I laid the new fabric inside the chest and began fastening it. I was in a hurry to get it done, so I took a shortcut and did not iron the fabric first, thinking I could stretch the wrinkles out. It didn't take long to see that my shortcut wasn't working. It looked awful! I had to waste precious time pulling out all the staples, then I literally had to go back to the ironing board!

Every day I rely on the Lord to apply His holy heat to the wrinkles in my life, in order to shape me in a way that brings glory to Him. There are no shortcuts in living a holy life; we reflect the glory of God through His power and patient teaching. Our wrinkles are smoothed out by the gracious hand of our loving God. Ephesians 5:25-27 says, "Christ loved the church. He gave up His life for her to make her holy and clean, washed by the cleansing of God's word. He did this to present her to himself as a glorious church without a spot or wrinkle or any other blemish."

No doubt about it, God sees us as holy people in Jesus Christ. Whatever hard things that come into our lives as "holy heat" will be circumstances God will use to conform us to look more like Christ until all our earthly wrinkles are gone forever!

"Iron on, Lord!" Next time you iron a piece of clothing, ask God to reveal any stubborn wrinkles in your heart. Place them on His ironing board of holy heat.

First Grade

The Lord keeps you from all harm and watches over your life.
PSALM 121:7

Remember your first day of all-day school? When I went to school, first grade was the initiation into a full school day from eight to three. No more kindergarten luxuries like lunch at home and nap time!

I'll never forget walking into Mrs. Attridge's first-grade classroom, my hand holding firmly on to my mother's. I looked at the desks lined up, the big chalkboard, and the teacher's desk at the front of the room and was scared to death. Clinging to my mama's hand, I looked up at her and said, "Will you meet me when I come out?" She assured me that she would. Only then did I let go of her hand, and I kept my eye on her as she left the classroom and went into the hall.

A little while later, when Mrs. Attridge walked us out of the room to go to the restroom, I burst into tears. My mother wasn't there when I got out! In my six-year-old mind, I thought she was going to stand in the hall outside the classroom door and guard me *all* day long.

My kind teacher came over, wrapped me in her arms, and asked me what was wrong. In between my "boo hoos" I repeated, "My mom said she'd be here when I came out! My mom said she'd be here when I came out!" Mrs. Attridge said that my mom meant that she would be there to pick me up after school. And true to her word, my mother was there after school, reassuring and comforting me.

What is even more comforting is knowing that God is constantly on guard and will never leave us or forsake us. He has promised to be with us always, every minute of every day.

Thank God today that He never leaves us for a moment. He is watching over our lives at all times, guarding our ways and our hearts!

Heavenly Hand-Holding

I hold you by your right hand—I, the LORD your God.
And I say to you, "Don't be afraid. I am here to help you."

ISAIAH 41:13

Please tell me that you're like me: sometime when you were in your teens, if you went to a movie with a boy you liked, you strategically placed your hand so that it was available . . . just in case he wanted to hold your hand as much as you wanted him to.

Holding hands can conjure up some of the sweetest memories as well as some of the most bittersweet ones, like holding the hand of a dying family member. I once received a wedding thank-you note from Sweet Meredyth with a photo from her wedding on the front. The image on the back of the note showed the couple with their backs to the camera, holding hands. It was so beautiful and so sweet!

Years ago, I had an enlargement made of a photo of my daddy's hand holding the hand of his only grandson—baby Elias, the son of my sister, Shawn, and her husband, Chuck. Seeing this tiny hand in Daddy's strong hand reminds me that God is holding my hand.

God gives it to us straight in Isaiah 41:13: He, the Lord our God, is holding our hand through life—all of life, the bitter as well as the sweet. Through whatever we deem as impossible, God still holds our hand! We don't have to physically feel His hand clasped around ours. We rest knowing that He never lets go of us, even when we may try to shake off His grasp so we can wander off our own way.

And there's more . . . there is always more with God! Because He always holds on to us, we are never alone and do not need to fear.

His words "Don't be afraid. I am here to help you" never grow stale and distant.

Hold tight to the truth of God's heavenly hand-holding every day. Read Daniel 10:1-12 to see a firsthand account of how God's hand was on this obedient man.

You Know . . . He Knows

*The LORD's light penetrates the human spirit,
exposing every hidden motive.*

PROVERBS 20:27

How many times have you caught yourself saying in a conversation, "You know, . . ." or "You know what?" It's surprising how often we use those words, whether we are sharing information or not!

I find today's enlightening proverb both convicting and comforting. Our God knows everyone inside and out. Just think how much information He has on each one of us. No computer could handle that amount of data. The Creator of every living thing, who knows even the number of grains of sand on every ocean floor, seashore, and swirling in the surf, knows what is really going on inside each of us.

Because His light penetrates your spirit and mine, we do not have to worry about how our prayers come out. Our praises, requests, conversations, desires, ugly thoughts, and tattling are all plain as day to Him.

He sees our hearts, and we cannot hide from Him. Since He is always with us, we can honestly say—even when we feel in the dark or ashamed about something—"You know, Lord. You know, Lord."

The Lord knows all that is going on in our human spirits and understands our failings and has also felt every feeling. He really understands. The Lord needs no clarifications or summaries. We can rest peacefully, despite our weaknesses, knowing He sees when our heart wants to be like His, and He offers us endless grace each time we fall short.

Even though He sees our thoughts and feelings, God still loves to hear from us. Talk to Him today: "Lord, thank You for knowing everything about me and still loving me."

268

Grading on a Complete Curve

Who then will condemn us? No one—for Christ Jesus died
for us and was raised to life for us, and he is sitting in the
place of honor at God's right hand, pleading for us.

ROMANS 8:34

When I was a schoolteacher, I dreaded and felt uncomfortable when report card time rolled around, not because it was difficult to fill in the little boxes and write sweet comments, but because what I wrote needed to be accurate and honest. Also, it was hard because I do know children really take their report cards to heart. Just like adults, children cannot be good in everything. A report card can never evaluate *all* that a child is, and I never wanted to make children think they weren't smart because they weren't good in every subject.

It's been a long time since I've received a report card, and yet I still remember how anxious I would get, not knowing what my final grade would be. Would I receive an A, B, C, D, or F? I will never forget failing a paper once and wishing my teacher had put a numerical grade on it instead of a big red F. I wished that she had graded on a curve. I decided then and there that if I ever became a teacher, I would try to refrain from marking a big red F on anyone's paper.

Fortunately, God grades us on the highest, most complete curve ever—His Son, Jesus Christ. Jesus' life in us raises our standing with God to the point that God erases our blackboard of sin through Christ's death on the cross. God views us as a perfect A—acceptable.

Sometimes we feel like our actions or circumstances earn all Fs. Recently, I was so focused on a particular failure (which felt like a bad report card) that I forgot about Jesus, my A+ Hope and Provider, who took my sins upon Himself.

Instead of condemning us, God evaluates believers based on the curve of Jesus' sacrifice for us. He used sinners in the Bible (like Moses, David, and Peter, among others) in spite of their failures, and He can use us for His glory too.

 Let's be encouraged that our spiritual report cards contain straight *A*s in Jesus Christ. Praise Him for grading on such a complete curve for our salvation and making us all *A*s forever!

Living the "Seek" Life

Solomon, my son, learn to know the God of your ancestors
intimately. Worship and serve him with your whole heart and
a willing mind. For the LORD sees every heart and knows every
plan and thought. If you seek him, you will find him.

1 CHRONICLES 28:9

This verse is an excerpt from a serious man-to-man, father-and-son talk. King David is close to death, and these are some of his last words of advice to his son, Solomon. We know David was far from perfect as a husband, father, and king. But he led a *seek* life and is known as a man after God's own heart (Acts 13:22).

As a child, I always loved playing hide-and-seek. But when it comes to God, I wonder sometimes if I'm searching well for Him. I know it's impossible to hide from Him, but what does it look like to actively *seek* Him?

Today's verse in 1 Chronicles reminds me of the greatest commandment: "Love the LORD your God with all your heart, all your soul, and all your mind" (Matthew 22:37). It's a great verse to meditate on when we want to learn what it means to seek the Lord. Seeking is assertive, and if you are seeking something, you initiate action, instead of waiting around for things to happen. We can personalize this verse with our own names as our heavenly Father speaks to us through His Word (fill your name in the blanks): "My daughter (my son), _____, learn to know Me, the God of your ancestors, intimately. Worship and serve Me, _____, with your whole heart and a willing mind. For I see your heart and know every plan and thought. If you seek Me, _____, you will find Me."

Living the *seek* life includes reading God's Word to know Him more. We can't help but fall in love with God the more we know Him because of who He is. He is all-perfect, all-loving, kind, just, merciful, and gracious. As we spend time in His presence, we take on His heart. Like King David, we can be people after God's heart.

 Ask God to grow your love for Him more deeply as you seek Him through His Word. He will give us wisdom when we live the *seek* life.

Be Clean, Smell Clean

God the Father knew you and chose you long ago, and his
Spirit has made you holy. As a result, you have obeyed him
and have been cleansed by the blood of Jesus Christ.

1 PETER 1:2

Have you ever forgotten a load of clothes in the washer? Do you recall the musty smell when you finally transferred them to the dryer? Stinky! Despite our best efforts to clean them, this one mistake means we've botched the job and need to start over.

God's children all have dirty laundry, and I'm not talking about clothing and linens. When you and I sit too long in sin in the washing machine of life and we don't hang out in the Sonshine to dry, our spirits start to stink and truly affect everyone else—and not for good!

But unlike laundry, God does not need special detergent to clean us up. He doesn't need to separate or categorize us by the sins we commit either. His cleanup formula works perfectly on all of us. Jesus took our sin stains to the cross with Him. We are separated unto God and made clean only in Christ.

Only God can clean us and remove our stain so that we smell like Christ in this dingy, dirty world. When we put ourselves in His hands and pull out the detergent of God's Word, the Holy Spirit reveals our dirty laundry and begins His method of cleaning our hearts white as snow. We just need to confess to God Almighty, who is without stain—pure and spotless—with arms open wide. He forgives our sin and makes us clean so that our lives send a Christlike fragrance rising up to God (2 Corinthians 2:15), which affects everyone else for His Kingdom good.

Be clean and smell clean with Christlike fragrance! And here's a practical tip about that stinky load in the washing machine. Do a rewash, adding a cup of vinegar along with a little more detergent, to get the odor out. It works every time!

More Pit Places

[The LORD] redeems your life from the pit
and crowns you with love and compassion.

PSALM 103:4, NIV

For more than thirty years, my parents lived in Gaffney, South Carolina. My dad told me that he wanted us to grow up in a small town so we would know the store owners and doctors, the people who served us and whom we served in our community. Besides being home to the beloved "Jesus Saves Shoe Store," as we called it, their small town is known for a big water tower painted to look like a mouth-watering giant peach. Every time they traveled "north" to Virginia for a visit, they'd be sure to load up the car with Gaffney peaches if they were in season. I loved to eat those peaches right down to the pit, and I still miss my daddy peeling them for me.

There's that word *pit* again. I mentioned it on September 16. We looked it up then and discovered that it could mean a literal hole, the actual place of hell, and an emotional state as well. When I hear the word, I think of peach pits, armpits, and the saying, "I'm in the pits," which always sounded unladylike to me.

Psalm 103 is a psalm of praise that David wrote later in life. Looking back, he certainly could have given many examples when he was trapped in a pit of his own making. In this verse, he reminds us that the Lord has redeemed us from the serious pit of spending eternity separated from Him.

Now and for all eternity, we praise God for His great love and compassion—for forgiving our sins and for healing all our diseases and hurts one day. We also praise Him because He "satisfies [our] desires with good things so that [our] youth is renewed like the eagle's" (verse 5, NIV). David unreservedly worshiped the Lord with his words. He knew without a shadow of a doubt that his life was in the hands of a loving God. Instead of being in the pits about his aging body and imminent death, he praised God for saving him from the pit of destruction. Do you have the same certainty?

Only God can redeem our lives from the pit places. Praise Him for His eternal place in our hearts!

Genuine Gratitude

[David] refused to drink it. Instead, he poured it out as an
offering to the LORD. "The LORD forbid that I should drink
this!" he exclaimed. "This water is as precious as the blood
of these men who risked their lives to bring it to me."

2 SAMUEL 23:16-17

What would our world look like without genuine gratitude and sacrifice? When I start to complain, I need a shot of gratitude instead of gripe-itude. Sometimes I think I am going to pop in gratefulness to God for all He has done for me and how He has used others to give so generously to our family.

Do you ever feel at a loss about how to thank people whom God has placed in your life, knowing that you can never begin to convey the fullness of your thankful heart? You feel *so* much gratitude, but the problem is, you don't know how to express it adequately. You know that nothing you have accomplished has happened because of you alone.

God uses the body of Christ to fulfill His purposes on earth. God has specific jobs for each of us to do. Nothing happens in our own strength, and certainly our growth in gratitude does not happen apart from God's power in us.

Indulge me for a minute. Just for this devotion, I want to adapt the words from 2 Samuel 23:9 (KJV) describing David's "mighty" men to describe the "mighty sweet men *and women*" God has placed in my life. When David was thirsty, three of his mighty men broke through the Philistine lines and drew water from the well near the gate of Bethlehem (where David was born) and carried it back to their leader. "But he [David] refused to drink it. Instead, he poured it out as an offering to the LORD" (2 Samuel 23:16). What I long to do is pour out my little cracked teacup filled with sugar cubes as an offering to the Lord to show my gratitude too.

We can all show genuine gratitude to God by purposely pouring out everything. You and I need to rest in the knowledge that God sees our gratefulness. It does not matter if anyone notices what we do to give back. When we offer ourselves wholeheartedly to God, our gratitude blesses Him, us, and others around us.

> Serving others sacrificially is one way to pour out gratitude to our gracious God.

Southern Spanish

I have summoned you by name; you are mine.

ISAIAH 43:1, NIV

Have you ever tried speaking Spanish with a southern accent? Even though I took two years of Spanish in high school and performed well on the written tests, I could never quite get the hang of speaking Spanish aloud—especially in front of other people! Because I did so well on the written tests, I was placed in the more advanced second-year class at Erskine College. Oh my, I was totally unprepared for that!

Lost does not even begin to describe the inadequacy I felt Monday, Wednesday, and Friday for two whole weeks! Our professor spoke Spanish fluently and very fast the whole class. We even played Spanish bingo, but not one square on my card was ever filled! When our teacher called the roll in our special Spanish names, I never uttered a sound (although I desperately wanted to scream "Adios!" because I couldn't even understand my Spanish name being called).

Sheer fear and embarrassment held me back from saying anything at first, but I finally made an appointment to see my professor after two weeks had passed. I admitted to her how lost I was. She told me she had assumed I had dropped the class. Since I had never responded when she called me by my Spanish name, she had marked me absent the six times I was actually there.

Once again, God used a life experience to help me appreciate that He summons me by name. The one and only true God, Creator of everything and the God infinitely involved with His people every minute of every day, has called me by name. He has called you by name too.

He wants us to know that He has us covered for all eternity and that we will not be counted absent "when the roll is called up yonder," as the old hymn says, because we belong to Him in Jesus Christ if we have received Him by faith.

We may not understand some of our circumstances in this life, but we can rest assured that God fully understands us. He knows the unique language of our heart. He speaks whatever language we speak (including Southern) fluently, and He delights in helping us learn His language of love.

 No name games with God! Ask Him to give you a glimpse today of His personal care for you, a child He loves to call by name.

Habakkuk's Heart

Even though the fig trees have no blossoms, and there are no grapes
on the vines; even though the olive crop fails, and the fields lie empty
and barren; even though the flocks die in the fields, and the cattle
barns are empty, yet I will rejoice in the LORD! I will be joyful in
the God of my salvation! The Sovereign LORD is my strength!

HABAKKUK 3:17-19

Habakkuk had a "cup half full" perspective on life—his empty cup overflowed!

At first glance we wonder how Habakkuk could have had such a great outlook. It appears as though he and the rest of the people lived in desperate circumstances, with little to no source of income or food for their next meal. But he knew life ahead was secured by God, even though the current environment looked bleak and resources were scarce. Habakkuk focused his heart on God and trusted that the Lord would see them through seemingly impossible circumstances.

Just as God's people had everything to look forward to in that situation, we have everything indescribably glorious to look forward to now! Our lot is sure. Yes, these days may be very difficult, with unknowns looming before us at every turn. It is tempting for us to curl up in fear or give in to discouragement and fatigue.

But one day we will see the Lord face to face and never know need again! We will never hurt or cry again. We will have glorious new bodies and a new home in heaven forever with Him. No matter what you and I or the people we love are facing at this very moment, no matter what fills our list of *even thoughs*, we still have the most amazing reason to rejoice.

Let's you and I list our own personal *even thoughs*—

- *Even though* I just lost my spouse, home, health, job, savings . . .
- *Even though* I can't have a baby . . .
- *Even though* I'm going through a messy divorce . . .
- *Even though* a serious illness lingers . . .

Even though my future seems hopeless, "yet I will rejoice in the LORD!"

"Lord, please give me a Habakkuk heart." Pour out your list of *even thoughs* to God and, by faith, offer Him praise anyway!

Comfort in Cancer

All praise to God, the Father of our Lord Jesus Christ. God is our merciful Father and the source of all comfort. He comforts us in all our troubles so that we can comfort others. When they are troubled, we will be able to give them the same comfort God has given us.

2 CORINTHIANS 1:3-4

In 2004, on Good Friday, the word *cancer* invaded our home.

The day after my routine mammogram, I received a call from my wonderful doctor while I was sitting in the Sweet Monday office with precious Paula. My first thought was, *God, You knew that spot was there,* and my second thought was, *How long will I live?* Other questions ran through my mind: *Will I get to see our one-and-only daughter walk down the aisle in her wedding dress? And what about grandbabies?* And then, *What are all the other women who are getting bad news today doing if they don't know You?* Then God brought to my mind that there are a lot worse things in life than a cancer diagnosis.

My very surprising news of an abnormality led to a lumpectomy, mastectomy, chemotherapy, and radiation—the most aggressive treatment for breast cancer. My sweet mother came from South Carolina to minister to me before being diagnosed with the same disease six months later. I sometimes wonder if God may have allowed me to go through it before my sweet mother so I could comfort her in the days to come.

God's Word doesn't tell us we have to experience the very same kind of trouble in order to comfort someone else. He tells believers in Christ that He comforts us in all our troubles so we can comfort those in any trouble with the comfort that we have received from God.

Anyone who experiences any kind of hurt can identify with pain in general. Whatever its source, pain gives us insight into specific ways we can provide comfort to someone else. Surely you have experienced some heartache in life—emotional or physical—that has grown your desire to ease someone else's suffering.

Focusing outward is a very practical way to reduce inward pain.

 Think of someone right now whom God would have you comfort. Write that person a note, give a gift of bright flowers, or make a phone call to offer sweet cheer!

How Are Your Relationships?

[Jesus] answered, "'Love the Lord your God with all your heart and with all your soul and with all your strength and with all your mind'; and, 'Love your neighbor as yourself.'"

LUKE 10:27, NIV

When it comes to marketing, Hallmark knows what to do. Their cards are all about wonderful ways to make connections with other people. You can even share your card story on their website. And then there are the commercials! They always make me cry because they draw me into what life is really about—relationships. The relationship between a mother and daughter, a teacher and student, one friend to another.

How are we doing in our relationships? Let's think about it. If you and I have an altercation with someone and do not do our part to resolve it, are we at peace? Of course not. We are either stewing at work or stewing at home, and heaven forbid, we may have gossiped about it to someone, and started that person stewing too.

Sweet friends, God set our priorities in Luke 10:27 with the two most important commandments—to love Him and to love people. If our relationships with God and people are full of strife or are simply lacking, then we need to do a heart check to see if our love priorities are in order.

If we have a personal relationship with God through Christ, we need to ask ourselves if we love Him with all our heart, soul, strength, and mind. If we do, then we should have greater love for others. As our relationship with God grows and we come to love Him more, in His strength and power He moves us toward restoration and reconciliation in our earthly relationships. We will not have time to look critically at others and judge them because our relationship with our holy, gracious God keeps our heart softened. When we live in light of God's perfect, infinite grace, forgiveness, and mercy with our own failings, then we will want to do what we can to offer grace and forgiveness to others rather than pushing to win an argument and get our way.

When we keep our relationship with God on His terms, it will carry over to our relationships with others.

Let's grow in our love for the Lord, and all our other relationships will grow and blossom too.

Only One Thing

Martha was distracted by the big dinner she was preparing. She came to Jesus and said, "Lord, doesn't it seem unfair to you that my sister just sits here while I do all the work? Tell her to come and help me." But the Lord said to her, "My dear Martha, you are worried and upset over all these details! There is only one thing worth being concerned about. Mary has discovered it, and it will not be taken away from her."

LUKE 10:40-42

Boy, does this sound familiar. Ugh! I have muttered a variation of Martha's words when I've been preparing a big dinner. I did not say them directly to Jesus, but I might as well have been talking to Him. Like Martha, I get worried and upset over a lot of details too!

Let's be honest. What woman hasn't had "Martha moments" from time to time, when she feels she has taken on more than she can manage?

Jesus responds quickly: "My dear Martha, my dear Kim, my dear sweet you, you are worried and upset over all these details! There is only one thing worth being concerned about. Mary has discovered it, and it will not be taken away from her."

Only one thing is needed, and that is connecting with the Lord Himself. Sweet Martha was distracted in the details, while Sweet Mary got the "only one thing" right: focusing on Jesus. As the old hymn says, we need to "turn our eyes upon Jesus, look full in His wonderful face, and the things of earth will grow strangely dim in the light of His glory and grace."

When we pause to focus on Jesus first, He either eases our stressed-out spirits or changes our attitudes in the circumstances that threaten to undo us. He wants us to pause in His presence and be mindful of who He is and the amazing things He has done for us. I know that sounds counterproductive, even a misuse of time when we are in a tizzy. Truthfully, He is just what we need to adjust our priorities and be able to encourage others around us.

 Let's be concerned about one thing—the Lord! Clear a space on your refrigerator and stick a note up there that says, "One thing!"

Sweet Submission

Wives, this means submit to your husbands as to the Lord. For a husband is the head of his wife as Christ is the head of the church. He is the Savior of his body, the church. As the church submits to Christ, so you wives should submit to your husbands in everything.

EPHESIANS 5:22-24

Sometimes women—married and single—get all worked up about these verses, especially the word *submit*. But when we understand what God's idea of true submission is, we can relax. God's purpose for submission has nothing to do with controlling us or keeping us under His thumb. Instead, God opens the door for His absolute best for us.

Nothing is sweeter than living in submission to God because He knows how the abundant Christian life works best. Following His commands is evidence of our submission, and we have a much easier time following them when we remember that His way *is* the best way. Living out God's commands in the power of His Holy Spirit sets us free in every single area of life!

In the first years of my marriage, I didn't listen well to God or to my husband, but when I read this passage, I knew God was at work to change me. God has not used anyone more than my husband, Mark, to help me see things in myself that I could not see and to encourage me to do things I never would have done.

After the first year of Sweet Monday in our home, Mark said, "Kim, write your ideas down. This outreach has been so successful in our home, other women can do it. If you write it down, I will go and make fifty copies." I *did not* want to do it, but when these verses in Ephesians kept ringing in my ears, I knew following Mark's advice was really an act of submission to God. More than ten years later, Mark used our savings to foster my idea of helping women become more confident and comfortable as they face breast cancer. I would not have done one thing without a few serious, sweet kicks in my pink pants from Mark! I would have missed God's best if I had refused to submit to my husband's leadership.

When we take the risk and submit to God's methods, we open the door for Him to come in and bless and grow us in miraculous ways.

Let's encourage one another in this sweet submission role. Joy follows obedience!

Fighting Your Battles

This is the LORD's battle, and he will give you to us!

1 SAMUEL 17:47

I envy David's confidence portrayed in this verse. He was facing a giant named Goliath, ready to fight him to the death with a few stones flung from a slingshot and plenty of big faith. David was able to fight confidently because he knew who was ultimately going to win his battle—the Lord! It wasn't little "d" fighting big "g." It was big G—God—fighting "little" Goliath.

Like me, you are probably fighting some personal battles. We can fight with faith, too, because our battles also belong to the Lord!

Faith assures us that Christ is beside us. He knows every detail about all the circumstances we're up against. Even in the darkest moments, we are not alone. Our comrade, Jesus Christ, is with us. He knows His victory is sure, and He guards us with His life. He camouflages us from being an unguarded target for the enemy. This knowledge about our great Warrior is our confidence to keep moving forward in life's battles.

During my mastectomy when I was under anesthesia, I was literally in the dark, hoping for a reconstructed breast when I woke up. When I awakened, I learned that both surgeons had made a judgment call and delayed reconstruction so my chemotherapy and radiation treatments would not be slowed down. When I saw myself in the mirror for the first time, I said to Mark, "Now I know why they call cancer a battle." I felt like a wounded soldier must feel when he or she is sent home from war.

But then God helped me see something: my battle with cancer was really His battle, not mine. I belonged to Him, and He would fight for me. God was doing an important reconstruction on my heart then, and thankfully, He continues to reconstruct me inside and out to this day.

We all know the feeling of being in the dark, unable to see something but believing it is there. Moving forward in the dark certainly requires faith. This faith fuels our hope when we faithful believers in Christ are in dark, painful places. We always need faith; we always need God.

 Be encouraged that the battle is not ours but the Lord's! Read 1 Timothy 6:12 to get your ongoing marching orders.

Source of Hope

*I love your instructions. You are my refuge and my
shield; your word is my source of hope.*

PSALM 119:113-114

Reading *The One Year Bible* has been a source of hope for me for the last ten years. My heart is being softened and my conscience pricked as God's Word reframes my earthly perspectives with His eternal hope.

It is not the structured reading plan that has been my source of hope, but God's actual words from the pages—moving through my mind, into my heart, affecting my choices. His Word speaks hope on a daily basis. I must confess, when Christian women tell me they have no hope, I carefully try to find out how much they are hearing God's voice through His Word over the voices of this despairing world.

God gives us hope like no other. We need to feast on what He says in the Bible. We cannot get hope at the frozen yogurt store. We cannot buy hope at the mall; it's not a special TV offer either! We cannot whip it up in our own kitchens. God is the source of hope and love and joy and peace and comfort—all the things you and I crave every day.

I have never heard God's voice audibly, but when I read His promises and see His perfect character and unconditional love throughout Scripture, I am encouraged for whatever is going on in my life. Every day, when we are by ourselves in the quietness of our homes, cars, offices, or vacation spots, may we open the Bible and hear His voice above the clamoring noise of the world. If we ever doubt the benefits of poring over God's Word, Psalm 119 can reaffirm its value. This longest psalm of the Bible has so much to say.

Let's help each other find a simple plan for a daily intake of hope through God's Word. You may prefer to pick a specific book of the Bible (the Gospel of John is a good place to start) and read through it over a few days, or you may choose a couple of chapters from the Old Testament and a couple from the New Testament each day. Maybe you can find a Bible study for accountability and structured teaching. Whatever your style, God's Word will fit.

Arrange each day to include a set time to read His Word and gain strength from the voice of God, the only Source of true hope.

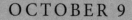

OCTOBER 9

Unnamed Hero

When the son of Paul's sister heard of this plot, he
went into the barracks and told Paul.

ACTS 23:16, NIV

Over the years, as I've read and reread God's Word, I cannot remember ever thinking about Paul's nephew or even recalling that Paul had one in the first place! But God used Paul's nephew, who is not mentioned by name, to save Paul's life. He is an unnamed hero who was used quietly by God to carry out His will.

In Acts 23 Paul had an opportunity to defend himself to the Sanhedrin and declare his hope about the resurrection of the dead. This proclamation caused such a disturbance that the situation became violent. The commander was scared that Paul would be torn apart, so he ordered his troops to remove Paul by force and bring him to the barracks. It appeared that prison was the safest place for Paul. What an encouragement for us today. Even our personal prisons can be places of God's provision when you and I cannot see what is ahead!

The biggest *wow* for me in this true story is the fact that God used Paul's nephew in a mighty way to protect Paul. All the nephew did was remain available, willing, and ready to act when God revealed a need. This story illustrates the power of simple, assertive faith—nothing flashy.

Who knows, perhaps you and I will be unnamed heroes as we obediently walk by faith and do the right thing, which is whatever God says. Who knows, it could be that we will be recipients of God's protection and provision through unnamed heroes. Who knows? God knows!

Our job is to stay tuned in to God's voice so we can hear when He tells us to move from the background to the front line to serve Him. Talk about walking the line—His!

Let's ponder this story today as we encounter unnamed heroes and be ready to fill that role ourselves as we walk God's line!

How Long, Lord?

*O LORD, how long will you forget me? Forever? How long
will you look the other way? How long must I struggle
with anguish in my soul, with sorrow in my heart every
day? How long will my enemy have the upper hand?*

PSALM 13:1-2

In this short psalm, David, whom God called a man after His own heart, cries out four times, "How long?"

As I read it, I think of all the times as a young child that I cried out when we were traveling to see grandparents. As the car kept winding through the mountains, every five minutes I'd cry out, "How long until we get there?" My parents were very patient, even though I'm sure they were thinking, *We can't wait until we get there either!*

I haven't ever stopped crying out to God even though I'm an adult. I still cry out as a child of God when I feel emotional pain in my heart or physical pain in my body: "How long, Lord? How long will it last?" Our desire to be rid of pain and discomfort doesn't disappear with age.

David is such a model of faith. He pours out his weary-of-waiting heart to God. Because of the simple fact that he knew where to look for comfort, his faith trumped his feelings. God had not forgotten him, nor was He looking the other way.

God has not forgotten you and me, either, and He is never avoiding our need for help! Skip to the end of David's song in Psalm 13. Verses 5 and 6 say, "But I trust in your unfailing love. I will rejoice because you have rescued me. I will sing to the LORD because he is good to me."

Our timing is not always God's timing; more often than not, it seems to be different. He makes all things beautiful in His time (right, Sweet Sherry? Ecclesiastes 3). Even when the waiting feels endless, we can take heart that God is still present and working in His sovereign wisdom and love. He will rescue us in His perfect way and time. Faith trumps feelings in our *how long?* hearts every time!

OCTOBER 11

Parched and Weary

O God, you are my God; I earnestly search for you. My
soul thirsts for you; my whole body longs for you in this
parched and weary land where there is no water.

PSALM 63:1

Parched, weary, and thirsty. David was hiding in a desolate wilderness when he
penned Psalm 63. He was in the wilderness of Judah, on the run from his rebellious son Absalom, who was trying to kill him.

I cannot imagine that particular wilderness situation, but I know what it feels
like to be so thirsty that nothing will quench it but good ole H_2O! Most of us
don't have to stay thirsty very long. We can quickly quench our physical thirst.
But when it comes to soul thirst, *nothing* will satisfy it but Jesus, our Living Water!

When we're in a "parched and weary" situation—the kind of wilderness experience that seems like it will never end, with circumstances that make us crave
relief for ourselves or for those we love—we don't know how much longer we can
last in the desert and wonder if help will ever arrive. Only the Lord Himself can
meet us with His life-giving water and satisfy our deepest needs.

Let's look at David's Living Water bottle of relief that's found in Psalm 63:

Seek God. (verse 1)
Tell God we long for Him. (verse 1)
Remember good experiences with God and God's power and glory. (verse 2)
Praise God for His unfailing love. (verses 3-4)
Compliment God and praise Him some more. (verse 5)
Think about God when we can't sleep. (verse 6)
Remember God is our keeper and sing for joy. (verse 7)
Follow Him closely and recognize that His strong hand holds us securely.
    (verse 8)
Turn all the bad guys over to God. (verses 9-10)
Rejoice in Him and show your trust by praising Him. (verse 11)

Talk about an energizing drink! Drink Him in and then fill up again.
You will be renewed and refreshed by all that He offers.

Sweet Homework

*God has given us this task of reconciling people to him. For
God was in Christ, reconciling the world to himself, no longer
counting people's sins against them. And he gave us this wonderful
message of reconciliation. So we are Christ's ambassadors.*

2 CORINTHIANS 5:18-20

What a sweet homework assignment we have as ambassadors for Christ! But what exactly does that assignment involve?

As Christ's ambassadors, we represent His name and Kingdom to the world. He chose us and appointed us to speak on His behalf to spread His message of salvation, love, and peace. When you and I joined the family of God by faith in Christ, He gave us full access to Himself, including 24/7 clearance to convene with Him. He is always in session to provide insight and wisdom for how best to accomplish His work.

He showers us with such gifts and privileges, too; it's as if we're both royalty and workers in His country, which is exactly what we are! We don't go around expecting to be introduced with trumpets and great pomp. Any position requires constant sweet homework behind the scenes before He places any of His children on the front lines.

He clearly tells us that our commitment involves sharing His wonderful message of reconciliation, which is the gospel, the Good News. We can be used by Him in a myriad of ways to take His Good News to others so that they can be reconciled to Him too. We all have the same task as ambassadors of Christ, but our roles will be as individual as each one of us! Some may sit at someone's bedside; others may write an e-mail. Some may travel great distances, and others may work from home. Still more will rescue the wounded and protect those in danger. All God's children are his ambassadors, offering God's truth and grace.

Most of all, as God's ambassadors we need to make sure we're conducting ourselves in a manner that honors Him as we extend the level of care He asks of us to those we serve. Only through our personal relationship with God in Christ will we be effective as His ambassadors.

Let's join forces and take our ambassadorship seriously by abiding in Christ and then carrying out our assignment faithfully.

Eternal Report Cards

But to all who believed him and accepted him,
he gave the right to become children of God.

JOHN 1:12

As I mentioned earlier, when I was teaching school, every year I wanted to quit the day I had to hand out report cards. Of course, I knew that evaluation was important, but marking in little black boxes on a report card could never show some of the special, delightful qualities of each child! Even though I filled up the space allotted for handwritten comments, I know everyone considered an A as "very good," and most girls, more so than boys, thought a C was very bad. Ds and Fs were much worse news for both boys and girls!

Grades really mattered to the children, thus they mattered to me. Although I was careful in my evaluations, I constantly wondered how to keep "my children" from thinking a report card was the total evaluation of them as a person. I longed for them to know their value was based on how much God loved them. More than anything, in my heart I wanted them to grasp God's acceptance of them. Knowing Jesus Christ means we receive an A+ on our eternal report card!

Who is our teacher? Our teacher is God Almighty, and His learning curve takes into account our unique strengths and weaknesses. He knows the ideal teaching strategy for each of His children. His methods are encouraging; He adapts them according to His purpose for us.

As students of our Savior, we are called to study His Word and follow His curriculum. This discipline becomes a joy because we learn to love and respect God so much as we experience what a wonderful, caring teacher He is. And someday when He deems the timing is right, we will graduate to heaven forever.

Wow! I just encouraged myself writing this and reminding myself what is true!

If you have given your life to Christ (you can do that right now if you haven't—just tell Him), celebrate your A+ in Jesus and get excited about what He has in store for you.

The Apple of His Eye

Keep me as the apple of your eye; hide me in the shadow of your wings.

PSALM 17:8, NIV

Every stage of my daughter's babyhood, from the sleepless nights to breast-feeding to changing dirty diapers, was a joy to me. I was ecstatic to finally have my long-awaited child, and I wanted to do everything right and not miss anything.

God provided us with the kindest pediatrician, Dr. Jaffe, who was a wealth of compassion, fatherly experience, and baby knowledge. He mentored me during every appointment through Kali's childhood and constantly reassured me of my abilities as a mother.

I will never forget one traumatic day when I rushed into his office, cradling my daughter and her burned hand.

Kali was in her crawling stage, and that morning I had put a still-warm toaster oven in a lower cabinet that didn't have child-safety locks . . . yet. Kali chose that morning to open her first cabinet. Before I could stop her, she put her sweet chubby hand on the toaster oven and cried out in pain. So did I!

I was really shaken! I was so sad that I did not guard her, the apple of my eye, as she needed. Her injury was my fault, and I could not hold back the tears. I rushed to Dr. Jaffe's office.

Dr. Jaffe assured me that day that I was still a good mother and these things happen, even when we're carefully watching over our children. He confirmed that my sweet baby girl was just fine and gave me ointment for her blistered hand. Dr. Jaffe's words of grace will never be forgotten. Grace and compassion always feel good.

Once I got home, my trembling turned to melting into God's strong arms. He was right beside me the entire time, just as He was with Kali.

In today's verse, David gives us a glimpse of how lovingly God guards us. David basks in the comfort of being the apple of God's eye. Even though I can never protect Kali from every danger, I know that God will always guard her under His wing, just as He guards every child of His.

Snuggle under a blanket and read Psalm 17. Bask in the reality of being guarded by the Grace Giver, as the apple of His eye, sheltered under His wing.

Pleasant Help

God is our refuge and strength, an ever-present help in trouble.
PSALM 46:1, NIV

When Kali was a toddler, I was explaining who we go to when we are in trouble. As soon as she began to form words, we began putting God's Word into our hearts together. Psalm 46:1 became a favorite of mine, but I especially loved her sweet spin on it. Instead of "God is an *ever-present help* in trouble," she said, "God is a *very pleasant help* in trouble." I think she was on to something there! I cannot think of anyone else I want by my side in trouble more than God Himself, can you?

We all have times of trouble. You may be surrounded by trouble now. I remember being stranded at a small country filling station. (That is a gas station, for some of you sweet ones who are younger than I am!) Mark was overseas. I was hours away from our home, traveling to my widowed mother's home with Kali, who was nine at the time. There was not a car rental place in sight, and the little motel nearby looked deserted and scary. We were hours away from our destination.

A young man getting food for his wife and nursing baby asked me if I was having car trouble. Once he and the owner of the station looked at the car and spotted the trouble, it became obvious it wasn't going to be a quick fix. Kali and I were not going anywhere. The kind young man offered to take us to the nearest airport to rent a car.

Now before you jump to all kinds of conclusions, be assured that I knew God saw my trouble. I knew God cared about my daughter and me. I knew God knew my husband was unreachable. I remembered Psalm 46:1, and I trusted the still small voice in my heart that said, "It's okay. This man's help is My provision." Because I saw the man's loving care for his family, I experienced God's peace that passes all understanding (Philippians 4:7). I would never want to put my precious child in danger, but I was uncomfortable staying in a place where others knew we were physically alone and stranded. So we loaded our stuff into the young family's car, rode to the airport, rented a car, and arrived home safe and sound.

God is an ever-present help in the very trouble you're facing now. Ask Him for His provision and for peace that passes all understanding. God is a Good Shepherd and His sheep hear His voice above all others.

BSSYP

Oh, that my actions would consistently reflect your decrees!

PSALM 119:5

It truly is the little things in life repeated over and over that make the most lasting impressions. Consistency is so important for connecting with people in a way that stirs love and warmth and builds trust in a relationship's stability. Consistency explains how family traditions become traditions.

Throughout our home, on license plates, art, and a mirror, the acronym "BSSYP" is on display. You see, when I went off to college, the first letter I received from home was written and addressed by my precious mother. My daddy had scribbled BSSYP in the upper left-hand corner of the envelope, along with a smiley face. For the life of me, I couldn't figure it out. I was so homesick that I called home and said, "Daddy, what is that BSSYP?"

He replied, "Sugar, it is what I've told you all your life: Be Sweet & Say Your Prayers."

For over twenty-five years until the day he died, Daddy consistently wrote "BSSYP" on every package or piece of mail from home. More than merely scrawling letters, my father's actions consistently reflected a parent's love. Mom's too—he'd say she did all the hard work! Those five letters have become a legacy that my own daughter surely will pass on to generations after her. In fact, my first text from Kali, away at college, closed with BSSYP.

I long to tell everyone I know to be consistent in the small things. They can grow to leave legacies later in life. Our actions will reflect God's desires if we are giving Christ full access to our hearts.

"Lord, I need Your help to BSSYP . . . and to be consistent in the little BIG things!"

SP (Sweet Pea): Sweet Dawn put BSSYP on her license plate in Florida, and my Virginia license has it too. Feel free to use BSSYP on your own state plate, and if you do, let us know at sweetmonday.org. It is a great conversation starter at gas stations. BSSYP . . . and be consistent in the little BIG things!

Relying on the Plumb Line

Then he showed me another vision. I saw the Lord standing
beside a wall that had been built using a plumb line. He
was using a plumb line to see if it was still straight.

AMOS 7:7

Until recently, I had not lived through a construction project since our "Jericho Room" was completed when Kali was around five years old. We actually marched around a play wall made of red cardboard blocks and sang the Jericho song before the actual room's wall came tumbling down.

Recently Dan, who built the Jericho Room, and Dave, his buddy from church, stopped by to brainstorm on a specific project I had in mind that quickly turned into several projects.

I could not decide how my idea could or should be done. We looked at the space many times, but I could not "see" what they envisioned and agreed upon. The industrial, architectural, mathematical, technical part of my brain is not wired like a builder's, and it never will be! I was so grateful for Dan's and Dave's strengths and really appreciated their expertise, but in order to move forward, I needed to see a visual picture. Dave quickly drew it out on a piece of drywall, and suddenly I was on the same page—er, wall—with them!

In the book of Amos, God gives a vision to Amos. In Isaiah 28:17, the plumb line refers to righteousness. It's comparable to a carpenter's level that construction men use often to check whether things are straight before the final nails go in. God was using a plumb line to show His people through Amos how their crookedness had caused them to fall short of His holiness.

God, by His Spirit, uses His Word as a plumb line in our lives to show us His righteousness and how we need to be made straight. The Good News is that Jesus truly made us straight and leveled us with His death on the cross!

As today's verse says, God used the plumb line to see if the wall was "still straight." His Holy Spirit in us continues to steady us when our faith gets shaky or our lives get out of balance so that we can maintain our clear vision of Him.

⚷ God's Word is a plumb line for us to keep us on His level path. His construction will bring the best outcome.

Boundless Love

*The LORD says, "Then I will heal you of your faithlessness; my
love will know no bounds, for my anger will be gone forever.
I will be to Israel like a refreshing dew from heaven."*

HOSEA 14:4-5

On almost every devotion I write, my heart is shouting, "I love God's Word." Actually, it is not the words I love, but God Himself. I fall more and more in love with Him as He reveals Himself through the Bible.

In the stories I read, I see Him forgive over and over again, and I am overwhelmed by His boundless love that was demonstrated by the sacrifice of His Son. I still can't get my mind around the fact that He lavishes His love on *me* because I feel so small in this big world.

His boundless love allows—no, it *invites*—me to rub shoulders with the King of kings and Lord of lords, Creator of all and perfect Father, who shares with His children all the riches of His endless wisdom, untiring kindness, mercy, grace, comfort, and care for everything that concerns me (and you). Again, I am purposefully reminding all of us reading this devotion today that God has endless love for you and me!

Only the Lord can refresh us from the inside and out. We can attempt to eat right and exercise and try to get enough sleep. We can take a day off to recoup. But we cannot invoke lasting joy, contentment, freedom, and comfort apart from God.

Need refreshment today? Read the book of Hosea and see a world gone wild restored. Be encouraged! Let's allow God's dew of heaven to pour out on us by His Spirit as we keep short accounts with God, repenting of our sin and allowing Him to restore us and refresh us.

Meditate on God's boundless love today. Write a love note to Him, telling Him what His love means to you. And maybe a family member would enjoy a surprise love note on his or her pillow too.

Truth Text

I will always remind you about these things—even though you already know them and are standing firm in the truth you have been taught.

2 PETER 1:12

Texting is a labor of love for me. I do not like to type and I'm not good at summarizing, as you will soon see. But with a busy college-age daughter, texting is a great way to communicate and truly a thing I do out of love.

I did not ever envision sharing this text exchange with you, but after reading 2 Peter 1:12, I asked Kali's permission to do so. I hope your heart will be lifted by Peter's words that inspired my truth text to Kali.

Sweetie, GOOD MORNING! While these thoughts are fresh on my mind, I want to ENCOURAGE YOU! My biggest regret in life is that I did not read God's Word daily until age 28! As we talked before, habits take almost 6 weeks! Like Nike says, JUST DO IT.

I am sure you will be soooo blessed and awed at God that reading His Word will become A WANT TO DO! Please don't get bogged down by underlining, and you can certainly decide what's manageable—whether that's just the New Testament and Psalms and Proverbs this busy year or just a Psalm and Proverb each day! FREEDOM is yours!

I am so confident that God will speak. I want to encourage you in any way I can so you can truly encourage others! We cannot piggyback on other people's walks with God. Oh Sweetie, you have so many wonderful decisions ahead of you. My prayer for you is that you will hear God's voice above ALL others . . . especially mine!

Kali's texted reply made my day:

This so warmed my heart. I love you, Mommy.

We all need the refreshment of an occasional reminder to stay immersed in God's Word. We can be givers as well as enthusiastic receivers of this encouragement.

🔑 Let's refresh our memories daily in God's Word and truth-text each other!

Pleasing God

Obviously, I'm not trying to win the approval of people, but of God.
If pleasing people were my goal, I would not be Christ's servant.

GALATIANS 1:10

Here's a riddle: What do you get when you cross a perfectionist with a people-pleaser? You get stressed-out me. When I'm overscheduled and feeling behind in my efforts to serve, I quickly plummet.

I take my identity as Christ's servant seriously, and I echo the apostle Paul—I'm trying to please God. However, the reality is that sometimes I waver between living to please God and going overboard trying to please other people.

When I get stuck on this seesaw, I have to stop myself in my own weak tracks and figure out why I am upset and lacking peace. God's Holy Spirit illumines my heart and shows me that many times it is because I have been trying to please people more than Him. This tendency is a human frailty—a weakness in my people-pleasing personality.

A simple example of this shift is when I get bossy with my family. Have you ever worked your fingers to the bone trying to get ready for company so that by the time your guests arrived you wished they weren't coming? You wanted everything to be just right, but you got caught up in the details.

Maybe you start ordering your family members around like I've been guilty of—barking at them to vacuum and empty the dishwasher—and in your haste, you become a stressful, not restful, woman. But then the doorbell rings . . . and you cheerfully greet your guests while you are still unsweet inside.

Getting bossy with my family is just one good indicator that I have crossed the line to perfectionistic people-pleasing. The crazy thing is, these actions certainly don't please God or the people in my family!

We already have God's approval in Jesus Christ. We please Him simply by being His. The wonderful result of being His is the contentment and peace that only comes from knowing Jesus Christ. This changes everything. You and I can cheerfully welcome others into our home or reach out in many other ways because of God's open heart to us.

⚷ Let's live to please God and not to gain others' approval!

OCTOBER 21

Full Life Even in Suffering

Then he died, an old man who had lived a long, full life.

JOB 42:17

The entire book of Job addresses suffering, yet I have laughed out loud at some of the things Job's friends said to him. Job's circumstances were awful and definitely not laughable, but some of the comments from his friends were so blunt I think I laughed in sheer shock. They sound like something a person might say today. For example, one man actually called Job a windbag (Job 15:2)!

Laughing aside, reading this poetic book has caused me to worship God. What a story of His sovereign Lordship and constant presence and care over a man whose heart belonged wholly to God.

Job lost everything. In one day, Job's camels and oxen were stolen, all his servants were killed, seven thousand sheep and their shepherds were killed by lightning, and all ten of his children were killed in a cyclone. Then Job was struck with a terribly painful disease. To make matters worse, everyone was talking about it, but no one offered lasting support. Being the brunt of gossip and feeling abandoned in the pain must have felt like being kicked while he was down. But through all of it, "Job did not sin by blaming God" (Job 1:22).

As believers, we sometimes struggle with the subject of suffering. We ask why, just as Job did. His whole book addresses the dilemma of suffering, and the "arguments" sound familiar today. Let's start asking *who* instead of *why*. God gets the last word, and it is always good, right, and perfect. In Job's life, God sets things right and blesses him more at the end of his life than at the beginning.

You and I will never get the subject of suffering figured out this side of heaven, but we can know without a shadow of a doubt who is in control. All of our suffering is tucked beneath God's outstretched arms as He governs the beginning, the middle, and the end. We can crawl into the arms of the One who truly knows and loves us and wait it out, trusting in His kind, generous, and constant care.

We never have to know *why*; we just need to know *who*. Only God can give us a full life, even in suffering.

SP (Sweet Pea): Surprise, Sweet Nancy Brown and Carol Holt! You both know the *who*. I'm cheering for you.

Sweet Ideas to Do

*Do to others whatever you would like them to do to you. This is
the essence of all that is taught in the law and the prophets.*

MATTHEW 7:12

Ever wonder whether God is asking you to meet a need? Maybe you feel unsure whether your efforts would really be helpful, thinking, *Surely, God, there must be someone more talented or well known who is ready to jump in and minister. They would be more effective than me.*

Well, we can let today's verse help us put those doubts to rest. If God brings someone to mind who needs help, we do not have to pray about it for five hours to discern whether He's telling us to do something. He is!

If we are God's child, then we have the "mind of Christ" (1 Corinthians 2:16), which means His giving nature is in us if we'll only let it thrive and express itself.

Whatever we can do with what He has given us, He tells us to just do it. Maybe we are making soup for our family—we can make a double batch to share. Maybe you cannot prepare a whole meal, so you choose a couple of favorite snacks to share, or you write a note of encouragement. Maybe you can help with yard work, cleaning, or transportation, or invite their children over to play.

There's no time like the present to offer what you have. After all, you are the only one who can offer what God gave to you to give. We need to take seriously our own gifts from the Lord and see them as resources to share.

I will never forget when I was going through sixteen unsweet weeks of chemo-therapy. Sweet Michelle from my daughter's school, whom I did not know very well, put a big cooler on my front porch and organized meals for our family. Even though my own appetite was limited, I felt so comforted that my family was well fed, and I felt more like a mother providing for them again. When someone gave us a gift card for pizza, Kali really loved that!

We all have different styles of giving, and God can use all of them. We can begin by giving as we would like to receive. Pretty simple!

Doing to others what we would like in return is Jesus' style! And it's a great way to keep moving and growing in faith. Let's not waste too much time just thinking about it.

In His Arms

Praise the Lord; praise God our savior! For each day
he carries us in his arms. Our God is a God who saves!
The Sovereign LORD rescues us from death.

PSALM 68:19-20

Each day the Lord, the God of all comfort, carries us in His arms. Imagine that. Our Sovereign God—who is the Lord of Heaven's Armies (Isaiah 48:2) and the Creator of all things—is tender toward His children.

I picture His love every Sunday at church when, right before the closing song, a small curly-haired toddler comes bounding through one of the rear doors into the sanctuary. Bubbling with delight, she runs down the aisle to her sweet mother, who stoops low with wide-open arms to snatch her up! I worship every time I have the privilege of seeing this precious sight—

because I see Jesus, stooped low to embrace us;
because He walked on this dirty earth around dirty people, but made us clean
   when He died on the cross for you and me;
because Jesus literally rescued us from death.

Not only does Jesus stoop low, but His arms are wide open just like they were when they were stretched out on the cross. You may have heard that body language makes up 90 percent of our communication. Well, Jesus communicates 100 percent of His abounding love with His arms wide open, calling out a welcome: "Come to me, all of you who are weary and carry heavy burdens, and I will give you rest" (Matthew 11:28). When we run to those holy arms, the God of all the earth scoops us up and carries us through sickness, grief, successes, loss, unemployment, and any other pain. Through it *all* He carries us!

Each day the Lord carries us in His arms. Make time to curl up for deliberate rest today—even if it is only fifteen minutes. Imagine yourself in the Lord's arms and revel in His love.

"Home Sweet Home" Missionaries

You will receive power when the Holy Spirit comes upon you. And you will be my witnesses, telling people about me everywhere—in Jerusalem, throughout Judea, in Samaria, and to the ends of the earth.

ACTS 1:8

When I was younger, I used to tune out sermons on witnessing, evangelism, and missions because I thought the messages were only for real missionaries who lived in the wild and had slide projectors. I honestly thought that to be a missionary and tell others about Jesus, you had to go overseas *and* then come back and make a presentation in front of the entire church! Even the word *furlough* sounded strange and not very fun to me.

Now that I am grown and have met real missionaries, I know better. I do have missionary zeal, the overwhelming desire to reach lost people before the Lord comes back. But now I know that you do not have to be able to put together an impressive PowerPoint presentation or take National Geographic–worthy photographs!

In the first chapter of Acts, after Jesus was resurrected from the grave but before He ascended into heaven, He answered a question the disciples kept asking Him: "Lord, has the time come for you to free Israel and restore our kingdom?" (Acts 1:6).

Jesus answered them clearly that God sets that time and it was not for them (or us) to know. Then Jesus lets His followers know that He has a game plan for them while He is gone physically from earth. He wants them to be ambassadors on His mission, going forth in His power, telling people everywhere about Him.

This assignment is for us, too, and our territory is not just our "Home Sweet Home" missionary assignments but also our town, throughout our state, across the United States, and around the whole world! Wherever God places you and me, we are His witnesses, His "Home Sweet Home" missionaries.

We don't need to be overwhelmed by our missionary assignment—the Great Commission (Matthew 28:19-20). God promised His power for His mission.

Ye Olde Crock-Pot

Thank God! He has made us his captives and continues to lead us along in Christ's triumphal procession. Now he uses us to spread the knowledge of Christ everywhere, like a sweet perfume. Our lives are a Christ-like fragrance rising up to God. But this fragrance is perceived differently by those who are being saved and by those who are perishing. To those who are perishing, we are a dreadful smell of death and doom. But to those who are being saved, we are a life-giving perfume.

2 CORINTHIANS 2:14-16

Don't you love walking into a home on a cold day and smelling the aroma of dinner cooking?

When fall brings the first chill in the air, I can't wait to pull out the old Crock-Pot that my grandmother Nana gave us as a wedding present. The convenience of throwing in a variety of ingredients in the morning and knowing that a no-fuss meal will be ready at dinnertime makes my day! And don't you wish your drop-in visitors would come on a Crock-Pot day and be so impressed with the mouth-watering aroma drifting through your home, instead of on a day you purposely planned to stay in your pajamas and were going to heat up leftovers?

God tells all believers that we smell like Christ to each other and to Him, because Christ's Spirit in His children is a scent that attracts us to each other. We recognize His fragrance in others because we know Him in ourselves. He is a unifier among His people, the fragrance of life that we share in Him. God's scent either draws or repels others, depending on whether their hearts are open to Him. Just as fragrances are undeniably pleasant or distasteful, His aroma carries the message of death to those still in opposition to Him.

As believers, living true to God's Word and in obedience to Him, we diffuse His aroma around others, and He always smells wonderful. Even those who don't readily recognize the true Source of the aroma may be curious about His signature scent of salvation, truth, and grace.

The next time the aroma from the Crock-Pot welcomes us home, let's be reminded that we smell like Christ to God, and that smells good! Plan to share a Crock-Pot meal with someone this week.

No Mold on Mercy

Yet I still dare to hope when I remember this: The faithful love of the LORD never ends! His mercies never cease. Great is his faithfulness; his mercies begin afresh each morning.

LAMENTATIONS 3:21-23

We have a bread drawer in our kitchen, a deep drawer lined with stainless steel. The drawer was there when we moved into the house, and I had no idea what it was until I asked someone.

At times, I actually forget that I store bread in there because it is hidden away in the cabinet drawer. When I finally remember it's there, I always hurry to pull it out before Mark finds the mold on it! Unfortunately, this week I wasn't fast enough, and he found it first. I told him that it was a good thing—we didn't need to eat all those carbohydrates anyway!

You and I do not order stale, moldy bread at our favorite sandwich shop, and we do not eat rotten meat. We like our food fresh, and for good reason. Food past its prime is distasteful and can even make us sick.

As much as I enjoy fresh food, I am perpetually grateful for fresh mercy every day! How grateful I am to our faithful, loving God that I do not have to try to store up mercy, hide it in the bread drawer, and hope it doesn't grow moldy! Every day our faithful God offers a fresh supply of mercy, along with love and every good thing you and I could ever need for sustenance.

Fresh mercy is one of the most encouraging benefits of belonging to Jesus Christ. We don't have to hoard it. It arrives in abundance, ready to reenergize and restore us.

Praise God that mercy never gets moldy! We wake up to fresh mercy each day. Let's remember Lamentations 3:21-23 as we go to sleep tonight and again tomorrow when we wake up to fresh mercy, just as He promises!

Bolder as I Got Balder

Since this new way gives us such confidence, we can be very bold.
2 CORINTHIANS 3:12

Who would have thought that boldness would come with baldness? Certainly not I!

When I was diagnosed with breast cancer, I thought I would want to stay inside, hide, and keep my head under the covers. I couldn't imagine becoming a member of "The Bald and the Breastless." I thought I would be afraid to come out and go about the days God had ordained just for me.

Only because of His sweet grace in my life was I able to push those covers back and get out of bed looking the way I did! It was—and still is—so comforting to know that God is personal and knows the number of hairs on my head (as well as the number of hairs that were no longer on my head). Although those specific dreaded days are past, I am still comforted to know that no matter what deformities I have, inside or out, my God-given femininity does not change. Yours doesn't either!

To be able to face days with big physical strikes against our appearance takes boldness and courage only He can give. We do not have that strength on our own. In Jesus Christ lies all our hope to smile at the future in the midst of life-altering changes. He should be our reason to get out of bed every morning, regardless of the way we look and feel, with or without hair, no matter if we are a bed head, redhead, or a wet head.

When we have Him, we have everything to offer the people He places in our lives. We can boldly live the hope within us! *Thank You, Lord.*

Find whatever cute accessory makes you feel like your boldest outward self (I sometimes pin on a fun pink flower!) and go out and live your inward Hope.

Eternal Inheritance

For you have heard my vows, O God. You have given me an
inheritance reserved for those who fear your name.

PSALM 61:5

I am comforted to know beyond a shadow of a doubt that nothing this side of heaven can interfere with the solid inheritance awaiting me in heaven. Death can't; crisis can't. The stock market can't, and no election or hurricane or even my own personal tsunamis of life can interfere with what Jesus and I have together.

You and I cannot lose anything in Christ. He is all gain, and what we receive when we meet Him face to face one day will be far grander than you and I could ever dream about.

Closing my parents' home after their deaths was sad for my family. My siblings and I were surrounded by so many memories. All of us live in different states, and for years we had gathered at my parents' home almost every holiday. Being together again without Mom and Dad and sorting through my folks' things was one of the most difficult tasks I have ever tackled.

My kind older brother, Ryan, handled the rigmarole of legal issues. My sweet younger sister, Shawn, who grew up in our parents' home while I was in college and who married a man from the same town, went the extra mile in organizing our parents' beautiful home to sell. Since I lived the farthest away, I could only help with the smaller things. We are all so different in our family, yet the hard process went about as well as I could imagine. Besides the pain of not seeing or hearing my dear parents' voices, the most difficult part for me was packing and deciding what to do with Mom and Dad's earthly treasures. Thank goodness Mama had diligently started purging before we went through this grueling process.

I took comfort in God's promises. The fact of eternity and our real inheritance can frame our attitudes toward temporal treasures. As meaningful as they can be for each one of us, God can use them to develop our eternal perspective. It can create a longing for what will really last in this world and our forever home in heaven.

Make sure that your inheritance is reserved in heaven in Christ. Plant Psalm 61:5 in your heart and trust that God will help you rest on His truth.

Mind Your Manna

He humbled you, causing you to hunger and then feeding
you with manna, which neither you nor your ancestors had
known, to teach you that man does not live on bread alone but
on every word that comes from the mouth of the LORD.

DEUTERONOMY 8:3, NIV

My parents were always telling us to mind our manners. That's good advice, of course. But I wish I'd known as a child the importance of minding our manna, too. Maybe I wouldn't have missed so many years of feeding on every word that comes from the mouth of the Lord.

For more than twenty years, I shied away from reading the Bible because I thought only pastors, Sunday school teachers, and seminary scholars could really hear God. I honestly did not know that the Bible was God's personal book for me, too.

This belief was so strongly entrenched in my mind that all through middle school and high school I did not even speak to a boy who went to my church because he told me he was going to marry me. Because he was a preacher's son, I thought he was closer to God than I was. If God told him about our future marriage arrangement and didn't tell me, that added to my insecurities about God and was too much information for me to handle as a young teen. I literally ran in the other direction when I saw the boy at church or school! I finally apologized years later at a high school reunion.

Minding our manna is simply an easy way to remember to make God's Word a habit. When we do what He says by the power of His Holy Spirit, we grow practically in our faith. Guess what follows? Joy! We feel good inside when we follow God's instructions. As minding our manners is important for our social skills, God's Word—our manna—is essential for our spiritual growth.

Read God's Word, chew on it, and do what He says. Remember, the manna did not fall from heaven into the mouths of God's people. They had to go out of their tents and gather this one-of-a-kind food. Mind your manna.

Glorious New Clothes

*We know that if the earthly tent we live in is destroyed, we have a building
from God, an eternal house in heaven, not built by human hands.
Meanwhile we groan, longing to be clothed instead with our heavenly
dwelling, because when we are clothed, we will not be found naked.*

2 CORINTHIANS 5:1-3, NIV

Every day I feel like a brand-new mother. Every stage is new when you only have
one child and have not passed this way before. Sometimes I can be too conscientious for my own good or for my family's. I want to do it right, but many times
I am not sure just what to do or say in certain circumstances. One thing I have
learned over the years is that the truth is always a great place to start.

When our daughter was five, we had to go to our first family funeral. As an
inexperienced mother, I was anxious about how to prepare her for the receiving line, the casket, the tears, and the grave. I told her the truth: We would see
her great-grandmother in a casket, but it was her body, a shell. Her spirit was in
heaven with Jesus, and she would never cry again or have pain. We would see her
again when we go to heaven!

Like any curious five-year-old, Kali wanted to touch her great-grandmother
when we went for the visitation. Later, on the way home, she said, "Mommy, why
did Grandmommy Newlen have her clothes on?"

I was so afraid I had ruined her for life by taking her, and I wanted to pass
over her question quickly. I simply said, "She just needed to be modest," knowing
full well that Kali did not know what the word *modest* meant.

The next day, out of sheer curiosity, I asked her why she had asked me that question. She said, "Because Mommy, when you go to heaven you get new clothes, and
she needs to be 'nekkid' to get them on. I can't wait to see Grandmommy Newlen in
her glorious new clothes!" *Glorious?* What a wonderful surprise word to hear from
the mouth of a babe. I'm *sure* it brought glory to God.

Casket closed!

Have some fun today imagining what your heavenly clothing will look
like. The possibilities are endless. No more worrying about what we
are going to wear. It will be glorious!

One Sweet Step at a Time

*Do not be afraid or discouraged, for the LORD will personally go ahead
of you. He will be with you; he will neither fail you nor abandon you.*

DEUTERONOMY 31:8

Being scared is not my idea of fun. I have never enjoyed being startled, and
spooky stuff has never been my cup of tea. Growing up, I never wanted to go into
any haunted houses at amusement parks with my friends. And at costume parties,
I always want to wear something beautiful rather than something scary and ugly.

One time, though, I did reluctantly go into an amusement park haunted house
with some friends from college simply because I didn't want to be left out. But
I was "so not liking it," as my daughter would say. My friends zipped through,
but I was scared and was left behind. In fear, I latched on to the shirt of the man
in front of me, who was holding his little girl's hand. I did not know him, but I
was so desperate I didn't care, and fortunately it was so dark he couldn't see me.
When we hit daylight, I ran!

The stranger's presence offered some comfort to me that day, but much more
comforting is the fact that God goes before us, with us, and behind us throughout
life. When I remind myself of this truth, it calms my many fears.

Sometimes I forget my safekeeping in Christ because either I'm busy with
my to-do list, or I get distracted from God's truth, or I am paralyzed by fear of
something I need to do but I'm afraid to do. But when I take one sweet step at a
time while hanging on to my Savior, even though I can't see what's ahead, I am
comforted knowing God is right there with me, cheering me on. God is so much
bigger than any set of circumstances you or I could ever face. He can navigate us
safely through our unknowns, one step at a time.

Step out in faith with God as your Guide. We cannot escape His
comforting presence . . . ever!
SP (Sweet Pea): Tonight your children may be bringing home
candy. One family tradition we had was a candy-only supper on
October 31, celebrating God and that everything good comes from
Sweet Him.

Don't Mute God's Word

Anyone who hears my teaching and doesn't obey it is
foolish, like a person who builds a house on sand.

MATTHEW 7:26

We have a habit of muting television commercials at our house unless they are genuinely funny. Sometimes we take a few minutes to interact with one another about what we just watched. But most of the time, we're just thankful for the moment of silence because the commercials are just too loud!

The crazy thing is that I just learned that this amplification is intentional. Advertisers increase the decibels on purpose, calling it—of all things— "sweetening." (Now one of my favorite words has gone sour!) Sweetening is one way the advertisers hope to get our attention and sell more products. Well, they received consumers' attention all right. There were enough complaints that the FCC established new rules in December 2012 requiring TV stations and paid providers to limit a commercial's average volume—it cannot be louder than the program itself.

Creating noise that's hard to ignore is one way to get attention. But sometimes soft-spoken simplicity speaks volumes in a powerful way. Jesus tells us in Matthew 7:26 that to ignore what He says is foolish, like building a house on sand. If you've ever built a sand castle on the beach, you know exactly what Jesus is referring to. After all your hard work, the waves roll in and—*whoosh!*—in less than a minute, your masterpiece is washed completely away.

If we ignore God's quiet counsel, we face the danger of falling apart, unprepared for any challenging circumstance that may engulf us. If we don't tap into His strength, we can be dragged into even rougher waters, get in way over our thick heads, and will probably get seasick.

God already sees the beginning, middle, and end of every situation we face. He knows when the waves will roll over us, and He knows how to shore us up to weather them. But we need to pay attention. He can shout if it's in our best interest, but more often it is His consistent, quiet voice speaking through His Word.

Don't mute what God says through His Word. Take it to heart, and in His strength, do what He says. That's true "sweetening"!

The Clock Is Ticking

Teach us to realize the brevity of life, so that we may grow in wisdom.

PSALM 90:12

Whenever I am in a shop, I gravitate toward unusual clocks and watches. Besides being time-conscience, I love the creativity of different timepieces. I'm fascinated by their colors and shapes and adornments, such as smiles, flowers, stones, and jewels.

I am sure I help our dwindling economy with all the watch batteries I buy! Instead of buying a souvenir when traveling, I usually purchase an inexpensive watch. My wardrobe is definitely not complete and I'm totally lost without a cute watch. A fun watch also becomes my bracelet.

In addition, our mantel is also decorated with a small collection of clocks as a visible reminder that time is so short on this earth! These earthly treasures remind me of wise thinking. Much like a clock's internal mechanism regulates the time, God uses His Word to regulate me. When I spend time reading the Bible, God grows me in thinking more like Him. I long to be a wise woman who brings honor and glory to God.

We all want to grow in wisdom. Wisdom comes from God through His Word. In today's verse, He reminds us to consider the shortness of life. Now that's practical advice! The way we plan our time and schedule our days is very important to make the most of what God has given us. Does how we spend our time, our talents, and our resources reflect our priorities, the Lord, and others? Thinking about the brevity of life can help us live our priorities in our day-to-day moments. The clock is ticking—not only for others to come to know the Lord but for us to know Him better.

"We want to grow in wisdom, Lord, so teach us to realize the brevity of life, and not just realize it, but live in light of this truth!"

Let's grow in our personal relationship with the Lord because we need wisdom for the brief time He has given to us on this earth. There's no time like now to share His truth with others who need to know Him as Savior and Lord.

Lasting Value of God's Word

It is the same with my word. I send it out, and it always produces fruit. It will accomplish all I want it to, and it will prosper everywhere I send it.

ISAIAH 55:11

As much as I enjoy my clock collection, this year I realized during the weekends of "spring forward" and "fall back" how much clock clutter I have. When I go to reset all of them, it becomes clear that I may have overindulged.

There have been too many times in my life when I have purchased something I did not need because it was convenient, cute, or sparked my creative juices. If you could see my tray full of lipsticks, you would understand what I mean. Please do not misunderstand me. Having a lipstick or clock collection is not wrong. They are just things, and they are temporary. They have no lasting value. In fact, their reward is short-lived, and that's probably why little things sometimes pile up and can become yet another distraction in life!

But God's Word? Everything God says prospers. His Word produces sweet fruit. His Word has eternal value and always accomplishes everything He wants it to accomplish in our lives. We will grow in our faith as His Word takes root in our hearts. But we must clear the clutter from our hearts and free up time for His Word to do its work.

We may need to rearrange our schedules, our homes, our habits, and anything else that will help us allot time to hear God. Perhaps we can use an alarm on a clock to keep us accountable to maintain our first priority. If we are having difficulty understanding God's Word, maybe it's time to try a different Bible translation with wording that resonates more clearly with our own personal learning styles.

This year I switched to the New Living Translation. Geared for the average "man [or woman] on the street," this is a translation that even a sixth grader can understand, and that's the grade I used to teach, so I love it! No matter what translation connects with you most, we can all trust God to speak to us.

First and foremost, we need to give Him our time. When we do, we can experience firsthand the fruit He grows.

It's about time we invest in what really prospers—God, His Word, and people! What can you do to bring a fresh element to your Bible reading?

There's a Whole Lotta Shakin' Goin' On

I know the LORD is always with me. I will not
be shaken, for he is right beside me.

PSALM 16:8

It sounds funny now, but this fifties song by Jerry Lee Lewis actually came to mind when a 5.8-magnitude earthquake hit my neck of the woods. Measurable earthquakes are rare in Virginia. The tremors struck without warning. I didn't have time to run for the bathtub, so I just shook and waited.

Although the unsettled floor beneath my feet felt strange, I didn't panic. My spirit remained calm, thanks to the Holy Spirit's power. I was not really alone. I know the Bible's promise in today's verse—that the Lord was right beside me. Repeatedly in His Word, He says that He will be ever present with His children.

It seems that every day there is some natural disaster happening somewhere in our world. Sometimes I catch myself wondering what I would do if I were caught in the midst of a devastating, seemingly hopeless catastrophe. Then I remember that God will be present in those crises, too, and my fears subside. We cannot get away from His presence; we cannot escape His watchful care over us. Because I belong to God, if the earth swallowed me one moment, I would be looking directly at the face of God the next.

Today's verse comes from what I call Psalm Sweet 16. No matter how much shaking is going on in our lives—financially, emotionally, physically, spiritually—we can confidently trust God. The Lord wants us not only to survive whatever we're going through but to truly thrive in His abundant presence even more deeply during shaky times.

He is our solid Rock who will keep us grounded now and forever. I like that it says in Psalm 18:36 from *The Message*: "You cleared the ground under me so my footing was firm."

Read Psalm 16:11 out loud, confidently repeating David's words: "You will show me the way of life, granting me the joy of your presence and the pleasures of living with you forever."

My People

They will be my people, and I will be their God,
for they will return to me wholeheartedly.

JEREMIAH 24:7

My sweet friend Faye was telling me about visiting her great-aunt in a nursing home. Her aunt was experiencing the effects of dementia, and she didn't recognize Faye. But then Faye's great-aunt said to her, "I know you are my people."

My people. Such a personal claim of belonging. It sounded so familiar to me, and God recalled to my mind that He refers to us as His people throughout Scripture. "My people" sounded like God speaking through Faye's great-aunt, and my heart was touched.

When God was directing Moses as His mouthpiece, God would tell him what to say to Pharaoh, and Moses would say it. Over and over Moses told Pharaoh that God said, "Let *My people* go!" How personal is that?

Even though He was speaking specifically to the Israelite nation in that instance, God adopts all believers in Christ as *His people* too. We are in God's immediate family, related to Him forever because of Jesus. Just as God claimed the Israelites, He claims us as His own. And like He did for them, God defends us. He is crazy about us and is always watching out for us as a capable Father.

If you're in God's family, you need to take courage in what God says about you: "You are *My people*!" We live in a hurting world where many people don't know they can be God's people too. We can introduce them to our heavenly Father and increase the joy at the family reunion in heaven!

Let's hear God say to us today in Christ, "You are *My people*." Write a note to God about what being a part of His family means to you. Read Colossians 3:12 to see a list of traits of God's family members.

Source of All Comfort

Share each other's burdens, and in this way obey the law of Christ.
GALATIANS 6:2

Think back to the last time you were truly uncomfortable. Perhaps you are experiencing discomfort right now. I imagine you are just like me. You, too, long for freedom from your distress as quickly as possible.

When I am uncomfortable, I want the pain to stop hurting my heart and my body. As I've said before, if I had to choose, I would take physical pain over emotional pain. I would rather lose a breast than a child; I cannot even imagine that kind of emotional pain.

But the God of all comfort (2 Corinthians 1:3-4) does more than just imagine our pain; He enters into it with us. There is not one thing that we feel that the God of all comfort has not felt first. "Since [Jesus] himself has gone through suffering and testing, he is able to help us when we are being tested" (Hebrews 2:18).

I take great comfort in the truth of today's verse. When I try to ease someone's burden, I send Band-Aid notes to people who are hurting. I always feel inadequate to know what to say. My heart hurts for them, but I realize that I cannot make their pain go away. However, I know for a fact that God will comfort them in ways that only He can, and He can use even my simple steps to comfort my hurting friends more deeply than I can.

One way to partner with God in offering His comfort is to pray for others every time God brings them to mind. (I am thinking today of Sweet Nancy, who has test results coming today.) We can also take them a meal, offer to run an errand, or let someone know they are loved with a hug. Once a sweet neighbor, Judy, brought me a package of chocolate-covered strawberries from the produce section of the "healthy" store. They were so beautiful and so tasty. Her sweet gift touched me so much that I went to the same store to purchase the same gift for someone else who was suffering, to let her know she was loved.

Let God comfort you today through His Word, and use it to share someone else's burden too! Continue to sow sweet.

Hope in Life and Death

*The time of my [Paul's] death is near. I have fought the good fight,
I have finished the race, and I have remained faithful. And now the
prize awaits me—the crown of righteousness, which the Lord, the
righteous Judge, will give me on the day of his return. And the prize is
not just for me but for all who eagerly look forward to his appearing.*

2 TIMOTHY 4:6-8

Sweet and spunky Anne of Green Gables is one of my favorite fictional characters. She spends much time with her friend and "kindred spirit," Diana Barry.

Kindred spirits share many things of the heart, but perhaps the sweetest
kindred-spirit relationship is one that shares the hope of eternity together with
Jesus. Jesus Christ is not only a kindred spirit with all who look to Him as Savior,
but He also ties us together with one heart of hope in Him.

The apostle Paul had another kindred-spirit friend named Timothy. Paul
was actually Timothy's mentor, but they shared a close bond as friends and
missionaries together. Paul wrote his last letter to Timothy while in a Roman
prison awaiting beheading. This is too gory for me to imagine, yet the whole
little letter cries *hope*!

Because life is so short, death is just around the corner for all of us. If we are
believers in Christ, we can echo Paul's cry of hope. We too can live our lives in
service to the Lord we love and in the fellowship of His hope with each other. We
can live life without regret, even on our deathbeds.

You and I have no idea when God will call us home to Him. This heavenly
home definitely will be worth waiting for. This home will not contain any pain or
tears, and it will hold such beauty, we will never have to decorate!

If we are in Christ, we are His kindred spirit as well as Paul's and Timothy's.
We can eagerly look forward to Him appearing again—His second coming—and
look forward to meeting Him face to face when we leave this earth to be with
Him. We can live with anticipation! It is all good with Him!

Kindred-spirit friend, in life or death, whether near or far—our hope
is sure in Jesus Christ! Let's live without regret until we see Him
face to face.

311

Perfectionism Trap

Did you receive the Holy Spirit by obeying the law of Moses?
Of course not! You received the Spirit because you believed
the message you heard about Christ. How foolish can you be?
After starting your new lives in the Spirit, why are you now
trying to become perfect by your own human effort?

GALATIANS 3:2-3

What a wonderful reminder that in no way, shape, or form can we be saved or made perfect by any works of our own. How about breathing a collective sigh of relief with me? I don't know about you, but I often need to hear this encouraging truth.

You may struggle with a tendency toward perfectionism like I do. We need to recognize it and reverse our thinking when the Holy Spirit convicts our hearts.

God's message about not trying to save ourselves was not directed to the pagans of long ago. He was telling early believers in Christ that they were not thinking clearly. They thought that obeying the Jewish law of circumcision was a requirement in order to belong to Him. But God freed those men and women (as well as us) from those restrictions when He sent Jesus to open the path to a personal relationship with Him, made accessible by Christ's death on the cross.

Our relationship with God is not based on how perfect we can be. Only God is perfect. If you are feeling inadequate and weary because you feel you're not keeping up with your Christian "to-do" list, tear it up in front of God right now.

"For when we place our faith in Christ Jesus, there is no benefit in being circumcised or being uncircumcised [binding ourselves to a law that He canceled a long time ago]. What is important is faith expressing itself in love" (Galatians 5:6). Out of love for us, Christ gave His own life to make us free, so we need to value His gift and live in that freedom that only He can grant.

This truth is so exciting, I have to contain myself from yelling out loud and waking up my family!

Galatians 5:1 says, "Christ has truly set us free. Now make sure that you stay free, and don't get tied up again in slavery to the law." Live in Christ's freedom!

312

Loading Up the Carts

Listen to my voice in the morning, LORD. Each morning
I bring my requests to you and wait expectantly.

PSALM 5:3

When I go to the grocery store, I always—and I am not exaggerating—*always* get more than what is on my list! This habit is my attempt to follow my sweet friend Sarah's advice to try something new every time I go to the store. Plus, I'll often see an item I need for a particular recipe that I forgot to put on my list.

In the same way, when I go to God's Word each morning with my grocery list of requests for His help, His strength, His courage, and His patience for the day, I always get more than I came for! God is so big, yet so personal; the biggest supermarket we could envision cannot begin to hold all of His awesome character qualities, but He stocks them up in our hearts.

As we read His Word, our finite minds are capable of processing only a glimpse of who He is. He, on the other hand, knows our every thought and request before we do. He supplies our every need, even if we have not revealed the exact list of all that's crammed in our heavy hearts.

What are some of His character qualities that He loves to load up in our hearts? Let's list some of them. He is

- our Friend
- our Rescuer
- our Savior
- our Forgiver

- our Protector
- compassionate
- loving
- merciful

The list goes on and on—and on and on! No matter how much we fill up on Him, the price at the checkout is always the same—free! We never have to worry about having enough funds to cover the cost of all He gives us because He took care of our account long ago through Jesus.

 What other attributes of God can you think of? Jot down how God spiritually nourishes you because of who He is.

Our Love Liner

You were cleansed; you were made holy; you were made right with God by calling on the name of the Lord Jesus Christ and by the Spirit of our God.

1 CORINTHIANS 6:11

When fall hits our neck of the woods and the leaves start to change, out comes my red Crock-Pot! You've already heard how much I love my slow cooker because it not only simplifies dinner preparation, it also fills our home with the most wonderful aroma of home cooking.

Until recently, I did not know they made liners for Crock-Pots. Wow! Now you don't even have to wash the pot before putting it away. I certainly don't miss the days of soaking my Crock-Pot overnight, then scraping and scrubbing off the caked-on remnants of food.

When I place my brand-new liner into my trusted Crock-Pot, it reminds me of Jesus. We are clean because of Jesus. We were made holy because of Jesus. We were made right with God by calling on the name of the Lord Jesus Christ, and we continue to be refined by His Spirit, who is a Master at scouring the stubborn sin we all have in common.

Before knowing Jesus, our lives were like dirty Crock-Pots. Our sinful nature built up ugly layers in our hearts. Even if our lives aren't always overcooking with wrong attitudes and actions, our lack of passion for the things of God will turn out mediocre results if we are not allowing the Holy Spirit to control us and keep us on the right setting.

By believing and receiving Jesus Christ, our Love Liner, we are made holy and clean for God. All He sees is a clean vessel, operating on the "Most High" setting. With the protective love liner of Jesus, God sees us as a brand-new Crock-Pot. (No, I did not say crackpot!)

If you have not done so, invite Jesus to be your Love Liner and present you clean before a Holy God!

God's Side Is the Good Side

*Hezekiah encouraged them by saying: "Be strong and courageous!
Don't be afraid or discouraged because of the king of Assyria
or his mighty army, for there is a power far greater on our
side! He may have a great army, but they are merely men.
We have the LORD our God to help us and to fight our battles
for us!" Hezekiah's words greatly encouraged the people.*

2 CHRONICLES 32:6-8

Hezekiah's words greatly encourage me. I love being in the Lord's army, which may explain why I also enjoy camouflage clothes—in *pink* and green, of course. Being in His army means we are always on God's side and He is always on ours. He has only one side—the good side—and we are on it!

The process of choosing sides for teams always brings up bad childhood memories for me. Someone was always chosen last and although it wasn't always me, I did not want to see that final person's face. It made my heart hurt whenever it happened, and it still does. Maybe God has used those experiences to quicken my heart's desire for everyone in this hurting world to be invited in, hear about God's good side, and be quick to respond to the only side that is going to win in the end for all eternity.

We can trust that God's plan is just and right, and that He fights on the front lines for those on His side. We can also live with bold courage, relying on His power in us rather than on ourselves. As we do, we will be amazed to see Him bless others in surprising ways as they observe Him in our lives. In fact, when we strive to live each day with vibrant faith in Him, God may use us to draw others to His side too.

God gave us His marching orders to proclaim the Good News to others! We can follow Him and His battle plan and gather the troops God places on our path, while we encourage each other in His Kingdom mission.

 Let's be strong and courageous on God's side! If you are facing a challenge right now, know that He is fighting for you even when you cannot see Him or feel the benefits just yet. Ask some of your fellow warriors to pray with you for a victorious outcome.

Failure and Forgiveness

The LORD is compassionate and merciful, slow to get angry and filled with unfailing love. He will not constantly accuse us, nor remain angry forever. He does not punish us for all our sins; he does not deal harshly with us, as we deserve. For his unfailing love toward those who fear him is as great as the height of the heavens above the earth. He has removed our sins as far from us as the east is from the west. The LORD is like a father to his children, tender and compassionate to those who fear him. For he knows how weak we are; he remembers we are only dust.

PSALM 103:8-14

I am lingering in Psalm 103 today. I am especially grateful for the generous gift of God's sweet grace I find in these verses because I'm dealing with guilt and remorse about my actions this past weekend.

My sweet daughter brought a precious friend from college home with her for the weekend. The friend was taking a test at another school close by, and Kali thought it made sense to have her stay with us. I'd like to say I was the picture of hospitality, but I wasn't. In not one but two situations I was *not* quick to listen, *not* slow to speak, and *not* slow to be angry.

Although the Holy Spirit is always living inside believers, I let my human nature show itself more than I left room for His character to shine! I failed to model Christlike behaviors and attitudes, even while writing these devotions. Can you see my tears? Do you know the feeling of failure too?

Where can we go when we mess up? Who can help us deal with our shame and regret? There is no one to turn to except God through the cross of Christ! He has a perfect plan for getting us through. He knows how weak we are on our own, but He is slow to get angry with us. His overflowing heart of unfailing love will not constantly accuse us, and He won't stay angry forever. He is not harsh with us, but instead helps us deal with our guilt and shame, and then puts it behind us forever.

"Lord, my love fails with the people I love the most, but Your love never fails! Thank You for forgiving me."

🗝 Camp in Psalm 103 every day . . . tomorrow . . . this week . . . forever.

Sad Isn't Bad

Sorrow is better than laughter, for sadness has a refining influence on us.

ECCLESIASTES 7:3

Sad isn't bad. This emotion points me in God's right direction.

I figured I'd jump-start this devotion with a boost of hope. I need one today, and I wonder if maybe you do too.

I feel sad today. I woke up missing our beloved Fluffy, our kitty cat of fifteen years that sat in my lap every morning for Purr-and-Praise time, perfectly content. Fluffy was a daily reminder to ask God to help me learn that same kind of contentment and to trust Him to direct me through all the challenges of the day.

I miss my sweet mama even more. I miss our regular early-morning conversations. Even though we were hundreds of miles apart, those minutes on the phone brought her closer to me. I still catch myself wanting to show her things and tell her things, but I won't see her again here on this earth. I miss Daddy, too. He gave me such good advice and loved people the way I want to. Although I feel so close to him when I'm in his Ford pickup, I wish I could roll back time and see him in the driver's seat.

And definitely not least, I miss seeing my one-and-only daughter every day, even though I am so grateful she is thriving in college. My nest just looks too empty this morning. It is a gray, rainy day, which adds to my inner gloom.

You may be struggling with sadness too. The one truth that lifts my spirit is to know Jesus understands, has felt sadness over loss too, and is right here just as sure as my feelings. If life falls apart, He is enough.

Our sadness can bring us to Him. He reminds us that a better day is coming and that all our "present troubles are small and won't last very long" in the scope of eternity. "Yet they produce for us a glory that vastly outweighs them and will last forever!" (2 Corinthians 4:17). Now *that's* sadness turned into gladness! He is using my sad times and yours as well to refine us.

 Sad isn't bad when it opens your heart to let Jesus refine you. Ask God to show you something beautiful today, even as you deal with your sadness.

No Substitutions

*This is how God loved the world: He gave his one
and only Son, so that everyone who believes in
him will not perish but have eternal life.*

JOHN 3:16

At a very young age, I memorized John 3:16. I knew God loved me and I knew He was in my life because I invited Jesus into my heart to save me from my sin.

But I did not begin to have a vital, growing relationship with God for a long time because honestly I did not feel I needed God very much. I was not dealing with any circumstance or disappointment that an ice-cream cone or, later, a new tube of lipstick would not fix.

At times, we all want to substitute things to mask a problem or put off dealing with an issue. These substitutions distract us from what really matters and what can really heal—a close relationship with God through Jesus Christ now and for all eternity.

When God says His Word is alive and powerful (Hebrews 4:12), He is not kidding. He is the Word. Any substitute we try for finding peace with God apart from Himself is dead and powerless.

When I began to recognize Scripture as God's very words, I learned that He is personal and wants us to know Him intimately. I learned God knows everything about us and loves us with an everlasting love. I learned He has a plan for my life and for yours. Spending time in God's Word was the beginning of a day-to-day walk of faith with Christ and the budding of a love relationship for all believers. God's Word tells us that there are no substitutions for His salvation plan and no way to grow spiritually without Christ and putting into practice His truth through the power of His Spirit!

There is no substitution for eternal life apart from Christ. If you have already made a commitment to Christ and are experiencing some "growing pains," that's good too! God draws us to Himself through His Word and by His Holy Spirit.

All in God's Hands

No one can come to Me unless the Father who sent Me draws him.

JOHN 6:44, NKJV

Jesus draws people! This truth frees me, relaxes me, comforts me, and makes me want to jump up and down with joy, even though I'm a grown woman.

You see, I love people, and I want everyone to know Jesus so they will have real, priceless hope, even in the heartaches of life. But I'm so relieved that it isn't up to me at all to change people's hearts—Jesus draws people to Himself.

I cannot do anything to change someone's heart one iota to desire God. When I finally realized this fact and that I was not responsible to give a "perfect" gospel presentation or be the perfect example of a Christian in order for someone to come to Christ, I relaxed. This was a huge burden off my shoulders.

Now, please do not misunderstand me. I am not relaxed about caring. I care about people. I care where people will spend eternity; I want to be in heaven with everyone. I want people to know Christ, not just because their eternal destination is at stake, but also because I cannot imagine experiencing the troubles in this life without relying on a loving and patient Savior, who never keeps any record of my wrongs (1 Corinthians 13:5) and is an ever-present help in trouble (Psalm 46:1, NIV).

Knowing that all the power for change and redemption is in the hands of God is so freeing. We can relax in God's faithfulness and provision, believing He will give us all we need to do what He wants us to do or say. He promised us that His Holy Spirit will reside in our hearts and will reflect Him to others in this hurting world as we go through our daily responsibilities.

Whew! Go God!

God does all the hard work in people's hearts. Let's ask Him to give us sensitivity to how He wants us to reach out to others with His Good News.

Parenting Tips

*So you must submit to [governing authorities], not only to
avoid punishment, but also to keep a clear conscience.*

ROMANS 13:5

As parents, we could be considered "governing authorities." There were times
when Mark and I had to say no to things our teenage daughter, Kali, was invited
to do. She wasn't always happy about it, because "everyone else is doing it."
Still, we believed some of those things could have put Kali in a compromising
situation.

Since I constantly felt like a brand-new mother in every stage of Kali's
development, I was grateful to know God because I needed His help and His
wisdom.

It finally dawned on me while spending time in God's Word how to explain
saying no to certain requests. My boundaries and standards did not necessarily
have anything to do with our daughter and her choices while under our roof, but
they had to do with me and my respect and love for God. As my perfect parent,
God cares for me. And just as Kali needed to submit to my parental authority,
I had to submit to God's authority! God picked me to be Kali's mother, and I took
my responsibility seriously.

I could not allow her to do something against my own conscience without
disobeying God. I wanted to obey God because I love Him. Even as an imperfect
parent, I wanted to honor God by listening to and obeying Him.

Lo and behold, when I shared this simple truth with her that the issue really
wasn't about her but about me answering to the God I love, she understood and
stopped insisting . . . until the next invitation came along.

Of course, I was glad that there were many opportunities to say yes to Kali,
too, but when that familiar unrest and lack of peace pounded my heart, I could
hear God's voice in my soul through His Word. I gained courage to keep a clear
conscience.

Whether you are a parent or not, keep a clear conscience and honor
God in everything. Enjoying His grace and peace feels good in any
situation! Is there something that has been nagging you that needs
to be taken care of?

History with God

"You are my witnesses, O Israel!" says the LORD. "You are my servant.
You have been chosen to know me, believe in me, and understand
that I alone am God. There is no other God—there never has been,
and there never will be. I, yes I, am the LORD, and there is no other
Savior. . . . From eternity to eternity I am God. No one can snatch
anyone out of my hand. No one can undo what I have done."

ISAIAH 43:10-11, 13

History was not my best subject in school. But ever since I began reading the Bible, I have become an avid history student.

Seeing God care for His people over and over again despite their continual disobedience has drawn me to worship such a patient, loving, merciful Lord.

God cares for His people from eternity to eternity, as only the one true God can. He reminds all of us that there is no other God—never has been, never will be!

The history of Israel recorded for us in the Bible is our heritage too. Through His people, God showed a lost world that He alone is God. Today's verses are just a taste of the precious relationship God has with His people—then, now, and forever. He claims us and gives us a place of belonging and hope in Him.

"But now, O Jacob, listen to the LORD who created you. O Israel, the one who formed you says, 'Do not be afraid, for I have ransomed you. I have called you by name; you are mine'" (Isaiah 43:1). When we accept the Lord's gift of salvation, we are His forever. In fact, He tells us that He called us by name—such an intimate, knowledgeable, and personal act on His part. He says no one can undo that fact: we are His and He is ours.

We have a history. We have a history with God through Jesus Christ! Please read all of Isaiah 43 in wonder and worship of God. Let's rejoice that our history with God will continue throughout our future with Him.

Soup Gone Bad

Jesus also used this illustration: "The Kingdom of Heaven is like the yeast a woman used in making bread. Even though she put only a little yeast in three measures of flour, it permeated every part of the dough."

MATTHEW 13:33

Ruined! After twelve hours of simmering soup, this "soup girl" is stewing! I just ruined a healthy and hearty pot of soup that I was excited to serve my family. I had bought a bag of at least sixteen colorful bean varieties that I could mix with a few leftovers and a can of tomatoes. I was feeling very domestic and "Betty Crocker–like." There is something about a big pot of soup on the stove that warms me inside and out, but this batch has me steaming.

It's my fault because I did not read the directions. You see, there was a little bag of spices enclosed with the beans. After soaking the beans overnight and rinsing them in the morning, I added fresh water and dumped the spices into the soup. However, hours later when I tasted a spoonful, I cringed. It was bitter! I discovered after the fact that I was not supposed to dump all the spices from the little bag into the soup immediately and simmer it all day. A lot of spices went a long way toward ruining what could have been a tasty meal because my timing and amounts were not correct.

In Matthew 13:33, Jesus talks about a little yeast permeating every part of the dough. The bitter spices I added permeated every part of the soup negatively. What a simple reminder to me that as believers in Christ, we are good spices; the hope we carry in Christ is the essential ingredient this world needs to recognize. He grows His kingdom in us individually as well as throughout the world. He permeates every part of our soul. His recipe is a sure success if we follow Him closely!

🔑 God can use the humblest effort on our part to grow His kingdom. Let's be open to sharing with others how our experiences of abiding with Him have changed our lives.

Grace Gratefulness

*He said to me, "My grace is sufficient for you, for my power is made
perfect in weakness." Therefore I will boast all the more gladly
about my weaknesses, so that Christ's power may rest on me.*

2 CORINTHIANS 12:9, NIV

Whenever I read the Bible and feel God shed His bright light on a dingy area in
my life, my "grace gratefulness" to Him increases. I realize I fall short of His perfect standard, but I am encouraged that I have company. The Bible is full of stories about God extending His grace to people who did or said the wrong things.

I'm especially guilty when it comes to saying what's on my mind, often without thinking. James, the half brother of Jesus, has a lot to say about the tongue in
his writings. He compares our tongues to tiny sparks that can set great forests on
fire (James 3:5). If you have been to places that have been ravaged by fire or seen
news reports about them, it's heartbreaking. Our unfiltered words can sear a person's heart in the same way. My tendency at times is a quick response, and this is
why I identify with the apostle Peter's impulsiveness. I am glad God knows us so
well and uses the approach of grace to change our weaknesses into strengths, just
as He did with Peter.

Peter spoke and acted impulsively, but Jesus still loved him. Peter did not
stop to think before he denied Jesus three times in a row. Yet Jesus forgave
Peter. As Peter grew in spiritual maturity, I'm guessing he also felt a lot of grace
gratefulness.

God Almighty's way of personally relating with His followers who keep blowing it increases my grace gratefulness. God is always showing us mercy as He
changes us to better reflect His good character. I've come to understand how
much I need His grace, which He lavishes on His own. The more I love Him, the
more I want to please Him and the more my grace gratefulness grows.

There is no way to ever be snatched from God's hand. His grace grips us in
every area of our life, including our tongues. God's grace frees us from being
paralyzed by guilt when we sin. Let's not waste a minute wallowing in guilt. Jesus
told us if we confess our sin, He "is faithful and just to forgive us our sins and to
cleanse us from all wickedness" (1 John 1:9).

What sweet encouragement to all of us. Read Jeremiah 15:16.

323

Little by Little

No, do not be afraid of those nations, for the LORD your God is among you, and he is a great and awesome God. The LORD your God will drive those nations out ahead of you little by little. You will not clear them away all at once, otherwise the wild animals would multiply too quickly for you.

DEUTERONOMY 7:21-22

God is so smart! He knows just how to lead us through this life, whether little by little, one moment at a time, or any way He deems best.

We wake up every morning to an all-knowing God who never needs sleep. He misses nothing. He knows all that happened yesterday, all that is going to take place in the next twenty-four hours (not to mention eternity), and all the repercussions of those events. He also knows everything about your future and mine! He maintains sovereignty over the big events and the little details, letting nothing slip through the cracks. I call this God's providence in tall supply.

In these verses from Deuteronomy, we get a glimpse of God's omniscience, His knowledge of *everything*. We also see His kind, wise commitment to lead His people each step of the way in His plan for them. We see God's specific system for destruction of the idolatrous nations that worshiped idols instead of Him. He worked out His plan for His people little by little, in His way and time, with His omniscient wisdom.

We are God's people in Christ. Everything He did for His people as recorded in the Bible, He can do for us. The ways He related to His people back then give us insight into how He relates to us now—with the added surety of Jesus' gift of salvation to us.

Often it seems we are taking baby steps of faith as we yield ourselves to Him. He knows that if we had to deal with our sins all at once, it would be overwhelming for us. That's why He provides His grace to us each and every day. We need it!

Be thankful today that God is willing to oversee our growth at a pace that works most effectively for us. This is a lifelong process. Let's not meddle with His methods.

This Is My Lord

*I love you, LORD; you are my strength. The LORD is my rock, my
fortress, and my savior; my God is my rock, in whom I find protection.*

PSALM 18:1-2

When we pass a particular church in our neighborhood, even though it is not
where we attend, at least one member in our family usually says in a childlike
voice, "This is *my* church!" We are imitating four-year-old Jack, one of the precious children Kali babysits. Every time the two of them were in the car headed to
the park or another fun excursion and passed Jack's church, he owned it!

This morning as I read the wonderful words in the first two verses of Psalm 18,
I am reminded of just how personal our relationship is to our Lord. Read the verses
out loud with me right now, emphasizing the word *my* every time it is used:

I love You, Lord:
My Strength, *My* Rock,
My Fortress, *My* Savior,
My God.

Because we are His, He is ours! We can pray about any need we have, any
emotional turmoil we are experiencing in our hearts, because we have His ears
and eyes and heart and Holy Spirit 24/7.

"Lord, I feel weak, emotionally and physically today, but You are my strength!"

"Lord, I feel like I am melting in a puddle—but You are my Rock, immovable
and unchanging!"

"Lord, I feel attacked, but You are my Fortress—You surround me. Nothing
can come in and out of my life unless it has gone past You."

"Lord, I feel like life is a daily battle with circumstances only You can really
see and understand. You know all that is happening, and I always win with You
because You are my Savior!"

"You are my God!"

 Take another minute alone today and read the list out loud to God.
He hears.

Lord, Help Me Listen

Spouting off before listening to the facts is both shameful and foolish.

PROVERBS 18:13

Are you a reactor or a responder? More often than I like to admit, I behave like a reactor. Even though my heart is loaded with care for others, sometimes I blurt out a response impulsively and interrupt others. I regret not pausing to think or quiet my spirit. "Lord, I want to become a responder, one who carefully monitors what comes out of my mouth so that my words and how I say them show respect and care for others."

God's Word is so practical! Its truths hits me right between the eyes, one more example of how His Word really is "alive and powerful" (Hebrews 4:12). I am thankful that He uses it to convict me of sin as well as to encourage my pink socks off!

Have you ever spouted off before listening—especially when you are in a hurry? Sometimes my brain is rapidly connecting lots of dots as a sweet person is talking, and I am afraid I am going to forget something, and I don't want the thought to be gone forever. That's different from when I spout off in anger, which is downright sinful.

A few days ago we looked at how Jesus lovingly forgave Peter after Jesus' impulsive disciple denied Him three times. Peter had assured Jesus that he would never deny Him, but sure enough, he did—just as impulsively as when he claimed he never would. Peter's weakness and Jesus' response to him gives me comfort. Peter's norm was to be a reactor, but Jesus was a master at being a gracious Responder.

God is at work in me. God is at work in sweet you. He wants us to reflect Him and bring glory to Him. "Lord, I long to be a better listener—to You and to others. It starts and ends with You, Lord. I need You!"

Today let's purpose in our hearts to be listeners who respond instead of being impulsive reactors. Read John 10:27 and ask God to make that true for you.

Best Friend

You are my friends if you do what I command.

JOHN 15:14

Do you have a best friend? There aren't too many relationships as sweet as those shared by best friends. Maybe you can name several who have filled that role for you throughout your life. Isn't it amazing that we can all share the same Best Friend, Jesus?

When I read a verse like the one for today, it makes me think what it must have been like to walk this earth as a friend of Jesus. The disciples were His companions, and He was always teaching them what it meant to be His friend. He knew all that was coming and how it would affect them, so He encouraged them to follow His lead. His words of caring direction showed how deep His love was for each of them.

Jesus was fully human, and He had best friends too. Of course, He chose His disciple friends wisely! If I were to guess which of them He'd call a best friend, I'd choose John. I call their twosome friendship "The Special Js."

John wrote about his firsthand experience with Jesus in the Gospel of John, followed by three very personal "sticky notes"—1, 2, and 3 John. John was known as the beloved disciple (John 13:23; 20:2), and he was the man Jesus entrusted with the care of His mother, Mary, as He was dying (John 19:26-27). John also outran Peter to Jesus' tomb (John 20:2-4) because he was so anxious to see what had happened to his Best Friend.

And how precious it is that Jesus' best earthly friend was the one God chose to write Jesus' words in Revelation, the last book of the Bible, to encourage us and prepare us for His final coming and to offer us a glimpse of what's ahead. John's life of obedience to Jesus' mission after He ascended to heaven attests to the fact that their friendship was genuine.

I love these examples of how personal Jesus is to His followers—He loves building friendships with us. He knows we need Him as a Best Friend, and He wants to help us all discover that special relationship with Him.

Let's seek the company of our Best Friend and spend time with those who share that same friendship with Him. Only in Christ can we all have the very same Best Friend.

Most High Place

*The high places, however, were not removed, and the people
still had not set their hearts on the God of their ancestors.*

2 CHRONICLES 20:33, NIV

Every time I read in 2 Chronicles of the ups and downs of kings either leading
God's people down a good path or clearly heading along a destructive one, I find
myself cheering under my breath for the ruler and his people to choose God!
"Choose the best! Choose to follow God's plan! There is no higher place than the
Most High God!" Sometimes I get so caught up in the story, I start getting anxious and say in my heart, *Uh-oh, don't go! Don't go there. Don't go up to those high
places where the pagan shrines are located.*

Time after time in the Bible, we find that high, mountaintop sites were used
as places to erect shrines to man-made gods. In erecting these shrines, the people
were breaking the first of God's Ten Commandments that He gave to Moses: "You
must not have any other god but me" (Exodus 20:3).

The books of 1 and 2 Kings and 1 and 2 Chronicles list the kings of Judah and
the kings of Israel. It appears that most of their downfalls resulted because they
did not remove the high places that were dedicated to false gods!

If we are wise, you and I should desire our Most High God to hold the most
high place in our hearts. Anything else we worship will eventually bring destruction to our lives, as well as to those we love. We may not notice the disastrous
effects right away, but they will come, just as they did to the kings in the Bible
who worshiped idols. God Most High always must be number one in our hearts.

 "Lord, is there anything that I have set high in my heart besides You
alone? You are the Most High God. I reserve the highest place in my
life for You!"

Peter, Paul, and Mary

Faith is the confidence that what we hope for will actually happen;
it gives us assurance about things we cannot see. Through their
faith, the people in days of old earned a good reputation.

HEBREWS 11:1-2

Peter, Paul, and Mary wannabes? Yes! Even though these three faithful people of God were not actually listed by name in the Hebrews 11 Hall of Faith, they sure have earned a good reputation with me (and I'm not referring to the sixties folk trio). The Bible's Peter, Paul, and Mary loved Jesus, and the more I read about each of them, the more I love how they personally demonstrated that love.

In 2 Peter 1:1, Peter calls himself a slave of Jesus Christ. I want to be that too. And Paul? His example of rejoicing and singing in prison and defending his faith inspires me (Acts 16:25; Acts 22–26). What an incredible passion he had for Jesus, his Savior and Lord. Finally there was Mary, the sister of Martha and Lazarus, who always chose the better way, which was spending time with Jesus (Luke 10:42). I want to be like Mary and prioritize my time with Jesus too.

Above all, I love Jesus, and I suspect you do too. We can't help but fall in love with Him as we discover more about Him and what He did for us. From the beginning to the end of the Bible—Genesis to Revelation—we get to know Jesus and how He relates to His people through individuals like Peter, Paul, and Mary. Reading about the heroes of faith who gave up everything for Christ—without any regrets—provides inspiration and courage to me to love Him just as fervently and to stay close to Him always through what He has to say.

Read the names of other faithful, godly people in Hebrews 11. Are any of them your personal heroes? What about the people who show Jesus' love to you now? Thank God for them.

A Smile in the Midst of Sadness

I heard a voice from heaven saying, "Write this down:
Blessed are those who die in the Lord from now on. Yes, says
the Spirit, they are blessed indeed, for they will rest from
their hard work; for their good deeds follow them!"

REVELATION 14:13

Yes, Lord, I am writing this down! (Please note that the exclamation point in the verse above wasn't added by me—it's part of Scripture!)

In the very first verse of the book of Revelation, the last book of the Bible, Jesus Christ dictates to His best friend, John: "This is a revelation from Jesus Christ, which God gave him to show his servants the events that must soon take place."

This entire book is a dramatic end to all the events in the Bible that precede it. But even more exciting, it's an introduction of the times to come. I don't think any of us—or even the best Bible scholar—will ever unravel what all of this prophetic book's mysterious events mean until they actually take place. That in itself should spark hope within us because Jesus is planning much more for His followers—this life isn't all there is. When a loved one dies, the loss is painful, but if that person was a believer, we can be comforted that the loss isn't permanent.

Bible scholars interpret the events in Revelation in a variety of ways. Regardless of all the different views concerning its message, most of them agree on some practical promises and warnings to all of us. I especially love the comforting promise of today's verse, since I have family members who believed in Christ and are now with the Lord. They are "blessed indeed," resting from their hard work, and their good deeds are following them.

Revelation's message is one of forever hope beyond temporary sadness. God didn't have to clue us in to His plans, but in His loving-kindness He did. He wants us to hold on to hope in Him while things are difficult here. It is yet another reason we can smile at the future in the midst of the sad things we experience.

 Christ is triumphant over death! This life isn't all there is. Read the apostle Paul's encouraging words about Jesus' return in 1 Thessalonians 4:13-18.

Daily Pep Talk

*Let us strip off every weight that slows us down, especially the
sin that so easily trips us up. And let us run with endurance the
race God has set before us. We do this by keeping our eyes on
Jesus, the champion who initiates and perfects our faith.*

HEBREWS 12:1-2

I need this pep talk from God every day, don't you? We are all running this race of life not knowing how long it will last, how many losses we will face, or if any earthly cheerleaders will ever show up by our side.

Life is full of unknowns, yet the clock is ticking and our choice for survival is faith in Christ, our true Life Coach. He has already won the eternal life "race" for us, so our goal really isn't about winning eternal life but about living by faith.

I love His practical advice here in Hebrews 12. When I get dressed every morning, I literally cut off every weight that slows me down—those tags in my blouses that itch the back of my neck, those ribbons stitched into the shoulders to keep your clothes on the hanger but that always manage to hang out when you don't notice. And pockets? I have most of them cut out and tightly sewn up because if I put anything in them, they literally bog me down with added weight to my thighs!

Jesus requires us to throw off anything—especially our sin—that slows us down from progressing in our faith. The very best way to live is to remain fixed on our constant, Jesus Christ. Life and faith are simpler if we are not holding on to anything that holds us back from Jesus. Focusing on Jesus in the race He sets for you and me is a game changer for sure!

Need a daily pep talk? Keep your eyes on Jesus and get rid of anything that distracts you from your primary focus, which is Jesus Himself!

Reminders

My child, never forget the things I have taught you. Store my
commands in your heart. . . . Never let loyalty and kindness
leave you! Tie them around your neck as a reminder.

PROVERBS 3:1, 3

Are you as grateful for reminders as I am? There is so much going on in life with both work and family responsibilities that I need something to keep me on top of things. If I don't jot down a note or send a text to myself, I'm sure to forget to pick up milk at the store or return a book I borrowed. Nowadays, we can even get phone or text reminders for our doctor and hair appointments! (I am definitely on overload since I forgot to make a hair appointment, which I really need!)

This may sound funny, but I even need a visual reminder to accessorize! I don't want to forget to grab a cute accessory before I head out for the day. After so many years of being disappointed because I forgot to wear something pretty, I finally hung my necklaces on a cute rack that I can't miss and put my watches on a dresser near the bedroom door. I simply grab something fun and go. No more wasting time trying to untangle a necklace or finding a coordinating timepiece!

When I slip on a necklace today, the verses above come to mind. I have never literally tied loyalty and kindness around my neck, but God knows how much I need to be reminded about the instructions in His Word.

We can be reminded to focus on Him in several ways. God longs for every believer to spend time reading His Word every day because we need reminders of His higher ways in our world that's packed with many of the lowest-common-denominator distractions! We also are reminded of Him when we spend time with other believers. When we are all growing together, God's Word is fresh on our hearts to encourage each other in this daily battle of life.

Let's remind ourselves to add "time with God" to our list for the day.

Pick some kind of reminder method that works for you to prompt you to spend time with God each day. Maybe it's a note on the fridge or a Post-it on the car dashboard or bathroom mirror. Maybe you'd even like to splurge and buy yourself a necklace that reminds you to be tied to God's Word whenever you put it on. Whatever it takes, let's keep His Word filling our hearts and minds.

Do You Have Reservations?

There is more than enough room in my Father's home. If this were not so, would I have told you that I am going to prepare a place for you? When everything is ready, I will come and get you, so that you will always be with me where I am.

JOHN 14:2-3

My husband is a very funny man with a quick wit. We've been married almost thirty years, and in certain situations I *still* cannot tell if he is teasing me.

The day before Mother's Day one year, Mark was frantically trying to get lunch reservations for our family to dine after church. He confidently advised me to give him a little credit because he was ahead of all the guys who waited until the day of the special occasion! When Mark was on the phone, he was talking loudly so Kali and I could hear everything clearly.

"Oh, is this the kind of restaurant where the portions are very small and it is very expensive? Well, that sounds just like the kind of place my girls like to eat!" I looked at Kali in horror, and she returned the same look to me. We were waving *no, no, no* in the background, trying to get Mark to hang up the phone!

But he got us good. We didn't know until he hung up the phone that he had been playing a joke on us. There wasn't anyone on the other end of the phone line when he called! Oh, the gift of laughter. It is so precious.

Did you know that God has reserved a place for each one of His children in His house? The comfort Jesus offered to His disciples before His crucifixion assures us today that there is more than enough room for all who trust Him as Savior. Not only that, He's getting His place all ready for us, and He will pick us up at just the right time.

Philippians 3:20-21 gives more clarity about what Jesus is preparing for those who believe in Him as Savior. What are you looking forward to most about your eternal reservation with Jesus? If you are not sure yours has been made, read John 3:16.

Sweet Slippers

Be still, and know that I am God!
PSALM 46:10

Back in college, my roommates used to tell me I walked hard! I would wake my friends with my stomping without even realizing I was doing it. My exuberance seemed to be coming out of my feet! Over the years, I've tried to help soften my tread with slippers. I have quite a few pairs. Not only do I appreciate how the slippers muffle the sound of my feet, but I also love the soft, cushiony feel of them. I'll take slippers over bare feet anytime!

As much as I love comfortable slippers, I am even more thankful that each new day God cushions me with His presence. The Creator of all—all that we see and all that we don't see, the Creator of me and the Creator of you—is our personal God. We can know Him and experience His comfort each day. He softens the rough way before us and helps us learn how to tread lightheartedly and gently around others.

Every day I am grateful to know Him but far more thankful that He knows me and loves me perfectly. He knows and loves you perfectly, too, more than anyone else in this world. He sees all that will transpire in our chaotic days that may threaten our ability to walk through the challenges.

God wants us to stop our perpetual moving and reflect on who He is. I think He wants us to literally stop all activity and know that He is God! When we do, He'll help us walk in His grace and rest in His strong arms, with slippers or not.

Slip into God's Word daily. Laugh, cry, and allow Him to encourage your heart. Then, when we put on our cute, regular shoes to carry out His plans, we can be the feet that bring Good News!

Pretty Pink Purse

An honest answer is like a kiss of friendship.

PROVERBS 24:26

Usually the first Monday in December is reserved for a special event—the annual Sweet Monday Purse Swap in our home. The December purse swaps are special because they fit well with the spirit of gift giving and Christmas shopping. Every woman brings a purse to exchange, and I share a five-minute devotion about the greatest exchange that ever took place when God sent His Son, Jesus, into the world. God's incredible gift is the true reason we celebrate Christmas.

At each month's Sweet Monday outreach, I display things on my foyer table that I've gathered from my own home for simple shoestring-budget decorations that tie in with the monthly theme. For one particular purse swap I set my new pink purse on the table, a surprise gift from my sweet friend Katherine.

Toward the end of the swap, it was time for a newcomer to make her choice. "I don't want any purses in this room," she said. "I want the purse on the foyer table!" *What did she say?* I couldn't believe it. My purse was a decoration, not part of the swap. I was so caught off guard that I didn't know what to do except give it to her! After everyone had left, I told Kali and Mark what had happened.

A week later Katherine stopped by to visit Kali and me. I dreaded telling her about the purse. When I finally did, I wasn't expecting her reaction.

"I wish you hadn't given her the purse," Katherine said kindly. "I wish you had said, 'A special friend wanted me to have that purse, so it's not part of the swap tonight.'" Kali, who was with me at the time, was as surprised as I was at Katherine's honest response. Her feelings had been hurt, and I felt awful.

"I am so sorry, Katherine," I said. "I wish I had been quick on my feet and thought of that. But instead, all I could think of was to give the purse up to Jesus and that He would have given it to this sweet newcomer."

As uncomfortable as this exchange was for me, I'm glad it happened. It was a true "kiss of friendship" and a teachable moment for all three of us. I was tickled pink when Katherine replaced the purse with another one. God desires honesty from us at all times, and an honest answer is loving in the long run.

🔑 An honest answer honors God! Read Psalm 51:5-6, verses that confirm we need God's help to be honest.

More Is Caught Than Taught

Remember your leaders who taught you the word
of God. Think of all the good that has come from
their lives, and follow the example of their faith.

HEBREWS 13:7

I cannot remember a time when I was not aware of God and His love for me through His only Son, Jesus Christ. My parents talked about Him and took us to church regularly. I remember saying the blessing, "Tank You," before a meal as a child and heading off to Sunday school.

My parents didn't have daily family devotions with us growing up, but they were leaders by example. Daddy read Luke 2 every Christmas, and Mama continued the tradition after Daddy died. Even though reading God's Word aloud was not a daily habit in our home while I was growing up, the power of love and forgiveness were evident in everyday living. I don't think I ever heard Daddy say the blessing without saying, "And Lord, thank You for forgiving us of our sins."

My mom and dad were genuine honest-to-goodness sinners just like you and me, and when I was younger they never tried to hide that condition! Now I realize how precious their honest, open example was. They were the same authentic people covered in Christ even after we left church. As a child, I caught their lessons of genuine faith. I'm grateful to God that in His sweet grace and providence, their genuine faith has rubbed off on me.

I am convinced that more is caught than taught for all of us—children and adults—whether those lessons are positive or negative. I think it is pretty much a given that someone is always observing our actions, watching how we live life and act on the faith we profess. Are we living a life of faith we want our children, friends, and coworkers to imitate? How will we be remembered?

More is caught than taught, so let's live like Jesus whether we think someone is watching or not. The one Someone who is always watching is God Himself. It is comforting that He sees all.

Eternal Gold Medal

*All athletes are disciplined in their training. They do it to
win a prize that will fade away, but we do it for an eternal
prize. So I run with purpose in every step. . . . I discipline my
body like an athlete, training it to do what it should.*

1 CORINTHIANS 9:25-27

Sports have always been a big part of my husband's life. Mark told me that when he was five years old and went outside to shoot hoops, he refused to come in for supper until he had made one hundred points! His strict personal training paid off when he was later offered a full scholarship to play basketball at the University of Virginia. At UVA, Mark was assigned to room with an athlete outside his sport, the first time this had happened. Mark and his roommate, Don Flow, a football player, helped start the first FCA (Fellowship of Christian Athletes) chapter there. (In his remarks at a recent FCA reunion banquet, Mark lightheartedly commented that he had to make it clear to the UVA football players that FCA didn't stand for "Follow Chicks Around.")

Mark coaches and teaches sports to this day, so you can understand why watching the Olympics every two to four years is a Newlen priority. I like hearing the athletes' stories and admire them for all the time and training it took for them to achieve their goal. It makes me ask myself, *What does my spiritual training look like?*

Paul knew his body was the temple of the Holy Spirit, and he knew how easily he could dishonor it through giving way to temptation. He encourages us to discipline ourselves like an athlete, always in training to do what we should for an eternal prize. Let's sweat a bit about our own weak areas and ask God to specifically show us where we may be flabby in running His race on this earth. Just as athletes tone muscle with use, we can tone our faith muscles for greater effectiveness in the marathon God sets before us by daily exercise in the Word of God and physically doing what He says.

We already have a gold medal in Jesus Christ, so we can run with purpose in every step. Let's make every step count today as we discipline our spiritual muscles.

Real Secret to Youth

He fills my life with good things. My youth is renewed like the eagle's!
PSALM 103:5

Have you noticed the great number of potions for ageless youth advertised on television or in women's magazines? The battle against aging rages on because there hasn't been a foolproof earthly formula found yet to prevent it from happening. And let me tell you a little secret: there never will be.

Psalm 103 is a song of praise for everything that God gives us who are His children. When you and I have a personal relationship with the Lord, we gain strength from Him. I have never met a Christian with a vibrant connection to Christ who was not a beautiful, seemingly ageless person at any age! And this is just the beginning. When we commit our lives to Christ, we can look forward to being with Him forever, without any of the effects of aging we experience now.

I am grateful that early in life I made the decision to go God's way and not mine. I purposed in my heart not to interfere with His plans, and I can say that His way has always proved to be the best. I had no idea that walking *with* God and not going ahead of Him with my own plans would prove to be the most fun, fulfilling adventure of my life.

He promises to fill our lives with good things, and I, for one, don't want to miss out. Okay, I'll admit that I buy face cream with sunscreen, but I know it cannot give me youth. A youthful spirit is something that only God can give. He gives it to all His people, along with other good gifts! Look what we have to look forward to—Jesus presenting us to God as His church, "without a spot or wrinkle or any other blemish" (Ephesians 5:27).

Feeling your age? You are young in Christ. He renews our youth when we put our faith and trust in Him. He is our best look!

Ready, Set, Roll

Commit to the LORD whatever you do, and your plans will succeed.

PROVERBS 16:3, NIV

One of the things that all the Newlen family has in common is matching planner pads. Although they are the same, we organize them differently. Nevertheless, our planners work well to help each of us carry out our many God-given responsibilities—for me as a wife, mother, coworker, and ministry leader; for Mark as a father, husband, teacher, and coach; for Kali as a college student, InterVarsity video team leader, and babysitter. While we may appear to have a handle on organization, sometimes our plans become so many that they move from being manageable to being big burdens!

Proverbs 16:3 gives us a specific plan to help us avoid being overwhelmed with our plans. We are to commit them to the Lord. He doesn't tell us not to plan, because that would be unwise. He tells us to commit our plans to Him, whatever we do. When we commit our plans to the Lord, we acknowledge that everything is ultimately in His hands. When we operate using our own efforts instead of depending on Him, we will grow weary (Isaiah 40:30).

A sweet friend named Debbie just shared with me what the word translated *commit* is in the original Hebrew: it is a word meaning *to roll*. I love that! Big or small, we can roll our responsibilities onto the Lord. We can drop our many plans off our burdened backs and dump them right down in front of the Living God.

He is not pacing back and forth wondering what He is going to do with His pitiful people who are trying to carry their plans by themselves. He did not create us to carry burdens but to roll them off our backs!

If we are wise, we want His plans. Our plans become His plans when we are faithfully walking with Him. And His plans will succeed, according to His will, in His time.

Let's roll those plans of ours off our backs and free ourselves from their limits. Then let's commit to God's plans for us, believing that His to-do list will be the most productive plan in every way.

The Power of This Moment

Make the most of every opportunity in these evil days.
EPHESIANS 5:16

When was the last time you had a professional photograph taken of yourself? Maybe your family gets them taken every fall for an upcoming Christmas card, or perhaps you've had a picture taken recently for work.

Professional photos are great because we have time to primp and prepare beforehand, the photographer shoots us in several poses, and sometimes we can even make clothing changes. When the photographic proofs arrive, we can choose the ones we think look the best. Heaven forbid if we have to start over!

As beautiful as a finished photograph may be, it doesn't usually present a truly realistic view of everyday life. Life is messy and spontaneous, and we're often thrown curveballs that make redos impossible. And sometimes we just don't look our best on the inside or the outside.

When it comes to living for God and preparing for Jesus' return, we need to make the most of each moment we have left on earth because no one knows the exact time and date when He will come back. We need to be ready as well as to help others be ready too. Although we don't know the timing of that momentous event, we can live life from one candid snapshot to the next, showing Christ's light developing in us. After we're gone, those snapshot memories will serve as a legacy to others that will glorify Him.

I believe that each connection we make with another person provides an opportunity to display an image of Christ's love to him or her. That's how we live out today's verse. The world is filled with images of sin and darkness, and what it really needs to see are images of Christ the Savior, Lord, King, Sustainer, Provider, Refuge, and Friend. Talk about the Power of a moment!

What characteristics of God will you show to a needy world today? Ask Him to help you leave His image everywhere you go and through everything you say in His strength and power, just as Colossians 3:17 says.

Bright Light

*You are a chosen people. You are royal priests, a holy nation, God's
very own possession. As a result, you can show others the goodness of
God, for he called you out of the darkness into his wonderful light.*

1 PETER 2:9

Wonderful light! As I mentioned in an earlier devotion, no forty- or sixty-watt
lightbulbs for me! Bright lightbulbs have been a staple for me since my college
days. I love the right lampshades, too—those that allow plenty of light to shine
through. In fact, I just changed two black shades to white ones for that very reason. I like light so much that I keep little white lights around the inside of most
windows in the back of our home year round. My sweet neighbor Muriel says she
enjoys them too.

Maybe like me, you enjoy driving through the neighborhood at Christmas to
see the lights. Some homes are ablaze with thousands of them. I pretend all those
bulbs are birthday candles for Jesus!

One of the reasons I'm a light lover is because Jesus is too. Actually, He calls
Himself the Light of the World. When we have a personal relationship with
Him, Jesus is forever our ultra-watt, bright and perfect Light who never needs
replacing! He never fades or flickers during life's storms. He doesn't rely on
unpredictable electricity sources—He is His own strong and unchanging power
source with infinite wattage.

He chooses us to shine His light far and wide. When we belong to Him, we are
chosen, holy lightbulbs that come in all shapes and sizes. He supplies the current,
and we carry that current out to a world that longs to be rescued from darkness.
That's definitely worth singing His praises.

Each day when we plug into Him, His glow will shine through us. When we
complain and argue and do not choose to give thanks in all circumstances, our
spiritual lightbulbs dim. But when we live our days in praise, our lights shine
brilliantly in Christ!

Let's shine on by declaring His praises! We are free from darkness
forever in Jesus Christ—our wonderful Light! Write Ephesians 5:8
on a card to hang among the lights on your Christmas tree as a
reminder of who you are as a follower of Christ.

Living by Faith

*My righteous ones will live by faith. But I will take
no pleasure in anyone who turns away.*

HEBREWS 10:38

For most of my life, I was afraid to step out in any direction that I was not sure would bring me 100 percent success. Failure was too painful for me. Failure in front of others? No, thank you!

In college, I did not want to play flag football unless I played a position where I didn't have to touch the ball! I was mortified by the thought that I might drop it. They made me the ineligible guard on offense. Now that may sound awful to you, but I liked the way it sounded—ineligible! On defense, grabbing for the flags ended up being my cup of tea. No offense for me.

I also loved to sing and was part of a huge choir that did a Christmas cantata each year. One year I was offered Mary's role. I went to all the practices, but I backed out the day before the performance because I was fearful I would fail. We all sang Mary's part in unison. As much as I was relieved not to be singing a solo, I was embarrassed that I had let down both the choir and the director.

Back then I thought it was too scary to live by faith. Living by faith requires movement, and I would chronically stall. As a result, I missed out on some of God's blessings and opportunities.

Fortunately, as I grew up and fell more in love with Christ, I started to take baby steps to do what God said in His Word as He placed situations before me. God always came through, and my faith journey had begun.

God tells us to live by faith—moving, growing, living faith—"no ifs, ands, or buts about it," as we say in the South! It's only when we live by faith that we see God changing us. It is clear from today's verse that there is only one direction in which we are to go. His direction—the direction of faith—is the right one every time.

Live by faith. God always comes through! The Bible is full of stories of many faithful heroes who moved when God prompted, even though what was on the other side was not visible.

Store Christ's Commands

My child, never forget the things I have taught
you. Store my commands in your heart.

PROVERBS 3:1

I'll admit it: I'm very sentimental. It's why I have many boxes, bins, and stacks of pictures that I haven't been able to part with yet because I need to go through them.

I even have a hard time throwing away people's family Christmas cards because their sweet faces are on them. Once I ended up wallpapering a whole wall in our powder room with family greeting cards, which became quite a conversation piece and kept a line at the door. Another year I covered a piece of black fabric with photos of family and friends and placed it under the glass tabletop in our den. We still enjoy seeing all of their faces there. (Other friends have been delighted to find one of their friends' photos under that glass tabletop, not knowing we shared a mutual friend.)

As sentimental as I am, I am a perpetual simplifier around our home. When I was unexpectedly diagnosed with breast cancer on Good Friday a number of years ago, everything in my life seemed to change so quickly. The cancer affected not only my body but my schedule, too. The seemingly endless tests, treatments, appointments, follow-ups, and living the "in sickness and in health" part of our marriage vows were hard to fit into an already abundant life. There was a lot to do, Lord willing, to get well! How grateful I was to have my personal priorities in place, knowing God loved me. I was His girl and I knew He had my best interest at heart. This made all the difference in my "royal" treatment.

On September 5 I explained how prioritizing God, His Word, and others became simple, sweet, and salty principles in my mind. Once again, here's a recap of Christ's commands that permeated my heart years ago and still shape how my days are arranged to live His priorities:

Simple: "Seek the Kingdom of God above all else." (Matthew 6:33)
Sweet: "How sweet your words taste to me; they are sweeter than honey."
   (Psalm 119:103)
Salty: "You are the salt of the earth." (Matthew 5:13)

Simplify your life today by storing Christ's commands in your heart.

Sweet Tweet

Calling the crowd to join his disciples, he said, "If any of you wants to be my follower, you must turn from your selfish ways, take up your cross, and follow me."

MARK 8:34

If Jesus had a smartphone, I wonder if "Follow me" would have been His first tweet. It certainly fits within Twitter's character limits! It's funny to think about Jesus pulling out His cell phone and typing that message, but you know, I believe He would do just that if He came to earth today. He met people where they were and connected with them in ways they understood. He would definitely be the master tweeter; I'd be very interested in how quickly His follower count would grow.

The crowd Jesus addresses in today's story was made up of people just like you and me who wanted to see for themselves what was going on with this man they had heard about. The news had spread about His miracles, like healing a deaf man and a blind man and feeding four thousand people with only seven loaves of bread and a few small fish. Not only did everyone there get more than enough to eat, but there were plenty of leftovers, too.

It is *amazing* how God can do so much with so little! He can communicate volumes with very few words, and He can reach anyone, anywhere, without the power of social media. His ability to reach people at their point of need has always been more spectacular than any man-made media can achieve. I echo the disciple John when he said, "Jesus also did many other things. If they were all written down, I suppose the whole world could not contain the books that would be written" (John 21:25).

Jesus is worth following, and following closely. His messages to us are like sweet tweets that went viral long ago and still bear retweeting.

When I imagine a modern-day crowd all with cell phones listening to Jesus and receiving His sweet tweet invitation to follow Him, I hope everyone is tweeting back, "Yes! I'll follow" and then retweeting it to all their friends.

⚷ Retweet: #Follow Jesus. Or respond to His sweet tweet today.

Songs of Confidence

My heart is confident in you, O God; my heart is confident.
No wonder I can sing your praises! Wake up, my heart! Wake
up, O lyre and harp! I will wake the dawn with my song.

PSALM 57:7-8

Psalm means "song," and even though we may have no idea of the original tune of Psalm 57 and may not have greeted the dawn with a song today, we can sing along with David about our confidence in Christ.

Why is it possible to have so much confidence in God? Well, not only has He delivered us from our enemies of sin, death, and the devil because of the victory Christ won on the cross, but we have a loving refuge in Him in the midst of upsetting circumstances. We have a Defender and a Conqueror who has unlimited capabilities to fight on our behalf. He wants us to be as confident in Him as He is in Himself.

In the introductory note for this psalm to the choir director, it says, "A psalm of David, regarding the time he fled from Saul and went into the cave. To be sung to the tune 'Do Not Destroy!'" David was fleeing for his life, finally admitting to God how weary he was from his distress (verse 6). If David, the man after God's own heart, became weary from distress, we can go to God to renew our confident faith too.

Going to God and taking hold of His peace is such a privilege. We must choose to put our confidence in Christ because He sees the before and after and ever after of every event in our lives.

"Lord, You loved David in his distress and You love me in mine! You know I'm upset about _____ (fill in the blank), but I trust You, Lord. I feel weary. I am tired of hiding, running, and complaining. I have You as my confidence builder. I open my heart to You right now."

Shout out with me whatever distress you are facing today. Then combat that circumstance with Christ's sure confidence, which is rightfully ours if we belong to Him! Read Ephesians 3:12 to see what that confidence compels us to do.

Standing on the Solid Rock

From the ends of the earth, I cry to you for help when my heart is overwhelmed. Lead me to the towering rock of safety.

PSALM 61:2

I will never forget the day my sweet friend Sherry showed us a painting at Community Bible Study. It was a big gorgeous scene painted with soft colors. It was so lifelike that we could almost see the wind blowing, sending the waves crashing into a big, solid rock that jutted out from the center of the sea.

A woman stood on the rock. Now mind you, she wasn't sprawled out on a beach towel getting a tan or tying up her sailboat. She was alone, with the wind and waves churning all around her. But she was standing upright on the rock, appearing to be unaffected by the wild water in turmoil around her.

This visual picture reminds me of our Solid Rock, Jesus. He is the only really firm place in life. He is the only Person who is immovable, unchanging, always loving, always strong, and solid as a rock!

When the waves of grief, disappointment, disease, death, divorce, and unmet expectations strike us and our hearts are overwhelmed, we need to see ourselves firmly planted on that Rock—with both feet balanced, not wavering, head high, eyes fixed on Jesus. Jesus Christ does not shift like the ebb and flow of ocean waves. He is always higher than our lowest point, always ready to raise us up to stand with Him. When we anchor ourselves to Him, no storm can drown us, no wind can blow us out of His range of protection.

Our lives in the midst of the storm can leave just as memorable an impression on others as that painting did for me.

When your heart is overwhelmed, imagine yourself as that woman standing on the Solid Rock of Jesus Christ. Read Psalm 19:14 aloud as a rock-solid prayer to our immovable God.

Lost My Marbles

Live clean, innocent lives as children of God, shining like bright lights in a world full of crooked and perverse people.

PHILIPPIANS 2:15

I lost my marbles. Seriously, I literally lost about a hundred of my marbles at the bottom of the kitchen trash can when I was discarding a seasonal fall decoration.

I wish you could have seen my work of art! I am not a very crafty person, but I do feel comfortable using a glue gun. The marbles acted as a weight to hold a brown twig with candy corn hot-glued strategically to its branches. It was very cute and sweet while it lasted.

When fall rolled into the Christmas season, I wanted to replace the arrangement with a holiday one. But when I went to discard it, I forgot about the marbles until it was too late! I laughed as I donned my fancy decorated kitchen gloves to transfer my trash into a new trash bag in order to save my marbles. One by one, I collected my marbles for future projects.

In a world full of crooked and unpeaceful people easily marred by the worries of life, God has chosen those in Christ to be His prized, shiny marbles, saved from the garbage can of sin, not only to reflect His light but to be used for His future projects. This is the gospel, the Good News we need to hear every day. God has given us everything we need to live clean, innocent lives as children of God. He sees us as clean and innocent before Him because Jesus came to earth as a human in order to rescue us.

Let's live clean, innocent lives as children of God and thank Him for rescuing us. Swap out an old home décor piece for a new one, and thank God that His Good News never grows old and never goes out of season.

The Gift God Has Given

Give as freely as you have received!

MATTHEW 10:8

When I am out and about and see something I can afford that reminds me of someone I love, I purchase it right then because I may not pass that way again. It saves me sweet time in the long run, trying to find just the right thing.

I also like to have things to look forward to, don't you? One of the reasons giving is fun is the joyful surprise on someone's face when the person opens something unexpected. At home I have a small chest of drawers for storing gifts. This organization helps me always know where I have stored the earthly treasures until the appropriate holiday arrives. Sometimes I cannot wait until a birthday or Christmas.

As believers in Christ, we have been given the greatest Gift, Jesus Christ, God's only Son. God gave His Son to us, and He will never take back this gift of salvation this side of heaven. No gift will ever compare to Him. I wonder who is more excited about all we receive in Him—God or us? I have to guess that it's God because He knows far better than we do all that awaits us, and He goes to such lengths to ensure our best.

In Luke 12, Jesus tells us to be ready for His return. In the meantime, He urges us to live faithful lives through His strength and power, which He fully and generously gives us. He says in verse 48, "When someone has been given much, much will be required in return; and when someone has been entrusted with much, even more will be required." He is talking about all we have—our time, possessions, spiritual gifts, everything! We, in turn, must follow His example and give of ourselves. We begin our giving with giving ourselves right back to God. We can live faithfully and purposefully, keeping the Giver of all things as our relationship priority!

 Let's give as freely as we have received. Remember that no gift is too small in God's eyes.

Hurry Worries

Paul had decided to sail on past Ephesus, for he didn't want to spend any more time in the province of Asia. He was hurrying to get to Jerusalem, if possible, in time for the Festival of Pentecost.

ACTS 20:16

The word that catches my attention in this verse is *hurrying*. The apostle Paul was trying to meet a deadline and had to travel as fast as possible. I feel his pain of possibly being late for some precious person or event. I truly take heart that someone like Paul, whom I admire for his incredible faith, actually experienced anxious human moments like I often do! What a great reminder to all of us that we need to place our hurry worries in God's hands.

I can relate to that human hurry, especially when I give myself too much to do in too little time. Most of us can relate to suffering, too—maybe not in as dramatic a fashion as what Paul endured, but suffering nonetheless. Yet Paul stayed true to the One who had transformed his heart and sustained him through his three missionary journeys with His power.

No matter how hurried we find ourselves, we can rest assured that God's timing will always be right for accomplishing His plans in our lives. He never gets behind, never overschedules, never feels panicked. He moves quickly, whether it is for the purpose of coming to our aid or opening or closing doors. His timing and sovereignty are perfect. His reign over our lives is not only comforting but brings us confidence in Christ. We can relax our hurried hearts and catch our breath in Him.

"Lord, I am so human! I get caught up in the rush more times than I'd like to admit. Please slow my racing heart and mind so that I can see Your timing and goals for me." By the way, Acts 21:17 says, "When we arrived, the brothers and sisters in Jerusalem welcomed us warmly." Paul made it in time!

349

No Hell

There is no condemnation for those who belong to Christ Jesus.

ROMANS 8:1

A precious friend called me and shared that she had attended a Christmas pageant that included young children singing. One little girl seemed to overpower some of the other children on the chorus of "The First Noel." Instead of singing the word *Noel* four times, she was belting out, "No hell, no hell, no hell, no hell! Born is the King of Israel!"

Afterward, the girl's mother asked her why she was singing that. She replied wisely, "When Jesus is in your heart, you don't go to hell." Oh, that simple fact, straight from the mouth of a babe, makes me want to belt out her words too!

What a cause for rejoicing on Christ's birthday, which we celebrate at Christmas. There is no condemnation for those who belong to Christ Jesus. He came as the greatest gift to mankind—a free gift, which cannot be earned. We have direct access to a holy God because Jesus died on the cross to pay for all of our sin—our decision to go our own way instead of His way. His purpose in being born was to die on the cross for our sin and be raised to life so we could live forever with Him. All we have to do is open the gift of Jesus by faith and ask Him to forgive us of our sin and come into our life.

He designed this whole eternal plan with His great love for us in mind. Since the beginning of time, He knew He'd make a way for us to avoid hell. Through Christ's sacrifice, there is no hell for a believer in Him. He wants us to be assured that when we die we will see Him in heaven. If you have not trusted in Christ, don't wait any longer!

Wherever you are, by faith in Christ, be assured of your eternal destination with Him and rejoice that there will be no hell for you.

Prayer of an Imperfect Mother

Don't worry about anything; instead, pray about everything.
PHILIPPIANS 4:6

I recently discovered this lone entry I wrote in a forgotten journal when our daughter was almost six and heading to dance class. (She is now twenty-one!) The crazy thing is that the day I discovered it, I was feeling the same "letting go" pains as I did when she drove away in her first car!

> *Oh, Lord, today I wanted to go home after dropping Special K off for dance and put my thoughts on paper. How good You are to remind me of Yourself in the everyday of life.*
>
> *The strangest sensation came over me as I watched Special K (turning six in two days) skip up the ramp by herself and look back with a wave to let me know she had arrived safely at the door. My baby didn't need me to walk her to the door anymore.*
>
> *I prayed, "Hold Special K tightly, Lord."*

That has been the prayer of my heart for her to this day, and God has faithfully answered it over and over again.

We all have many "letting go" aches in our lives. Thankfully, God never lets go of us. I need that assurance often, especially when I am struggling to do what He wants. "Thank You, God, for loving me much more than I deserve. Father, I have so many weaknesses. I am easily angered, I get hyper about being late, and I keep things inside. And when my faults surface, I don't like them. I am recommitting myself to be Your woman, a God's girl in every way."

And by the way, here was the PS in my journal all those years ago that has turned into an SP (Sweet Pea).

> *PS: Before I forget, thank You for using Special K to make me laugh today when she sang, "Hark! the herald angels sing, 'Glory to the newborn King; peace on earth, and mercy mild, God and sinners Frankenstein!'"*

☐— Fearful of "letting go"? God will fill the hole in our hearts with His presence through any letting-go pains.

Put on God's Armor

*Put on every piece of God's armor so you will be able to resist the
enemy in the time of evil. . . . Stand your ground, putting on the belt
of truth and the body armor of God's righteousness. For shoes, put
on the peace that comes from the Good News. . . . Hold up the shield
of faith to stop the fiery arrows of the devil. Put on salvation as your
helmet, and take the sword of the Spirit, which is the word of God.*

EPHESIANS 6:13-17

What are you wearing today? Maybe it's one of your favorite outfits or maybe it is
the first thing you grabbed that didn't need ironing. Some women, like me, enjoy
creating new looks and shopping in their own closets to stay in touch with the current styles. But today's verses focus on the real essentials needed to dress for success.

God's wardrobe for us—His armor—may not seem to fit your fashion style,
but we would be wise not to leave the house without it. This outerwear is actually
our innerwear, protecting us from the enemy and helping us defend God's truth
and stand our ground. Here's what's included:

Belt of truth: Truth guards our core against the onslaught of misleading
standards.

Body armor of righteousness: God's righteousness covers our whole being.

Shoes of peace: The Good News gives us peace, and we can share the story of the
Prince of Peace with others.

Shield of faith: Faith protects us like a shield over our heart, where Jesus resides
when we have a relationship with Him.

Helmet of salvation: Jesus' death secured our salvation, and when we focus
on that fact, we don helmets of confidence for what lies ahead.

Sword of the Spirit: The Word of God is our only offensive piece of armor. When
we carry the sword of the Spirit we'll be ready to wage war against the enemy
using the power of God's Word.

 As you dress each day, think of each piece of spiritual armor you're
putting on too. Then listen to what our Commander in Chief, Jesus,
asks you to do and wear Him well!

Tooth Tale

*O Lord, there is no one like you. We have never
even heard of another God like you!*
1 CHRONICLES 17:20

When our daughter, Kali, started kindergarten, it was such a fun time around our house. She was so excited about starting school and getting a new backpack. And after the first day, she couldn't stop talking about the tooth chart in her classroom. Whenever anyone lost a tooth, his or her name was added to the chart and everyone celebrated!

One morning when Mark was getting ready for work, Kali said to me, "Mommy, will you please pull my tooth? I'm afraid it's going to come out at school and I'll lose it. I want to be on the tooth chart." Inside I'm thinking, *I don't like blood. I wish Mark could pull it. There's no time.* Out loud I said, "Okay, sweet one," and wrapped one end of a piece of string around the loose tooth and tied the other end to the doorknob, my daddy's tried-and-true method.

Just then Mark appeared and said, "What are you doing? You may do that in South Carolina, but we don't do that in Virginia!" Needless to say, we had run out of time, and Kali went to school with her tooth still hanging on.

When she got home that day, our plumber, Mr. Trexler strolled to the kitchen after fixing a leak under Kali's bathroom sink. He and his wife had a lot of children, so when he saw her wiggling her tooth, he said, "Do you want me to pull it for you?"

"Yes," she replied cheerfully, while I'm thinking, *Maybe you should wash your hands first!*

Mr. Trexler quickly grabbed a paper towel and yanked gently. Suddenly, Kali was grinning with a noticeable gap where the tooth had been. She drew a picture of herself smiling—without a tooth—to thank him. Later she asked, "Could Mr. Trexler come back and pull all my teeth? Nobody can do it just like him!" Tears of joy welled up in my eyes.

Doesn't that describe God, too? After all, nobody can do it just like God!

What small thing do you need to place in God's hands right now? Take a moment and prayerfully give it to Him too.

Jesus, the Real Mr. Wonderful

A child is born to us, a son is given to us. The government will rest on his shoulders. And he will be called: Wonderful Counselor, Mighty God, Everlasting Father, Prince of Peace.

ISAIAH 9:6

I have a Mr. Wonderful talking doll that I cannot bring myself to stick in a yard sale. If something makes me laugh, I intend to keep it, and Mr. Wonderful makes me laugh. As the package promised, "He always knows just what to say." Mr. Wonderful says, "You know, honey, why don't you just relax and let me make dinner tonight?" and "The ball game really isn't all that important. I'd rather spend time with you." When I pull the doll's string, he responds idealistically to expectations we sometimes put on the "Mr. Wonderfuls" we actually live with.

When I first saw this doll at a friend's home and listened to the remarks that were unrealistic expectations that every woman wants to hear, I thought of the real Mr. Wonderful, who has made us promises that He really does fulfill. Jesus is our true Mr. Wonderful. He is God, and His name is Wonderful Counselor, Mighty God, Everlasting Father, and Prince of Peace. Getting to know Jesus and focusing on His attributes gives us so much more than repeated recorded messages.

The man-made Mr. Wonderful can only *say* "I love you," but our Creator God *shows* His love by first sending His Son, Jesus Christ, to die in our place and then sending the Holy Spirit to reside in us and help us. God initiated and implemented the way for us to have a love relationship with Him for all eternity. He's not all talk, like my animated doll.

When the doll says, "You've been on my mind all day. That's why I bought you these flowers," it isn't really thinking of me at all. But we can be assured that God is always thinking of us and seeing to our needs. God, our Wonderful Counselor, is our *living* Mr. Wonderful.

🔑 We all have a real Mr. Wonderful named Jesus! Jot down some of the ways He shows He cares for you and meets your every need.

His Favor Rests on Us

Glory to God in the highest heaven, and on earth
peace to those on whom his favor rests.

LUKE 2:14, NIV

Every Christmas morning when I was growing up, my mom or dad read the Christmas story from Luke 2. Sometimes I tuned out the all-too-familiar words, causing them to skid off my heart rather than take root. Because I had heard them so often, I neglected to appreciate the meaning those words always bring to each holiday season.

When we hear something over and over again, we sometimes become deaf to what is being said. But repetition is necessary and helpful for remembering truth. God's Word never gets old and is worth reviewing over and over again. It is full of repeated messages of God's love, grace, care, and redemption for lost people. It is alive and powerful (Hebrews 4:12). Amazingly, His Word can set the tone for all that is going to take place today, tomorrow, and forever. It's really as if God's Word follows us around throughout the day.

To read it daily brings delight because no matter how many times we read a passage, God's Spirit makes His Word fresh in the hearts of all His children who are sensitive to His voice. Our hearts become tender when we know what God says, and we not only want to live by it but we actually *do* what He says by faith. This is called obedience.

This past Christmas, God showed me fresh truth in the familiar verse Luke 2:14. He clearly reminded me that His favor rests on *me*! What a wonderful thought.

God approves of me in Christ Jesus. I do not have to win His favor or approval because He already proved His love and favor toward me by sending Christ into the world. On that first Christmas Jesus came to earth as a baby so we could experience God in human form.

God's favor rests on you, too—forever. Let the deep meaning of the Christmas story move your heart closer to His heart this season.

⚷ Let's live like we are favored! Thank the Lord that His Word always offers something fresh like the story of Jesus' birth. Read the account in Luke 2:1-20.

Generous God-Givers

Everything we have has come from you, and we
give you only what you first gave us!

1 CHRONICLES 29:14

Although not everything I've ever done may be described as logical, this truth about giving is very logical: We can be generous God-givers to a depleted world because nothing really belongs to us. We freely give what God has lavished on us. His giving nature is a primary motivation for us to follow His lead and become givers ourselves.

No human can motivate us to do anything like God can! I'm sure someone has said somewhere that God's Word is the only self-help book we need. It should be on the top of our book stack, worn from use! His Word motivates me like no other book.

Whether the Lord wants to urge us to give, to clean, to forgive, to go the extra mile, to cook, to call, to write, to exercise, to commit, or to change by the power of His Spirit, God prompts us through His Word. But we need to sensitize our hearts to listen for His direction and then accept His nudge to act on that gentle push He gives us. Every time I have personally held back from giving something, I have regretted it, haven't you? We need to develop the doer aspect of giving and move beyond merely dreaming of the possibilities.

The fact that everything we have belongs to Him should motivate us to not hold back. If we have a resource, whatever it is—not just money, but time and talents as well—we just need to let it go! When we give to people, we give to God and we point others to Him, the best Gift Giver there is.

Let's be generous with all God's gifts. He gave them to us so that we would pass them on to others as a way to share His generous love.

A Christmas Moment by the Cash Register

*He does not punish us for all our sins; he does not
deal harshly with us, as we deserve.*

PSALM 103:10

This verse describes one of the most encouraging benefits of belonging to Jesus Christ. His mercy is extended to us every morning, even though we are undeserving. We don't have to store up His mercies because He gives us a brand-new batch of mercy every day. Are you hootin' and hollerin' "Hallelujah" with me?

One December when I was returning an item that I had bought impulsively, I was surprised to see that there wasn't a long line at the cash register. It seemed odd that the popular store appeared empty a week before Christmas. As the clerk processed the transaction, I gave her a piece of wrapped "smiley faith" candy.

She was so excited that she called out to a passing associate, "Look! One of my customers just gave me a piece of candy." I was somewhat embarrassed, but I told her that I liked sweet surprises too.

She said, "I'll never forget when my mother spoiled a sweet surprise for me. She brought cupcakes to my class for my birthday. Mom slipped and dropped the cupcakes. I laughed along with everyone else." Then she continued. "I did the exact same thing recently for my own daughter's birthday party in her classroom at school. I slipped and fell, too, and the cupcakes went everywhere. I guess God got me back for making fun of my mother all those years ago."

Although my heart was thumping, I quickly said something like, "Oh, no, God is not like that! God loves you. He is a forgiving God, and He loves to offer us fresh starts because He is so merciful. His fresh start for us is why we celebrate Christmas. Jesus was born in order to die on the cross and save us from our sins."

Her eyes lit up with wonder as she listened. As I briefly shared the Good News of Jesus, I was in awe that God had given us this time alone, with no one else at the checkout. The woman never stopped smiling, even as I walked away. I thanked God that I had an opportunity to worship Him by the cash register.

Thank God this Christmas for giving us His gracious, forgiving Spirit, who loves new beginnings. Share the Good News with others so they can have a fresh start with God too.

Take Time to Ponder

All who heard the shepherds' story were astonished, but Mary kept all these things in her heart and thought about them often.

LUKE 2:18-19

I want to be like Mary! I want to think often about who and what really matters in life.

In today's verses, the Son of God was just born to Mary, a young teenager who was a virgin! How wild is that? I can't imagine "all these things" that she was keeping in her heart, but I'm guessing she would have been overwhelmed by them had she not shared a deep personal relationship with her Lord.

When we have a close relationship with the living God, we, too, have hidden away what He says in our hearts. But let's be really honest with ourselves. How much time during Christmas and Easter and every holy day God gives us on this earth do we spend pondering the real meaning of the holiday? The word *holiday* means "holy day." We have been made holy through faith in Jesus Christ, so a holy day is personal to believers.

When we ponder His Word daily, we are thinking about Him often. We can even think of Him in the bustle of a busy office with clamoring coworkers or in a kitchen with busy hands and little helpers, as well as when we're relaxing by ourselves in our favorite places.

Christ is our constant companion through all our to-do lists and pending responsibilities. He brings peace even in the midst of great unknowns, such as Mary experienced during the nine months the Savior of the world grew inside her. Just as Mary couldn't snap her fingers for instant peace, we cannot create it in our own strength either.

Mary modeled the true meaning of Christmas through her quiet attitude of trusting faith. She was able to do so because she spent time pondering God's Word in her heart. Instead of being swayed by the "what ifs," she planted her mind solidly in God's great throne room and let Him settle her heart. We can follow her lead and quiet ourselves with God through His Word this season.

Let's take time today to ponder who God is and the power of His great love for all of us! Enjoy the quiet with Him.

It's a Boy—Jesus!

*Because Joseph was a descendant of King David, he had to go to
Bethlehem in Judea, David's ancient home. He traveled there from the
village of Nazareth in Galilee. He took with him Mary, his fiancée,
who was now obviously pregnant. And while they were there, the
time came for her baby to be born. She gave birth to her first child,
a son. She wrapped him snugly in strips of cloth and laid him in
a manger, because there was no lodging available for them.*

LUKE 2:4-7

It's a girl—our girl! Kali Sutton Newlen was born Christmas week. To be honest, that year the many gifts under the tree seemed insignificant once she finally arrived. Our hearts were filled with gratefulness to God that we finally had a long-awaited child! She certainly was a gift that would keep on giving . . . and taking!

My sweet mom was the best gift giver. I think that God's chosen season for her granddaughter's birth was an extra-special gift to us both. December is known as a gift-giving month, and people are often looking for ideas for the perfect present to buy for the special someone (or someones) in their lives.

My sweet sister, Shawn, gave me an idea that has become part of our family's Christmas tradition. On the first day of December, I place a big basket in our foyer filled with brand-new, unwrapped seasonal gifts. They are tied with beautiful Christmas ribbon so that everyone who comes to our door that month can grab a gift from the basket. Visitors can choose what they need or take something new to surprise someone else with.

This time of year we give Christmas gifts because we celebrate God's great gift in the birthday of Jesus. God wrapped His Son in the flesh as a human baby, who grew up and gave His life so that we might have forgiveness of sin and eternal life!

We open not only the gift of salvation by faith in Christ, but also the gifts of love, joy, peace, and comfort. And God's gifts aren't just reserved for Christmas—they keep on coming throughout the year. How exciting is that—we can celebrate Jesus' birth every day! It's a boy—it's Jesus!

Happy birthday, Jesus!

Our Search Stops Here

I want them to be encouraged and knit together by strong ties of love. I want them to have complete confidence that they understand God's mysterious plan, which is Christ himself. In him lie hidden all the treasures of wisdom and knowledge.

COLOSSIANS 2:2-3

The Bible is a big book, and sometimes it can be difficult to locate the shorter books because they can easily get lost in the shuffle of pages.

Recently when I was looking for Colossians, I kept saying to myself, *General Electric Power Company.* Do you think GE knows that because of their name I can always find Galatians, Ephesians, Philippians, and Colossians? Those four books of the Bible are tucked in between two other "ians," 2 Corinthians and 1 Thessalonians. These potent little letters written by the apostle Paul are tucked away in the last fourth of the Bible, and thumbing through to find them after all these years, I still think *GEPC*! (Maybe that tip will help you find them too.)

Once we arrive in one of these letters, we are in for some strong doses of God's wisdom. For instance, when I am not living free in Christ, I turn to Galatians. Is there contention in the church? Ephesians. Lack of joy? Philippians. Need reminding that Christ is God and all sufficient? Look to Colossians. Of course, this is a quick summary, but it is a starting point for tackling truth from God about what really matters.

And *what* really matters? Rather, I should say *who* really matters? One reading of any of these books will give strong evidence that Jesus Christ is who matters. Everything in the Bible—from Genesis to Revelation—points to Him.

Paul reminds us of this truth in today's verses. Our search for wisdom and knowledge stops in one place—Christ! "In him lie hidden all the treasures of wisdom and knowledge." Paul was yearning for all believers to have this complete confidence.

Our personal relationship to Jesus Christ—God in the flesh, our Savior, our Everything—is the answer to God's redemptive plan.

 Rest in Christ because our searching is over! Ask Him for wisdom to handle the challenges you're facing today.

Unpackers Anonymous

All these people died still believing what God had promised
them. They did not receive what was promised, but they
saw it all from a distance and welcomed it. They agreed
that they were foreigners and nomads here on earth.

HEBREWS 11:13

We, too, are only foreigners and nomads on this earth because our real home is in heaven. It is certainly okay to avoid getting too comfortable here because a better, more glorious day is coming, and each moment we live moves us closer to it! Since we are always wandering as nomads on earth, we do not need to worry if we die with our suitcases still packed. When we have believed in Christ, we will always be ready to go!

For some unexplained reason, I am the only one in our family who does not unpack immediately after returning home from a trip. Maybe I like that the clothes in my suitcase are neat and covered up—out of sight, out of mind. After a trip, I try to tackle my priorities at home and at work first, so I procrastinate in unpacking because I know it can wait. Maybe I ought to start a group called Unpackers Anonymous.

In Hebrews 11, we can be inspired by the great examples of men and women packed with faith because they simply believed what God had promised them. "They placed their hope in a better life after the resurrection" (verse 35). They kept their greatest treasures—God's promises, His love, protection, and power—packed in their hearts at all times.

Maybe I could defend myself for not wanting to unpack with the fact that my loaded suitcase serves as a reminder that I am a wanderer on this earth! I praise God that my final destination in heaven is secure.

If you are not packed for heaven with faith in Christ, please take that step now. Believe and receive Jesus Christ. This is a one-way ticket only. God tells us in John 14:6, "I am the way, the truth, and the life. No one can come to the Father except through me."

Faith on Fire

Nebuchadnezzar, we do not need to defend ourselves before you. If we are thrown into the blazing furnace, the God whom we serve is able to save us. He will rescue us from your power, Your Majesty. But even if he doesn't, we want to make it clear to you, Your Majesty, that we will never serve your gods or worship the gold statue you have set up.

DANIEL 3:16-18

My favorite phrase from this story is "but even if he doesn't." I never get tired of reading how the three friends of Daniel refused to bow down to a man-made statue—a god with a little *g*. They knew and loved the only capital-G God, the Creator and Sustainer of every living thing.

King Nebuchadnezzar was infuriated with them for refusing to follow his edict. In order to save face, he sentenced them to a grisly death—being burned alive in a furnace. Shadrach, Meshach, and Abednego stood up for God and told Nebuchadnezzar that God could get them out of that hot situation, but even if He didn't, they would not give in to the pressure of the world and put anything above their one true God—the only One worthy of praise, worship, and glory.

Nebuchadnezzar ordered that the fire be made seven times hotter than the normal furnace temperature. These three "wise men" expressed their faith in God in word and action. They knew God. Do we know God as personally as they did? Are we getting to know Him so well that we can say that we will never put anything above Him? Will we stay true to God even if He doesn't do what we want Him to do—even to the point of death?

Whatever fires you and I face in this life, we need to get fired up by the fact that God is almighty and He is able to deliver us. But even if He doesn't, we are still His for eternity. We win either way!

"Lord, we need You to light a flame under our faith too! Help us respond to the furnace of life in ways that bring glory and honor to You!"

Consistency

I have not kept the good news of your justice hidden in my heart; I have talked about your faithfulness and saving power. I have told everyone in the great assembly of your unfailing love and faithfulness.

PSALM 40:10

When my daddy died unexpectedly, the Lord mercifully gave me everything I needed to be able to pay tribute to him at his memorial service. I wanted people to know what it was about Daddy that reminded me of Jesus. Getting my thoughts out helped me grieve.

Consistency was the quality about my earthly father that reminded me most of my heavenly Father. Daddy's early-morning back-porch quiet time was just one pattern of consistent faithfulness that led me to trust God's faithfulness. This was one habit of his that I wanted to share with our family and friends.

Other ways that Daddy showed consistency included harvesting his yearly crop of tomatoes, volunteering for Meals on Wheels, the time he spent fixing breakfast every morning for our family, doling out treats from his pocket, writing BSSYP (Be Sweet & Say Your Prayers) on my mail for more than twenty-five years, telling me to always hold my shoulders up for good posture, and so many other examples.

Dad's good habits affected our whole family for good, and they gave me the precious experience of having someone follow through on his word. When we are consistent, others come to rely on us and know what to expect. Our reputation with them builds confidence and security.

The lessons I learned from observing Daddy's consistent life make me think about our perfect Father's unfailing faithfulness. As consistent as my earthly father was, I know that God is the only perfect Father who comes through for us all the time. No parent is perfect, but my heavenly Father is. God is consistent in showering us with love, mercy, grace, pardon, justice, and fairness. We can truly trust Him to do what He says, and we can feel secure in our standing with Him.

Learn about God's perfect reputation and consistency by reading what He says in His Word every day. Be reminded that His character is unchanging—yesterday, today, and forever!

Share the Joy

I will rejoice even if I lose my life, pouring it out like a liquid offering to God, just like your faithful service is an offering to God. And I want all of you to share that joy.

PHILIPPIANS 2:17

We've all heard the slogan "Share the love." In Paul's precious thank-you letter to the Philippian church, he tells God's people to "share that joy."

What joy is he talking about? The joy that comes from faithful service found in obedience to God. Just like one of my favorite hymnlines says, "Trust and obey, for there's no other way to be happy in Jesus, but to trust and obey."

Your faithful service will look different from mine. You and I need to be encouraged that any faithful service—whether it be housekeeping, child rearing, or running a business—can glorify God just as much as serving in a soup kitchen or preaching a sermon.

Even though you may not be called to be a Sunday school teacher, vacation Bible school leader, or attend a women's Bible study because of work responsibilities, whatever you do for God by being available to others counts as faithful service. There is no extra credit for being in full-time Christian work, and there is no reduced reward for simply living faithfully and reaching out from the little corner of the world where God has placed us.

Whether we are serving our family a meal, taking a meal to someone in need, calling a friend, sending a word of encouragement by mail or e-mail, composing a sweet tweet or text, or inviting an acquaintance into our homes, let's give generously of all we have—"Whatever you do, do it all for the glory of God" (1 Corinthians 10:31).

Joy is a by-product of obedience to God. Faithful service pours out of us when we have offered ourselves wholeheartedly to God in obedience. In return, He showers us with the joy of being useful for His work.

🔑 Let's share the joy of serving faithfully!

Forget and Look Forward

*No, dear brothers and sisters, I have not achieved it, but I focus
on this one thing: Forgetting the past and looking forward to what
lies ahead, I press on to reach the end of the race and receive the
heavenly prize for which God, through Christ Jesus, is calling us.*

PHILIPPIANS 3:13-14

I had the privilege of speaking at a Sweet Monday outreach in Sweet Shannon's neighborhood. Her theme was "Pretty in Pink," and she encouraged all the women to wear pink that particular night. Putting on my pinkest, fluffiest—some may say gaudiest—pink sweater set was so much fun. Shannon also asked me to please drive my beloved pink truck to her house so her children could see it.

When I arrived, her two young children were peering out through the glass front door. They were wearing their pink pajamas, anxiously awaiting the arrival of my pink truck—which I had simply forgotten to drive! I felt sick to my stomach and so embarrassed. I try so hard not to disappoint anyone if at all possible, and definitely not a sweet child.

After a heartfelt apology and sweet laughter from the children, I was reminded of God's Word to us through Paul in Philippians 3:13. Even though I believe he was exhorting us to forget past successes, the phrase about forgetting what is behind and looking forward to what is ahead kept running through my mind in a concrete way. Forgetting to drive the pink truck that day was not a sin, but I was still weighed down by my error.

I felt the sweet soothing of God's grace, reminding me to forget everything holding me back from peace and joy. He removes our sin completely when we admit and ask for forgiveness. That frees us to move forward confidently with Him in all life situations.

When we focus on what's to come, the serious troubles of sin in this life diminish in their power to crush us. But what is ahead for us? Heaven and an inheritance "that can never perish, spoil or fade" (1 Peter 1:4, NIV). This anticipation should tickle us pink and be truth we never forget.

 Wear pink tomorrow or just think pink. Forget what is behind! Look forward to forever in Jesus Christ. Remember that the fields are pink for harvest as we tell others the Good News about Jesus.

Thank you for helping me blossom!

Daddy and Mama (Claud "Bo" Bowman and Maxine "Honey" Bowman) . . . "Lord, please tell them thank you for living and passing on the legacy of BSSYP (Be Sweet & Say Your Prayers). Let Daddy know I painted his beloved blue '86 Ford pickup pink! Tell Mama the book is finished now and I'm so happy she knew about it before she saw You!"

Carl "Grandy" Newlen and Charlene "Grammy" Newlen . . . "Lord, please tell Sweet Charlene thank you for always saying she couldn't have picked any two daughters-in-law she loved more for her sons, and please tell Grandy that I eat jalapeños on my pizza now and I still wear the wild fur vest he picked out just for me!"

. . . And more of my sweet family living in the Carolinas and Virginia! Bubba and April, Claire, Chuckie, Shawnee, and Elias, Aunt Doris and Uncle Eddie, Aunt Shirley, Aunt Ruth, Rocky and Robert, Gary and Becky, Lindsay, Katie and Tony, Mrs. Gilbert, David and Rita, Aunt Gladys, Aunt Thelma, Aunt Donna, Uncle Jimmy, Aunt Bonnie and Uncle Red, Uncle Charlie. My Gaffney "family": Dorcas, Jean and Joe, Joyce and Oscar, Ann and Bill, Betsy and Billy. My Virginia Beach "sister," Daphne.

John Van Diest . . . God knew I needed a father in the faith this side of heaven as I was missing my own dad's wise advice. I "adopted" you after hearing your heart and you seeing mine. Thank you for introducing me to Jan Long Harris of Tyndale House Publishers, who gave me her sweet time and believed that books and me go together! Sweet love to Bonne Steffen, whose love and laughter reverberate on every phone call, and to the rest of my very Sweet Tyndale team!

Richard Sharp . . . You and your Sweet Sherry, besides being fun, have always encouraged my ideas! Thank you for answering my many questions about serving in nonprofit ministry and tutoring me in new business vocabulary!

Sweet Monday Board . . . Where do I start with you, my Sweet Board? I always liked that it rhymed with my Sweet Lord! It was your idea to e-mail the devotions every Sweet Monday. Jacquelin Aronson, Katherine Arthur, Amy Bohlen, Cheryl George, Pamela Hoade, Stuart Holt, Aimée Mestler, Joyce Minor, Diann Mitchell, Michele Rhudy, Faye Rivers, JoNell Robertson, Richard and Sherry Sharp, Steve Shelby, Debbie Spencer, Donna Sharp Suro, Kristine Tedeschi, Annhorner Truitt, Debbie Weber, John Whitlock, Janet Wills. In sweet memory of Skip Wilkins. Accountants Jenifer Cryer, Allison Hearn, and Carla Becker.

Sweet Tuesday . . . Faye Rivers, Sherry Sharp, Paula Dozier, Christy Thompson, Kristin Kessler, and Bonnie Smith. We served together at Community Bible Study for many years and we still stick together over long lunches, lasting love, and precious prayers. And in sweet memory of Mary Ann Griffin and Susan Kinney.

The Ukrop family . . . Jayne, you were my first Collegiate mom to welcome Mark and me to Richmond before I even knew about Ukrop's Super Markets! I have loved you ever since. Bobby, you put my *Sweet Monday* booklets in eleven of your stores, where God multiplied the five cupcakes and two pieces of candy! You and your children Jacquelin, Nancy Jo, Jeff, and Rob continue to spur on so many others in our Richmond community to *Lead Like Jesus*. (Go Ken Blanchard!)

Anna Barron Billingsley (William and Mary), Cecilia Thrailkill Pitts (Erskine College) . . . We met at Montreat as juniors in college 7-7-77. We got together 8-8-88, then 9-9-99, and again 10-10-10. Just think! In heaven, our reunions will never end.

Meg Hogshire Bogue, Mimi Larsen Beggs, Karen Loving Branagan . . . In 1981, you angels introduced me to Mark, the most eligible bachelor in Charlottesville. Funny, he was always stopping by our Angel House for dinner!

Amy Sansom Bohlen and Kay Sansom, my South Carolina mother-daughter mentors! Amy, having you (my former "3rd Greater" from The Covenant School in Charlottesville, Virginia) as a close friend now is one of God's greatest gifts to me. Kay, I wanted to be a godly mother just like you. I still do!

Krayton Davis, Robin Vaughn, Missy Patterson, John Robinson, Bob Mooney, Tom Byrd, Rhonda Day, Laurie Chalifoux, Giff Breed, Debbie Fisher, Katie Gilstrap, University of Richmond Robins School of Business, TJ and Rhonda Tanir, Bill Bevins, Shelly Perkins, the Shmoos, Walter and Heidi Class, Herbert and Christine Bschor, Peter and Heidi Poschl, and West End Presbyterian Church . . . A loud, sweet shout-out to you all for spurring me on to love and good deeds!

Sweet Monday volunteers . . . Lots of BIG sweet love! Think *World's Largest Tea Party*, *7,250*, and *Guinness World Record*! That's my heart for you! Your names will not fit on these two pages! Here's a shoestring list from our 1995 roots in sweet memory of my neighbor, "Grandma Hazel" McLennan: Brenda Johnson, Linda Tuskey, Fannie Lou Melton, Paula Nelson, Dawn Goodrich McKee, Leslie Kuhfuss, Sue Miner, Aimée Mestler, Lin Wang, Margie Breeden, Wilda Corbin, Faye Parker, Rick Schofield, Joey Burrough, Gary Wilson, Marj Newcomb, Elane Huprich.

Scripture Index

John 1:12   *June 27, October 13*
John 3:3   *March 3, September 4*
John 3:16   *November 14*
John 4:14   *August 8*
John 4:35   *February 15*
John 6:40   *June 5*
John 6:44   *November 15*
John 6:47   *July 2*
John 7:38   *July 17*
John 8:7   *April 5*
John 8:10-11   *September 7*
John 8:12   *June 20, August 4, August 16*
John 8:31-32   *September 9*
John 8:32   *January 23*
John 11:25-26   *July 31*
John 14:1-2   *February 11*
John 14:2-3   *November 29*
John 14:6   *June 3*
John 15:1-2   *July 15*
John 15:11   *June 14*
John 15:14   *November 23*
John 16:33   *July 19*
John 20:29   *August 23*
Acts 1:8   *October 24*
Acts 4:32   *August 10*
Acts 17:28   *February 7*
Acts 20:16   *December 15*
Acts 23:16   *October 9*
Acts 24:15-16   *January 28*
Romans 3:23   *February 21*
Romans 5:5   *January 25*
Romans 7:18-25   *August 7*
Romans 8:1   *December 16*
Romans 8:1-2   *July 28*
Romans 8:15-16   *June 16*
Romans 8:26-27   *September 14*
Romans 8:28   *August 19*
Romans 8:34   *September 26*
Romans 8:38-39   *July 26*
Romans 10:15   *May 24*
Romans 12:2   *March 19*
Romans 12:9   *September 18*
Romans 12:13   *September 17*
Romans 12:15   *June 24*
Romans 13:5   *November 16*
Romans 14:8   *June 10*
Romans 15:3-4   *May 27*
1 Corinthians 2:9   *January 14*
1 Corinthians 3:10-11   *August 26*
1 Corinthians 6:11   *August 25,
    November 10*

1 Corinthians 7:28   *March 7*
1 Corinthians 7:31   *April 14*
1 Corinthians 9:25-27   *December 3*
1 Corinthians 12:31; 13:4-7   *February 4*
1 Corinthians 13:4-5   *January 31, May 14*
1 Corinthians 13:12   *February 2*
2 Corinthians 1:3-4   *October 3*
2 Corinthians 2:14   *August 31*
2 Corinthians 2:14-16   *October 25*
2 Corinthians 3:12   *October 27*
2 Corinthians 3:18   *February 17*
2 Corinthians 4:6-9   *March 22*
2 Corinthians 4:10   *August 20*
2 Corinthians 4:16-18   *March 23*
2 Corinthians 5:1-3   *October 30*
2 Corinthians 5:7   *July 29*
2 Corinthians 5:17   *March 1, June 17*
2 Corinthians 5:18-20   *October 12*
2 Corinthians 9:7-8   *April 30*
2 Corinthians 10:12   *January 4*
2 Corinthians 11:23   *August 12*
2 Corinthians 12:9   *November 19*
Galatians 1:10   *March 20, October 20*
Galatians 2:20   *June 28*
Galatians 2:21; 5:1   *July 8*
Galatians 3:2-3   *November 8*
Galatians 3:26-28   *April 22*
Galatians 6:2   *November 6*
Ephesians 2:4-5   *September 13*
Ephesians 2:8-9   *February 8, July 11*
Ephesians 2:19   *January 24*
Ephesians 4:29   *April 28*
Ephesians 5:16   *December 6*
Ephesians 5:20   *September 8*
Ephesians 5:22-24   *October 6*
Ephesians 6:13-17   *December 18*
Philippians 1:6   *January 3*
Philippians 2:3-4   *February 9*
Philippians 2:14   *April 4*
Philippians 2:15   *December 13*
Philippians 2:17   *December 30*
Philippians 3:8   *March 11*
Philippians 3:13-14   *December 31*
Philippians 3:20   *May 13*
Philippians 4:6   *December 17*
Philippians 4:11-12   *March 30*
Colossians 1:5   *April 12*
Colossians 1:6   *June 11*
Colossians 1:19-21   *July 12*
Colossians 2:2-3   *December 26*
Colossians 3:13   *April 6*

Sweet Monday is creative evangelism that "reaches out to women one sweet invitation at a time for Christ." Women laugh a lot, learn from each other, and leave with a simple introduction to Jesus Christ. Sweet Monday is also a homegrown, tiny tool that God is using in a BIG way to connect women to each other and Himself.

♥♥♥♥♥♥♥♥♥♥

Visit www.sweetmonday.org to learn more!

CP0677